PLACE IN RETURN BOX to remove this checkout from your record.
TO AVOID FINES return on or before date due.
MAY BE RECALLED with earlier due date if requested.

DATE DUE	DATE DUE	DATE DUE
12 13 12 SEP 27 '02	DEC 21 2023	

2/05 p:/CIRC/DateDue.indd-p.1

John Collier's
Crusade
for
Indian Reform

John Collier's

for

Indian Reform

1920–1954

Kenneth R. Philp

with a foreword by FRANCIS PAUL PRUCHA

⊔⅃ The University of Arizona Press

Tucson, Arizona

Crusade

About the Author . . .

KENNETH R. PHILP, holder of a Ph.D. in history from Michigan State University, first became attracted to the life and work of John Collier while attending a graduate seminar on the New Deal. Since that time he has pursued his interests in the history of the American Indian and federal Indian policy, publishing his research findings in such journals as *Arizona and the West, Rocky Mountain Social Science Journal,* and *The Journal of Ethnic Studies.* In addition to his own authorship duties, Philp has reviewed manuscripts for the *American Indian Quarterly* and the *Western Historical Quarterly* and served as co-editor of the book *Essays on Walter Prescott Webb.* Philp and his wife have lived in Arlington, Texas, since 1968, at which time he joined the faculty of the University of Texas.

E
93
.C7
P48
42

THE UNIVERSITY OF ARIZONA PRESS

I.S.B.N. 0-8165-0472-5 paper
I.S.B.N. 0-8165-0595-0 cloth
L.C. No. 76-4427

For My Parents

HAROLD AND ALBERTA PHILP

Contents

Foreword, by Francis Paul Prucha   ix

Preface   xiii

1. Discovering a Red Atlantis   1
2. Protest From the Pueblos   26
3. Indian Dances Defended   55
4. A Provisional Revolution   71
5. Herbert Hoover's New Era: A False Dawn   92
6. The Indian New Deal Begins   113
7. Failure To Create a Red Atlantis   135
8. A Partial Restoration of Tribal Sovereignty   161
9. Thunder Over the Southwest   187
10. The Quest Continues   214
11. The Collier Legacy   237

Bibliographical Essay   245

Abbreviations   252

Notes   253

Index   291

ILLUSTRATIONS

John Collier	Frontispiece
Wintertime at Taos Pueblo	2
Taos Pueblo Church	3
John Collier in the Appalachians	6
Cooper Union	11
Immigrants Attending a Concert	13
Bohemian Children in the Pageant and Festival of Nations	17
Mrs. Stella Atwood	27
Albert Bacon Fall	29
Holm Olaf Bursum	31
Ray Lyman Wilbur	94
Charles Rhoads and J. Henry Scattergood	95
Harold L. Ickes	116
Formal Portrait of Commissioner Collier	119
Workers at the Yakima Indian Work Camp	121
Woodrow Crumbo and his Mural, "Wild Horses"	124
Caricature of Collier	136
Blackfoot Indians and John Collier	146
Secretary Ickes Signs the Flathead Constitution	168
Joseph Bruner	171
Tribal Council Meeting, Window Rock	191
Elwood A. Towner	203
John Collier at CCNY	221
Collier and Reporter at Knox College	233
John Collier at his Taos, New Mexico, home	235

Foreword

quote

United States Indian policy changed dramatically at the beginning of the second quarter of the twentieth century. Behind that change stood one man, the clearest symbol of the end of the old and the beginning of the new — John Collier. No one can understand Indian affairs in this century without a full knowledge of that remarkable man and his influence.

Collier appeared at a time when many of the old verities that gave form to American society were under attack, and he sided with the innovators. The last decades of the nineteenth century and the first decades of the twentieth had witnessed a flowering of evangelical Protestantism as a dominant element in the character of the nation, with an outlook that emphasized the individual and his conversion and salvation, that saw in thrift and hard work the path to righteousness, and that came close to equating religion with Americanism. Americanization of all foreign elements became a high priority.

Indian policy formulated in the 1880s and 1890s was part of that world view. Having failed to protect the Indians in the West from the onrush of white population, the federal government determined upon an all-out effort to turn the American Indians into Indian Americans, to destroy the tribal communities and to absorb the Indians as individuals into the mainstream of American society. Reforming groups like the Indian Rights Association, the Board of Indian Commissioners, and the Lake Mohonk Conference of Friends of the Indian campaigned mightily in the public press and in congressional halls to bring about the transformation. They insisted, above all, on breaking up the communal land holding patterns of the Indians and on the allotment of reservation lands as homesteads to individual Indian families in the pattern of white America. Thus individualized on his own parcel of land, encouraged to cultivate it for his livelihood and to improve it for his heirs, the Indian would be Christianized by zealous missionaries, educated in American customs at government schools, and soon disappear as a singular element in the body politic. "The Indian as a savage member of a tribal organization cannot survive, ought not to survive, the aggressions of civilization," the Indian Rights Association declared in a typical statement in 1884, "but his individual redemption from heathenism and ignorance, his transformation from the condition of a savage nomad to that of an industrious American citizen, is abundantly possible."

By concentrated effort the reformers got what they wanted. On February 8, 1887, the Dawes General Allotment Act became law — authorizing the president to allot portions of the reservations to individual Indians and granting United States citizenship to those who received the allotments. The humanitarians rejoiced at the passage of the act; they hailed it as the "Indian Emancipation Act" and spoke of the beginning of a new epoch in Indian affairs. "The supreme significance of the law in marking a new era in dealing with the Indian problem," one reformer noted, "lies in the fact that this law is a mighty pulverizing engine for breaking up the tribal mass. It has nothing to say to the tribe, nothing to do with the tribe. It breaks up that vast 'bulk of things' which the tribal life sought to keep unchanged. It finds its way straight to the family and to the individual."

The schools that were to help prepare the Indians for this momentous change were to be government schools, but inculcation of Christian principles was to be insisted upon, for it was citizenship in a Christian nation that was the goal. The formulators of Indian policy were convinced of the position enunciated by the presiding officer at the Lake Mohonk Conference in 1893:

Only as men and women who are full of the light of education and of the life of Christ go in and out among these savage brothers and sisters of ours, only as the living thought and the feeling heart touch their hearts one by one, can the Indians be lifted from savagery and made into useful citizens. . . . As we get at them one by one, as we break up these iniquitous masses of savagery, as we draw them out from their old associations and immerse them in the strong currents of Christian life and Christian citizenship, as we send the sanctifying stream of Christian life and Christian work among them, they feel the pulsing life-tide of Christ's life.

The ambitious program of Americanization and Christianization did not work as its advocates had intended, for their outlook was too narrow to allow them to take the Indian cultures into account. Under the allotment provisions of the Dawes Act the Indians lost much of their land,

and the educational programs broke down the Indians' heritage and cultural pride without substituting anything in its place, until many Indians became demoralized, lost between their historic identity and the white American culture they could not totally accept. Poverty, disease, and defective education were increasingly recognized as serious problems in the Indian communities as the twentieth century advanced.

Into this scene came John Collier, with a radically different approach to the Indian question. Not only was he a strong advocate of protecting and guaranteeing Indian rights to their own religion and culture, but he saw in the communal existence of the Native Americans a model for reforming society at large. Beginning as an outspoken critic of existing Indian policy and Indian service administration, Collier soon became the architect of a new program, and as commissioner of Indian affairs under Franklin Delano Roosevelt he established an Indian "New Deal." He sought to reestablish Indian societies, to give them status and responsibility, and above all to restore a communal land base.

His was a vastly different world from that of the Lake Mohonk Friends of the Indian with their Christian individualism. Indian corporate life was to be regenerated and individualism rejected as the highest good. Cultural and religious freedom — no matter how it might go against the established American cultural grain — was to be ensured. A secularized democracy replaced American Christianity as the essential *end* to be sought. Scientific research — the Indian administration was to be "a laboratory of ethnic relations" in Collier's view — replaced the "strong currents of Christian life" as the indispensable *means* of reform.

Kenneth R. Philp, in this first full-length study of Collier and the Indians, provides an admirable account of Collier's philosophy and of his program. He makes us understand what motivated the man and how his life experiences influenced his Indian policies. It is a thoroughly fascinating story, told in rich detail, and it should destroy for the future any simplistic approaches to Collier and the Indian New Deal.

I have on occasion spoken figuratively of changes in American Indian policy as the swinging of a pendulum, as though there were a clean movement from one extreme to another, from the assimilationist policy of the 1880s to the cultural pluralism of Collier's program in the 1930s. Philp's study will no longer permit the luxury of such simplicity. In his discussion of the criticism Collier received, he has convincingly shown that tensions between the two philosophies existed throughout the Collier period, on the part of Indians as well as whites. He has vividly demonstrated that panaceas — whether the individualized Americanization of the reformers of the 1880s or the collective democracy of Collier and his anthropologist brain trust — are not capable of solving the age-old "Indian problem."

John Collier was a highly controversial figure, who engendered strong support from his friends and strong antagonism from his critics. By his well-balanced, scholarly judgments of the man and his work, Philp will no doubt revive the old debate — he will be too kind to Collier for some, too hard on him for others. So much the better. The problems Collier faced in seeking the proper place of the Indians in American society were real ones, and they have not yet all disappeared. If this story of Collier forces us to think deeply — even passionately — about them, much good will surely come of it.

FRANCIS PAUL PRUCHA

Preface

While many historians regard the two decades after World War I as a turning point in federal-Indian relations, there has been no comprehensive analysis of government Indian policy during this era. Many books and articles have provided information about this watershed in Indian history, but none have examined carefully the career of John Collier, the individual most responsible for shaping alternatives to the Dawes General Allotment Act of 1887. This volume attempts to fill that void.

Collier developed his approach to ethnic relations during the Progressive period while he was a social worker at the People's Institute in New York City. There he searched for ways that would allow Americans to harness the disruptive forces unleashed by the Industrial Revolution. Convinced that the rise of capitalism had caused anarchic individualism, wasteful competition, and an unhealthy obsession with materialism, Collier sought to construct a new set of values to replace the philosophy of social Darwinism. Unlike most of his contemporaries, Collier had little interest in destroying the folk cultures of the immigrants who resided on Manhattan Island. Instead, he worked to strengthen their former community life where individuals and groups had supposedly acted in harmony.

Essentially a conservative who was not afraid of radical innovation, Collier looked to preindustrial cultures, not rigid social doctrines, to discover the secrets of a democratic communal form of existence. After a trip to Taos Pueblo in 1920, Collier concluded that these Indians had in fact established a cooperative commonwealth. Persuaded that culture was more important than politics as a method of providing social cohesion and unity, Collier began a crusade to protect tribal institutions and property rights.

His activities on behalf of Native Americans, while research agent for the General Federation of Women's Clubs and executive secretary of the American Indian Defense Association, clearly demonstrate that it is a mistake to view the 1920s as simply a conservative interlude between two eras of reform — the Progressive movement and the New Deal. Collier contributed to the progressive impulse that surfaced after the 1918 armistice when he helped the Pueblo Indians organize opposition to legislation that threatened their Spanish land grants, discredited the government's attempt to suppress Indian dances, and insisted that the Indians receive all of the royalties from their water power sites and mineral land. Collier was ridiculed and sometimes despised for his harsh criticism of the Indian Bureau, but he managed to pave the way for the sweeping changes that took place during the presidency of Franklin Roosevelt.

Collier's appointment as commissioner of Indian affairs in 1933 altered the sense of hopelessness that had overcome Indian America. He gave many Native Americans a renewed sense of destiny by including them in most of the New Deal's relief and recovery programs. And he enkindled enthusiasm among his supporters at the Indian Bureau by arguing that the federal government had to implement bold new ideas drawn up by social scientists to honor its guardianship obligation. The Indian Reorganization Act of 1934, the heart of Collier's effort to revitalize Indian civilization, was based on the concept of cultural pluralism. It ended land allotment and enabled some tribes to secure once again a measure of political and economic control over their own futures.

While many of Collier's achievements were impressive, tensions and inconsistencies also underlay the Indian New Deal. Like the earlier reformers who formulated the Dawes General Allotment Act, Collier often imposed his notion of welfare — a collective democracy — upon a reluctant Indian population. Beset with the dilemma of synthesizing theory and reality, Collier discovered that his idealistic perceptions about the mystical qualities of Indian culture were often inaccurate. And he never located the specific engines of change that would enable him to use Indian tribal life to help transform American society as a whole into a cooperative commonwealth.

After his resignation from the Indian Service in 1945, Collier continued to work for the preservation of preindustrial cultures. As advisor to the United States delegation at the first General Assembly of the United Nations, he took up the cause of dependent peoples throughout the world. A short time later he became president of the Institute of Ethnic Affairs and accepted a professorship at the City College of New York. In this capacity, he pointed out the need for civilian self-government on

America's Pacific islands and opposed the policy of Indian termination which threatened the country with another century of dishonor.

A prophetic thinker, Collier envisioned an Indian renascence that would bring about a new consciousness wherein individuals would find meaning as members of a specific group. The first signs of that idea becoming manifest were evident in the early 1970s. Numerous tribes have used the Indian Reorganization Act as the basis for their survival in the postwar world, while many Indians have reaffirmed Collier's previous initiatives by stressing the importance of their native religions, Pan-Indianism, and tribal heritage as a means for ensuring cultural independence. But as yet it is too early to determine whether the potential for collective action that exists in Indian America will become vibrant enough to have a significant impact on the social malaise that dominates American life in this century.

During the course of my research for this book I have accumulated debts that can never be repaid, and some that cannot be recalled. While accepting responsibility for all shortcomings, I would like to give credit to the many people who made this volume possible. I am grateful to the librarians and archivists at the following institutions: the Library of Congress, the National Archives, the New York Public Library, Yale University, the Franklin D. Roosevelt Library, the University of Oklahoma, Michigan State University, the State of Michigan Library, the University of Michigan, and the University of Texas at Arlington.

I owe special thanks to Archibald Hanna and his excellent staff, who graciously made available the facilities of the Beinecke Rare Book and Manuscript Library at New Haven; Robert Kvasnicka, Richard S. Maxwell, and Jane F. Smith, who provided assistance in uncovering materials at the National Archives; Jack D. Haley, the assistant curator of the Western History Collection at Norman, Oklahoma; and Elizabeth Drewry at Hyde Park, New York. Grants from the Organized Research Fund at the University of Texas at Arlington eased the financial burden.

It is a pleasure to record the support that I received from Madison Kuhn, my mentor at Michigan State University. He served as a model of what a teacher, historian, and intellectual ought to be. I am also indebted to the following individuals: Robert E. Brown, John Harrison, and Vernon Lidtke, who were members of my doctoral committee; colleagues in the history department at Arlington, who provided criticism at faculty seminars; F. Ross Peterson, whose friendship and encouragement I deeply appreciate; and Glyndean La Plante, who typed the entire manuscript.

For authorization to quote from the Private Papers of John Collier,

I would like to thank his wife and literary agent, Grace V. Collier. Portions of this book have appeared elsewhere in somewhat different form: *Arizona and the West* (Autumn 1970); *The Rocky Mountain Social Science Journal* (April 1972); Leon Blair, ed., *Essays On Radicalism In Contemporary America* (Austin: The University of Texas Press, 1972); and the *Journal of Ethnic Studies* (Spring 1973). Permission from the editors to publish copyrighted material from these periodicals and books is gratefully acknowledged.

I started work on this volume in 1967. One year later Marjory Kay Donovan became my wife. She has been interested in the story of John Collier as long as we have been married and has taken time from her own career to participate in every stage of the book's development. My most concerned critic and editor, and my closest friend, she has contributed in ways that cannot be measured by mere words.

Finally, I would like to thank the University of Arizona Press for effecting publication of this book.

KENNETH R. PHILP

1. Discovering a Red Atlantis

During November 1920, John Collier, social worker and adult educator, left the Bay area of California with his wife, three young boys, and five dogs, intending to spend a year or longer in the Sonora wilderness of Mexico. En route they paused for a month, pitching their big balloon tent just above the high tide marks to enjoy the desolation of the Redondo, California, seaside with its rocky islets and seabirds. At Redondo Collier received a letter from Mabel Dodge, a bohemian friend whose pre-war Greenwich Village salon he had attended, asking him to detour his trip to visit Taos, New Mexico. Because he no longer visualized "the occidental ethos and genius as being the hope of the world," Collier became curious about Dodge's letter which described "a magical habitation" of Pueblo Indians: he decided to investigate it for himself.[1]

At the Santa Fe Railroad office in Los Angeles, Collier inquired about travel arrangements, but the personnel at the ticket window had never heard of either Santa Fe or Taos. After consultation in the main office he finally received tickets and started out for New Mexico. Following a short rest in a Santa Fe hotel, the Colliers decided to take a narrow gauge railroad as far as Embudo station, twenty-six miles from Taos. After renting a municipal ash cart for fifty cents to move their luggage to the train depot, they departed early in the morning. When they reached Embudo station, the Collier family met John Dunn, a stagecoach driver, who took them on the old highway along the Rio Grande Canyon until the road climbed onto the Taos plateau in the midst of a whirling snowstorm.[2]

Mabel Dodge, "a richly appareled and gracious woman," welcomed the Colliers at her home "in front of a blazing fireplace."[3] She introduced

[1]

National Archives

Wintertime at Taos Pueblo. John Collier discovered his Red Atlantis here in 1920.

Collier to Antonio Luhan, a Pueblo Indian, who took them into various Indian homes. They also participated in the dramatic Christmastime activities at Taos, where Collier watched the Virgin and Child carried on Indian shoulders from the adobe Catholic church along an avenue of ground fires to a tribal dance and song over a thousand years old. Three days later he witnessed the Red Deer Dance, "a communal art remotely impersonal while very passionate and very joyous, exquisite in myriad detail and as massive-seeming as the Sacred Mountain beyond it."[4]

These powerful religious dances and the dramatic physical beauty of northern New Mexico had a profound impact upon Collier; he believed he had discovered a "Red Atlantis" which held secrets desperately needed by the white world. Mabel Dodge was correct, he thought: Pueblo Indian life did possess a mystical social significance because its societies, unlike those of the white world, were alive and sources of power to their members. He was convinced that the integrated social organizations at the Pueblo offered an example of community life that had eluded him while a social worker in New York City. These Indians maintained the attribute, lost in the white world, of communal and cooperative experience — the profound sense of living found in primary social groups; they had discovered a way to become both "communists and individualists at one and the same time."[5]

Collier thought he had found on the New Mexico frontier a solution to the question of whether materialism and selfish individualism would dominate and destroy man. He concluded that Pueblo culture offered a model for the redemption of American society because it concerned itself very little with the material aspects of life; its goals were beauty, adventure, joy, comradeship, and the connection of man with God. To Collier, Pueblo life held the secrets to social education and personality formation urgently needed by the white world.[6]

This fascination with the Taos Indians was an extension of Collier's earlier attempts to create a sense of community among immigrants in New York City. Like other urban middle-class progressives, Collier had tried to restore a sense of unity lost in the industrial age.[7] At first, he attempted to bind the masses together through spontaneous public forums, voluntary film censorship, school community centers, and a school for settlement-house leaders. When these efforts failed, he joined the National Community Center Conference and the National Community Councils of Defense which he hoped would provide nationwide social planning after World War I.

Armistice Day, however, brought with it the end of reform, and

Taos Pueblo Church — where John Collier witnessed Christmas religious ceremonies.

National Archives

Collier headed to the Southwest where he met the Pueblo Indians. They attracted him because of their group life existing in the midst of an individualistic oriented white society. As a mystic who had previously found a romantic sense of rebirth in the North Carolina mountains, Collier was impressed with the Indians' "reverence and passion for the earth and its web of life."[8] He concluded that their survival on the harsh frontier raised the pregnant hypothesis that culture might be just as important as economics in the development of community life.[9]

Being convinced that Indian culture must be preserved for the benefit of all mankind, Collier continued his efforts at social reconstruction, making the twenties a seedtime for reform in Indian affairs.* In 1933, when President Franklin D. Roosevelt appointed him Indian commissioner, the groundwork had been laid for the Indian New Deal. Collier, a consistent supporter of social engineering during the thirties, attempted to strengthen tribal relationships because he hoped that they would offer an example of the communal life he had discovered at Taos.† But, as in his earlier efforts with New York's immigrant population, he met with limited success.

Collier's profound concern for group living began in his childhood. Born in Atlanta, Georgia, in 1884, to a union of Southern and New England families, he was the fourth of seven children. His father, Charles A. Collier, a distinguished lawyer and banker, helped build the new South by promoting a series of expositions culminating in the Cotton States and International Exposition of 1895. As mayor of Atlanta for the next four years, he struggled for the public ownership of utilities. Young Collier would eventually identify with his father's public service, while he learned from his mother, Susie Rawson Collier, a sensitivity toward plants and animals as well as a love of literature acquired through her reading aloud to him for several hours at a time.[10]

Much of Collier's life was determined by the early death of both his parents. This tragedy stemmed from his father's involvement in a financial scandal. His mother, deeply distressed by these events, died in 1897 from

---

*Clarke Chambers neglects to discuss Collier's successful efforts at Indian reform when he describes the persistence and expansion of social welfare activity by former progressives during the twenties. Clarke Chambers, *Seedtime of Reform, American Social Service and Social Action, 1918–1933* (Minneapolis: University of Minnesota Press, 1963).

†Interestingly, Collier's background supports Otis Graham's thesis about the type of progressive who supported the New Deal. He was a social worker from New York City, a reform Darwinist, acquainted with urban poverty, studied in Germany, and fought for social justice after World War I. Otis Graham, Jr., *An Encore for Reform* (New York: Oxford University Press, 1967), pp. 55, 109, 167–68.

addiction to laudanum, a drug used as a relaxant.[11] During the year after
his mother's death, Collier, then thirteen years old, lived in Sharon,
Georgia, the home of a Roman Catholic convent school operated by the
Sisters of the Sacred Heart. There he became close friends with several
nuns, turned away from the Methodism of his family, and temporarily
embraced Roman Catholicism.[12]

Three years later Collier's father committed suicide after grieving
over his wife's death and the family's tarnished honor. While in a "condition of deep physical and spiritual depression" for six months after this
event, Collier made a promise that would influence all of his adult years:
he vowed not to seek "any success in the society" that had led to his
parents' downfall.[13]

Despite the shock surrounding his parents' untimely deaths, Collier
finished his education at Atlanta High School. A reporter for the *Atlanta
Journal,* impressed with a speech Collier gave about Robert E. Lee during the school's Christmas exercises, remarked: "we predict for this
talented young man a brilliant future, and many honors from his coun-
trymen."[14] Collier did graduate valedictorian, but not because of scho-
lastic merit. Along with most of his classmates he had cheated during
final examinations, and the principal responded by expelling two boys
from poor families. Upset at this unfair punishment, Collier warned that
he would expose the whole cheating system and the mediocre nature of
the school unless the boys were reinstated. The principal agreed and
nominated him valedictorian.[15]

Finished with high school, Collier went camping with his brother
Charles in the southern Appalachian Mountains of Georgia during the
summer of 1901. They walked from Tallulah Falls toward Porter Springs
through the beautiful Nacoochee Valley where their parents had first
met. Upon entering a country store to purchase food, they encountered
several mountaineers who offered them whiskey; they soon became drunk,
staggered out of the store, and fell into a haystack. The next day they
met a woman who remarked "you look sort'er wore out."[16] Accepting
an offer to rest at her house, they eagerly jumped into a double bed but
were soon attacked by a host of fleas. After an hour's misery they left
the house and slept on the ground. When the two boys reached Porter
Springs, Charles decided that he was tired of camping, so Collier continued alone toward Tranquilia, North Carolina.*

There he discovered spiritual rejuvenation — a sense of "cosmic
consciousness" — to combat the loneliness and isolation which came after

---

*Collier's interest in native folk cultures began during such camping trips to
the Appalachian Mountains. John Collier, *From Every Zenith* (Denver: Sage Books,
1963), pp. 27–30.

"I am too glad to live":
John Collier on one of his
restorative visits to the
Southern Appalachians.

Mrs. John Collier, Sr.

his parents' death. Once, at sundown following a severe thunderstorm, he experienced the vision of a bird which summoned him to continue "onward, into the struggle not lost and not won," and toward the "immortal effort toward creation in which I, the bird, need you."[17] Later Collier composed a poem about these experiences. He wrote:

> *Vast landscapes, glimmering wide from marge to marge;*
> *Huge hills, like the titans of unrestful dream!*
> *Back and yet back they tower, away, away*
> *Far to the glimmering limit of the new born day;*
> *Range upon range they climb in purple majesty.*
> *The vales are mazed in mist; the cloudbanks gleam*
> *High to the central crimson, where the rays*
> *of the unrisen sun do shimmer and steam.*
> *Vast winds, born in the dreamland of the dawn,*

Swell, roaring inward; leagues on first leagues
Blind their wild scent and sound.
The tide is full,
The tide of glory past all fathoming,
The vision of everlasting God
Forth-shadowed on the everlasting hills,
Can rise no more.
The concentrated splendor of a thousand days
Climbs the triumphant east.
My God, my God,
Told me this moment home: too beautiful!
I am too glad to live: I know Thou livest![18]

After he returned from the wilderness, Collier used money from his father's estate to enter Columbia University during 1902. Sponsored by Professor Brander Matthews, a friend of the family, Collier enrolled as a special student taking graduate courses in literature. Although he could not read French, Collier signed up for Matthew's graduate class dealing with nineteenth-century French drama. Using great mental exertion, he soon read in French most of the works of Victor Hugo for his thesis. It was not long, however, before he came under the influence of Miss Lucy Graham Crozier, a free-lance New York teacher, who directed his interest from literature to biology. Accepting a summer scholarship during 1904, he studied natural science at Woods Hole Marine Laboratory in Massachusetts. In his leisure hours he showed great physical stamina by swimming far out to sea, which surprised his colleagues because he had been living as a vegetarian on a diet of fruits and nuts.[19]

Collier soon became distracted from biology to larger social problems, especially after reading Prince Peter Kropotkin's book, *Mutual Aid*. A well-known Russian anarchist who lived in exile in London, Kropotkin used biological data to buttress his utopian vision of a classless society. He rejected the ideas of social Darwinists who argued that man made progress by competition and survival of the fittest. Kropotkin suggested that a law of mutual aid between members of the same species was by far a more important factor in the evolutionary process. After discussing mutual aid in various classes of creatures such as bees, ants and wolves, he described the importance of cooperative life in precapitalist societies. Reviving the theme of the noble savage, Kropotkin showed how Eskimos and other primitive peoples shared their food, lived on communal tracts of land, and generally followed the rule of "each for all." The growth of the Roman Empire had disrupted this mutual aid, but it grew again during the medieval period only to face disruption because of the industrial age.[20]

Mutual Aid profoundly impressed Collier, and he believed that it was "one of the great books" on community life.[21] It proved that "cooperation and reciprocity" had accompanied human life through thousands of generations. Kropotkin had demonstrated that these village communities "like countless flowers in a long April" held the secrets of "informing, enriching, tempering and socializing" the human personality.[22]

Delighted with the intellectual curiosity of her student, Miss Crozier exposed Collier to the writing of William Morris, an unorthodox British socialist. He immediately became interested in Morris' *Sigurd the Volsung,* an epic Icelandic saga, which substituted heroic deeds for the crass and sordid aspects of industrialized life. Collier admired Morris for his "sustained labors in behalf of the social revolution," which included lectures before the Socialist League.[23] In these talks Morris had challenged the British middle classes to reject their Victorian values that regarded wealth as the only means to advancement and create instead a civilization consisting of federalized local communities where the work of the laboring man would be admired.[24]

During this period of his life, Collier absorbed ideas from such men as Friedrich Wilhelm Nietzsche, the German philosopher, and Lester Frank Ward, an American sociologist. From Nietzsche he discovered that the task of life was to order society "to invoke the beyond-man from present man." Collier thought that Nietzsche was the "flaming, winged, and thundering apostle" of a personality development that sought "self-improvement and self-transcendence."[25] And when he read the works of Ward they excited him "like nothing else in life but life itself when experienced in some inscrutable, beautiful human relationship."[26] Accepting Ward's concept of sociocracy which advocated the "scientific control of social forces by the collective mind of society," Collier believed that through *social telesis* the psychic forces of mind and spirit could control and direct the evolutionary process.[27] Nevertheless, he had moments of despair because Ward's synthesis was "inertly familiar but unused in the minds of the thinkers of our generation."[28]

Because of his growing interest in human relationships, Collier followed Miss Crozier's suggestion that he convince southern railroads and chambers of commerce to establish a system of resettling unemployed immigrants on land in Georgia and neighboring states. Worried that his scheme might fail, he contacted Lester Frank Ward at the Smithsonian Institution who gave his "unconditional endorsement" to this experiment in the cross-fertilization of biological stocks and cultures. Collier hoped that his plan would relieve the congested northern cities and enrich the ethnic character of the new South. In March 1905, when this effort failed due to the lack of financial support, the young idealist became executive officer of the newly formed Atlanta Charities. He suggested that all relief should be based on work, but after four months of meager results the board of directors asked for his resignation.[29]

After his second experience with failure, Collier decided to camp again in the southern Appalachians, equipped with only bare necessities such as a water bag, frying pan, and a knife. He lived in the wilderness for about six months, returning in November 1905 to accept the position as a "cub" reporter for the *Macon Telegraph*. Because of rapid staff changes due to alcoholism, he soon became acting editor. Collier's working days began at nine in the morning with a breakfast consisting of whiskey and buckwheat pancakes. He did not eat again until the office closed after midnight, when he went to a Greek restaurant to dine on sweet potato pie.[30]

But Collier became bored with small town existence and felt that his learning experience as a newspaperman had ended, so he sailed for Europe in 1906 to meet a friend in Leipzig. While on shipboard he met Lucy Wood, a young woman from Philadelphia who was bound for Paris. After he visited Germany, Collier rejoined Lucy in France, and they fell in love while touring Brittany. Returning home, they married and soon departed again for Paris where Collier attended Pierre Janet's psychology classes at the College de France. He immersed himself in Janet's "psychology of the unconscious" and became close friends with the professor, who unsuccessfully tried to treat an alcoholic friend of Collier's.[31]

While they resided in Paris, Collier and Lucy met James Ford, a professor of social ethics at Harvard, who helped them study the Belgian labor movement and French syndicalism. A short time later the trio traveled to England and Ireland. After arriving in Dublin, they set out on foot across valleys and mountains toward the northwest coast. At one point they became lost in the fog on one of the mountains and eventually arrived at the home of an Irish Anglican priest who invited them indoors, served whiskey, and talked for hours about the Gaelic Renaissance and the Irish cooperative movement.[32]

Back in the United States during 1907, Collier became a social worker, spending a twelve-year period of experimental activity among the immigrants on Manhattan Island. His concern about an "unplanned and inhuman urban America" was not surprising considering his social philosophy.[33] The influence of Miss Crozier and his trip to Europe had caused Collier to reject the biological and mechanistic determinism found in the writings of men such as Herbert Spencer. He disliked free market and laissez-faire doctrines which portrayed the world as an aggregation of persons controlled by universal economic laws. Collier was a reform

Darwinist and self-made sociologist who argued that man must mold society's future through deliberate innovation and individual creativity. He cast aside all values that justified wealth as an end in itself and focused on subjective and spiritual motivations in history.[34]

According to Collier, whose arguments sounded similar to those found in Kropotkin's *Mutual Aid,* there were four epochs in history: prehistory, the classical-Christian period, the advent of modern science, and the industrial age. He believed that all through prehistory the common man felt a sense of social purpose because he had depended on small groups for his existence. Then came the classical period, which witnessed the growth of large centralized states and cities. The average person no longer felt that the destiny of the world rested on his shoulders, but the growth of Christianity once again enabled him to identify with the hope of the race. This religious unity, however, started to disintegrate with the beginning of modern science.[35]

The dilemma of modern man in the fourth epoch of history, the industrial age, especially concerned Collier. He worried about the impact of industrialization and urbanization on the quality of human life, believing that organic society with its sense of community was being replaced by one in which the individual found himself isolated. Collier felt that the supremacy of machine over man led only to the uprooting of populations, the disintegration of neighborhoods, and the starvation of the soul. He knew that only through social planning could man regain a social consciousness and control over his future.[36]

Because of his interest in promoting community life to combat the social upheaval caused by the Industrial Revolution, Collier accepted the position of civic secretary for the People's Institute, an organization devoted to giving the immigrant masses a sense of brotherhood in their local neighborhoods. Founded in 1897 by Charles Sprague Smith, the former head of Columbia University's department of comparative literature, the institute was not a settlement house but an educational institution.[37] Smith attempted to assist in the "peaceful reorganization of society" by supporting the advance of social democracy through a union of intellectuals and the working class. He hoped to establish a political and social alternative to Tammany Hall and redeem the immigrant's leisure hours.[38]

The institute's activities centered in the large meeting hall at Cooper Union. There adults met for a free evening school, which offered lectures on history, literature, and related social sciences. Theories such as the single tax, socialism, and the European cooperative movement received attention as long as they proved "not inconsistent with evolutionary progress."[39] A people's forum also met at Cooper Union to give "knowledge, leadership, and public voice to wage earning masses."[40] At

New York Public Library

Cooper Union, headquarters of the People's Institute,
announces free public lectures.

these forums over 1,000 Jewish and Italian immigrants met three times
a week to discuss local, state, and national politics. At the end of their
"perpetual mass meetings," they passed resolutions supporting measures
such as the public ownership of New York's transit system, the popular
election of senators, women's suffrage, and self-determination for the
Philippine Islands. On Sunday the institute operated a people's church
that sponsored congregational singing and a series of addresses on ethical

questions. All denominations could state their views but attempts at conversion were prohibited. By 1903 over 140,000 people attended 120
lectures at Cooper Union.[41]

These forums excited Collier because they implemented Lester Frank
Ward's concept of sociocracy or the scientific control of social forces by
the collective mind of society. By educating the immigrant masses, the
leaders of the People's Institute used the concept of *social telesis* to promote progress.* Collier believed that the people's forums brought forth
the inner strivings of the human soul and he warned that the manifesta-
tions could be "positive and terrifying," inaugurating upheavals such as
the French and Russian Revolutions. They might even start social change
in America, demonstrating that the people were determined "to override
constitutional limitations, to defy repressive laws and to force upon judges
and lawmakers new and disturbing principles of government." This did
not bother him because he confidently looked forward to the "dawning
soul of society."[42]

While working at the institute, Collier concluded that the "problem
of the twentieth century" would focus on "the utilization of leisure time"
to secure economic justice and political freedom, rather than on the creation of wealth.[43] He thought that machine industry and the growth of
science had destroyed the fabric of society by alienating man from his
work, weakening the social bond of Christianity, and destroying the cohesion of the family. Worse yet, man's emotional, social, and aesthetic
nature was being ministered to by secularized amusements such as the
saloon, dance hall, and movie theaters. Collier believed that the community had to extend its control over these "irresponsible, money making
agencies" because emotional forces were the dynamics of mankind and
should not be left to private exploitation.[44]

During February 1908, Collier completed a study of commercial
amusements, his first assignment for the People's Institute. He reported
that the nickelodeon had become "an unwieldy excrescence on the body
politic," often "openly immoral in influence."[45] It threatened church
activities, caused children to cut school, and led to empty libraries. Collier
indicated that the city should inspect movie houses because they menaced
the community with their poor ventilation, congested rooms, and fire

---

*The large turnout of immigrants at the People's Institute supports J. Joseph
Huthmacher's thesis that the urban lower class played an active role in the Progressive movement. In New York City this group joined the middle class and helped
determine the course of American liberalism. J. Joseph Huthmacher, "Urban Liberalism and the Age of Reform," *Mississippi Valley Historical Review* 49 (September
1962): 231–41.

Immigrants attending a concert sponsored by the
People's Institute.

hazards. He recommended stricter moral censorship to improve the minds
of the people while giving them entertainment.[46]

This report caused Charles Sprague Smith to establish a National
Board of Censorship under the guidance of the People's Institute. Directed
by Collier, the board cooperated with exhibitors of motion pictures who
agreed voluntarily to remove undesirable scenes such as overacted love,
the wanton heroine who turned lightly from man to man, and fighting
women or hairpulling girls.[47] The board was careful, however, not to
censor political, sectional, and controversial films such as *Birth of a
Nation*.[48] Under Collier's leadership it persuaded Mayor William Jay
Gaynor, in 1910, to cancel the licenses of New York movie operators
until they met safety regulations drawn up by the National Board of
Censorship.[49]

Aware of the potential of the infant movie industry, Collier appeared before a joint session of the Wisconsin legislature in October 1911. He advocated a state-owned motion picture library that would rent educational films to school districts. Hopefully, this would stimulate the school curriculum and prevent rote lessons.[50] Collier favored censorship and municipal ownership of amusement places so films would concentrate on the universal strivings of mankind, thus raising the level of the working class. But he admitted that these efforts failed to thwart Hollywood, which preferred to focus on sensationalism, hero-worship, obscenity, and victorious criminality.[51]

Collier's other duties included co-editing the *People's Institute Bulletin*, a paper that dealt with topics such as the need for rapid transit and parks.[52] In October 1909, he became sole editor of an expanded publication called the *Civic Journal*. Usually limiting himself to the discussion of New York civic matters, Collier claimed that his weekly newspaper, which contained no advertising, supported the cause of "progressive democracy."[53] Consistently, his columns proved sympathetic toward the reform program of Tammany Hall opponent, Mayor William Jay Gaynor, and a variety of Progressive causes such as ending the sweatshop, unionizing women shirt makers, and home rule.[54]

Although he emphasized municipal problems, Collier occasionally commented on world events. In the October 6, 1909, issue of the *Civic Journal* he composed an impassioned poem in memory of Francisco Ferrer, an anarchist and anti-clerical educator, executed by the Spanish government after an abortive revolt in Barcelona.

Francisco Ferrer

They shot him down, far off in ancient Spain.
A gentle man, soft-voiced, and spirit clear,
A man like you and me, greater through pain,
Holier, and happier for through conquered fear.

They shot him down, calm enemy of all wars,
Herald of peace, who waged his lonely fight.
They shot him down, coward and murderers.
They slew the herald, they can not slay the light.

Brothers, have we forgotten how late we dealt
Fiercely, and wrenched the Southern Isles from Spain?
I have seen Moro Castle, and I have knelt
Where hundreds knelt never to rise again —

Knelt as I knelt against a sun warmed wall,
Old-world, and harrowed with an old world sign,
Where brains were scattered with the leaden ball
That bit the stone. And they had souls like mine!

He was an anarchist. Well, and so were we
Who scourged Spain from the Caribbean shore.
He fought at home, alone and terribly,
What we drove from this West forevermore.

He fought to save a nation from within,
Grappled with monstrous vampires from the grave,
Asked for his people what we need not win,
Whose fathers won our freedom. Oh how they rave.

Dull, far off, strange to us, those restless seas
That broke our dungeon, and that are not done,
Though feared and named by us as anarchies,
Till the last mortal cavern sees the sun.

And we, who cry because they shot him down —
We are less happy, we have not conquered fear.
Subtler, stranger our war which is not won.
Oh that we had this epic chance and clear!

Oh that we heard a clarion-call, as they
In old-world countries with their tangible foes!
We fight in multitudes and terribly
And know not whither the endless battle goes.

Only we bear a spark from earlier time,
And in the simplified distance still may wait
An age heroic, a clarion-call sublime.
We are as bridges between Fate and Fate.[55]

Despite such eloquence, the *Civic Journal* ceased publication during April 1910 because of financial problems due to a small circulation.[56]

Undeterred by this failure, Collier cooperated with Edward Barrows, who had lived with boys' gangs in the Hell's Kitchen district of Manhattan, to begin research on child life in New York City. They discovered that schools closed after classroom hours, while the street front made up the only playground for 95 percent of the city's children. In 1911, Collier and other reformers helped deal with this dilemma by persuading the New York Board of Education to open several schools for recreational activities in the evening and on holidays.[57] They convinced the police commissioner that he should close selected streets several hours each afternoon for playground use. Three years later, Collier and Barrow published their findings in a booklet entitled *The City Where Crime Is Play*.[58]

Their activities led to the growth of "school community centers" throughout New York City. Patterned after a similar experiment in Rochester, several public schools became the focus of educational, political, and recreational projects. One of the most active centers, Public

School 63, was located on the east side of Manhattan. Directed by Clinton S. Childs, a representative of the People's Institute, it became the focal point for civic discussion and ethnic pride. A Jewish club was formed to revive national songs, while other activities included open-air dances, · political forums, and an educational motion picture exhibit.[59] Collier added to this effort by attempting to revive Italian marionette shows for educational use and as a device for drawing immigrants to the community centers.[60]

In a similar effort Collier helped organize a Pageant and Festival of Nations at Public School 63. He explained the purpose behind this event in a feature article written in March 1914 for the *New York Press*. He warned that industrialism had made people collective beings in an economic way but wreaked havoc with social institutions. The "new giant" of machinery had caused class alignments, dehumanized labor, and led to the migration of immigrants on a vast scale. It shredded collective units, such as the family, the neighborhood, and the church, where life had gathered up its beauty and hope. Instead of freeing man from the economic system forever, machinery had become a "new form of human slavery."[61]

According to Collier, mankind urgently needed to "strive together" in order to harness the forces of industrialized society. Salvation would come by creating positive social institutions "of liberation, joy and group achievement." He argued that pageantry would "bring out in the average man a more burning and positive vision of collective life . . . than any other art device" and help preserve the human "heritage of beauty, loyalty and civilization."[62] It might provide a nucleus where human interests could organize in a city that was a "conglomeration of factories, terminals and mercantile houses."[63]

The Pageant and Festival of Nations began during the first week of June 1914, when different ethnic groups met at Public School 63 to present songs and dances from their homeland. These activities culminated on June 6, when over 300 Jews, Italians, Irishmen, Bohemians, Russians, Poles, and other nationalities marched in their native dress accompanied by bands and maypole dancers down the east side of Manhattan. Over 15,000 people watched this spectacle, many from the windows and rooftops of tenement buildings. Notable guests included Miss Margaret Wilson, daughter of President Woodrow Wilson, and Miss Lillian Wald, a settlement-house worker.[64]

Mabel Dodge, whose Fifth Avenue salon Collier often attended, vividly described his efforts to preserve the culture of various nationalities. She saw Collier "as a small blond Southerner, intense, preoccupied, and always looking windblown on the quietest day. Because he could not

Bohemian children in the Pageant and Festival of Nations, June 1914.

seem to love his own kind of people, and as he was full of a reformer's enthusiasm for humanity, he turned to other races and worked for them." Dodge pointed out that Collier had attempted against tremendous odds to stem the tide of Americanization by persuading immigrants to "keep their national dress, their customs, and their diets, their religion, and all their folk ways." [65]

After residing in Paris and Florence, Mabel Dodge had returned to New York in 1912. Her weekly salons at 23 Fifth Avenue brought together many radical intellectuals such as Max Eastman and John Reed, editors of *The Masses;* Bill Haywood, an organizer for the International Workers of the World; Walter Lippmann, a well-known social critic from Harvard; and Isadora Duncan, an avant-garde dancer. Hutchins Hapgood, a liberal journalist, introduced Collier to Dodge's circle of friends; in return, he brought Emma Goldman, an anarchist, to Dodge's apartment.

At these salons a speaker presented a topic that was discussed by all present. Collier's subject usually centered on some phase of his community work.[66]

Dodge's salon had proved a valuable experience for Collier, but he was "overstimulated, mentally and emotionally" after seven years of social work.[67] So he temporarily resigned from his position at the People's Institute in order to spend several months with his family near Andrews in the North Carolina mountains. Unfortunately, Collier's youngest son caught pneumonia and his wife, Lucy, had to take the child to Asheville for pediatric care. There she learned that her mother was dying from cancer, so Lucy returned to Philadelphia, witnessing the unexpected sudden death of both her parents, who suffered from malignant tumors.[68]

Collier remained in the wilderness with his two sons and camped along the Nantahala River. He read the books of two French social thinkers, Henri Poincaré and Henri Bergson, both of whom questioned positivistic explanations of man and the universe. Collier also wrote a great deal of poetry patterned after the work of William Morris.[69] Most of his poems invoked a vision of a happier arcadian world free from the frustrations of being unable to alter the social order in New York City. In June 1914, Collier wrote *Ruined Land,* which beckoned the reader to "come away from the grapple of nations and classes" to the Appalachian Mountains with their "dawn flowery sky meadows" and "pungent fog-wreaths cold." Collier further noted that in a past golden age "the heart of humanity had throbbed" there and a "noble folklife" existed. But this was all being ruined by lumbering, a product of the industrial age, which had turned the "forest and humanity to an ashen thing."[70]

When not composing poems or camping, Collier carried on a lengthy correspondence with Mabel Dodge, one of the "most stimulating people he knew." They discussed hashish, homosexuality, poetry, the writings of William James, and the role of the subconscious in human behavior. Enthralled with the beauty of the Blue Ridge Mountains, Collier wrote Dodge that:

... the ground is nearly as white as snow with apple-blossoms now, the nearby knoll is a fountain of green, the lilac hangs heavy, the blooming sourwood has stormed the mountains to their crest. And a thousand puffs of white are shot skyward along the foothills — the dogwood in full bloom. And the bees — their moaning is louder than Junaluska's.[71]

During his year of seclusion Collier began writing for *Survey Graphic* a series of articles entitled "Lantern Bearers," which dealt with the history, philosophy, and potentiality of the theatre to unite men in groups.[72]

Concerned about the growing impersonalization of life "into business enterprises encircling the earth," Collier called for the creation of community theatres in America similar to Belgium's "Maison du People" and the Free Folk Theatre of Berlin (*Freie Bühne*), an organ of the Social Democratic Party.[73] He hoped that a people's community theatre would bring a concern for humanity in an age where the "economic stud had run away with its rider."[74] By performing naturalistic plays similar to Gerhart Hauptmann's *The Weavers,* which dramatized the revolt of the Silesian peasants in 1844, Collier thought that the theatre might help the masses regenerate their moral ideals and harness "the cosmos for social service."[75]

At the end of 1914, Collier and his family returned to their prerevolutionary Dutch farmhouse in Sparkhill, New York. There the Colliers established the Home School, a utopian educational experiment which operated for five years. It consisted of their three sons and nine other children. Under the supervision of Miss Mattie Bates, a teacher who followed the tenets of John Dewey, the children combined academic study with carpentry work and recreation. In the summer they went naked and swam in the farm's millpond. Collier and his wife, Lucy, visited the school during weekends, spending the rest of their time in New York City.[76]

Collier resumed his activities at the People's Institute, and he soon became involved in a bizarre incident involving Isadora Duncan. An unconventional "free spirited woman" who took up "the cudgels for free love" and raised her children without getting married, Isadora was the first American to reject the orthodox ballet tradition for a free dance form that expressed "the emotion of humanity." Because her talents failed to attract enough support in the United States, she moved to Europe and received financial assistance from wealthy patronesses in London, Paris, and Berlin. There she became famous for her flowing "transparent tunic" and bare feet.[77]

The first meeting between Collier and Miss Duncan took place at Mabel Dodge's salon in 1915. The famed dancer had just returned from Europe, and she became close friends with Collier after reading four of his poems praising her artistic endeavors. Entranced by Isadora's dance performances at various New York theatres, Collier, Dodge, and Juliette Poyntz, the educational director of the International Ladies Garment Workers' Union, decided to secure the city armory to enable her to teach dancing to 1,000 working-class girls. Collier invited Mayor John Purroy Mitchell to Isadora's studio where they planned to present a petition that requested permission to use the armory. Unfortunately, Isadora had become a psychotic "self-abandoned alcoholic," and she grasped the mayor's hand and drew him onto a couch. He fled in terror and their project became a fiasco.[78]

According to Collier, this type of occurrence caused "bewilderment, exasperation, even distrust" among his colleagues at the People's Institute.[79] But the fundamental cause of this tension lay in Collier's unique personality. An "energetic, persistent, ingenious, and inventive person," he often began more projects than he could finish. And, being concerned with mainly the ideas relating to social engineering and achievements, he often lost "a sense of responsibility for things which the idea or vision had produced." In addition, Collier differed with some of his associates over the role of the institute. He was determined that it carry forward the work of "experimental sociology in action" rather than rely on "sterile successes" and "mere executive hustling."[80]

Because of his dissatisfaction, Collier established the Training School for Community Workers, an independent organization having only a loose affiliation with the People's Institute. Its purpose was to equip young men and women with skills to staff existing public school community centers, settlement houses, and neighborhood associations.[81] As director of this unusual educational endeavor, Collier hoped that his students would become pioneers, expanding New York's community activities into a national movement. In August 1915 he placed an advertisement in a local newspaper calling for thirty-five individuals "of an adventuresome disposition" who were in a position to risk two or three years of their lives with the knowledge that the project might be a failure.[82]

The Training School opened in October with the exact number of students Collier requested, and it remained in session until May. It offered a flexible two-semester curriculum that reflected the influence of John Dewey, a renowned philosopher and progressive educator who taught at Columbia University and directed the Training School's educational committee. Each week the students attended three lectures or seminar sessions and engaged in fifteen hours of practice experience at local public school community centers.[83] They used William McDougall's *Social Psychology* for a textbook and read from the voluminous writings of Lester Frank Ward. According to Collier, a great deal of learning took place at "intimate nightly discussions" between beginners and veterans in the field of social work.[84] At these sessions Collier stressed that human behavior was rooted in psychic instincts; he emphasized the importance of social rather than physical heredity and tried to prove that the former was transmitted through psychic mechanisms when people associated with one another.[85]

Collier believed that the modification of social institutions made up the "leading problem of sociology," so he invited guest lecturers to speak on questions concerning the impact of industrialism, problems caused by immigration, and the study of "the group mind."[86] They included Charles Beard, a well-known progressive and professor of political science at Columbia, who spoke about the evils of Tammany Hall, Professor James Ford of Harvard, whose lectures focused on the consumer cooperative movement, and Dr. A. A. Brill, who expounded the psychoanalytical system of Sigmund Freud.[87]

Many of Collier's students did their fieldwork at the Wingate Community Center located at Public School 40 in the Gramercy District. Established by the People's Institute in July 1916, it organized the local neighborhood and started activities such as folk dancing classes, concerts, playground games, and a variety of clubs. Collier's students carried out New York's first experiment in the use of a public school by organized labor. In the evening young Italian and Jewish girls from Local 25 of the Ladies Waist and Dressmakers' Union used the Wingate Community Center to hold business meetings and engage in educational activities such as a workers' free university.[88]

The Training School remained in operation until 1919 when it closed for several reasons. It had stressed theory while neglecting such practical matters as teaching students the knowledge of crafts, bookkeeping, and recreation games for adolescents. Fieldwork at the public school community centers faced trouble because of inadequate supervisory personnel for the students. Other problems included difficulty in attracting volunteer experts for so few students and lack of sufficient funds.[89] Since it was financed only by small contributions from the People's Institute and declining tuition receipts, the Training School went several thousand dollars in debt.[90]

In conjunction with his activities at the Training School, Collier worked to organize various community endeavors into a nationwide organization. On April 16, 1916, social workers from all parts of the country met in New York to establish the National Community Center Conference. They elected Dr. Luther Gulick, the director of physical training at the New York public schools, as president and Collier as secretary. Hoping that the community centers would follow the European cooperative movement, Collier and his friends wanted to move from cooperation in the field of leisure and recreation "toward the distribution of physical necessities."[91]

Their dreams vanished when Edward J. Ward, an expert in community center organization from the United States Bureau of Education, spoke for the more conservative delegates at the conference. He claimed that "a little coterie of New York extremists" headed by Collier represented the syndicalist philosophy of Bill Haywood, a leader of the International Workers of the World. According to Ward, any proposal to turn the public schools over to private individuals would be "removing the Stars and Stripes . . . and putting up the two-headed eagle." Collier ridiculed the contention of Ward, whom he called a modern-day Don Quixote, but his dreams for unity among community workers lay in shambles.[92]

At the New York convention, Collier had accepted the position as editor of the *Community Center,* a magazine-newspaper issued by the National Community Center Conference. He began publication during February 1917 and welcomed as subscribers all persons "interested in the liberation of the human spirit through the use of leisure time, be the channels what they may."[93] He published articles on all aspects of the community center movement and brought attention to the need for health reform. Citing an investigation made by Dr. Haven Emerson, New York's health commissioner, which recommended inexpensive medical services, Collier called for the passage of state "compulsory health insurance" and the creation of neighborhood clinics for the poor.[94]

Editorial work engaged much of his time, but Collier managed to help the People's Institute establish the Community Clearing House and the Social Clinic for Unadjusted Children in the Gramercy District. Settlement workers at the clearing house compiled a directory of public and private agencies that dealt with human needs in New York City. They brought together the heads of thirteen city and county departments in a cooperative effort toward better understanding between government and the citizens it served, while the Social Clinic for Unadjusted Children provided assistance in solving the problems of truancy and juvenile delinquency.[95]

Collier's activities in behalf of social reconstruction ended in 1917. In the autumn he worked actively to renominate John Purroy Mitchell, a liberal-minded mayor. When this effort failed and the people elected a Tammany Hall candidate, the political atmosphere of New York changed decisively toward conservatism.[96] More important, America's entry into the First World War caused the New York Board of Education to issue a proclamation stating that all public schools must remain open after hours for use by voluntary agencies "organized to promote national purposes."[97] Since they were taken over by the patriotic National Community Councils of Defense, the school community centers no longer focused on urban concerns. Instead, they sold war bonds, issued propaganda for conserving food stuffs, dispatched relief materials, held military drills, and secured enlistments in the army.[98]

Collier watched these events with some dismay, but like many other progressives he supported the war because he felt there was a chance to nationalize local reform. In a keynote address made in Chicago on April 17, 1917, at his inauguration as president of the National Community Center Conference, Collier spoke about "The Crisis of Democracy." He warned that to maintain the values of Western civilization, the democratic nations would have to adopt a centralized organization similar to the one that made Germany efficient. This raised the question of whether a country could have efficiency and preserve democracy at the same time. Collier thought that both were possible, and he hoped that the National Community Councils of Defense would remain after the war to engage in nationwide social planning. Because he knew that isolated community centers affected only a few individuals, he wanted to federalize his experiments in New York "in order to work effectively toward the regeneration of local democracy."[99]

When the Great War ended on November 11, 1918, Collier believed that the United States had the power "to emancipate the human race — if only she had the will to do it," but that determination faltered and Armistice Day "proved to be a day of delusion."[100] On the national level the government forced the disastrous Treaty of Versailles on Germany and followed conservative demobilization practices at home, while at the local level reforms such as the community centers failed to reemerge.[101] Because his activities in New York were beset by monetary problems, political reaction, and by the Americanization drive of World War I, Collier moved to Los Angeles, California, in September 1919 and accepted a position as director of the state's adult educational program. Sponsored by the State Immigration Commission, the State Board of Education, and the regents of the University of California, Collier once again embarked upon efforts to restore community life to urban America.[102]

Initially his efforts focused around a district of immigrant wage earners near Custer Park in Los Angeles where he worked with local educators who had agreed to keep schools open for evening citizenship classes and provide increased services at playgrounds.[103] Collier's major task, however, consisted of traveling across the state on "a continuous lecture tour," where he established public forums similar to those of the People's Institute. During his lectures, he talked at length about two of the "most important issues on everyone's mind," the cooperative movement and the significance of the Russian Revolution.[104] Collier believed that the Bolsheviks had "provided the most important single sociological experiment of our time" in their effort to revive community life growing out of peasant institutions such as the mir.[105] One year later, during the Red Scare, he came under the surveillance of Department of Justice agents who sat in his classes. They became suspicious of his ideas and cooperated with the Better America Federation of California, a lobby of reactionary businessmen, which convinced state legislators to remove Collier's salary from the state budget.[106]

Harassed and finding his salary cut, Collier left for the wilderness of Mexico, but his trip became permanently interrupted after visiting Taos during the winter of 1920. There he found answers to the questions that had vexed him in his pursuit of community life in New York and California. He believed that these Indians had personality-forming institutions that produced "states of mind, attitudes of mind, earth loyalties and human loyalties, amid the context of beauty which suffused the group."[107] Collier concluded that Pueblo culture, and tribal life in general, must survive, not only in justice to the Indian but in service to the white. The Indians offered examples of gemeinschaft relationships, in which people in communal life were motivated by shared purposes, instead of the white-oriented gesellschaft mode of life, in which individuals lived isolated from each other. They demonstrated how organized groups of people, joined together in community life, could save mankind from the negative consequences of the industrial age.[108]

The vision that Collier experienced at this time dramatically changed his life. Intermittently through the next two years he occupied a house in the art colony at Spanish-American Taos, but he rejected the life of the colony with its "severe individualism," which left each artist "at the center of a wistful and socially undernourished solitude."[109] Instead, Collier held evening conversations with selected writers around the fireplace at Mabel Dodge's home where they discussed the meaning of Indian life for the white world.[110] Mary Austin, author of books sympathetic to the American Indian, proved especially influential with her ideas about the importance of the group consciousness that existed in the New Mexican Pueblos.[111] Austin and others soon enlisted Collier in a regional movement to revive and preserve Indian culture. He became so zealous that his next-door neighbor, the English novelist D. H. Lawrence, feared that he would destroy the Indians by "setting the claws of his own benevolent volition into them."[112]

Lawrence's perceptive comment touched on a dilemma that had plagued Collier's altruistic efforts on behalf of the immigrants and, later, the American Indians. Like those of other middle-class settlement workers, his efforts to close the gap that existed between the urban lower classes and the rest of society through various techniques of social control were marred by internal contradictions.[113] Collier found it impossible to apply his mystical vision of a classless agrarian community, where people discovered meaning and spiritual values in their work, to the social chaos of New York City. He failed to establish a new system of primary group relationships in the unstable tenement neighborhoods because of the confusion produced by the great variety of nationalities.[114] This frequently caused him to abandon the democratic goals of the People's Institute and impose coercive measures to secure his reforms. He discovered that it was often easier for an elite to direct the immigrants rather than listen to their aspirations.

Despite these problems, Collier's experience with minority groups uniquely prepared him for the upcoming struggle to assist the American Indian. His interest in bringing social science and rationality to philanthropy made it possible for him to perceive the weakness in the government's land allotment and assimilation policies and to see the need to work for the organization of the Indians into self-governing communities. Committed to the efficient utilization of the nation's human and physical assets, Collier would continue his devotion to conservation by advocating the planned development of the Indian's natural resources.

2. Protest From the Pueblos

Collier remained at Taos until August 1921, when he returned to California to accept the position of psychology and sociology lecturer at San Francisco State College. He settled down with his family at Mill Valley, a suburb of San Francisco, where he found teaching both easy and stimulating.[1] Collier began work on a book to be entitled "Crowds, Groups and the Great Society: With a Study of the American Community Movement," but his mind dwelt on the Indians in New Mexico. He wrote Mrs. Frank Gibson, a supporter of many Progressive causes in California, asking whether the General Federation of Women's Clubs might be interested in the Pueblo Indians. She responded by introducing him in November to Mrs. Stella Atwood, who resided at Riverside.[2]

Mrs. Atwood, chairman of the federation's Indian Welfare Committee, had her first contact with the Indians while serving on a draft board during the First World War. She had listened to their complaints concerning the ineffectiveness of the Indian Bureau and decided that it was time to investigate the government's handling of Indian affairs. In June 1921, Mrs. Atwood brought the Indian problem before a federation meeting at Salt Lake City. This resulted in a unanimous resolution that requested the formation of an Indian Welfare Committee with herself as chairman. After consultation with Collier, she began to organize her colleagues by appointing state chairmen of Indian welfare who were directed to set up local publicity and legislative committees.[3]

For several months Collier frequently corresponded and visited with Mrs. Atwood, discussing the need for Indian reform. His effort to get her financial aid and an assistant proved successful during May 1922 when

[26]

Mrs. Stella Atwood, who led the Women's Clubs in the struggle against the Bursum bill.

Mrs. John Collier, Sr.

Mrs. Kate Vosburg, a philanthropic woman from Azusa, California, agreed to help on the condition that Collier become Mrs. Atwood's field worker.* Quickly accepting the offer, Collier resigned from San Francisco State College and accepted the position of research agent for the federation's Indian Welfare Committee. He received $10,000 from Vosberg to start a survey and investigation of the reservation system.[4]

Collier left for New Mexico during September 1922, visited all the Pueblos except Acoma, and met with their tribal councils. He surveyed the economic and health problems of these Indians by conferring with Indian Bureau officials, doctors, teachers, and farmers.[5] While at Espanola, the superintendent for the northern Pueblos handed him a copy of the Bursum bill which threatened the Pueblos' Spanish land grants.[6]

*The support Collier received from these California progressives continued throughout the twenties. Their reform efforts, which included articles in *Sunset Magazine* and support for Collier's American Indian Defense Association, conflict with George Mowry's thesis that the Progressive impulse collapsed and disappeared in California shortly after 1916. George E. Mowry, *The California Progressives* (Chicago: Quadrangle Books, 1963), p. 274.

The Bursum bill had been sponsored by Albert Bacon Fall who became secretary of the interior in 1921.* Soon after his appointment as head of the Interior Department, Fall told Indian Commissioner Charles H. Burke that Congress needed to pass legislation concerning disputed land titles within the Pueblo grants of New Mexico.† His desire to solve this land controversy was understandable, because a threat of armed conflict existed between the Indians, Anglos, and Spanish settlers. In the winter of 1922, violence had been narrowly averted when the Tesuque Indians ripped down a settler's fence. Fall explained to the commissioner that he had arranged with Attorney General Harry Daugherty for the appointment of Colonel R. E. Twitchell, a lawyer and scholar of Spanish history from Santa Fe, as government attorney for the New Mexico Indians. Twitchell's task was to prepare a historical and legal report concerning Pueblo land tenure.[7]

Fall had appointed Twitchell because of the complicated history surrounding the Pueblo land quarrel. Under the terms of the treaty of Guadalupe Hidalgo which ended the Mexican War in 1848, Congress confirmed to the Pueblo Indians the ownership of thirty-five Spanish land grants which totaled 700,000 acres. The Anglos and Spanish-Americans in New Mexico assumed that these Indians had every right to sell their land without the interference of the federal government. In 1876 the Supreme Court supported this view by ruling that the Pueblos, because of their advanced civilization, were not wards of the government. Many non-Indian settlers purchased Indian land in good faith, while others, who were usually squatters, used the technique of open encroachment.[8]

The right of the Pueblos to sell their land, however, became questionable when New Mexico entered the Union. Under the provisions of the 1910 Enabling Act, Congress forced the State of New Mexico to

---

*Born in Frankfort, Kentucky, in 1861, Albert Bacon Fall eventually settled in Las Cruces, New Mexico, where he became an active Democratic politician and newspaper editor. In 1893 he was appointed associate justice of the Territorial Supreme Court. With statehood looming for New Mexico and realizing that the Republican party was deeply entrenched in the territory, Fall switched his political allegiance and became one of New Mexico's first senators. He served as secretary of the interior from 1921 until his resignation in 1923. *Biographical Directory of the American Congress, 1774–1949* (Washington: Government Printing Office, 1961), p. 1144.

†Sixty years old at the time of his appointment on March 21, 1921, Charles H. Burke was known for his old style party regularity. Elected as a Republican congressman from South Dakota in 1896, Burke served on the House Committee on Indian Affairs, eventually becoming its chairman. After losing a bid for the Senate in 1914, he returned to his home town of Pierre, where he became "a fairly rich man" in the real estate business. He also engaged in relief work during World War I prior to his selection as Indian commissioner. Herbert Corey, "He Carries the White Man's Burden," *Collier's* 71 (May 12, 1923): 13; and *Biographical Directory of the American Congress, 1774–1961* (Washington: Government Printing Office, 1961), p. 628.

Albert Bacon Fall —
sponsor of the Bursum bill.

Arizona and the West

surrender all jurisdiction over the lands of any Indians deriving their title from the United States or any prior sovereignty. The constitutionality of these provisions came up in the Sandoval Case in 1912, when a Spanish-American named Sandoval was arrested for introducing liquor into Santa Clara and San Juan Pueblos. The government, represented by Francis Wilson, upheld the jurisdiction of the United States over the Pueblos. A. B. Renehan, the attorney for Sandoval, claimed that the provision of the Enabling Act applying to the Indians was unconstitutional, because it resulted in the admission of New Mexico into the Union on a basis different from the other states. The federal district court upheld Renehan's argument, so Wilson appealed the government's case to the Supreme Court. In 1913, the Court reversed itself, reaffirming the responsibility of the United States for the Pueblo Indians because they were wards of the government.[9]

This decision meant that the Pueblos had not been competent to alienate their land since 1848, and it threw into question the validity of

3,000 claims by 12,000 non-Indians within the Pueblo grants. These claims represented a relatively small acreage estimated at roughly ten percent of the total area granted to the Pueblos, but they posed a serious threat to the Indians because most of the claims were for valuable irrigated acreage. Almost all of the water that flowed through the Tesuque irrigation ditches had been taken by whites, while San Juan had lost the use of 3,500 of its 4,000 irrigated acres. A severe drought in New Mexico made the Indian position even more desperate.[10]

The settlers as well as the Indians faced a dilemma in this controversy, for they often found it difficult to prove title to the land that their ancestors had purchased or seized through open trespass. The lack of reliable probate records in New Mexico during its territorial period further complicated the situation. Although many of the settlers had lived on Pueblo grants for generations, the Sandoval decision meant that they could not plead a statute of limitations against the government, which exempted itself from such provisions as a guardian of dependent wards.[11]

Fall's problems began when he asked Senator Holm O. Bursum of New Mexico to introduce a bill designed to quickly settle the land controversy in their state. On the last day of May in 1921, Senator Bursum complied with this request and submitted a bill that would have solved the crisis by confirming all non-Indian claims of title held for more than ten years prior to 1912. Representatives of the missionary-oriented Indian Rights Association protested against this bill in person to Fall and denounced it in their annual report as legislation "obviously in aid of the trespassers and not of the Indians."[12]

Consequently, the secretary refused to push this bill but instead waited until Colonel Twitchell submitted his report dealing with the problem. In the meantime, he asked Attorney General Daugherty to inform District Court Judge Colin Neblett of the government's decision to postpone four cases pending in the New Mexico courts against 600 non-Indian claimants to Pueblo land. Fall's advisors believed that if these cases were prosecuted they would cause the wholesale eviction of white settlers and possible bloodshed between Anglos, Spanish-Americans, and Indians.[13]

Twitchell's report on the Pueblos along with a draft of a bill to solve the controversy arrived at Secretary Fall's office during the spring of 1922. Mainly historical in nature, this legal brief revealed Twitchell's Spanish-American bias by recommending that Congress enact special legislation to offset the Sandoval decision, which would have removed all non-Indians from Pueblo land. But Twitchell called for the government to protect Indian water rights and end forever the settlers' "trespasses which have been the rule rather than the exception."[14]

Holm Olaf Bursum,
senator from New Mexico.

Museum of New Mexico

Nothing was done with this report because Commissioner Burke had departed for the Southwest to discuss the situation with several Indians at Santa Clara Pueblo. While in Santa Fe, the commissioner held a conference with A. B. Renehan, the attorney representing the settlers, and Twitchell, the government lawyer for the Indians. Since both men had drawn up legislative guidelines to solve the land dispute, Burke asked them to meet him later in Washington. Twitchell and Renehan arrived at the Indian Bureau during July, and after several days of discussion each presented a bill to Fall at a special conference.[15]

At this meeting the secretary agreed with Twitchell that legislation was necessary to protect the settlers, but showed little concern with the rest of his recommendations. Fall followed Renehan's advice that he accept secondary evidence to help the non-Indians validate their land claims by adding sections 15 and 16 to a compromise bill. Section 15 used the Joy Survey of 1913 as secondary evidence against the Indians. The Joy Survey had been authorized by the government to determine all of the claims the settlers chose to make against the Indians, in order to portray the tangled land situation, not to confirm title. Section 16 further assisted the settlers by allowing them to appeal to the courts for a special ruling from the secretary of the interior if they still were unable to prove title to their land.[16]

The final draft which emerged from this meeting proved a misfortune for the Warren G. Harding administration. Introduced by Senator Bursum on July 20, 1922, at the request of Fall as an "administration measure," the Bursum bill confirmed by law almost every non-Indian claim. It enacted a statute of limitations which normally would not run against wards of the government. Under this bill's provisions Anglo and Spanish settlers would receive title to Pueblo land if they could prove continuous possession, with color of title, before or after 1848. Any non-Indian who proved continuous possession since June 29, 1900, without color of title, could claim title to Indian property. Any trespasser who found it impossible to obtain land under these provisions had the privilege of appealing to the courts and the secretary of the interior to make a special ruling in his favor.[17]

Other features of the Bursum bill proved detrimental to Indian interests. One section proposed that Pueblo water rights and contested land fall under the jurisdiction of the unfriendly state courts. Another provision required the New Mexico District Court to accept as prima facie evidence the Joy Survey. It stipulated that the government should compensate the Pueblos with adjacent public agricultural lands, which were often non-existent, or with cash for the lands they might lose. Opponents of the bill estimated that it would deprive the Indians of at least 60,000 acres and destroy their unique self-government by placing all domestic quarrels under the jurisdiction of the district court.[18]

Collier had received a copy of the Bursum bill while visiting the northern Pueblos at Espanola, but he probably already knew about this piece of legislation. As early as December 1921 Mrs. Atwood had met both Albert B. Fall and Colonel Twitchell, who were attending a conference at Riverside, California, on water power development and settlement of the Southwest. Cooperating with Mrs. Atwood, they discussed Pueblo matters and sent her a copy of the Bursum bill during May 1922.[19] Three months later, she visited with S. M. Brosius, the Washington representative of the Indian Rights Association, who warned her about the adverse effect of this proposed legislation on the Pueblo Indians.[20] After obtaining copies of the bill she sent them to her lawyer and a number of friends, who reported that it was unfair to the Indians.

This adverse report caused Collier and Atwood to start a campaign to prevent the passage of the Bursum bill. They used their influence to orient the *Survey*, a progressive bi-monthly, toward the Pueblo problem. Its staff consisted of a small group of reformers, who had formed a voluntary association called Survey Associates. Haven Emerson, one of the journal's associate editors, knew Collier during their years in New York City and asked both Collier and Atwood to provide him with lengthy essays for the October 1922 issue of the magazine which the editorial staff devoted to the Pueblos.[21]

Collier also used the *Sunset Magazine,* a liberal periodical, to bring the Pueblo situation before the American people. While in California he had developed a close contact with Walter Woehlke, an editor of the journal, who encouraged him to contribute feature articles on the government's injustices to the Indians.* Collier severely castigated Secretary Fall, accusing him of burning "into ashes" the Pueblos' ancient land guarantees. The editors of *Sunset* then distributed marked copies of their magazine concerning the Bursum bill to government officials and to every member of the House and Senate.[22]

Mrs. Atwood and Collier did not limit their activities to writing journal articles, for they used the power of the federation's two million members to lobby actively against the Bursum bill. With the assistance of Collier, Francis Wilson, a Santa Fe attorney hired by Atwood, prepared a critical analysis of the bill which they incorporated into a blue book. Entitled "Shall the Pueblo Indians of New Mexico be Destroyed," it called for the defeat of the Bursum bill and the creation of a three-man presidential commission to solve the Pueblo land controversy. After its publication on October 18, 1922, it was sent to members of Congress and distributed all over the country. Atwood also wrote several of her state chairmen asking that they mail protests to Congress and the Department of the Interior. Women from various parts of the country complied with this request by sending letters and telegrams.[23]

When the purpose of this bill became publicly known, several groups including the New Mexican and Eastern Association on Indian Affairs and the Indian Rights Association began to voice their protests. Soon condemnation of the measure and the men who proposed it became nationwide. Bursum's and Fall's own constituents at the artist colonies in Santa Fe and Taos were among those who raised their voices against the bill.

After World War I, New Mexico had been discovered by intellectuals seeking the refreshment of primitive life and escape from American society. Writers such as Mabel Dodge had moved to Taos in 1917. Three

---

*Almost every issue of the monthly western periodical *Sunset* from November of 1922 through December of 1923 carried one or more articles on the plight of the Indian. Many of Collier's titles were self-explanatory: "The Pueblos' Last Stand," "Pueblo Land Problem," and "Persecuting the Pueblos."

years later she convinced Collier to visit and in 1922 successfully persuaded D. H. Lawrence to come and write about American Indian life.[24] Other important intellectuals who centered their activities around the Taos and Santa Fe art colonies included Mary Austin, Alice Corbin Henderson, Elizabeth S. Sergeant, and Witter Bynner. These "nerve-wracked ascetics" found contentment in the beauty and intensity of Pueblo life. Each artist had a favorite Indian village. According to one contemporary, "it was obligatory to go to every Pueblo dance. Failure to appear on a sunny roof on every saint's day marked one as soulless and without taste." Convinced that the Bursum bill threatened the culture they treasured, these New Mexicans rallied to the slogan of "Let's save the Pueblos."[25]

During the autumn and early winter of 1922–23, the artists and writers replaced their poems and paintings with resolutions and essays. Many of them signed a "Proclamation to the American Public," protesting the destruction of Pueblo land rights.* Others, like Witter Bynner, wrote for *Outlook,* while Alice Corbin Henderson and Elizabeth S. Sergeant submitted their writings to the *New Republic.* The Henderson article suggested that if the Bursum bill originated from the Department of the Interior as Fall claimed, it would be a "blot on the administration." The *Nation* took a similar position in one of its editorials, which indicated that the secretary and his associates had betrayed the Pueblos because most of the claimants to their land were Republican Spanish-American voters. This allegation contained some truth, for the Republican party of New Mexico at its state convention in Albuquerque during the autumn of 1922 had adopted a resolution favoring the enactment of the Bursum bill.[26]

The Santa Fe and Taos intellectuals appealed to many of their editor friends to carry feature stories against Fall's solution to the Pueblo land dispute. Elizabeth S. Sergeant contacted Walter Lippmann, and he persuaded the *New York World* to print an editorial entitled, "Justice for the Pueblo Indians." The *Christian Science Monitor* ran a series of columns against the bill, while Miss Sergeant and D. H. Lawrence wrote material concerning the Pueblos for the *New York Times.* Sergeant warned that the Bursum bill would turn the Indians "into homeless wanderers on roads that have no ending." Lawrence agreed with this estimate, calling the bill "a cool joke" which played "the Wild West scalping trick a little too brazenly." Many adverse articles, however, came not from the East but from the Santa Fe *New Mexican.* Under the militant leadership of

---

*Names such as Vachel Lindsay, Edgar Lee Masters, Carl Sandburg, and William Allen White appeared on this manifesto. "Proclamation to the American Public," Collier Papers.

Dana Johnson, it consistently gave favorable space to artists and writers and supported their criticisms.[27]

This chorus of protest grew with the formation, in 1922, of voluntary organizations whose purpose consisted of defending the Pueblos against the policies of the Interior Department. The New Mexico Association, centered around Santa Fe, actively opposed the Bursum bill. It appealed for money to help the Indians at the Tesuque and San Ildefonso Pueblos where conditions were so deplorable that they had to live on rations.[28]

The Eastern Association consisted of a group of people living near New York City. Because of their interest in preserving Pueblo arts and crafts, they sent out pamphlets and circular letters that questioned many provisions of the bill.[29] Herbert Spinden, president of the association and a distinguished anthropologist, called the Bursum bill "totally iniquitous" because it took land the Indians had salvaged from the desert and gave it to the white trespassers controlling the Pueblos' water supply. He was joined by Herbert Welsh, president of the older Indian Rights Association, who asked all friends of the Indian to oppose the bill.*

This publicity proved quite successful. Senator William Borah of Idaho, after receiving a critical letter from Francis Wilson, the attorney representing Mrs. Atwood, took the unusual step of recalling the Bursum bill from the House by unanimous consent. The bill was again sent back to the Senate Committee on Public Lands and Surveys.[30]

In the meantime, Collier rallied the Pueblo Indians against Fall's answer to the land controversy. He started at Taos and told the governor and council about the threat that the bill posed to their land and tribal life. They agreed and provided Collier with a letter of introduction to the other Pueblos. Both he and Antonio Luhan, a Taos Indian, began informing the rest of the Pueblos about the bill. When they visited Cochiti in October of 1922, they met the Indians in a sacred room. As the meeting drew to a close, one of the Indians named Alcario Montoya suggested that they must organize "as we did long ago when we drove the Spaniards out." The requests for this Pueblo meeting were signed by the governor of Cochiti and mailed to the several Pueblo governors. Both Father Fridolin Schuster, a Franciscan missionary from Laguna Pueblo, and Collier assisted in the preparation of these invitations.[31]

---

*Herbert Spinden's protest was countersigned by scientists working in the Peabody Museum at Harvard. The Indian Rights Association attacked the Bursum bill in its 1922 *Annual Report* and in the *Southern Workman,* a periodical published by the Hampton Normal and Agricultural Institute in Virginia, which was affiliated with the association through one of its trustees. *New York Times,* November 19, 1922, 2, p. 6, and January 7, 1923, 8, p. 6.

On the morning of November 5, 1922, the 121 delegates of the All Pueblo Council met at Santo Domingo to discuss the Bursum bill. According to Collier, this meeting took place inside a quadrangular windowless kiva, or secret ceremonial chamber, with the council sitting "Indian-fashion against the wall on the floor, two ranks deep."[32] Between the men were ancient ceremonial pots, while above their heads were dim yellow paintings of the sun, the eagle, and the moon. The Indians passed a community tobacco sack and rolled their cigarettes from corn husks stacked at the center of the room. The smoke rose densely and "half-hid" the paintings of outstretched human hands on the ceiling beams. At the far end of the room a six-foot mural of a green serpent "floated above the old men's heads through the milky air, lighting and darkening with the flickering fire."[33]

A number of white guests attended all or part of this two-day meeting. They included John Collier, Margaret McKittrick, Elizabeth S. Sergeant, Francis Wilson, and a number of Franciscan fathers.[34] With their assistance, nine Indian delegates, sitting in a horseshoe formation, drafted "An Appeal by the Pueblo Indians of New Mexico to the People of the United States," which stated that the Bursum bill destroyed "their common life and will rob us of everything we hold dear — our lands, our customs, our traditions." Using shorthand, Father Schuster took down the ideas for this appeal, while Collier typed them into a resolution. All of the 121 delegates approved of what had been done by rising to vote. The Indians also decided to raise $3,500 in order to send a delegation to Washington, D.C., to make an appearance at the hearings of the Senate Committee on Public Lands and Surveys.[35]

Albert B. Fall responded to this nationwide outcry against his plans by threatening the wholesale eviction of settlers from Pueblo land. He asked Attorney General Daugherty to give R. E. Twitchell, the government attorney for the Pueblos, the authority to bring to a favorable conclusion the law suits pending in the New Mexico District Court against non-Indian claimants. Collier believed that Fall hoped to create panic among the Spanish and Anglo settlers in order to secure a friendly sentiment toward the Bursum bill in and out of New Mexico. The secretary never clearly stated his motives, but he evidently thought that the threat of eviction would make the opponents of the bill appear as ruthless extremists driving thousands of innocent non-Indians off their lands.[36]

Fall's tactics proved disastrous, for they brought only an increasing flood of protest and further isolated him from the confidence of the administration. On December 6, 1922, Mrs. Atwood sent a letter to her friend Brigadier General Charles Sawyer, the president's personal doctor, asking that he take up the Pueblo matter with Harding. She warned that eviction proceedings would be political suicide, pointing out that "over a hundred leading newspapers and periodicals were giving publicity to Pueblo affairs." Sawyer complied with her request and forwarded the telegram to the White House, where it was intercepted by Harding's personal secretary, George Christian, Jr., who sent the message to the secretary of the interior. Fall replied to Christian that he had left unanswered, except as official duty required, "the propaganda which has been filling the newspapers of the United States and reaching you through general letters and otherwise from artists and ministers." Fall told Christian that he would not withdraw his approval of eviction proceedings and intimated that Mrs. Atwood had caused the present crisis by refusing to compromise on the Bursum bill.[37]

When the controversy over eviction proceedings continued, Fall wrote a lengthy letter to Senator Borah defending the Interior Department and its formulation of the bill. He pointed out that the government intended to provide a quick settlement of all claims in order to prevent armed conflict in New Mexico. The secretary admitted that the controversial Joy Survey was not a legal claim against the Indians but had been inserted in the bill as secondary evidence to safeguard the non-Indians' property rights. He believed that the settlers needed this special consideration because they were the merchants and businessmen who inhabited the villages within the Pueblo grants and paid their taxes, while the Indians were exempt from such obligations.[38]

Fall's defense of the Bursum bill failed to prevent a growing clamor against his threat to evict the non-Indian settlers. On December 20, Collier, Father Fridolin Schuster, and General Hugh Scott, a member of the Board of Indian Commissioners, wrote a letter to Attorney General Daugherty asking that the government delay eviction proceedings to prevent violence. The attorney general forwarded this request to Fall and indicated that his plan might result in bloodshed, making mutual cooperation impossible. This letter did not alter the secretary's position, for he still claimed the right to take action if Congress refused to give "equitable consideration" to a measure similar to the Bursum bill.[39]

This uncompromising position resulted in more objections from associations concerned with protecting the Pueblo Indians. On December 22, a day that Fall called "a little significant," Stella Atwood sent telegrams all over the country protesting against his threat to start eviction proceedings. She dispatched one of them to the White House which warned President Harding that Fall's scheme "would lead to grave political consequences." Mrs. Amelia E. White, secretary of the Eastern Association on Indian Affairs, wrote a similar telegram on December 23, urging the president to exert his authority to "prevent this projected abuse of legal procedure which may cause bloodshed and which will have a political aspect of national importance." The president did not respond publicly to these warnings, but as December drew to a close unconfirmed reports circulated that Fall would resign from the cabinet. As these rumors intensified, Harding issued a statement denying Fall's possible retirement. The secretary, vacationing in Virginia, said nothing for publication.[40]

Early in January of 1923, the White House announced that, effective March 4, Fall would leave public office because of the pressure of "private business interests." No mention was made of the Teapot Dome oil scandal which broke during the spring of 1922 or the uproar over the Bursum bill. Instead, friends of the secretary intimated that he was resigning because of the failure of Congress and the Harding administration to carry out his recommendations concerning the 1921 Washington Naval Conference on Disarmament, the reorganization of the Alaskan administration, and the transfer of the Department of Agriculture to the Department of the Interior.[41]

Fall spent his remaining days in office trying to defend himself against the criticism leveled at his department, including those offered by Indian reformers at hearings before the Senate Committee on Public Lands and Surveys. During the first part of January, seventeen Pueblo Indians left New Mexico to appear before this committee in order to raise money and arouse public opinion against the Bursum bill. Under the direction of Collier, they wanted to promote their alternative, the Jones-Leatherwood bill, which proposed to establish a commission of three persons to examine contested claims and authorized appropriations for needed irrigation projects.[42]

On their way to Washington, D.C., the Indians and their white friends stopped at two major cities to denounce the Department of the Interior in front of private organizations. In Chicago, their speaking engagements included an appearance before the Union League and the Cliff Dwellers. The latter organization's membership included artists, businessmen, and bank presidents who were interested in Indian affairs. They enlisted the support of the Chicago Indian Rights Association and received the endorsement of such prominent citizens as Harold L. Ickes, who later became secretary of the interior under Franklin Roosevelt.[43]

Next, they visited New York City, where Collier renewed old contacts from the Progressive era. They helped him arrange speaking engagements at the Explorers' Club and the People's Institute at Cooper Union. Escorted by Collier, seven Pueblo Indians appeared at the Explorers' Club on January 14, wearing feathered headdresses, blue blankets, and beaded moccasins. They held the silver-topped staffs which Abraham Lincoln had given them symbolizing their right to "perpetual possession" of their land. Antonio Romaro, an Indian from Taos, spoke for the whole delegation when he insisted that the government remove non-Indian squatters, assist the Indians in irrigation, and allow them a measure of self-government. In the evening this delegation made a similar appearance at the People's Institute, but their most dramatic engagement took place before bankers and businessmen at the stock exchange. Because of a rule forbidding speeches, the Indians sang songs and beat drums. The stock exchange "went wild," and many bankers sent telegrams to their congressmen suggesting that they "kill the Bursum bill."[44]

Shortly after arriving in the capital city this delegation appeared at the Ebbitt House before a forum of the National Popular Government League. Swamped with publicity problems, Collier contacted his old friend Judson King, the executive secretary of the league. King agreed to handle publicity against the Bursum bill. He assisted the Pueblo cause by issuing a league bulletin that criticized Secretary Fall for pushing an administration bill through the Senate that would "put the Pueblos on the double-quick to destruction."[45]

On January 15 the Pueblo delegates and their friends appeared before the Senate Committee on Public Lands and Surveys. Their spokesman, Mrs. Atwood, expressed the opposition of the General Federation of Women's Clubs to the manner in which the Interior Department had handled the Pueblo land problem. She warned that the passage of the Bursum bill meant that the Pueblos could no longer hope for a tardy justice from the United States. Aside from its adverse material effects, Atwood suggested, it "would break their spirit and annihilate the hope that still burns in their souls, the hope that was kindled there when Abraham Lincoln gave them their treasured guarantees sixty years ago." She rejected Commissioner Burke's belief that the Bursum bill was a question for lawyers, when she stated that it presented "a humanitarian question . . . of elementary justice."[46]

Robert Walker, a railroad lawyer and a representative for the Eastern Association on Indian Affairs, supported Atwood's testimony. Walker indicated that it was improper for a guardian to give away the land of its ward. He praised the unique self-government and culture of the Pueblos and reminded the senators that "artists and scientists have votes, and they are good American citizens, most of them as good as the rest of us, and they should be heard." He ended his testimony by suggesting that the senators take up the "white man's burden" and show altruism toward a weaker brother.[47]

Francis Wilson, whom the General Federation of Women's Clubs had employed as legal counsel for the Indians, offered the most devastating critique of the bill. He rejected the provision which gave the district court control over the internal affairs of the Indians and expressed concern about a section that enabled the New Mexico state courts to have jurisdiction over much of the land in dispute. Wilson asked why secondary evidence should be admissible only in the Pueblo situation. But the statute of limitations provision received the brunt of Wilson's attack. He pointed out that this section went much further than giving title to white settlers who obtained land under the territorial decisions. The provision "without color of title" meant that a squatter could claim Pueblo property, and this would cause the Indians to lose 60,000 acres of their land.[48]

Wilson demonstrated that the provision for compensating the Pueblos with adjacent public lands or cash was "equally a joke," because public agricultural lands were nonexistent in the vicinity of the Pueblos. He suggested that to give cash to landless Indians would be of little value and criticized the section of the bill that failed to offer the Indians any compensation for lost water rights.[49] Wilson ridiculed the provision which accepted the Joy Survey as prima facie evidence of land boundaries. He stressed that the Department of the Interior had made the Joy Survey in order to give the Indian Bureau data concerning all the claims against the Indians regardless of the validity of these claims. Wilson pointed out that the Joy Survey did not recognize or establish right of occupancy or title; its purpose was to help the government defeat fraudulent claims, instead of confirming them.[50]

Senator Irvine Lenroot, chairman of the committee, evidently agreed with Wilson's analysis, for he forced Colonel R. E. Twitchell, the government attorney for the Pueblos, to answer a rigorous cross-examination. Twitchell, upon being questioned by Senator Lenroot, acknowledged that the bill promoted few Indian equities and agreed that the government should abandon or rewrite most of its sections.[51] According to Collier, Senator Lenroot at the end of this cross-examination stated: "Colonel Twitchell, I do not see how any lawyer could have drawn this section. And how the Government. . . ." The senator did not finish his sentence.[52]

The committee also listened to the testimony of Pablo Abeyta, an Isleta Indian who was a member of the Pueblo delegation. Abeyta told the senators that the time had come for the Indians to "raise our voices and demand justice." Opposing the Bursum bill because it would turn "us into the wild," he called for the ejection of all non-Indian treaspassers and the building of fences to keep their stock off Pueblo land. Abeyta pointed out their need for better cattle breeds, more water, and help with advanced irrigation methods.[53]

When Fall appeared at this hearing he refused to discuss the merits of the Bursum bill but claimed that propaganda had misled the public in the Pueblo controversy. He told the committee: "I have long since learned to see the words that I have uttered twisted by knaves to make a trap for fools." The secretary warned that "if we are to have a government by propaganda, not by the three departments of government, the present conditions in Soviet Russia would constitute a political paradise . . . compared to what we might have here." Fall made clear his opposition to the Jones-Leatherwood bill, when he declared that a Pueblo lands court and irrigation system would cost the government too much money. Finally, he explained to the committee that his effort to prosecute Francis Wilson on charges of conspiracy to defraud the government and the Indians out of their lands, during Wilson's tenure as a federal attorney for the Pueblos, had been rejected by the Justice Department. The proceedings ended after the secretary of the interior refused to undergo a cross-examination by Wilson.[54]

Collier and the Indians then returned to New York City where they condemned the secretary of the interior and the Bursum bill. At the Town Hall they raised $1,400 for their cause, while at the New York Economic Club the delegation received unanimous support from the club's 1,000 members and guests for their alternative Jones-Leatherwood bill. Fall, upset that this endorsement of his opponents came without the usual debate found at the club's meetings, sent its members an open letter of protest. He stated that if there were any truth to the "propaganda" that he desired to deprive the Indians of their rights or reap financial gain from the Bursum bill, the club's members should "insist upon impeachment proceedings against himself, the Indian commissioner, and others in the Interior Department." Collier followed this letter with a rebuttal which indicated that although no "thought out conspiracy" existed, the secretary of the interior had exhibited "an ineptitude, an incompetence, and an utter disregard for the rights of the Pueblos."[55]

On March 4, 1923, Secretary Fall wrote a "confession" in the *New York Times* that discussed his decision to resign from the Harding cabinet. He admitted that public life had been a "mixture of roses and thorns," but chose to discuss the latter. Fall complained about the failure to discuss both sides of important issues, citing as an example the meeting of the New York Economic Club. He denounced the public attacks which had falsely charged him with being motivated by selfish interests.[56] The secretary evidently referred, in part, to a column which appeared in an earlier issue of the *Times* claiming that he had a financial interest in the Pueblo land controversy.*

---

*The *Times* publicly regretted the unjust implication that Albert B. Fall was interested in Pueblo lands for financial reasons. *New York Times,* February 4, 1923, 2, p. 1.

Fall, however, declined to mention that the Bursum bill may have influenced his decision to resign because it resulted in a serious uproar in New Mexico, which challenged his political stature in that state. The endorsement of the bill by the Republican party had proved disastrous, for the New Mexico Democrats were victorious in the November state-wide elections "all the way from grave-digger to the Governor and Senator." The secretary also neglected to refer to the letters of protest from Indian reformers to Colonel Sawyer, Attorney General Daugherty, and President Harding as factors contributing to his growing isolation within the administration.[57]

Contemporaries believed that a direct connection existed between his resignation and the uproar over the bill.* Carolyn Vance, a journalist writing for the *Nashville Tennessean,* indicated that "it was the protestations of the two million members of the General Federation of Women's Clubs against the legislation sponsored by Secretary Fall of the Interior, that caused him much unhappiness and perhaps his ultimate decision to resign." An editorial in the New York *Journal of Commerce and Commercial Bulletin* drew a similar conclusion by noting that the resources of the Southwest included both oil and water. It suggested that "possibly no feature of the aftermath which attended the retirement of Secretary Fall has aroused so much severe criticism in influential circles as the scheme to expropriate the Pueblo Indians . . . in the form of the Bursum bill."[58]

Delighted that Fall had resigned, Collier told the homesick and tired Pueblo delegation to return to New Mexico after their appearance at the New York Economic Club. But Collier and his associates remained in Washington, D.C., during the first two weeks of February 1923 in order to testify in favor of their Jones-Leatherwood bill at hearings before the House Committee on Indian Affairs.[59] Led by Homer Snyder, a Republican from New York, who had sponsored legislation similar to the Bursum bill in the House, most committee members showed little interest in assisting the Pueblo Indians. They attacked the reformers who had embarrassed them over their earlier failure to protect Indian property.

Indian Commissioner Charles H. Burke, who had "the round, hard eye and the square jaw and lip smile of a fighter," appeared first at these

---

* In his excellent revisionist study, Burl Noggle has suggested that the oil inquiry concerning Teapot Dome may have had little effect upon Fall's decision to leave office. Loss of influence in New Mexico politics, growing isolation from President Warren G. Harding, and disappointment over his relative unimportance in the cabinet supposedly turned the secretary's thoughts toward resignation as early as February of 1922. Noggle's explanation, however, failed to focus on the opposition that Fall encountered from Indian reformers. Burl Noggle, *Teapot Dome, Oil and Politics in the 1920's* (Baton Rouge: Louisiana State University Press, 1962), pp. 52–53.

hearings.[60] Because he hoped to discredit his critics, Burke called for a special executive session to inquire into the "campaign of propaganda ...waged throughout the country" in behalf of the Pueblo Indians. If the committee felt that it did not have this power, the commissioner suggested that it create a joint investigating committee from both the House and the Senate to deal with libelous charges. After meeting in a closed session, members of the committee decided to go beyond the narrow scope of analyzing the Jones-Leatherwood bill, but they declined to refer the matter to the Senate for further action.[61]

Francis Wilson, the attorney for the General Federation of Women's Clubs Indian Welfare Committee, followed Commissioner Burke, and he explained the complicated background of the Pueblo controversy. Wilson offered an extensive criticism of the Snyder bill, the House counterpart to the Bursum bill, but he admitted that some compromise might be desirable. Under pressure from members of the House Indian Affairs Committee, Wilson supported a separate bill for Pueblo irrigation because he agreed that the Senate Committee on Public Lands and Surveys had no jurisdiction over appropriations. He abandoned "to a limited extent" the section of the Jones-Leatherwood bill which called for a separate judiciary to solve the Pueblo land dispute, because he felt that Congress might refuse to pass such an expensive proposal.[62]

It soon became apparent, however, that certain members of the Indian Affairs Committee had little interest in reaching a compromise. When Wilson suggested that the Pueblo Indians were an industrious people who needed government help, Chairman Snyder replied that "if these Indians are really thrifty, hard working Indians, they are the first tribe or bunch of Indians that I ever saw that were."[63] This attitude made it clear that committee members had little desire to discuss the legitimate opposition of Indian reformers. They hoped to discredit the federation's Indian Welfare Committee by demonstrating that it misrepresented that organization's two million members.

This purpose became apparent when Mrs. Atwood took the stand. Cross-examined about whether the federation's National Board of Directors had officially approved or financed her activities, she answered no, explaining that a group of wealthy California women had paid her expenses and the salaries of both Collier and Wilson. Mrs. Atwood admitted that she was unaware of Collier's critical attitude against government officials in the January issue of *Sunset* or his publicity activities with Judson King.[64] Miss Alice Robertson, a representative from Oklahoma, continued this interrogation when she accused Atwood of collecting over $6,000 for the Pueblo Defense Fund without approval of the federation's Board of Directors. Robertson warned that all funds should have been turned over to the national treasurer because "anyone who touches Indian work must, like Caesar's wife, be above suspicion." She criticized Mrs. Atwood for sending only $400 back to the Indians for medical care, while spending more funds on publicity.[65]

Angry at the way his close friend had been treated, Collier appeared before the Indian Affairs Committee on February 10, 1923, to clarify her testimony. Showing displeasure, he told the representatives that their three-and-one-half-hour cross-examination of a frail woman past middle age "was nothing less than a crucifixion of her." He pointed out that Mrs. Atwood had become confused during this "grilling" and had forgotten many things which demonstrated that her Indian Welfare Committee did represent the federation's two million members. As early as June 1922 she had appeared before its biennial conference held at Chautauqua, New York, where she made a verbal report explaining the $10,000 gift from California friends and her plans to hire a specialist to investigate Indian affairs. Collier stressed that this report went unchallenged and was published in the July and August issue of the *General Federation News*. She had also conferred with the chairman and other officers of the federation to warn them that "there was going to be a strenuous time," and they supported her.[66]

His defense of Mrs. Atwood completed, Collier attempted to demonstrate that the Bursum bill was just one aspect of government neglect toward the Indians. He used the findings of Dr. Esherf Shevky, a scientist from Leland Stanford University who had visited the Pueblos during the fall of 1922, to show that the Taos Indians lived on a per capita income of $30, while their neighbors at San Ildefonso and Tesuque existed on incomes that ranged from $13.66 to $16.46. These figures, however, meant little to Congresswoman Robertson who suggested that both the Indians and whites in the Southwest suffered "because of drought, the boll-weevil, and the failure of other things, but it was survival of the fittest."[67]

This callous behavior made Collier even more determined to expose bad health conditions among the Pueblo Indians. Citing a letter from Dr. Frederick Hoffman, health statistician for the Prudential Life Insurance Company, he criticized the inadequacy of the Indian Bureau's medical service. Many of its doctors earned only $1,000 to $1,600 a year which caused them to engage in outside practice and neglect the rapid growth of such Indian afflictions as tuberculosis, dysentery, and venereal disease. Collier pointed out that only two doctors treated all of the Pueblos north of Santa Fe and they were unable to prevent the growth of an eye disease called trachoma which partially blinded 19 percent of these Indians.[68]

The hearings ended with the testimony of Indian Bureau officials. Assistant Commissioner Edgar B. Meritt appeared first to criticize Collier's statement concerning government neglect toward the Pueblo Indians. He admitted that the bureau lacked reliable figures on per capita income, but Meritt claimed that only 214 out of 8,000 Indians had requested relief. If they suffered, it was because of the drought and the excessive time they spent executing their "pagan dances," instead of cultivating land not under irrigation. Meritt stated that in recent years the bureau had constructed over eighty wells in the Pueblo country and increased appropriations for medical work from $40,000 to $370,000.[69]

When Commissioner Burke testified before the Indian Affairs Committee he explained that before the present controversy he had cooperated closely with Mrs. Atwood. They had corresponded weekly but trouble had started soon after she employed Collier, who conducted "a sort of revival meeting" at Santo Domingo Pueblo. Burke warned that in the future the bureau would prevent "unconscionable propagandists" from stirring up trouble in areas under its jurisdiction.[70] The commissioner called for legislation similar to the Bursum bill to solve the Pueblo land dispute. He pointed out that Wilson had abandoned the federation's Jones-Leatherwood bill "almost immediately after being interrogated by members of the committee." Burke emphasized that this measure was an unacceptable alternative because the government opposed the creation of an expensive land claims commission. Already having problems with the Bureau of the Budget, he doubted if Congress would accept its one million dollar price tag. The commissioner stressed that Congress should solve the question of land tenure before appropriating irrigation funds.[71]

Collier believed that the House and Senate hearings had killed the Bursum bill, but on February 28, 1923, five days before Congress adjourned, the Senate Committee on Public Lands and Surveys, unexpectedly reported a substitute measure.[72] Known as the Lenroot bill, this legislation established the Presidential Lands Board of three persons to determine Pueblo land titles. The board was required to use a statute of limitations which assisted non-Indians. A settler could claim land if he possessed it with color of title for twenty years or without color of title for thirty years. Title to disputed real estate outside these provisions came under the jurisdiction of the New Mexico District Court. This substitute measure eliminated obnoxious provisions of the Bursum bill, such as the use of the Joy Survey, but neglected to offer the Indians compensation for lands and water rights lost to the settlers.[73]

The Lenroot bill passed the Senate because Francis Wilson, the attorney for the Pueblos and the Federation of Women's Clubs, had given his approval. Consulting with members of the Senate Committee on Public Lands and Surveys, Wilson agreed to accept this compromise after he realized that the federation's Jones-Leatherwood bill contained a section on irrigation appropriations that failed to come under the committee's jurisdiction. Wilson sympathized with the settlers who had taken possession of Pueblo land between 1849 and 1913 when the territorial courts had established the right of the Indians to sell and alienate their lands. Because he thought that many settlers had acted in good faith under these decisions, Wilson persuaded Senators Andrius Jones and Reed Smoot that the Pueblos would offer little opposition to the Lenroot bill.[74]

The New Mexico and Eastern Association of Indian Affairs sided with Wilson because they sympathized with his concern about the claims of non-Indians. They feared the extreme position taken by Collier that 75 percent of the Anglo and Spanish-American claims were not based on legal title but on an ex post facto statute of limitations that was inoperative against Indian wards. Jealousy also had developed between the reform associations over the influence of Collier among the Pueblos. A member of the Eastern Association accused Collier of organizing the All Pueblo Council as a "personal instrument for coercing the government."[75]

Collier learned about the Lenroot bill after joining the Pueblo Indians on their trip back home to New Mexico. Judson King, the executive secretary of the National Popular Government League, had wired Collier and explained that Wilson arbitrarily gave their endorsement to legislation similar to the Bursum bill. When he returned to the nation's capital to find out what had happened, Collier "had it out with Wilson," and terminated his employment with the federation during the spring of 1923. According to Collier, this action "set off a feud which continued across years, and which divided Santa Fe into warring camps."[76]

The continuing controversy over the Pueblo land grants led to the formation of the American Indian Defense Association. Organized in New York City during May 1923, it was led by Collier who filled the important position of executive secretary. He received $5,000 a year for his services which included direction of the executive committee that made significant policy decisions. Collier's primary responsibility consisted of working as a lobbyist out of the association's Washington, D.C., headquarters, where he constantly issued bulletins on a variety of subjects concerning the Indian. Starting in 1925, he published every few months *American Indian Life,* a magazine which kept its readers informed on the struggle to reform the Indian affairs system.[77]

Collier explained the objectives of the Defense Association in a pamphlet entitled "Announcement of Purposes." It reflected his interest in preserving Indian civilization by proposing that Indian education encourage rather than suppress group loyalties, that Indians be allowed to develop their arts and crafts, and that they have religious and social freedom in all matters not contrary to public morals. Collier opposed the Dawes General Allotment Act of 1887 because it had dissipated Indian land by dividing reservations into 160 acre or smaller plots, and encouraged the rapid assimilation of the red man into American society. He suggested that Indians receive agricultural credit and called for the extension of the trust period on all allotted lands in order to make the tribes self-supporting, self-reliant, and prosperous.[78]

In this pamphlet Collier requested a reorganization of the Indian Bureau to end its monopoly over the personal affairs of the Indians. He proposed to enlist the cooperation of other federal and state agencies to bring the Indians government services already rendered to non-Indians. Medical responsibility, for example, should be transferred to the United States Public Health Service, while the bureau's Forestry and Irrigation Divisions needed to come under the supervision of the Agriculture Department and the United States Reclamation Service.[79]

At first, Collier's association attempted to incorporate everyone crusading for Indian reform into its membership. Its board of directors consisted of Stella Atwood, of the Women's Federation; Margaret McKittrick, chairman of the New Mexico Association of Indian Affairs; D. T. MacDougall, representative of the American Association for the Advancement of Science; Ralph Fletcher Seymour, secretary of the Chicago Indian Rights Association; and Amelia E. White, secretary of the Eastern Association of Indian Affairs.[80] Although this broad-based support would soon diminish, the Defense Association grew constantly during the next decade, reaching a membership of 1,700 persons. It spent about $22,000 a year for legal aid services and had branches with local boards in a number of cities. The leaders of these local boards included people such as Dr. John R. Haynes, at Santa Barbara, Charles de Y. Elkus, an attorney from San Francisco, and Reverend O. H. Bronson at Salt Lake City.[81]

Unfortunately, the unity of the Defense Association shattered in disagreement over the Lenroot bill. At an All Pueblo Council meeting held at Santo Domingo on August 25, 1923, Margaret McKittrick, Francis Wilson, Witter Bynner, and others representing the New Mexico Association on Indian Affairs, recommended that the Indians accept the Lenroot bill as a realistic compromise. Collier, who attended this gathering, disagreed with his colleagues. When he asked the Indians whether they had ever given Wilson the power to endorse the Lenroot bill for them, they shouted back, "we never did."[82]

Under Collier's direction the Pueblos adopted a "Declaration" repudiating the Lenroot bill, and they authorized the Defense Association to represent them before Congress concerning the question of disputed land titles. Using this "Declaration" as his guide, Collier drafted "The Indian bill" which Senator Charles Curtis from Kansas introduced on January 16, 1924. It rejected the concept of a statute of limitations and called for the creation of a three-man commission to visit the Indians to determine what lands they would voluntarily give up. Once these claims were settled out of court the government would begin eviction proceedings to determine the legality of non-Indian claims. Both the Pueblos and settlers would receive compensation for relinquished land.[83]

Collier's attempt to defeat the Lenroot bill gained momentum at the May 1923 Atlanta meeting of the General Federation of Women's Clubs. His close friend Mrs. Atwood informed the president of the federation, Mrs. Thomas Winter, that the fight over Pueblo lands would intensify and if she did not favor this approach she would resign. Fearful that Atwood might join the League of Women Voters, the president agreed to support her activities, and a strong resolution passed demanding justice for the Indians.[84]

Next, on September 11, 1923, Collier wrote a letter to the Pueblo governors and delegates to the All Pueblo Council, suggesting that the Indians remain cautious and continue to reject the confusing advice of certain people from Santa Fe, especially Miss Margaret McKittrick and Francis Wilson who had joined the New Mexico Association of Indian Affairs. He indicated that Wilson's defense of the Lenroot bill and statement that the Indians could get compensation from a future Congress was "a cruel and dreadful mockery of the Pueblos," which demonstrated that the New Mexico Association had betrayed them. Finally, Collier warned the Indians to discard the advice of writers such as Witter Bynner who had urged them to accept this compromise.[85]

Collier continued his assault against the Lenroot bill by writing a lengthy letter to the Santa Fe *New Mexican*. He made it clear that the bill failed to receive support from the Pueblos or the General Federation of Women's Clubs. He criticized Wilson for being inconsistent and argued that the main feature of both the Bursum and Lenroot bills was the confiscation of Pueblo land through a retroactive statute of limitations made to operate against the Indians. Collier noted that the Lenroot bill offered no compensation for nullified Indian land claims, making it worse than the Bursum bill. Because he believed that a statute of limitations was inapplicable for Indian wards of the government, Collier stressed that the courts, rather than the legislature, must solve the controversy over Pueblo land.[86]

Angered by the defection of the other reform groups, Collier attempted to purge the Defense Association of members who supported the Lenroot bill.[87] At a Defense Association Board meeting he indicated embarrassment over the membership of Amelia E. White and Margaret McKittrick. He suggested that since their groups lacked intellectual honesty and fair play, "any concession to get their help would be burning the house to roast the pig."[88]

Following this meeting, Collier wrote a letter to the board of directors of the Defense Association, which outlined the tactics they must follow regarding Indian reform. This letter marked the deep break that had occurred between Collier and many of the other Indian rights leaders. It indicated his taking firm control over the machinery and policy of the Defense Association. Collier told his colleagues that they must proceed positively in the matter of Indian reform and defeat the Lenroot bill even at the risk of alienating Francis Wilson and the executive committee of the New Mexico Association. He proposed that the Defense Association immediately start preparing for the publicity which would kill the Lenroot bill. Stella Atwood should continue to inform the women in all parts of the country about the Indian situation, while every member of the House and Senate had to be reached and systematically warned against the measure and the terrible condition of the Indians.[89]

During November 1923 Collier visited the new secretary of the interior, Dr. Hubert Work, to explain his opposition to the Lenroot bill.* He talked about the alternative Indian bill which had received endorsement from the All Pueblo Council. Work listened sympathetically but remained non-committal, waiting for recommendations from his National Advisory Committee, commonly known as the Committee of One Hundred.[90]

Work had appointed this committee during May 1923 in response to the national uproar over the Pueblo Indians. Aware of his predecessors' problems, he wanted to obtain recommendations on how to proceed in Indian affairs from a variety of persons.[91] During the second week in December seventy-seven concerned citizens traveled to Washington, D.C., in order to attend a two-day conference. They represented educated

---

*President Warren G. Harding appointed Dr. Hubert Work secretary of the interior in March 1923, after the resignation of Albert B. Fall. Sixty-two years old at the time he took office, Work had a distinguished record. He graduated from the University of Pennsylvania Medical School and practiced medicine at Pueblo, Colorado, where he founded the Woodcroft Hospital for mental diseases. He soon participated in politics and became a member of the Republican National Committee and a delegate to the Republican national convention that nominated William Howard Taft for the presidency. When Harding won in 1920, he received the position of first assistant postmaster general, eventually becoming postmaster general on March 4, 1922, when Will Hays resigned. He served in that position until his appointment as secretary of the interior. Eugene P. Trani, "Hubert Work and the Department of Interior, 1923–1928," *Pacific Northwest Quarterly* 61 (January 1970): 31–32.

Indians, missionaries, scientists, conservatives, reformers, and most of the Board of Indian Commissioners.[92] Notable guests included Bernard Baruch, the public-spirited capitalist; Oswald Villard, economic radical and pacifist; and the fundamentalist politician William Jennings Bryan.[93]

Collier believed that the first meeting of the Committee of One Hundred determined its destiny. He noted with amusement that "those who stood for the continuance of the existing order in Indian affairs gradually concentrated at the right of the hall, while the group standing for a new order concentrated to the left." The rightists won control of the meeting when General Hugh Scott, a progressive member of the Board of Indian Commissioners, lost by one vote in an election to determine the permanent chairman of the conference.[94] Instead, the delegates picked the more conservative Arthur C. Parker, a Seneca Indian ethnologist who worked at the New York State Library in Albany.*

Once the chairmanship question was settled, Collier told members of the conference that the agenda, which had been drawn up before the meeting, omitted any reference to the Pueblo land controversy. He proposed to devote twenty minutes to this topic on the two-day program, especially since Secretary Work had requested advice from the committee concerning the Pueblos. Miss McKittrick immediately arose and pointed out that this "was a very complex question for lawyers and would require thirty-six hours" of discussion. After much debate, Collier's resolution passed by a narrow vote.[95]

Although the reformers failed to control this conference, the Resolutions Committee, headed by Dr. F. A. MacKenzie, president of Fisk University, sent several positive recommendations to Secretary Work. It requested that the government start a survey of Indian health conditions, hire more trained physicians, and open public schools for Indian use. The Resolutions Committee encouraged the work of missionaries and suggested that the bureau discontinue Indian dances if they interfered with the "laws of the land or interests of morality." Its most decisive resolutions called for the creation of an Indian court of claims, plus the protection of Indian gas, oil, and mineral rights on executive-order reservations.[96]

Little progress was made concerning the Pueblo Indians, but the Resolutions Committee requested a prompt determination of all legal

---

*Arthur C. Parker was one of the founders of the Society of American Indians. Organized in 1911 by Indian progressives, it advocated assimilation and self-reliance. Most of the Indian delegates at the Committee of One Hundred had been leaders of this organization. Hazel Hertzberg, *The Search for an American Indian Identity* (Syracuse: Syracuse University Press, 1971), pp. 52–53, 202–3.

questions and indicated that both settlers and Indians receive compensation for relinquished land. According to Collier, so much disagreement existed over this question that the committee sent two conflicting resolutions without any comment for Secretary Work's consideration. The first one, sponsored by the New Mexico Association, endorsed the Lenroot bill, while the other, drawn up by Collier, expressed opposition "to any measure which would settle by legislative *fiat* questions of Pueblo land titles now being litigated in the courts."[97] The delegates further disappointed Collier when they rejected his effort to make the Committee of One Hundred a permanent advisory body.[98]

The conference ended with a visit to the White House. President Calvin Coolidge, responding to a request of a member of the Board of Indian Commissioners, had invited the delegates over to discuss Indian affairs. According to Collier, "no one spoke for the committee and President Coolidge did not speak to it."[99] This impasse abruptly ceased when Miss Ruth Muskrat, a young Cherokee student from Mount Holyoke College, approached the president. Sponsored by Miss Edith Dabb, head of the YWCA Indian Department, she was clad in deerskin, her head bound with beads.[100]

Miss Muskrat's mission became evident after she delivered a memorized speech and handed Coolidge a copy of G. E. E. Lindquist's book, *The Red Man in the United States*.[101] Published in 1923, this volume contained the findings of an "American Indian Survey" started four years earlier under the auspices of the Inter-Church World Movement to provide data that would help Protestant churches in their missionary efforts.[102] Valuable for its investigation of conditions on reservations throughout the country, the survey exposed widespread poverty and inadequate housing conditions. It revealed that diseases such as trachoma and tuberculosis had ravaged many tribes and recommended that the bureau transfer its health facilities to the Public Health Service.[103] In the area of education, the survey discovered that over 20,000 illiterate Indian children remained out of school, and it recommended increased appropriations for boarding schools and other facilities.[104]

Despite these criticisms, Lindquist's book, which contained a favorable introduction by Commissioner Burke, offered a defense of the Indian Bureau. It praised the land allotment system as a "far-sighted and benevolent policy" although its own findings demonstrated that the Dawes General Allotment Act had failed to protect Indian property.[105] Lindquist commended the bureau for cooperating with the missionaries in their effort to take the Indians down the "Jesus road" and for helping discourage the use of peyote by the Native American Church which he called the "Cult of Death."[106] The book also supported the government's efforts to discourage Indian dances such as the "Indian two step and the 49 dance" which had supposedly resulted in "race demoralization."[107] Evidently Coolidge agreed with these generalizations because, without saying a word to anyone, the president invited Miss Muskrat and Miss Dabb to lunch.* Frustrated by this gesture, other members of the committee "seeped out of the White House . . . like a stream disappearing in the sand."[108]

Disappointed with the Committee of One Hundred's achievements, Collier traveled to New Mexico to meet with the All Pueblo Council on January 17, 1924. He warned the Indians that during the previous December Senator Holm Bursum had introduced a new bill similar to the Lenroot bill. He suggested that a delegation of Pueblo Indians should "go once more to Washington and to the great cities like Chicago and New York, to tell Congress and the American people" about their opposition to Bursum's second bill. He asked the Indians to pick excellent dancers and drummers because "our ability to win this fight . . . depends on arousing the feeling of the American people." The Indians agreed, choosing thirteen delegates. They passed a resolution stating their "opposition to the second Bursum bill and to the kind of resolution of the Pueblo land questions which that bill represents."[109]

Proceeding east under the auspices of Collier's Defense Association, the Indians again visited New York City. Officially greeted by Acting Mayor William T. Collins at City Hall, they tried to create a favorable impression for their "Indian bill" introduced by Senator Curtis.[110] Next, using three kettle drums, they danced before a luncheon at the City Club and a meeting at Town Hall. Dressed in white feathers, with bells jingling from their waists, the Pueblo Indians chanted the corn grinding song and offered a prayer to the eagle for strength. Collier supplemented these dances with speeches against the second Bursum bill.[111]

While in Washington, the Indians were officially received by Commissioner Burke, Secretary Work, and President Coolidge.[112] More important, their Defense Association attorneys held protracted conferences with attorneys who represented the settlers at a meeting before the Senate Committee on Public Lands and Surveys. Under the direction of Olva Adams of Colorado, the committee's chairman, they reached a compromise that made significant concessions to the Pueblos.[113] This revised bill passed the Senate on May 13, the House on June 3 without amendment, and President Coolidge signed it four days later.

---

*Mrs. Calvin Coolidge belonged to the National Indian Association, which believed that the most vital thing for the Indian was to follow the "Gospel of Christ." *Annual Report of the National Indian Association,* 1921 (New York: National Indian Association Press), p. 9.

Known as the Pueblo Lands Act, this legislation established a Lands Board at Santa Fe, New Mexico, consisting of two representatives selected by the secretary of the interior and the attorney general. A third member was appointed by the president. It empowered this board to "investigate, determine, and report" the status and boundaries of all Pueblo lands. The board had to reach a unanimous decision when it recommended extinguishing Indian claims, and its findings went to the attorney general who had authorization to bring suit to quiet title.[114]

The Pueblo Lands Act required that the board use the controversial statute of limitations concept. Non-Indian claimants, to substantiate their claims, had to demonstrate either continuous adverse possession under color of title since January 6, 1902, supported by payment of taxes on the land, or continuous possession since March 16, 1889, supported by payment of taxes, but without color of title. The Indians, however, had the right to hire attorneys and to "assert and maintain unaffected by the provisions of this act their title and right to any land" in court prior to the filing of the field notes by the board.[115]

Other provisions included the principle of compensation at fair market value for all lost Indian lands and water rights, which might have been recovered by seasonable prosecution on the part of the government. If the Indians disliked the board's findings they could appeal within sixty days to the District Court of New Mexico for a more favorable ruling. Non-Indian claimants would receive compensation after the secretary of the interior reported their losses to Congress.[116]

The Bureau of Indian Affairs had to use all money awarded to the Pueblos for the purchase of lands and water rights to replace those abandoned to the settlers or for irrigation works. The act directed the board to find land and improvements of successful non-Indian claimants that the government might purchase for the Indians' benefit. Finally, the Pueblos were prohibited from future transfers of land unless agreed to in advance by the secretary of the interior.[117]

Successful in his attempt to amend the second Bursum bill, Collier believed that the Pueblo Lands Act demonstrated "the difference between honest adjustment and mere theft." He agreed to compromise because he thought the act upheld the right of the Indians to compensation for relinquished land and water rights. Other desirable features prevented future seizures of Pueblo land and directed the government to use all awards in needed irrigation projects. Collier thought that the act avoided "in explicit language any imposition of a retroactive statute of limitations" by allowing the Indians to challenge this concept in court. Because he saw the statute of limitations as an unconstitutional ex post facto measure, he falsely hoped that the courts would overthrow it before the board made its definitive recommendations.[118]

The All Pueblo Council, the General Federation of Women's Clubs, and the American Indian Defense Association had been only partially successful in the Pueblo land controversy. But these setbacks did not upset Collier, who found satisfaction in the resignation of Secretary Fall, the defeat of the Bursum and Lenroot bills, and the creation of the Committee of One Hundred. He told the Defense Association's board of directors that "whether in the future we take up the allotment question . . . the subject of heathen customs, or any basic issue, especially of an economic character, we shall have to cope with such devious and stubborn resistances as we are dealing with in this Pueblo matter." Collier insisted that a clear-cut attack on the Indian affairs system would dispose of these problems and "win the larger public."[119]

The protest from the Pueblos had awakened the country to the plight of the Indians, and the stage was set for an assault on the Coolidge administration which tried to speed up the process of assimilation by suppressing Indian religious ceremonies. This episode made up part of the larger intolerance that surfaced during the twenties in the form of prohibition, the Red Scare, and immigration restriction. Collier, who participated in the intellectual rebellion at Greenwich Village before the First World War, would insist that the government take a cosmopolitan approach toward Indian culture, which included respect for their sexual freedom. But he faced opposition from missionaries, congressmen, and Indian Bureau officials who wanted to safeguard an old-fashioned small-town moralism that denied the divisions in American society: they would work for the preservation of religious orthodoxy and attempt to compel by statute their ethical code on the Indians.

3. Indian Dances Defended

While he fought to safeguard Pueblo property rights, Collier opposed the bureau's effort to crush Indian culture. As early as 1920, Herbert Welsh, the president of the missionary-minded Indian Rights Association, had complained to the bureau about the Hopi Snake Dance and situations among other tribes in the Southwest which needed correction. Welsh became alarmed after reading a report made by Reverend E. M. Sweet, an inspector for the Interior Department. This report used the testimony of whites and Protestant Indians who had repudiated their own heritage to prove that certain evils accompanied dancing festivities — in particular sexual excesses among the Hopi. According to Welsh, the report revealed that students who returned from government boarding schools were forced in secret ceremonies before and after public dances to engage in activities that abandoned "moral and legal restraints imposed by marital obligations."[1]

Welsh and other officers of the Indian Rights Association had quickly accepted the findings of Sweet's report because they thought the Pueblo Indians were a relic of the dark ages and little short of barbarians. Welsh found nothing beautiful in Pueblo civilization; in fact he wanted to lift these Indians "out of a stone-age condition of human society by the spiritual force of the Christian religion."[2] Welsh opposed Indian dances because he wanted to discredit the Roman Catholic missionary effort in New Mexico. He believed that since the Spanish reconquest of the Pueblos in 1696, Catholic priests had followed an evasive policy over the question of when to eliminate pagan customs. He also hoped to weaken Pueblo

[55]

tribal self-government because he thought the governors ran a "boss system" which held "the progressive and educated Indians chained to an
old system worse than feudalism."[3]

The association used its journal *Indian Truth* to put pressure on the
bureau to discourage Indian dances. Matthew K. Sniffen, the editor,
pointed out that several tribes engaged in immoral ceremonies, such as
the Koshare Dance at Santo Domingo where whites had to hide their faces
and leave the village. He claimed that a further description of Pueblo
dances would be too indecent to print or send through the mails, but
indicated that interested persons could read copies of Sweet's report at
his Philadelphia office.[4]

The Board of Indian Commissioners, a non-partisan organization
created to oversee the administration of Indian affairs, joined this protest against Indian dances. In 1918, one of the board's members, Father
W. H. Ketcham, the head of the Bureau of Catholic Missions, had completed a study which claimed that many Indians engaged in the "vilest
sexual practices."[5] On October 21, 1920, after receiving complaints from
missionaries about the injurious effects of dancing among the Sioux, the
board passed and sent to Commissioner Burke a resolution recommending adequate supervision of all dances to maintain order and suggesting
that the bureau put a stop to ceremonies that interfered with Indian industrial pursuits.[6]

Burke agreed that some Indian dances were harmful, and they made
it difficult for him to follow Congressional mandates such as the Dawes
General Allotment Act which required that he work to assimilate the
Indian into white society. The commissioner had no intention of keeping
the Indians as objects for the study of artists or bored intellectuals because
he thought that they needed to learn self-reliance in order to survive in
the modern world.[7] An avid supporter of missionaries who sought "the
highest welfare of the Indians," Burke issued regulations requiring that
Indian children at government boarding schools attend Sunday school
and church. Furthermore, he told his superintendents to extend impartial
privileges to all denominations.[8]

The commissioner implemented the recommendations made by missionaries, the Board of Indian Commissioners, and the Indian Rights
Association, on April 26, 1921, in Circular 1665. In this directive Burke
stressed his approval of many ceremonials which brought "pleasure and
relaxation," but he listed as Indian offenses punishable by fines and
imprisonment, the Sun-Dance and "so-called religious ceremonies" that
involved self-torture, the reckless giving away of property, prolonged
periods of celebration, the use of injurious drugs and intoxicants, or excessive performances that promoted idleness, superstitious cruelty, and dan-

gers to health. Burke also requested that his superintendents encourage missionary activities that prepared the Indians for citizenship and "a higher conception of home and family life."[9]

Two years later, on February 14, 1923, the commissioner strengthened Circular 1665 with a "Supplement" which "heartily endorsed" recommendations made at a conference of missionaries in Fort Pierre, South Dakota.[10] He asked his subordinates to abolish an Indian form of gambling known as *"ituranpi;"* limit dances to one each month in the day, in mid-week, at the center of each Indian district (except during the planting and harvesting months from March through August when most dances were banned); and prohibit anyone under fifty years of age from participating in ceremonies that revealed immoral or degrading influences. Burke, however, showed moderation when he told his superintendents to use tact and persuasion in their implementation of his order.[11]

To secure full compliance with his previous directive, Burke wrote a "Message to All Indians" on February 24, 1923. He criticized customs that caused the neglect of farming and the raising of livestock and warned against the handling of poisonous snakes. The commissioner then stated that he could arbitrarily issue orders against "these useless and harmful performances" but opened the door for compromise by suggesting that the Indians give them up of their own free will. Burke indicated that if after one year they had not made progress he would take "some other course" of action.[12]

Hubert Work, the new secretary of the interior, agreed with these restrictions on Indian dances. His Committee of One Hundred, which met in 1923, had cordially commended "the substance and spirit" of Circular 1665 and called for the discontinuance of dances when they contravened "the laws of the land, or the interests of morality."[13] Work supported Burke because he believed that the government should continue its efforts "toward the absorption" of the Indian into the mainstream of American life. He felt that the fundamental problem for the Indian Service consisted of encouraging individual thrift, industry, and responsibility. He approved of the bureau's attempt to modify Indian ceremonies into "harmony with the forms of Christian religion which civilization has approved, from which our rules of life are drafted and from which our government is founded." But he doubted whether the Indian could afford any more than the white man to exaggerate the sex instinct which might "contribute to his spiritual and physical downfall."[14]

This policy of degrading Indian culture met the opposition of Collier who wanted to preserve Indian heritage. He claimed that the government could not save or usefully assimilate the red man by crushing his soul, stripping him of "racial memories, and forcing him to become

a premature social half-breed."[15] Collier assumed that Indians such as
the Pueblos represented not an inferior but simply a different world, holding the secrets of communal life. He was especially impressed with
Frank Hamilton Cushing's book *Outlines Of Zuni Creation Myths,* which
maintained that these Indians had mastered rituals that solved the problem of merging diverse peoples together without a surrender of "richness
and freedom." He believed that the Zuni and other Pueblos lived by
organizational principles that would be adopted by a future "democratic,
pluralistic, holistic world order."[16]

At House hearings held during February 1923, Collier publicly
explained his position concerning the suppression of Indian dances. He
admitted that some of the Picuris Indians belonged to the Penitente cult
which applied self-torture, such as whipping its members who carried
huge crosses during Good Friday services, but he was still infatuated with
their "wonderful and weird music."[17]

Collier rejected the commonly held notion that the Pueblos held
secret ceremonies because they were wicked and disgraceful. He suggested that although these Indians carried out certain festivities dealing
with mating and fertility which had "an erotic significance" offensive to
some whites, the Indians considered these ceremonies decent and sacred.
Collier pointed out that he had inquired at Taos about allowing his three
sons to participate in adolescent initiation rites and found nothing immoral
or hurtful to a well-brought-up white boy. The Indians refused his sons
permission, however, because they feared their secrets might become
public information.[18] Collier stressed that the Pueblos were "sexually the
purest, sweetest people" he had ever known, and he called for statutory
protection to safeguard them from Indian commissioners who had a "rav-
enous attitude" toward native culture.*

The bureau paid little attention to Collier's plea for laws to protect
Indian religious freedom. Following the advice of missionaries, it started
a campaign to educate public opinion against Indian ceremonials. During
December 1923, Miss Edith Dabb, head of the YWCA Indian Department and a supporter of assimilation, wrote a letter to the *New York
Times* which supported Commissioner Burke's attempt to abolish certain
tribal dances. She pointed out that there were two ways of looking at the
Indian problem: the government could keep the Indians artificially isolated or it could prepare them for citizenship and progress. Dabb warned

---

*Collier qualified this with a statement that he would later regret. He indicated
that Commissioner Burke had "a fine humane attitude" and appreciated the "cultural
value of the Indians." U.S. Congress, House, Committee on Indian Affairs, *Hearings
on H.R. 13452 and 13674, Pueblo Land Titles,* 67th Cong., 4th Sess., 1923, p. 212.

all sentimentalists who dwelled on the beauties of the quaint and primitive that this type of splendor was frequently found in close company with ugliness. She claimed, without specific evidence, that young Indian girls who had started to enjoy school and adolescence were made to take part in ceremonial dances, which meant child marriage and usually mother-hood. She criticized giveaway dances because they caused destitution among families and sometimes the loss of a daughter or wife to other tribal members.[19]

Collier started his fight against the bureau's policy of degrading Indian culture when he wrote a letter to the *New York Times* entitled "Indian Dances Defended." Dismayed at Miss Dabb's insensitivity, he argued that almost all Indian rituals were religious in nature and "of a kind that our modern unsophisticated world knows little about." He admitted that he knew four Americanized Pueblo Indians who had repudi-ated their past heritage, but he doubted the wisdom of divesting the Indian of his own personality for that of an Anglo-Saxon.* Collier pro-posed that the government study the French and British colonial experi-ence, which attempted to blend native culture with modern civilization.[20]

But Collier's protest failed to stop the Indian Bureau from continuing its effort to discredit native institutions. It distributed, in cooperation with the Indian Rights Association, copies of documents from Reverend Sweet's report. Consisting of about one-hundred affidavits and sworn testimonies by missionaries, Christianized Indians, and bureau personnel, these documents criticized the immoral and revolting character of sev-eral Indian dances.[21] According to Collier, one of these exhibits written by William E. "Pussyfoot" Johnson, a former chief officer of the Indian Service and director of the World League of Alcoholism, was "a foot deep on the desk of Commissioner Burke's secretary."[22]

Johnson had supported the Indian Bureau by suggesting that Pueblo secret dances were hideous, obscene, and revolting. He claimed that these Indians participated in rites more degrading than the phallic worship of the ancient Greeks and Hindus.[23] Johnson quoted the testimony of Miss Mary E. Dissette, an Indian who stated that Zuni girls were "debauched in these dances under the guise of religious liberty," and he cited other unnamed witnesses who stated that at one sacred dance every female participant became pregnant.[24] Johnson criticized the frequent fiestas of the Southwest, which interfered with successful farming, but his testimony

---

*The Eastern Association on Indian Affairs supported Collier on the dance issue by sending out an illustrated brochure in which four scientists denounced Miss Dabb for claiming that certain Indian dances were indecent and immoral. Matthew K. Sniffen, ed., *Indian Truth* 1 (April 1924): 3.

reached the apex of its accusation when he condemned the Pueblos for
withdrawing their children from school in order to give them a two-year
course in sodomy under pagan instructors. He concluded his statement
with the names of the Indian Rights Association, the Bureau of Catholic
Missions, and "every known Protestant missionary organization," as institutions which actively supported the bureau's attempt to eliminate tribal
dances.[25]

These rash statements angered F. W. Hodge, curator of the Museum
of the American Indian, and he joined Collier in opposition to the bureau.
Hodge wrote two letters to the *New York Times* that questioned the
accuracy of such statements concerning the indecent and immoral nature
of Pueblo dances. He criticized the reams of affidavits supplied by the
bureau to substantiate its charges by asking how the government could
have documents about secret dances no white person had ever seen. He
had witnessed these ceremonial dances for thirty years and claimed that
all such statements were based on the grossest misinformation. Even the
Zuni Indians, who adhered closely to their primitive customs, engaged
in essentially religious ceremonies.[26]

The bureau made its first attempt to enforce previous bans on
dancing at Taos, a Pueblo which had cooperated closely with Collier. On
April 18, 1924, Commissioner Burke, accompanied by Secretary Work,
traveled to Taos and spoke before a meeting of the tribal council. Burke
told the Indians that on the next Monday they must return two boys
temporarily withdrawn from government school for religious training.
This withdrawal took place once in a lifetime and lasted for about
eighteen months.[27] After Burke and Work departed, the Indians still
refused to send the boys to school, so Superintendent C. J. Crandall called
on the officers of the Pueblo and repeated Burke's order.*

This led to open resistance on the part of the Indians at an All
Pueblo Council meeting held on May 5 at Santo Domingo. Seventy-four
delegates from fifteen Pueblos attended, and Collier helped them draw
up a statement concerning religious liberty. This declaration, which passed
unanimously, called Burke's order forcing the boys to attend school an
instrument of religious persecution. The Indians also agreed with Collier
that they should formally state their position to the Indian Bureau.[28]

In a letter dated May 7, 1924, which Collier helped compose, the
governor and council at Taos told Commissioner Burke that they wished

---

*The bureau had also prohibited the withdrawal of Zuni children from school
for four days during their sacred initiation rites. John Collier, *The Indian and His
Religious Freedom* (pamphlet), July 2, 1924, Collier Papers.

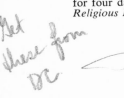

to have their boys take full advantage of the government school and had urged that any boys withdrawn temporarily for religious training make up lost time. Nevertheless, they refused to obey his order because their religion "was more important to each of us than money, horses, land, or anything else in the world." It taught them "about God and the earth, and about our duty to God, to earth, and to one another."[29]

This debate over the question of religious freedom divided the Indians into hostile camps. On May 2, 1924, thirty Pueblo Indians had met at Santa Ana village to assert their individual right to religious liberty and to form the General Council of Progressive Christian Indians. Composed of delegates from eleven Pueblos, this assembly claimed to represent approximately 2,000 out of 10,000 Indians. Led by Matthew K. Sniffen, secretary of the Indian Rights Association, and Mrs. Nina Otero Warren, a government inspector, the council sided with the Indian Bureau. These Indians passed resolutions which criticized the domination of caciques or priests who forced them to conform to old pagan customs and retarded their economic and social progress.[30]

Despite this support, the open defiance by Taos Pueblo forced Secretary Work to back off from his previous confrontation concerning the religious training of Indian boys. On June 2, 1924, he publicly stated that the government contemplated no definite action until the fall term.[31] When he continued to vacillate in September, the Indian Rights Association criticized him for refusing to suppress "ignorant and reactionary caciques" who persecuted the progressive Pueblos.[32] Work replied that "persecution by a Pueblo official of the progressives will not have my approval," but he conceded religious liberty and toleration for all Indians.[33]

Pleased with this victory, Collier told the board of directors of his Defense Association that the religious issue was more fundamental than the land problem. He pointed out that the destruction of tribal culture, the historical policy of the bureau, had turned into fanaticism in recent years. Because tribal life revolved around religion, Burke's orders would have destroyed Indians as a social group and as a race. Collier urged his colleagues to continue their attack against the bureau before the upcoming presidential contest because the government would compromise until after the election and then "laugh in spite of thunder."[34]

Thunder struck first during the Federation of Women's Clubs June 1924 biennial convention held in Los Angeles, but it brought defeat for Collier. The question of Indian religious freedom became paramount when Miss Clara D. True, associate secretary for the Indian Rights Association, appeared with a delegation of seven progressive Pueblo Indians. Using Collier's publicity tactics to win over the emotion of the women, she protested against the pagan priests who supposedly persecuted the

Christian Indians.[35] She successfully prevented the convention from supporting Charles Fletcher Lummis, a writer and authority on southwestern history, who pushed for a resolution which would have condemned Commissioner Burke's ban on dancing.*

Lummis appeared at this convention because he agreed with Collier, who had often entered his home where they "were silent together."[36] Officially representing the Defense Association, he told the women that the religious controversy was closely allied with the failure of discredited politicians who had attempted to rob the Indians of their land. Lummis warned that, having failed with the Bursum bill, the government followed a new and less obvious line of attack. The recent assault on religious freedom at Taos contained "the entering wedge of a campaign to destroy the whole Pueblo system and drag from under the Indian's feet the last acre of their lands."[37]

The women in Los Angeles responded to these contradictory pleas by refusing to take a stand on religious freedom. Instead, they passed a resolution which called on President Coolidge to reorganize Indian affairs immediately.[38] They also removed Stella Atwood from her chairmanship of the Indian Welfare Committee because of the continued controversy she brought the federation. Undaunted, she would continue her reform as a director of the American Indian Defense Association.[39]

This defeat, however, did not deter Collier, who wrote a letter to Mrs. John D. Sherman, president of the Women's Federation, stating that the history of religious persecution held no more disgraceful episode than the bureau's attempt to prevent Pueblo boys from entering into the priesthood. He rejected as monstrous the charge by William "Pussyfoot" Johnson and others that Pueblo priests gave Indian boys a two-year course in sodomy. Johnson's real motive, he claimed, lay in economic rather than religious matters. Collier reminded Mrs. Sherman that Johnson had quoted such people as Miss Clara D. True, whose record as a promoter of the Bursum bill, which cancelled Pueblo land titles, was well known.[40]

Collier's most devastating criticism of the Indian Bureau came in a Defense Association pamphlet entitled "The Indian and Religious Freedom." In it he traced the history of the government's "inquisition" and

---

*Born on March 1, 1859, Charles Fletcher Lummis was city editor for the *Los Angeles Times* from 1885 to 1887. Strenuous work caused paralysis, so he went to New Mexico to live for five years at Isleta Pueblo. There he learned Pueblo customs, languages, and folk ways. In 1905 he became a librarian at the Los Angeles Public Library, built an excellent collection of Southwestern material, and made phonographic records of more than 400 Indian songs. In 1922 he joined the struggle to reform Indian affairs and remained active in it until his death on November 25, 1928. Dumas Malone, ed., *Dictionary of American Biography,* Vol. 11 (New York: Charles Scribner's Sons, 1961), pp. 501–2.

questioned the use of the "thumb screw" to make converts. Collier cited the General Council of Progressive Christian Indians as an example of the property motive behind the attack on ceremonials at Taos. He believed that this council represented only fifty Indians out of a population of 10,000 and was a puppet of the bureau. Furthermore, it had the assistance of Mrs. Nina Otero Warren, a government inspector who had been appointed by the discredited Albert B. Fall, and A. B. Renehan, the attorney for the white settlers, who wanted to deprive the Indians of their land.[41]

In this pamphlet Collier stressed the importance of religion on the continuance of the Indians as a social group. United in their spiritual beliefs, the Indians could stand up together as men, cling to the remnants of their land, and resist becoming slaves of the 6,000 Indian Bureau job holders who made their living civilizing the Indian. Sensing the universal significance of Indian life, Collier wanted to preserve "their treasure of the soul which no man yet has known enough to be able to estimate."[42]

Collier continued his defense of the Pueblos in a letter to the *New York Times* that rejected a statement by Herbert Welsh, president of the Indian Rights Association, claiming that their religions involved immoral behavior. Collier indignantly argued that the government's campaign of injury against the Indians, with the aid of missionaries and certain welfare agents, was "unprecedented in a long history of struggles for the emancipation of subject peoples and the establishment of liberties."[43] The Indian Rights Association countered this argument by insisting that Collier wanted to perpetuate an obsolete type of civilization under the plea of religious liberty.[44]

Collier also questioned Catholic support of the bureau's infringement of Indian religious freedom. He criticized the activities of priests such as Father Fridolin Schuster, a Franciscan monk, who had campaigned against Indian dances, and Monsignor William Hughes, the director of the Bureau of Catholic Education, who syndicated material through the Catholic press in defense of Commissioner Burke.[45] Collier admitted that he knew the bureau held these missionaries under duress because Catholic schools received $191,000 out of tribal funds without the Indians' consent. He realized that the government patented the land from reservations for the use of various mission groups without compensation to the Indians. While it was impractical for the missionaries to initiate reforms in the Indian Service, Collier suggested "they at least might be silent and not appear as open and wholesale advocates of a state of affairs that was truly indefensible."[46]

In the *Christian Century*, Collier warned that the country owed an old debt to the Indians, a whole branch of the human race which faced the agony of a spiritual and physical slaughter. He asked the Christian churches to assume some responsibility for the preservation of precious Indian qualities, such as the beauties of art, secrets of moral education, profound values of comparative religion, and knowledge of the coopera- tive way of living. And he reminded his readers that the importance of institutions was not measured by the numbers of individuals who lived in them. He told the churchmen to look to their past, when they suffered as tiny minorities, and they would understand the issue of religious persecution.[47]

These arguments may have influenced some Christians, but they had little impact on the bureau. The conflict over religious freedom reached its zenith at Taos during the summer of 1925 when officers of the Pueblo disciplined two Indians who were members of the peyote-using Native American Church for invading traditional religious ceremonies dressed in non-ceremonial costumes. The imposters had been given the choice of paying a two dollar fine or receiving a single stroke with a piece of leather delivered on the back through a blanket and clothes. The two Indians chose the whipping, and one admitted publicly that he had made his choice in order to break up the Pueblo's government.[48]

The Indian Bureau sided with the two Indians and against the officers of Taos. C. J. Crandall, the superintendent of the Northern Pueblos, obtained authority from Commissioner Burke to arrest all but one mem- ber of the governing body at Taos just before the most sacred and manda- tory of that year's religious ceremonies. Charged with assault and battery, these nine officials were taken under armed guard to Santa Fe and held under $500 dollars bail for each man, but Collier's Defense Association provided bail money and lawyers. The next day Judge Colin Neblett released the officers of Taos after they appeared before the New Mexico district court. He repudiated the bureau's action by ruling that his court had no jurisdiction because Congress had determined by statute that the Pueblos should govern their own internal affairs according to their own customs.[49]

The Pueblo Indians responded to this imprisonment by calling a meeting of the All Pueblo Council at Santo Domingo on August 31, 1925. Under the influence of Collier, seventy-seven delegates from fifteen Pueblos issued an appeal to "The President of the United States, the Congress, and Our Friends the American People." This resolution denounced the bureau's effort to destroy their self-government through the imprisonment of the Taos officials and thanked white friends for employing lawyers to defend them. It criticized the "reckless and hostile persons" who distributed "the shameful documents" collected by the Indian Bureau which demeaned their religion. The Indians stated that these documents contained false, slanderous, and libelous statements, and they asked the American people whether they would tolerate their continued circulation in an effort to destroy what the Indians held sacred.[50]

Collier then convinced the Indians that they should accept invitations from local chapters of the Defense Association and visit California and Utah. While on this trip they could explain their plight and raise money to hire lawyers to appeal questionable decisions of the Pueblo Lands Board. When the twelve Pueblo delegates reached California, social leaders in the Bay area received them warmly and opened their homes to listen to the Indians. Groups such as the Commonwealth Club, the Oakland Forum, and the Berkeley Playhouse also provided receptive audiences.[51] When the Indians gathered over $13,000 dollars in a few weeks, officials in the bureau spread innuendo, which appeared on the front page of the *Albuquerque State Tribune,* suggesting that the turmoil among the Pueblos stemmed from outside influence financed by "money from Moscow."[52]

Discouraged by the Indians' open resistance to his policies, Commissioner Burke drafted an administration measure called the Leavitt bill. It directed that all federal civil and criminal laws apply to the Indians with the United States district courts having jurisdiction over these crimes and misdemeanors.* For other offenses, not punishable by federal law, the bill gave authority to existing Indian reservation courts which could levy six-month jail sentences and $100 fines. This legislation abolished future Indian custom marriage and divorce. If the Indians knowingly violated this section one year after the bill passed, they faced imprisonment for up to one year and a fine of $200.[53]

Collier believed that the Leavitt bill contained unconstitutional features, so he appeared on February 13, 1926, before the House Indian Affairs Committee to criticize its provisions. First of all, Collier objected to section 2, which recognized the existing authority of Indian reservation courts. He pointed out that they were run without law codes or jury trial by superintendents and their ten-dollar-a-month Indian judges. These courts followed the "whim" of the superintendent or "bizarre" regulations, such as the prohibition of religious ceremonies, drawn up by the secretary of the interior. Collier warned that by failing to establish due process of law, the bill sanctioned rule similar to that "maintained by the Czar in Russia" or by "Leopold of Belgium" toward his Congo victims.[54]

---

*Previously Congress had directed that only eight major crimes apply on the reservations. They included murder, manslaughter, rape, assault with a dangerous weapon, arson, burglary, larceny, and assault with intent to kill. U.S. Congress, House, Committee on Indian Affairs, *Hearings, on H.R. 7826, Reservation Courts of Indian Offenses,* 69th Cong., 1st Sess., 1926, pp. 1–2.

Section 4, which outlawed Indian custom marriage and divorce, received the brunt of Collier's attack. He explained that these rituals made up part of the entire complex of Indian social life, especially among the Navajos and Pueblos. The substitution of state law would disintegrate their moral and institutional life without substituting any adequate control. If this part of the bill became law, Collier believed that the Indians in the Southwest would disregard it because they would find it hard to readjust their lifestyle in one year. He doubted whether any advantage existed in making these individuals criminals.[55]

Collier ended his testimony by suggesting that Congress replace the Leavitt bill with legislation that Defense Association lawyers had drafted. Introduced by James A. Frear, a Republican from Wisconsin and member of the House Indian Affairs Committee, it abolished the reservation courts and guaranteed Indians due process by giving the United States district courts exclusive jurisdiction over all felonies, misdemeanors, and civil matters on a reservation. Where federal statutes failed to apply, the court could consult state law codes. But if tribal authority still existed, Indian custom would prevail in all civil and criminal cases other than felonies. In order to allow the district courts to handle this additional work, the Frear bill authorized them to appoint special commissioners who could arrest and bring Indians to trial. No bail was required if individuals held property under government trust worth $500, and Indians could appeal the commissioner's decisions to the district court judge. Finally, Indian marriages and divorces remained lawful where tribal custom prevailed.[56]

S. M. Brosius, the Washington agent for the Indian Rights Association, followed Collier, and he also opposed the Leavitt bill. Brosius expressed concern about legalizing the courts of Indian offenses, which he considered a step backward. He pointed out that Congress had made the Indians citizens in 1924, and he favored placing them under federal jurisdiction but thought Collier's cumbersome proposal might have to go before the Judiciary Committee. He suggested that whenever possible the Indians should come under the state courts, but he did support the bureau's effort to abolish Indian custom marriages and divorces.[57]

The testimony of Mrs. Amelia E. White, secretary of the Eastern Association on Indian Affairs, further undercut the bureau's position. She favored the use of reservation tribunals because Indians would find it difficult and expensive to travel to the nearest district court. But Mrs. White criticized the bureau for refusing to give the Indians a greater voice in choosing judges, who should limit their activities to misdemeanors and short sixty-day sentences. She stressed that the government must respect Indian custom marriages and divorces because of the principle of religious freedom.[58]

When Assistant Commissioner Meritt appeared at these hearings to speak for Commissioner Burke who was sick, he vigorously defended the Leavitt bill. Meritt emphasized the importance of increasing the scope of federal jurisdiction over the reservations beyond the eight major crimes. This would help the bureau prosecute several offenses such as "unlawful cohabitation, fornication, seduction, carnal knowledge, incest, polygamy, lewdness, soliciting females for immoral purposes, and desertion of wife."[59]

Meritt defended the continued use of the courts of Indian offenses because he believed that Indians remained sufficiently unadvanced for the bureau to subject them to the severe punishment contained in many state laws. In the meantime, the assistant commissioner warned that he had to have some method for providing law and order. He indicated that the reservation tribunals suited this purpose because superintendents selected Indian judges who held progressive ideals and they provided quick as well as inexpensive justice. He claimed that the bureau planned to prepare a new modern set of regulations to guide these courts.[60]

Meritt next discussed section 4 of the Leavitt bill which abolished Indian custom marriages and divorces. He cited a report made in 1918 by Father Ketcham, a former member of the Board of Indian Commissioners, which deplored the shameful laxity in morals and marriage relations among members of Indian tribes. According to Meritt, he and Commissioner Burke were following the board's recommendations, which proposed to give state courts jurisdiction in such matters to help the bureau fight this growing evil.[61]

Finished with his formal presentation, the assistant commissioner attacked his critics. He opposed Collier's alternate plan because it would require an expensive new system of judicial procedure and lengthy consultation with the Justice Department. Meritt complained that Congress had been flooded with circulars which contained malicious falsehoods, evidently referring to a Defense Association bulletin entitled, "A Bill Authorizing Tyranny." He emphasized that he disapproved of paid propagandists who falsely criticized him for trying to reach out for more power. That was "all bunk" because the bureau wanted only to "improve moral conditions on the reservations."[62]

Representative Scott Leavitt from Montana consistently defended the bureau during these hearings but received lukewarm support from some of his colleagues. Leavitt stated that the Montana Indians had never complained about their reservation courts, and he favored the bill because it would help the Indians "carry on as part of the American people."[63] These arguments, however, failed to impress George Brumm from Pennsylvania, who declared that he saw nothing incompatible between Indian marriage ceremonies and state common law. William Williamson from South Dakota agreed, and he doubted if any member of the committee would declare himself for the bill as submitted by the Interior Department. Faced with this open hostility, Leavitt consented not to report the "bill out at this session."[64]

Although the bureau failed to secure passage of the Leavitt bill, it continued to apply pressure to discourage Indian religious training. On March 1, 1926, C. J. Crandall, superintendent of the Northern Pueblos, wrote to the Taos school principal and instructed him to read his letter to the Pueblo officials. It stated that "in every case where a boy is taken out of school for any purpose and kept out . . . I shall hold the parents responsible and cause arrest upon your recommendation." The bureau threatened Jemez Pueblo when S. A. Young, superintendent of the Southern Pueblos, wrote a similar letter to the governor of Jemez. It warned that Commissioner Burke opposed the continued withdrawal of thirty children from school for four days a year to engage in religious instruction.[65]

Collier responded to this renewed threat by writing letters to Scott Leavitt and John Harreld, chairmen of the House and Senate Indian Affairs Committees. He warned the two men that the issue squarely before the American people and Congress consisted of whether the Indian Bureau should be "permitted to invade the last sanctuary of dignity and holiness in the life of the Indians . . . making it a crime to worship God."[66]

Leavitt rejected Collier's appeal and, after consultation with the Indian Bureau, he reported his bill out of committee with only minor changes. This infuriated Collier, who published a letter in Montana's *Great Falls Tribune* that called Leavitt a "careless, ignorant, and obedient Representative," who had maneuvered through committee a bill of "absolute ruthless, even fantastic oppression and enslavement."* Confessing that he wanted to see someone else made chairman, Collier asked for a person who would not be a "tool of the Indian Bureau . . . and of the predatory interests which that bureaucracy serves."[67]

Because he believed that the Leavitt bill threatened the Pueblos' right of self-government, Collier organized an All Pueblo Council meeting at Santo Domingo on November 28, 1926. Other white friends of the Indians who attended included Stella Atwood, Charles F. Lummis, and Defense Association attorneys.[68] But officials from the bureau refused

---

*The Indian Bureau modified its demand to imprison Indians without trial but still insisted that its regulations govern the reservation courts of Indian offenses. *Great Falls Tribune*, October 9, 1926, Collier Papers.

an invitation to come because it challenged their newly formed United States Pueblo Indian Council. Established two weeks earlier in Santa Fe, this council was led by Herbert J. Hagerman, the special commissioner to the Navajos and a member of the Pueblo Lands Board. Hagerman, who had successfully organized the Navajo Tribal Council, told the Indians that this new council would offer them an official forum to air their views, needs, and grievances. He explained that private meetings were fine, but they would have "no official recognition without govern-ment representation."[69]

When Collier spoke before the assembled delegates at Santo Domingo, he advised them to reject the Leavitt bill. He warned that it interfered with their self-government by providing that Indian marriages come under state instead of tribal law. He explained the Defense Association alternative, the Frear bill, which proposed to "give a new Congressional confirmation of your right to live according to your tribal customs and govern yourselves in your own way." The Indians agreed, and they passed a resolution which opposed the Leavitt bill while endorsing Collier's substitute measure.[70]

Collier then discussed whether the Indians should continue to attend meetings of the government-sponsored United States Pueblo Council. He told them to boycott its proceedings because they could not trust the bureau, which had tried to abolish Indian dances.* He questioned the propriety of allowing Hagerman to lead the council when the Indians might have to dispute his decisions on the Lands Board. As usual the delegates followed Collier's advice, and they were "practically unanimous in asserting their wish to retain their own pueblo council, to control it themselves, and not to participate in the United States Pueblo Council called by Herbert Hagerman."[71]

Because of this opposition, Congress refused to pass the Leavitt bill. Thus ended the last major threat to Indian religious freedom. Although Collier failed to secure approval for his alternative legislation, he continued his reform activities by helping to expose and defeat bills sponsored by the Interior Department that threatened Indian oil, water, and mineral rights.

This controversy over resource development in the West began when Secretary of the Interior Albert B. Fall, who believed in the unrestrained

---

*Collier also suggested that the Indians refuse to meet with the United States Pueblo Council because he knew that it was an effort by the bureau to undercut his influence through the All Pueblo Council, which had become a power center for reformers and a serious nuisance since the struggle in 1922 against the Bursum bill. John Collier to the All Pueblo Council, 1926, Collier Papers.

use of natural wealth, opened up Indian executive-order reservations for private exploitation by local interests. Neglected by historians, this attack on Indian land resources was just as important as the Teapot Dome scandal for an understanding of the progressive conservation movement that continued during the twenties. Influenced by ideas in vogue during his career in New York, Collier worked to bring scientific management, efficiency, and rational planning to an expanded regional economy.[72]

4. A Provisional Revolution

The threat to Indian oil reserves began on February 25, 1920, when Congress passed a bill known as the General Leasing Act, opening up the public domain to the mining of coal, oil, and phosphates. Two years later, E. M. Harrison, an oil prospector, applied for leases on the Navajo reservation.[1] The General Land Office denied this application, ruling that the General Leasing Act was inapplicable to executive-order reservations.* Harrison then appealed his case to Secretary of the Interior Albert B. Fall, who declared on June 2, 1922, in a report to the House Indian Affairs Committee, that the act did in fact apply because executive-order reservations "were merely public lands temporarily withdrawn by executive-order."[2]

Fall's ruling empowered the Department of the Interior to lease portions of executive-order reservations for mining purposes under the terms of the General Leasing Act, and it placed in jeopardy Indian property rights to over 22 million acres of land.[3] The secretary decreed that the Indians would receive no royalties; instead, 52.5 percent of the bonuses went to the general reclamation fund, 37.5 percent to the state where the reservation was located, and 10 percent to the federal government. Prospectors filed over 400 applications in the General Land Office

---

*The United States dealt separately with various tribes, defining their legal rights by treaty until 1871, when Congress prohibited further treaty making. After this date reservations were established by executive order or by acts of Congress. The federal government had recognized Indian property rights on both types of reservations until Fall's decision in 1922. Felix Cohen, *Handbook of Federal Indian Law* (Washington: Government Printing Office, 1942), p. 299.

to explore for oil and other resources on Indian land, but Fall had granted only twenty leases before his resignation.[4]

Herbert Welsh, the president of the Indian Rights Association, believed that the secretary's decision "was an act in keeping with the Teapot Dome, but on a larger scale," and he sought to have it reversed.[5] On November 4, 1922, he wrote a letter to Moorfield Storey, the honorary president of his organization and former president of the American Bar Association, requesting a careful study of the law and court decisions pertaining to Fall's ruling. Three days later Storey replied to Welsh: "I am clearly of the opinion that the construction placed upon the law by the Secretary in this case is not warranted." To prove his contention, Storey cited the 1896 *Spaulding vs Chandler* decision of the Supreme Court which confirmed Indian title to executive-order reservations. The Indian Rights Association submitted this opinion to Fall but it "had no effect."[6]

The matter came up again, however, when Herbert Work assumed control of the Interior Department.* On March 31, 1923, Commissioner Burke sent Work a letter which refuted the idea that the General Leasing Act applied to executive-order reservations. Because he agreed with the position taken by the Indian Rights Association, Burke cited Storey's brief and requested that his superior refer Fall's ruling to the solicitor of the Interior Department for a reevaluation. Work replied on November 15 that due to complicated circumstances he felt unwarranted in overruling his predecessor, but he did favor a legislative solution to the dilemma. He promised to recommend a bill which would give the Indians a "fair share of the receipts from oil and gas produced on these lands."[7]

This failed to placate the Indian Rights Association which feared that the government would not protect Indian title to executive-order reservations. On November 27, Storey wrote Work to request that he reconsider reversing his predecessor's position, which had overruled the decision of the Supreme Court in various cases. Storey indicated that whenever the Indians had anything particularly desirable some method of taking it was always devised. He warned that "a vastly more scrupulous regard for the rights of the Indians should be shown by the Department of Interior."[8]

---

*Not only did Albert B. Fall fail to heed these warnings, he "heartily" favored an Indian Omnibus bill which passed the House early in 1923. It sought to end all federal responsibility for the Indians by having Congress individualize their tribal property and pay to each Indian the cash value of his assets. Late in the legislative session Senator Robert La Follette blocked this bill when he refused to agree on unanimous consent for its consideration, claiming it had "to do with the wrongfare of the Indians." *Congressional Record*, 67th Cong., 4th Sess., February 3, 1923, 64, Part 3: 2972–77, and Ibid., March 3, 1923, Part 6: 5389.

Work declined this advice after he discussed the matter with his subordinates. Instead, he drafted a bill on December 6, 1923, and secured its introduction in both the House and Senate. This measure gave the Indians all royalties from the development of oil and gas on executive-order reservations while the government continued to issue oil permits in accordance with the General Leasing Act, but it failed to emerge from committee.[9]

Irritated that Work had refused to repudiate the decision of Fall which clouded Indian title, the Indian Rights Association sent a letter to President Calvin Coolidge, on January 11, 1924, urging that he refer the controversy to the attorney general for an opinion. The president forwarded this request to Work who answered his critics five days later. The secretary claimed that an opinion by the attorney general "would be no more conclusive than the one rendered by my predecessor," and he suggested that the question would have to be settled by a "decision of the court of last resort or by an act of Congress."[10]

Work's equivocal attitude caused the Indian Rights Association to seek assistance from Senators Charles Curtis from Kansas and Henry Cabot Lodge from Massachusetts. They interceded with President Coolidge and insisted that he refer Fall's contentions to the attorney general's office for reevaluation.[11] This effort proved successful, because on May 27, 1924, Attorney General Harlan Stone repudiated Fall. Stone indicated that the General Leasing Act of 1920 was inapplicable for executive-order reservations and suggested that the failure to provide the Indians with royalties violated "practically all legislative precedents." He cited previous congressional and Supreme Court decisions to prove that executive-order reservations were not public domain but belonged to the Indians. A short time later, the attorney general initiated legal action to void the permits issued to E. M. Harrison and other prospectors.[12]

Because he anticipated future legislation dealing with Indian land resources, Stone publicly discussed his views about this problem. He pointed out that it was possible to take the position that the Indians owned their executive-order reservations by a governmental act of grace, owning only surface rights. On the other hand, one could stress that Indian possession remained intact including subsurface rights. Stone suggested that if it were necessary to decide between these opposing views, he would incline strongly to the latter, because the Indian possession has always been recognized as complete and exclusive until terminated by treaty or an act of Congress.[13]

Stone's decision meant that Congress would have to enact special legislation if it wanted to open up executive-order reservations for mineral exploration. On December 30, 1924, Senator John W. Harreld from

Oklahoma reintroduced the bill sponsored by Secretary Work, which proposed that the General Leasing Act apply to executive-order reservations with the provision that the government pay all royalties to the Indians. This bill eventually passed the Senate, but the House amended it to allow the states to tax the production of Indian minerals the same as on private lands.[14]

The Senate rejected this amendment because it wanted the states to receive money from royalties rather than a production tax. Consequently, the bill went to a conference committee which provided that the government pay 37.5 percent of Indian royalties to the state. When the House considered this report, Representative Frederick Dallinger of Massachusetts blocked it on the ground that the conferees had "changed the text to which both Houses agreed."[15] He took this action at the request of Commissioner Burke and the Indian Rights Association, who wanted all royalties for the Indians' benefit.[16]

During the next session of Congress, Representative Carl Hayden of Arizona entered the controversy by introducing a measure known as the Indian Oil bill. It stated that the leasing of executive-order reservations would follow the Indian Oil Leasing Act of May 29, 1924. That legislation had established procedures for mineral development on treaty reservations, and it allowed the states to tax Indian gas and oil production the same as non-Indian property. Hayden's bill, however, substituted this production tax with a provision that the government give 37.5 percent of Indian royalties to the states where the reservations were located. But to protect the Indians the states had to spend these funds on public roads within the reservations or for the support of Indian education. The remaining 62.5 percent would go directly to the tribes.[17]

The Indian Oil bill validated approximately twenty oil prospecting and leasing permits issued by Secretary Fall. It made this concession because of complications surrounding the oil permits made under the terms of the General Leasing Act. On April 27, 1925, the United States District Court of Utah, in a case involving E. M. Harrison, had repudiated Attorney General Stone's ruling invalidating these permits by holding that the General Leasing Act applied to executive-order reservations. The government had supported the Indians and appealed this case to the Supreme Court where it was still pending.[18]

Commissioner Burke defended the Indian Oil bill in testimony before the House Committee on Indian Affairs. He favored the measure because it followed the terms of the Indian Leasing Act, placing the development of Indian oil lands under the jurisdiction of the Indian Bureau rather than the General Land Office. This implied that executive-order reservations were the same as treaty reservations. Burke wanted a quick legislative solution since he feared that the Supreme Court might refuse to uphold the Indians' right to receive royalties. The commissioner believed the bill a fair compromise because, even though it gave them 37.5 percent of Indian royalties, the states had to spend this money in some way that benefited the Indians.[19]

To gain these concessions Burke agreed to accept legislation validating the twenty permits issued by Fall. At stake was the royalty oil prospectors would pay. Under the provisions of the General Leasing Act a prospector had to pay a 5 percent royalty on one-fourth of his permit, instead of a flat 12.5 percent under the Indian Oil Leasing Act.[20] According to an editorial in the *New York World,* this assisted "the soldiers of fortune seeking wealth in the [Navajo] desert" such as "that veteran prospector, Secretary of the Treasury Andrew Mellon."[21]

When he arrived in Washington, D.C., early in January 1926, to lobby before the forthcoming legislative session in behalf of the Indians, Collier learned about the provisions of the Indian Oil bill. His sentiments paralleled those of the *New York World,* which had stated that it was "another pretty kettle of fish . . . about as pleasant as passage aboard a freight vessel lying alongside a cannery in the salmon land of the Yukon."[22]

Upset with the position taken by the Indian Bureau, Collier caustically attacked this bill in several Defense Association legislative bulletins, which he distributed to members of Congress. One bulletin, entitled "The Albert B. Fall Indian Title Cancellation Scheme Revived," claimed that by validating the permits made by Fall and by giving 37.5 percent of the Indians' royalties to the states, the bill implied that executive-order reservations had the same legal basis as ordinary public lands.[23] If the Indians possessed no vested interest in this property, Collier warned that they would have the status of a guest who might be told to leave or "of cattle allowed to graze in their owner's field."[24] He wrote similar protests in such newspapers as the *New York Herald Tribune* and the *New York World.*[25]

On March 5, 1926, Collier appeared before the Senate Subcommittee on Indian Affairs to explain his association's opposition to the Indian Oil bill. He agreed with Burke about the tremendous need to develop executive-order reservations but rejected any measure which tended to invalidate Indian title. Collier claimed that section 2 of the Indian Oil bill gave the Indians only a permissive right to 62.5 percent of the royalties, thus setting the precedent for the neglect of Indian vested rights. Furthermore, he doubted the wisdom of section 3, which allowed a prospector who obtained a permit under Fall's ruling to drill under the provisions of the General Leasing Act. This meant that executive-order reservations were only public lands, and the Indians in the future might be robbed of their valuable resources. In place of the Indian Oil bill, Collier called for legislation that would treat executive-order reservations the same as treaty reservations — legislation that would give all royalties to the Indians after the deduction of a state tax on production.[26]

Several members of Congress agreed with Collier's position. The most important was Representative James A. Frear.* A liberal Republican from Wisconsin, Frear had been removed from the House Ways and Means Committee in 1924 because he actively supported the Progressive ticket instead of Calvin Coolidge. Demoted to the Indian Affairs Committee, Frear quickly joined Collier's crusade against the Indian Bureau for political and ideological reasons.[27] Frequently he used Defense Association circulars to denounce the Indian Oil bill in the House.[28] Two Progressive members of the Senate Indian Affairs Committee, Burton K. Wheeler, a Democrat from Montana, and Robert La Follette, a Republican from Wisconsin, also supported Collier. Wheeler inserted in the *Congressional Record* a lengthy article by members of the Indian Defense Association criticizing Commissioner Burke, while La Follette publicly attacked the Indian Oil bill from the floor of the Senate.[29]

Not content with this Congressional protest, Collier worked closely with Stella Atwood to bring the matter directly before President Coolidge. On March 27, 1926, Mrs. Atwood sent a telegram to the White House warning that the Women's Federation considered the Indian Oil bill one of the most destructive measures ever to appear in Congress against the Indians, and she specifically objected to taxing the Indians 37.5 percent of their oil income for state use. Mrs. Atwood indicated that the precedent of treating executive-order reservations separately from treaty reservations might prejudice the Supreme Court against the Indians in the case involving E. M. Harrison. She asked Coolidge how the bureau had the audacity to endorse a measure that was similar to Albert B. Fall's previous ruling.[30]

When the president refused to reply, Collier and his associates used their successful technique of public meetings to bring pressure upon the administration. On June 3, 1926, sixty members of the Defense Association attended a dinner at New York's Town Hall to hear their president,

---

*Born in Hudson, Wisconsin, on October 24, 1861, James A. Frear practiced law in Hudson, where he became city attorney and district attorney of St. Croix County. Elected a member of the state assembly in 1903, he served in the state senate two years later. On March 4, 1913, he was elected as a Republican to the House of Representatives and continually served until he voluntarily retired on January 3, 1935. *Biographical Directory of the American Congress, 1774–1961* (Washington: Government Printing Office, 1961), p. 913.

Dr. Haven Emerson, attack the Indian Oil bill.[31] Collier also secured the services of Judson King's National Popular Government League, which had opposed the Bursum bill in 1922. King provided Collier and his association free office space, contact with publicity sources, advice on political strategy, and consultation on technical matters.[32] The league helped by sponsoring a forum at Washington's La Fayette Hotel where Collier charged the Indian Bureau with a gigantic conspiracy to deprive the Indians of their coal, oil, and gas lands — similar to that which led to the resignation of Albert B. Fall. Progressive congressmen such as Burton K. Wheeler, Lynn Frazier from North Dakota, and Representative Frear attended this meeting, and they voiced complaints against the government's handling of Indian affairs.[33]

This type of protest continued when Judson King wrote an article for *Labor* entitled "Scheme Before Congress to Loot Rich Indian Lands." King warned President Coolidge that former Secretary of the Interior Albert B. Fall had "cast an eagle eye" upon the executive-order reservations and "said, in effect to his friends, come on boys, and let's grab these tax exempt oil lands for twenty years at a 5% royalty." King wondered if the president would allow Fall's "stain to be put on his administration, which, by comparison, makes the Teapot Dome episode an insignificant thing."[34]

Although Coolidge preferred not to respond to this adverse publicity, members of Congress did by enacting a substitute oil bill introduced by Senator Ralph H. Cameron of Arizona. This measure provided that prospectors could explore for oil and gas on executive-order reservations under the terms of the Indian Oil Leasing Act of 1924. The Indians would receive 100 percent of their royalties subject to a state production tax. Section 2, initiated by Commissioner Burke, provided that only Congress could make changes in the boundaries of executive-order reservations. The Cameron bill validated those permits where the prospector had already made a substantial investment, such as spending money for a geological survey, building a road, or drilling an oil well.[35]

Congress passed the Cameron bill in 1926 but the president vetoed it on July 2. Coolidge claimed that the bill discriminated against four hundred applicants and in favor of twenty prospectors who had received permits before Attorney General Stone reversed Fall's ruling. He warned that the prospectors' legal rights were still pending before the Supreme Court, but the president expressed his approval concerning the rest of the bill and promised to sign a new measure if it treated all applicants fairly.[36]

During the winter of 1927 Congress amended the Cameron bill to meet the president's objections and he signed it on March 3. Known as the Indian Oil Act, this piece of legislation gave the Indians all of their royalties, subject to a state production tax, prohibited altering the boundaries of executive-order reservations except by an act of Congress, and placed all prospectors who received permits to drill on an equal basis.[37] According to Collier, it "ended a legislative declaration that the Indians were but tenants of the land surface, subject to eviction when the executive might so decree." He summed up the satisfaction of all Indian reformers when he stated that "this victory was the largest gain for the Indians in our generation."[38]

On another issue, the question of reimbursable debts, Collier lost in the spring of 1926, but not until a new principle had been thoroughly aired. In 1914 Congress had passed legislation authorizing the construction of Indian irrigation facilities with the provision that the Indians eventually repay the government out of tribal funds.[39] Over the years this type of financing grew to include other public projects resulting in a $31 million debt, and often the government required Indians to pay half the cost of projects that mainly aided whites.[40]

Disturbed by the bureau's practice of using tribal funds for such purposes, Collier chose the Lee's Ferry bridge as a test case. On February 25, 1925, Congress passed an appropriation bill which contained an item favored by the Interior Department. It authorized the expenditure of $100,000 from Navajo tribal funds "now or hereafter placed in the treasury" to construct a bridge near the head of Marble Canyon over the Colorado River. Located six miles below Lee's Ferry, Arizona, on the northwestern part of the reservation, this proposed bridge cost $200,000 of which Arizona was to pay 50 percent.[41]

A year earlier, in a letter to Homer Snyder, chairman of the House Committee on Indian Affairs, Secretary Work had recommended that the Navajos share the cost of building this bridge. Work indicated that the bridge would connect the western part of the Navajo reservation with the public domain on the other side of the Colorado River. The secretary claimed that the bridge would furnish an important outlet for the Indians, facilitate their communication with whites, and assist them in their progress toward a more advanced civilization. Work frankly admitted that the bridge would benefiit the "general traveling public," but he believed it necessary "for the proper development of that section" of the country.[42]

Because the act of 1925 only authorized the use of tribal funds to build Lee's Ferry bridge, Collier lobbied to block any appropriations during the next legislative session. In the House, Representative Frear proved his most dependable ally. The progressive Republican attacked the Lee's Ferry bridge and all other reimbursable debts in several inflamatory speeches before the House. On February 4, 1926, Frear told his colleagues that he refused to "let this outrageous looting of the Navajo tribe pass the House without a strong protest." He cited statements prepared by Collier's Defense Association that ridiculed every attempt to justify the bridge and stated that he knew of no proposal as indefensible as this reimbursable proposition. According to Frear, the bureau had never consulted with the Indians about the bridge, and its cost would wipe out their modest $116,000 tribal fund. Frear rejected the notion that the bridge would serve the Indians; instead, it was primarily an automobile travel route for the National Park Service and tourists visiting the Grand Canyon.[43]

Frear then asked the broader question of how the bureau could justify squandering Navajo tribal funds for a bridge when these Indians desperately needed assistance. He indicated that one-third of the tribe suffered from trachoma, an eye disease that caused blindness, while most of their reservation remained useless for grazing because the government had failed to dig wells. Turning to the area of education, Frear pointed out that over half of the school-age Navajo children lacked classroom facilities. Because of the above reasons, Frear told his colleagues to stop "this wicked misuse of funds" and support his bill, which deleted any reimbursable charge to the Indians.[44]

Collier received additional support in the Senate for his fight against Lee's Ferry bridge. Senator Ralph H. Cameron from Arizona indicated that few Indians lived within the extreme western part of the reservation due to its arid condition, and he doubted "whether ten Indians a year would cross this bridge at Lee's Ferry" because the government had prohibited them from shooting deer and antelope.[45] Senator Sam G. Bratton from New Mexico supported this testimony by inserting evidence in the *Congressional Record* demonstrating that the Navajos at their July 7, 1925, council meeting had questioned spending tribal funds for the bridge.[46]

Matthew K. Sniffen, secretary of the Indian Rights Association, joined this public outcry after visiting the area where the government planned to construct the bridge. He failed to find one Indian who lived within twenty-five miles of the reservation side of the Colorado River, while the nearest settlement appeared eighty miles across the river. He warned that no approach to the site existed, thus making it necessary to construct a road across the Navajo reservation near Tuba City, which would cost an additional $300,000. Sniffen called the bridge a "white man's proposition" and noted that "no stretch of the imagination" could justify the use of Navajo funds for such a purpose.[47]

Despite this criticism from all directions, officials at the Indian Bureau continued to defend their decision to construct the bridge. Assistant Commissioner Edgar B. Meritt stated that it would open up the western part of the reservation and encourage the development of Indian resources. Meritt suggested that the recent discovery of oil meant the Navajos could afford to pay their share of the construction costs, and he indicated that the government would defer its request for the money until the Indians had ample funds available for that purpose. Meritt noted that the Navajos should help pay for the bridge because the State of Arizona lost "many thousands of dollars each year due to the non-taxable status of Navajo land."[48]

In the end, Collier's efforts to defeat the construction of Lee's Ferry bridge proved unsuccessful. The Senate eliminated the reimbursable item from its appropriation bill, but the House passed the measure without a recorded vote. When this legislation went to a conference committee, members of the House successfully argued that the $100,000 debt remain, and President Coolidge signed the bill into law on February 26, 1926.[49] Although Collier lost this fight, he consoled himself with the hope that Congress had been alerted to the misuse of Indian funds. He believed that the protests inside and outside Congress meant that any future attempt to build public facilities at Indian expense would encounter crystallized opposition.[50]

Undaunted by this setback, Frear and Collier worked harder than ever to reform the Indian affairs system. On March 4, 1926, Frear delivered a scathing attack against the policies of Commissioner Burke and Assistant Commissioner Meritt from the floor of the House. Because he concluded that these officials had failed to protect Indian rights or property, Frear introduced a joint resolution authorizing the appointment of a ten-member committee from both chambers to investigate and report "any charges of neglect, dissipation of funds," or improper treatment stemming from the bureau's mismanagement of Indian affairs.[51]

Frear used material assembled by Collier to offer several arguments that supported his request for a joint Congressional investigation. First, Burke and Meritt had supported "highway robbery" in the Lee's Ferry bridge scheme by looting the Navajo Indians, while simultaneously pushing the Indian Oil bill that drew oil manipulators like "a cloud of buzzards obscuring the sun." Frear questioned the bureau's use of "ten-dollar-a-month" subordinate Indian judges who could give sentences of six months imprisonment or a $100 fine for breaking arbitrary rules drawn up by the secretary of the interior. This violation of constitutional rights had resulted in situations such as the case of Paul Moore, an Indian from Odanah, Wisconsin, who was thrown into a cell six by eight feet, with a ball and chain fastened to his ankle, for committing a misdemeanor. In addition, the bureau had neglected the health of its wards until diseases such as tuberculosis and trachoma menaced the white population of several states.[52]

Angry at this criticism of his administration, Commissioner Burke accused Frear of making statements without any personal knowledge of the Indians. Frear knew that this accusation contained some truth, so he accepted an invitation from Collier to investigate conditions on approximately twenty reservations in western states. During most of September and October 1926, the two men traveled 4,480 miles in Collier's Pierce-Arrow car.[53] They attended several tribal council meetings and talked with sympathetic white friends who provided them with a forum to attack the Indian Bureau. At Salt Lake City, Frear reaffirmed his demand for a congressional investigation because he had discovered that many Sioux faced famine, while approximately 25 percent of the Crow Indians suffered from trachoma. Collier joined this protest when he declared that the bureau was destroying the Indians as a race because it still had a "hangover" from the "original military policy which regarded the Indian as an outlaw and danger to society."[54]

Assistant Commissioner Meritt publicly responded to Frear and Collier's charges on December 1, 1926, in an address delivered before the Oakland Forum in California. He accused both men of making unwarranted criticisms and claimed that the Indians owned valuable real estate that provided them with a per capita wealth nearly twice as great as other Americans. Furthermore, Indian judges were prominent leaders who seldom gave over thirty-day sentences and any Indian could appeal his case, but to protect tribal funds the secretary of the interior had to approve all contracts with attorneys. Turning to the case of Paul Moore, Meritt indicated that this unruly Indian had led astray a young Indian girl while visiting the Lac du Flambeau reservation. Because of previous escapes, the jailer had to attach a ball and chain around his leg. Meritt refuted charges that the government neglected Indian health when he cited increased appropriations for such purposes and explained the bureau's reorganization of the Indian Medical Service along lines similar to the Public Health Service.[55]

The assistant commissioner told his audience that he saw no reason for a congressional investigation of the Indian Bureau. On June 12, 1926, Secretary Work, with the "cordial approval" of Commissioner Burke, had contacted the Institute for Government Research, a private organization at Washington, D.C., to make a comprehensive general survey of Indian affairs. The secretary had asked for such a survey "on account of harmful attacks and propaganda" that created the false impression that the government neglected Indian welfare.[56]

Meritt had loyally defended the bureau, but Secretary Work candidly set forth other reasons for his private investigation in an article entitled "The Poverty of the Indian Service."[57] Work stated that he had made many reforms such as calling together the Committee of 100 and reorganizing the Indian field service to improve the bureau's performance.[58] Nevertheless, he realized that it had failed to keep "pace with progress elsewhere along health, educational, industrial, and social lines."[59]

Work blamed the cumulative effect of many years of financial neglect by Congress for the Indians' plight.* Between 1923 and 1928 appropriations for the bureau remained inadequate and without increased financial assistance he had little power to prevent the frequent turnover of personnel in the Indian Medical Service. This shortage of funds resulted in the hiring of teachers in name only, who possessed neither education nor attainments to impart knowledge to classes of Indian students. It also meant that school plants were in a dilapidated condition and without proper repair. More importantly, the land allotment system had faltered because of niggardly appropriations. Work stressed that the Indians needed two years' agricultural experience and a minimum of $2,000 credit to make a living on irrigated farms in the West. Unfortunately, the government had placed them on raw land where they received rations or per capita payments.[60]

When they returned from their western trip in the autumn of 1926, Collier and Frear were unmoved by the announcement that Work had contacted the Institute for Government Research. Instead, they appeared before hearings of the Senate Subcommittee on Indian Affairs to support a resolution introduced by William King of Utah. This resolution authorized the Committee on Indian Affairs to make a general survey of Indian conditions and report its findings "together with recommendations for the correction of abuses that may be found to exist, and for such changes in the law that will promote the security, economic competence, and progress of the Indians."[61]

---

*In 1923 Indian Bureau appropriations were $10,316,221 and they had increased by only $2,338,463 in 1928. This lack of sufficient funds stemmed from two sources. In 1920, Congress created the Bureau of the Budget, which imposed strict economy in the federal government and favored lower taxes to promote industrial recovery after World War I. Louis C. Cramton, chairman of the House Subcommittee on Appropriations for the Interior Department, added congressional sanction to this policy. Indian Commissioner Charles H. Burke told his superintendents on June 28, 1923, that the Indian Service would have to cooperate in recovering from "the war's excesses." He warned that "more business in government" contained the "gospel of our financial practice." U.S., Department of the Interior, *Annual Report of the Commissioner of Indian Affairs* (Washington: Government Printing Office, 1923), p. 16; and Lawrence Kelly, *The Navajo Indians and Federal Indian Policy* (Tucson: University of Arizona Press, 1968), pp. 142–44.

Representative Frear testified before these hearings on February 23, 1927. He reiterated his previous charges against the bureau and told members of the subcommittee that he had already introduced a similar resolution in the House. He referred to his recent trip, which confirmed his previous suspicions about the terrible state of Indian boarding schools. He believed that if Harriet Beecher Stowe were present, she could write a story "far worse than anything that ever appeared in *Uncle Tom's Cabin,* about the children today on some of these reservations."[62]

Collier supported Frear when he appeared before the subcommittee. He called for a Senate investigation to fix responsibility for past scandals and to expose the mishandling of Indian property. Collier reminded the senators that Congress could not pass fundamental reform legislation until it conducted its own investigation and obtained "a new total view of the Indian problem."[63] He insisted that Congress reevaluate the Dawes land allotment law of 1887 because the bureau had misled Congress and the public; it had created the false belief that Indian wealth was increasing at a rapid rate by padding statistics with recent income from oil royalties. Actually, most tribes faced impoverishment because of the failure of land allotment. During the last four years alone, Indian land held in trust diminished 16 percent, while the total Indian real estate decreased 4 percent. Collier estimated that at this rate the Indians would be disinherited from their property within twenty-five years and suggested that Congress could remedy this situation by ending reimbursable debts, providing the Indians with rural credit, and equipping them with the modern instruments of business life.[64]

Collier told the senators that several emergency reasons made a congressional investigation necessary. Because of bureau neglect, the Indian death rate from tuberculosis was six times that of whites, while trachoma threatened the eyesight of 60,000 people. Collier believed that all of this had been deliberately hidden by the bureau when it withheld a Red Cross report critical of the Indian Medical Service. Indian education needed urgent attention because the government had filled boarding schools to 38 percent beyond their physical capacity. This unhygienic herding of children into "overpacked concentration institutions" cost three and one-half times more per capita than public day schools.[65]

Commissioner Burke followed Collier and suggested that he had been placed in a false light for the last three or four years. Burke indicated that Collier's call for an investigation was superfluous because one had already been underway for sometime under the direction of the Institute for Government Research.[66] But this testimony failed to convince members of the Senate, who authorized the Committee on Indian Affairs to start a survey of Indian conditions. It appointed a special subcommittee led by Democratic and Republican malcontents such as Robert La Follette, Jr., from Wisconsin; W. B. Pine, from Oklahoma; and Burton K. Wheeler, from Montana; who continued to harass the Coolidge administration.[67]

One of the subcommittee's first agenda items concerned Commissioner Burke's handling of the Jackson Barnett case. An illiterate Creek fullblood, Barnett had become one of the wealthiest Indians in Oklahoma after oil was discovered on his allotment in 1912. Cato Sells, Indian commissioner during this period, planned to give part of Barnett's several million dollar estate to charities benefiting other Indians, but he dropped this idea after learning that Barnett had become involved with Anna Laura Lowe, a former prostitute who had the reputation for involvement in various extortion schemes. On February 20, 1920, Miss Lowe had persuaded Barnett to get into her car, plied him with whiskey, and married him in Coffeyville, Kansas.[68]

Shortly after becoming commissioner, Burke revived previous plans to distribute part of Barnett's estate to charity, but he had to recognize the interest of Anna Laura in the property. On December 15, 1922, with the approval of Secretary Fall, Burke divided $1.1 million in liberty bonds held by the Interior Department for Barnett in the following manner: He created a trust of $550,000 for the Baptist Home Mission Society, which had to pay Barnett a yearly $20,000 income for the rest of his life, while a similar fund gave $200,000 to Anna Laura and she had to pay her husband $7,500 a year. She also received $350,000 cash and her attorney collected a $137,500 fee.[69]

This agreement, however, was successfully challenged in 1927 by Elmer Bailey, Barnett's newly appointed guardian. In conjunction with the Justice Department, he started a suit in the United States District Court of New York to nullify the donation given to the Baptists. Judge John C. Knox repudiated Burke and Fall when he declared Barnett incompetent and ordered the money returned to the supervision of the Interior Department.[70]

The Senate investigating subcommittee focused on the Jackson Barnett case during 1928 and 1929. Collier appeared frequently at these hearings and worked closely with Lynn Frazier, the subcommittee's chairman. Collier used the Barnett scandal to question the Indian Bureau's probate system, and he received support from Frear, who called the distribution of Barnett's funds "the most miserable thing I have ever seen in public life."[71] This testimony angered Burke, who told the senators about his role in this affair. He explained that he wanted to provide Barnett with an adequate income to prevent the Indian from living in squalor. The money that went to the Baptist Home Mission Society had enabled Bacone College to start an expansion of its facilities, and this helped all Indians who lived in Oklahoma. He had quickly settled Barnett's estate to prevent spurious heirs from starting litigation which would only enrich attorneys. He pointed out that under state law Barnett's wife was entitled to fifty percent of the Indian's estate.[72]

Not impressed with this testimony, Senators W. B. Pine and Burton K. Wheeler put Burke through an extensive cross-examination. This caused the commissioner to lose his temper, and he accused Pine and Collier of engaging in a "conspiracy" to destroy him for political reasons.[73] Burke claimed that Charles B. Selby, a special assistant to the attorney general, who had declared at the New York trial that his actions warranted indictment for malfeasance, was a friend of Pine. When Senator Wheeler demanded that Burke substantiate these charges, the commissioner indicated that it was merely "his opinion" that Collier and Pine had ulterior motives.[74]

Almost simultaneously with his appearance before the Senate subcommittee, Collier became involved in a controversy concerning 2,800 Flathead Indians. Early in February 1927, Commissioner Burke and other bureau officials, without inviting the Indians, held a meeting with the Montana Power Company and some white irrigation farmers to discuss the development of the Flathead Indian water power site, located six miles south of Polson, Montana, on the Flathead River. The bureau wanted private enterprise to develop this site because previous government efforts had proven unsuccessful, leaving both white and Indian members of the Flathead Irrigation District saddled with large debts. The government had spent nearly six million dollars and built hundreds of miles of canals and laterals but never used them because in 1909 the newly finished Newell Tunnel project failed to pump irrigation water.[75]

After meeting with bureau officials, the Montana Power Company signed a "gentleman's agreement" on February 17, 1927, which gave it the exclusive right to develop this 175,000 horsepower site, paying an annual rental of one dollar per developed horsepower. The company agreed to deliver at cost to the Flathead Irrigation District 10,000 horsepower, for pumping water, at the price of one mill per kilowatt-hour, and another 5,000 horsepower, for miscellaneous purposes, at the rate of two and one-half mills per kilowatt hour. Other provisions included paying the government $101,000 for the discredited Newell Tunnel. Finally, the Federal Power Commission received twenty-five cents out of every dollar paid in rental for its surveys and field expenses, while the remaining amount was divided up in the proportion of one-third to the tribe and two-thirds to the white settlers.[76]

Secretary Work attempted to secure legislative endorsement for this compact by supporting an amendment to the Second Urgency Deficiency bill which contained the provisions of the "gentleman's agreement."[77]

Representative Louis C. Cramton from Michigan, chairman of the House Appropriations Subcommittee for the Interior Department, sponsored this amendment that denied Indian ownership of the Flathead power site because it promised to deliver inexpensive power to indebted white settlers who "had been hanging on by their finger tips waiting for the time when they can share in the national prosperity."[78]

When Collier learned about this bill he believed it "worthy of the great days of Albert B. Fall."[79] Collier favored public ownership of the Flathead power site but doubted its feasibility given the climate of opinion in Washington. Instead, he worked for the immediate issue of securing for the Flatheads their vested right to the water power property.[80] On February 28, 1927, Collier issued a Defense Association bulletin entitled "The Pending Flathead Indian Outrage." Sent to members of Congress, it warned that the bill proved "identical in its confiscatory action with that contained in the bureau's oil bill which Congress rejected last year."[81]

In this and other publications Collier gave several reasons why the House and Senate should defeat the measure. He stressed that it violated the Treaty of 1855, which secured Indian property rights to all land around Flathead Lake and the adjoining timberlands, and section 17 of the Federal Water Power Act of 1920, which guaranteed that the Indians would receive all proceeds from power development on their reservations. Collier argued that the Montana Power Company should offer a royalty at least three times larger than the one dollar per horsepower rental. Finally he questioned giving the settlers power at cost and reimbursing the government $101,000 for Newell Tunnel because these features of the bill siphoned off revenues belonging to the Indians.[82]

Collier's arguments had little impact on most members of the House because the Second Urgency Deficiency bill passed without a debate. But in the Senate it faced the opposition of Lynn Frazier, Robert La Follette, Jr., and Burton K. Wheeler. They agreed with Collier that the bill was detrimental to Indian interests and, therefore, they helped block its passage during March 1927.[83]

In addition to his other bulletins, Collier sent two letters to President Coolidge requesting that the chief executive intervene in the Flathead controversy. In February 1927 he asked for action by the Department of Justice on behalf of the Indians; in July he warned that this effort to "rob" the Flatheads of their valuable property threatened "a scandal . . . of national interest and consequence."[84] In order to prevent this, Collier asked the president to stop all proceedings involving the water power facility until Congress publicly debated the proposal and the government officially consulted with the Flathead tribal council.[85]

President Coolidge neither answered Collier's letters nor intervened in the Flathead problem, but he did respond publicly to the growing criticism about his administration's treatment of the Indians. While staying at his summer White House near Rapid City, South Dakota, the president prepared an address that he planned to deliver to the Sioux Indians, who had decided to give him the honorary name of either "Still Waters" or "Sullen Warrior," but the bureau favored "Leading Eagle." On August 18, 1927, "Leading Eagle" addressed over 10,000 Sioux at Pine Ridge.[86] In this speech the president reviewed his efforts to assist the Indians but he neglected to mention the Flathead tribe. Coolidge told the Sioux that he took special pride in the passage of the 1924 Indian Citizenship Act which merged "the Indians into the general citizenry and body politic of the nation." The president praised the Dawes General Allotment Act of 1887, which had provided the Indians with individual ownership of land, and the progress made by the bureau in the area of Indian education. He believed these programs more practical than "appeals to sentimentality, by loose talk, by ill considered legislation, or by hysterical campaigns."[87]

The president's reassuring rhetoric failed to persuade Congress which repudiated the "gentleman's agreement" made between the Indian Bureau and the Montana Power Company. On February 21, 1928, it passed an appropriation bill confirming Indian ownership of all rentals from the Flathead power project, but Congress left the Federal Power Commission free to make the Flathead lease unhampered by any previous commitment of the Interior Department. Due to House pressure, the Senate agreed not to limit the terms of any future agreement, including the possibility of selling power at cost to the white settlers.[88] This refusal to solve the specific terms of the lease set the stage for future conflict with the Federal Power Commission over the question of competitive bidding.

The last major issue concerning Indian affairs during the Coolidge years involved the Pueblo Indians and the Rio Grande Conservancy District. Formed under the laws of the State of New Mexico, this public corporation proposed to spend $11,829,000 to provide flood control, drainage, and irrigation for 132,724 acres of land that had become swampy because of a rise in the level of the Rio Grande River. Situated adjacent to the river, this land extended 150 miles and varied from 1 to 5 miles in width. The conservancy project proved impossible to implement, however, without including interspersed Indian lands, which consisted of 23,607 acres or 17 percent of the area.[89]

Consequently, congressmen from New Mexico introduced bills in both House and Senate to solve this dilemma. Amended in joint meetings by all concerned parties, this legislation became known as the Middle Rio Grande Conservancy bill.[90] It authorized the secretary of the interior to make an agreement with the conservancy district providing for the reclamation of land affecting 3,500 Indians living in the Pueblos of Cochiti,

Santo Domingo, San Felipe, Santa Ana, Sandia, and Isleta. The government insisted that the cost of this work should not exceed $1,593,011, thus resulting in a debt of $67.50 per acre.[91]

Several other provisions of the bill specifically guaranteed Indian rights. The government provided a gratuitous appropriation of $593,011 to improve 8,346 acres of land already irrigated by traditional Pueblo methods, while it exempted this land from any future cost of irrigation work. The Indians, however, had to repay the government approximately one million dollars in forty annual payments, for the cost of developing the remaining 15,000 acres. Finally, all Pueblo water rights to the 8,346 irrigated acres remained "prior and paramount to any rights of the district," but the Indians could not relinquish remaining land, equal in stature to white lands, by non-use or abandonment as long as they held title to this property.[92]

When Collier appeared before hearings of the Senate Indian Affairs Committee on January 20, 1928, he offered little opposition to the amended conservancy bill. Authorized by the Pueblos to speak for them, he pointed out that they opposed any reimbursable debt but would approve of the measure due to the various safeguards protecting Indian interests.[93] Despite his previous harsh criticism of the bureau, Collier agreed with the assessment of Assistant Commissioner Meritt, who believed that for the last twenty years Congress had never presented a more generous bill concerning the Indians.[94] Because of this unanimous consent, the Senate Indian Affairs Committee reported the bill favorably.

The conservancy bill easily passed the Senate, but Representative Louis C. Cramton opposed it on February 6, 1928, from the floor of the House. Although the House Indian Affairs Committee had approved of the bill, Cramton offered amendments that were accepted without debate. The first one eliminated the $593,011 gratuitous appropriation to improve the 8,346 irrigated acres of Pueblo land. The Indians had to pay for this money out of revenues coming from improvements on their remaining 15,000 acres, which faced an increased indebtedness of $109.50 an acre, and Cramton struck out the provision that the Pueblos pay this debt in less than forty annual payments.[95]

Cramton favored these changes for several reasons. Concerned with keeping the budget in balance, he opposed the Indian Bureau's "gift of half a million dollars from the treasury." He saw little "gain for the Indian in teaching him to be a mendicant or to expect gifts from the government." According to the representative, "the day of rations proved the insanity of that policy, and we have abandoned it." He stressed that his amendments followed the positive policy of helping the Indian assist himself.[96]

The conservancy bill passed with Cramton's amendments, but Senator Lynn Frazier, at Collier's request, recalled it from the House.[97] This gave Collier time to send several Defense Association bulletins to members of Congress. These circulars stated that they should defeat the amended bill because it charged the Pueblos an additional debt of over $500,000 on the fiction that the conservancy district would substantially benefit their 8,346 irrigated acres. In reality, the Indians had already obtained an intensive crop yield from this region, which sustained one human being for each two and one-half acres. The bill meant that the government would indebt the remaining 15,000 acres $109.50 per acre as compared to the debt of $77.00 on contiguous white land. This large reimbursable debt also prevented the Indians from farming any newly reclaimed land. Finally, Collier feared that Cramton's elimination of protection against an "extortionate rate of collection" might create in the future a "new era of confiscation and dispossession" of Pueblo land.[98]

Representative Cramton, upset with this interference in his assistance to white irrigationists, violently attacked Collier from the floor of the House. He called the Indian Defense Association a destructive organization whose members allowed Collier, a sensationalist and opponent of the government, to exploit their names in a mistaken cause. He then focused attention on Collier's recent pamphlet entitled *The Sacco and Vanzetti Horror* and warned that even it was "less destructive than this constant parading of propaganda in order to bring the government into disfavor and disrepute concerning its handling of Indian affairs."[99]

In the end Cramton won only a partial victory because a bitter debate occurred in the Senate against his amendments. After three hours of discussion on March 1, 1928, the Senate finally agreed to accept the conservancy bill with an amendment proposed by Charles Curtis of Kansas. It allowed the Pueblo Indians to farm their 8,346 irrigated acres free of debt while giving them the right to farm 4,000 additional acres without any reimbursements. The remaining 11,000 acres, however, faced a reclamation debt of $149.66 per acre.[100]

President Coolidge signed this revised conservancy bill on March 13, 1928, despite Collier's letter requesting a veto.[101] Dismayed over this action, Collier left for Albuquerque, New Mexico, to make a last ditch fight against the conservancy measure. He threatened to halt work in the district by appealing the act to the Supreme Court because it violated the Fifth Amendment, which prohibited the government from taking private property for public use without just compensation. Collier wanted to force the Interior Department to interpret the regulations of the act favorably with regard to the Indians. Although Louis Marshall, a prominent attorney from New York, offered free legal advice for the Pueblo Indians, he had made little progress when Coolidge left the White House a year later.[102]

Back in Washington during June 1928, Collier received a copy of *The Problem of Indian Administration,* which contained the findings of the private investigation of Indian affairs made by the Institute for Government Research. Named after its director, Lewis Meriam, this report offered a lengthy analysis of such topics as Indian health, education, administration, economic conditions, and law. Although critical of the performance of the Indian Bureau, it placed most responsibility on Congress for refusing to appropriate adequate funds.[103]

The Meriam Report's harshest criticisms of the bureau came in the areas of health and education. It pointed out that the Indians suffered from an inadequate diet, lacking in vegetables, fruit, and milk. This made infant mortality, tuberculosis, and trachoma commonplace on many reservations. In order to solve this problem, the Meriam Report recommended that Congress raise boarding school appropriations from a per capita expenditure of eleven cents to thirty-five cents a day. It chided the bureau for operating overcrowded boarding schools that were "grossly inadequate," and it called for the increased use of day schools for all children through the sixth grade.[104]

The Meriam Report also criticized the land allotment policy, which it claimed had "resulted in much loss of land and an enormous increase in the details of administration without a compensating advance in the economic ability of the Indians."[105] To correct this mistake it recommended that the bureau exercise extreme conservatism when issuing fee patents, curtail the leasing of Indian land to whites, and regulate the use of inherited lands, which were often sold to non-Indians.[106] The bureau could end this dilemma, by establishing a revolving fund to purchase inherited land, consolidate it, and then sell it back to the Indians subject to restrictions. Where a tribe owned vast natural resources not susceptible to allotment, the government should help set up a corporation to manage the property on a tribal basis.[107]

Collier believed that the Meriam Report had "blasted apart" the walls of the dungeon called the Indian affairs system and provided the single most important indictment of the bureau since Helen Hunt Jackson's *A Century of Dishonor.* Nevertheless, Collier attacked this private investigation for its failure to place responsibility for bad conditions on officials such as Burke and Cramton.* He pointed out that the "placating

---

*No longer able to run the bureau effectively and in poor health, Charles H. Burke resigned from office early in 1929. Lawrence Kelly, *The Navajo Indians and Federal Indian Policy* (Tucson: University of Arizona Press, 1968), pp. 147–48.

euphemism" of its summaries revealed no information about such scandals as the use of Navajo tribal funds for Lee's Ferry bridge or the controversy over the Flathead power site. But these were minor shortcomings, and Collier indicated that the Meriam Report had set the stage for a fundamental change in Indian policy.[108]

The years between 1923 and 1928 were certainly a seedtime for Indian reform. Representative Frear wrote Collier that this effort on behalf of the Indian was one of the most significant humanitarian achievements during his congressional career.[109] Collier thought that his Indian Defense Association had brought about "a provisional revolution" in the Indian situation during the twenties. He gave credit to progressive-minded congressmen and to voluntary groups such as the Indian Rights Association, the General Federation of Women's Clubs, and the National Popular Government League. But Collier insisted with pride "that the main initiative and burden of detailed work" had rested on his American Indian Defense Association.[110]

More importantly, this "provisional revolution" would influence the next president of the United States. One of Herbert Hoover's accomplishments consisted of extending the benefits of his New Era to the American Indian. Unfortunately, Hoover, like his predecessor, never shook off the corrupt legacy of Albert B. Fall. The president's appointees in the Interior Department soon became involved in political disputes, such as the Rattlesnake Dome oil controversy, which stymied his altruistic Indian program.

5. Herbert Hoover's New Era: A False Dawn

During the 1928 presidental campaign Herbert Hoover demonstrated his interest in the cause of the American Indian by responding favorably to a letter from Dr. Haven Emerson, president of the American Indian Defense Association, which warned about the starvation of Indian children, widespread disease on the reservations, and boarding school atrocities.[1] Hoover answered that he was not in a position to confirm or deny such assertions, but if they did exist, he would demand quick remedy of these evils.[2] But this positive answer failed to prevent Collier's Defense Association from supporting the candidacy of Alfred Smith in a pamphlet entitled "For President Vote for Governor Alfred E. Smith."[3] The association had openly backed the Democratic nominee because he promised to support a comprehensive Indian reform program drawn up by Collier.

Despite his disappointment in the outcome of the election, Collier hoped that President Hoover would inaugurate a New Era for the American Indian. His expectations rose when Hoover publicly identified with the Indian cause by nominating Ray Lyman Wilbur, the president of Stanford University, as secretary of the interior. Wilbur had previously supported the missionary-oriented Indian Rights Association, centered in Philadelphia, and he maintained a membership in the California branch of the more militant Defense Association.[4] Hoover further demonstrated his commitment to a new policy when he accepted the resignation of Commissioner Burke and transferred Assistant Commissioner Meritt to the budget department.[5]

In his search for new Indian Bureau personnel, Hoover accepted the recommendations drawn up by the Indian Rights Association and the Eastern and New Mexico Associations on Indian Affairs. These groups in a memo entitled "The Reorganization of Indian Administration and the Indian Commissionership" called for a commissioner who would carry out the reform proposals of the Meriam Report. They submitted the names of five candidates known for their "unimpeachable character" and administrative experience in "financial as well as human affairs."[6]

From this list Hoover picked Charles J. Rhoads as Indian commissioner and J. Henry Scattergood as assistant commissioner. Rhoads, a wealthy Philadelphia banker, had served as president of the Indian Rights Association, while Scattergood, a successful businessman, was involved in the association's philanthropic activities. Both men were Quakers and known for their humanitarian efforts in European relief and reconstruction programs after World War I.[7] Collier spoke for his Defense Association when he welcomed the new officials and expressed confidence that there existed every "condition favorable to a large reorganization of Indian affairs."[8]

To insure this confidence Collier helped Vera Connolly write a series of three articles for *Good Housekeeping*. Published during the winter and spring of 1929, they summarized the Indian scandals during the Harding and Coolidge years and traced the efforts of the General Federation of Women's Clubs and the Indian Defense Association to inaugurate Indian reform.[9] The final article urged women to write their senators, congressmen, and President Hoover about the need for a reorientation of Indian affairs. It promised that "the righteous wrath of American womanhood . . . aroused to deep indignation and banded together in a crusade to obtain justice for the oppressed" could "rescue the American Indian."[10]

Between March 1929 and February 1930 a honeymoon period existed between Department of the Interior officials and Indian welfare groups. The Hoover appointees worked earnestly to carry out the Meriam Report's "Recommendations for Immediate Action," which included increased appropriations to improve the diet of children in boarding schools, the creation of new positions in the fields of health and education, the construction of more Indian day schools, and the repair of Indian Service buildings.[11]

Daily contacts between government officials and reformers resulted in many innovative ideas about how to assist the American Indian. Collier's Indian Defense Association proposed several legislative programs which received the endorsement of the Hoover administration. They included the California Indian Plan or Swing-Johnson bill, calling for transferring to the states some of the responsibility for the education,

Secretary of the Interior
Ray Lyman Wilbur,
1929–33.

National Archives

health, and general welfare of their Indians. Commissioner Rhoads agreed
to push an Indian arts and crafts bill that had been formulated by James
Young, a member of the Defense Association's directorate. It would have
opened markets for Indian crafts and used a government trademark to
insure that the Indians rather than white imitators produced the art object.
Bureau officials also accepted Collier's suggestion that Congress pass legislation to protect Indian civil liberties and to start the phasing out of
boarding schools.[12]

In consultation with Matthew K. Sniffen, secretary of the Indian
Rights Association, and Lewis Meriam, a member of the Institute for
Government Research, Collier continued to advocate reform by helping
Commissioner Rhoads draft four letters to Lynn Frazier, chairman of the
Senate Indian Investigating Subcommittee.[13] Rhoads proposed that Con-
gress change "in its entirety" the 1887 Dawes land allotment law, which
permitted the division of tribal property and its sale to non-Indians. In
place of the Dawes Act, he suggested that Congress allow the tribal

Charles Rhoads and J. Henry Scattergood — Indian commissioners who pushed for reform during the Hoover years.

incorporation of Indian estates, provide loans for Indian farmers, and give tribal councils power and responsibility for the operation of their real estate. Rhoads further asked for an end to the financing of public works from reservation income, the transfer of reservation irrigation projects to the General Reclamation Service, and the creation of a court of claims to reimburse Indian losses.*

A short time later, Secretary Wilbur, who had endorsed these letters, formulated specific administration programs for the consideration of Congress. In May 1930, he sent a proposal for an Indian court of claims to the chairman of the House Committee on the Judiciary. A bill emerged from committee but was killed on the floor due to opposition from the Department of Justice and the Budget Bureau for being in conflict with the president's economy program. Similarly, the secretary's plan to trans-

---

*The Wheeler-Howard Act of 1934 stemmed, in part, from these proposals. *Congressional Record,* 71st Cong., 2nd Sess., December 21, 1929, 72, Part 1: 1051–53.

fer reservation irrigation to the General Reclamation Service died when the House Appropriations Committee, under the leadership of the economy-minded Republican Louis C. Cramton from Michigan, inserted a provision forbidding it in the Interior Department appropriation. Congress refused Wilbur's request to cancel the large reservation indebtedness for public works, but it did relieve Indians on the Gila River reservation of $1.37 million debt incurred for irrigation work in Arizona.[14]

Although the depression and its stress on the economy frustrated many reforms, the Hoover administration managed to raise appropriations for the Indian Service from fifteen million dollars in 1928 to twenty-eight million dollars in 1931. Especially significant was an increase of $800,000 that would immediately improve the diet and clothing of children in boarding schools.[15] Unfortunately, the bureau spent the rest of this money to enlarge its employee force by nearly 300 percent. After hiring over 2,000 new people and increasing their salaries 25 percent, the bureau had a supervisor for every 36 Indians. Thus the money desperately needed for direct relief during the depression went instead into an often unresponsive bureaucracy.[16]

The Department of the Interior took other steps besides legislative ones to humanize the Indian Service. During March 1931 Wilbur responded to recommendations made in the Meriam Report by reorganizing the bureau into five divisions: health, education, agricultural extension, forestry, and irrigation. Each division had a technical or professional director to insure a more direct relationship between the reservation superintendents and Washington.[17]

Quite naturally, Wilbur, as former president of Stanford University, made educational reform the essence of the New Era for the American Indian.[18] He agreed with the Institute for Government Research that Indian reform had failed in the past because of the lack of a sound educational program and appointed Dr. W. Carson Ryan, a professor of education at Swarthmore College, as director of Indian Education.[19]

Ryan introduced progressive education, replacing the obsolete "Uniform Course of Study" with one which stressed practical education and vocational work. He formed a guidance and placement division which helped promising young Indian students find jobs and provided exceptionally intelligent Indian children with opportunities for a college education. Ryan converted many of the boarding schools into day schools, and he added a high school program to others. He abolished the positions of girl's matron and disciplinarian for boys and reduced "vocational work" such as the scrubbing of school floors.[20]

Although the Hoover appointees achieved many humanitarian improvements, the unity of the Defense Association and the Indian Bureau had started to disintegrate as early as February 1930. Part of the problem stemmed from the failure of the Department of the Interior to actively support legislation needed to end the land allotment law and its inability to persuade Representative Louis C. Cramton to jump on the reform bandwagon. More fundamental was the ideological difference over the future of the American Indian between administration men such as Wilbur and critics like Collier.

Secretary Wilbur believed that the government should direct all of its energy toward assimilating the Indian into the mainstream of American life. He hoped that in twenty-five years the Indian Bureau would cease to exist. "The redman's civilization must be replaced by the white man's," he wrote, and "the Indian must give up his role as a member of the race that holds aloof, while all other races enter into our melting pot and emerge as units of a great new purpose."[21] Using the homely idiom of the family physician, he compared the Indian to a child that continued to nurse too long. He suggested that just like the dependent child, "the thing to do" was to hand the Indian "a pickle and let it howl."[22]

Because the Indians had failed at farming after the passage of the Dawes General Allotment Act, Wilbur stressed that their future lay in finding a place in the industrial life of the nation. He wanted educated Indians kept as far away from their reservations as possible, while those Indians who remained on the reservation should increase their contact with white neighbors. Wilbur believed that continued allotment of tribal lands would break down the Indians' isolation and give them an opportunity to associate with white society.[23]

In opposition, Collier favored a policy of cultural pluralism that would not turn the Indian into a white man, but let him contribute elements of his culture to white civilization. He believed that the Indian heritage offered examples of viable communal practices, potent educational disciplines, and the composite art of blending speech, song, and dance.[24] He dreamed of preserving the institutional life especially of the Southwestern Indians because it provided a social alternative for the "frustrated but struggling Aryan individualized consciousness."[25]

Collier wanted to develop and conserve Indian life through government-assisted self-activity on the part of the Indians. He had traveled to Mexico during 1930 and 1931 where he met that country's "Indianist" leaders, and learned about the *ejido* agrarian reform program which restored land under communal title to Indian villages.[26] According to Collier, the Mexican experience proved that the Indian as a member of a "commune" or corporation would be satisfied and productive. He hoped that a cooperative society could evolve that was neither acquisitive nor clearly communist but one that would combine individual initiative with an even distribution of wealth. If the American Indian Service adopted such a program, he thought it would "open a new heaven and a new earth to the Indians within the term of one presidency."[27]

The first break between Collier and the bureau resulted less from a difference in philosophy than from the expediency of providing food allowances for 22,000 Indian boarding school children. On December 4, 1929, President Hoover tried to implement recommendations made by the Meriam Report when he sent Congress a special message supporting a $1.1 million emergency appropriation for food, clothing, and other necessities needed by Indian children. It would have increased the food allowance from 20 to 37.8 cents a day and the annual clothing allowance from $22 to $42 for the balance of the school year, with a provision for a later appropriation to maintain the same standards through 1931.[28]

This message pleased Collier but Louis C. Cramton, chairman of the House Appropriations Subcommittee, shocked him by responding to the president's food and clothing request with a warning that he would "not allow himself to be stampeded by talk of starving children."[29] As subcommittee chairman since 1921, Cramton had controlled the purse strings of the Indian Bureau and allowed appropriations for food and clothing to remain at substandard levels. Proud of that record in an era of Coolidge-Mellon balanced budgets, he refused to double appropriations without a struggle. The beginnings of the depression made him even more adamant.

During November 1929, Rhoads and Scattergood appeared before Cramton's subcommittee and detailed the dire needs of Indian children. This had little effect on Cramton who questioned the findings of the Meriam Report and pointed out that it was too late in the 1930 fiscal year for the government to administer additional appropriations effectively. Because of this hostility, Commissioners Rhoads and Scattergood consented to reduce the president's food request on January 30, 1930, by about 75 percent and the clothing allowance by 80 percent. They agreed with Cramton that the government should divert the remaining money into machinery, furniture, livestock, additional bureau salaries, and a day-school lunch program.[30]

In private discussions Collier attempted unsuccessfully to persuade the two commissioners not to surrender to Cramton's request. As Collier related the conversation, Scattergood lost his temper, told him that outside people should leave discussions to the men who had to live with the situation, and asked him to be content with "the Quaker way of doing business."[31] They considered any adverse action by Collier an "unfriendly act and a parting of the ways."[32]

Collier believed their attitude unrealistic and impractical. In a

Defense Association bulletin issued from his Washington office, he lamented the "melancholy spectacle" of Rhoads and Scattergood surrendering to Congressman Cramton and pointed out that "to those who hailed their appointment as the dawn of a new day for the Indians this was the culminating disappointment."[33] In a public statement given to the press Collier castigated Cramton for administering a "great rebuff" to President Hoover and asked whether the Senate would cooperate in the outrage of allowing hungry children to shiver "in humiliating rags."[34]

The Senate, backed by Collier's publicity, restored most of Hoover's original request for food and clothing. But at a conference committee, Cramton lowered these figures, resulting in a twenty-eight cent per day food allowance, while the additional money for clothing restored by the Senate was permanently diverted into equipment, livestock, and salaries for bureau personnel. The Indians' condition improved, however, in 1931, when an increased Department of the Interior appropriation bill enabled the bureau to raise its food and clothing allowance to meet the recommendations of the Meriam Report.[35]

The renewal by the Indian Bureau of its corporal punishment regulation on March 20, 1930, in a circular called "Student Control," accelerated the split between Collier and Commissioner Rhoads.[36] This was a sensitive matter because previous testimony before the Senate Indian Investigating Subcommittee revealed the floggings of Indian boys and girls during the Coolidge years. Employees of the Indian Bureau had whipped Indians with leather straps, knocked them down for sarcasm, and struck children with their fists and hard objects until blood ran from their faces to their knees.[37]

The Senate investigation disclosed that girls eleven and twelve years old, who escaped from Rice Boarding School, at the San Carlos Apache reservation in Arizona, had been forced to walk with heavy cordwood packs on their shoulders while being beaten with a club. At Rice, when runaway children entered their dormitories for the night, they were chained to beds in order to prevent them from leaving again. Using similar tactics, bureau officials marched runaway children to meals with chains fastened to their necks.[38] This testimony had motivated Commissioner Burke, on January 10, 1929, to forbid corporal punishment at boarding schools and to abolish school jails.[39]

But one year later Commissioner Rhoads modified these orders in his circular entitled "Student Control," because the end of corporal punishment had caused discipline to disintegrate at several boarding schools. Instead of the jails formerly maintained at some schools, Rhoads ordered his subordinates to provide a "quiet room," inaccessible to other students

Rhetoric

or employees, to restore discipline. If this method failed to bring satisfactory results, he authorized the superintendents "to adopt emergency measures" to solve discipline problems.[40]

Rhoads asked school employees to submit detailed reports concerning their actions to the bureau. But Collier feared the return of jails and corporal punishment, so he issued Defense Association bulletins which attacked Rhoads and Scattergood for neglecting to end cases of extreme abuse by superintendents and school principals.[41] At hearings before the Senate Indian Investigating Subcommittee, Collier attempted to prove these charges when he cited the case of the Phoenix Boarding School, where authorities had flogged and beaten children.[42]

Despite these charges Commissioner Rhoads refused to withdraw his circular. In a confidential letter to Haven Emerson he explained that Collier's onslaught concerning the whipping of Indian children was offensive and unbecoming to such a group as the American Indian Defense Association.[43] With regard to the Phoenix situation he warned that he would not dismiss personnel without proof of brutality.[44]

Another point of contention between Collier and the Department of the Interior grew out of the controversy over the development of the valuable Flathead Indian power site in Montana. In 1928, Congress had repudiated the "gentlemen's agreement" made between Indian Bureau officials and the Montana Power Company, which left the Federal Power Commission free to lease the Flathead site (see Chapter 4). A short time later the Montana Power Company applied for a license to develop one of the five power sites, where it proposed to generate 68,000 horsepower and pay the Indians $68,000 a year rental. A second bidder, Walter Wheeler, from Minneapolis, promised an initial development of 214,000 horsepower. He offered the Indians $240,000 in annual royalties and indicated that he would eventually develop all of their power sites.[45]

Collier disliked the bid of the Montana Power Company because this corporation was related to the Anaconda Copper Company and the American Power and Light Holding Company. He wanted government ownership of the power site, but that being impossible he favored Walter Wheeler who offered the Indians more money.[46] In several Defense Association circulars and before Senate hearings, Collier attacked the Indian Bureau for neglecting Indian interests by secretly negotiating with the Montana Power Company.[47]

Secretary Wilbur and his colleagues opposed Collier's position because they feared that Wheeler's proposal was based on the shaky premise that he could bring industry to Montana to develop a market in the chemical, fertilizer, and metallurgical fields. The Indians might lose valuable royalties if Wheeler were unable to find buyers for his power in the midst of desolate Montana and during a depression. The Montana Power Company, on the other hand, could give the Indians a guaranteed rental not possible "in a speculative enterprise."[48]

The Federal Power Commission agreed with the Interior Department and granted the Montana Power Company a license on May 23, 1930. But Collier's agitation did cause the company to offer the Indians more advantageous terms. Although it agreed to pay only $60,000 annually during the first five years for an estimated 50,000 horsepower, the rate would rise to $125,000, $150,000, $160,000, and $175,000 in subsequent five-year periods. The Montana Power Company also agreed to supply up to 15,000 horsepower for pumping on the Flathead irrigation project and to reimburse the government $101,000 for the partially constructed Newell irrigation tunnel.[49] Collier had helped bring about a partial victory for the Flathead Indians but at the expense of further destroying lines of cooperation between himself and the Indian Bureau.

As early as February 1930, Collier intimated in a confidential letter to Haven Emerson that the Department of the Interior must take certain steps to avoid the permanent hostility of their Defense Association. The most significant step consisted of promoting and incorporating into legislation the program which Wilbur had laid before Congress in 1929 in the form of four letters to Senator Frazier. If swift action did not come from the secretary, Collier promised to promote a "critical and muckraking publicity" in Congress. He stressed that "the injurious effects of such a method would be incalculable," but his crusade for Indian reform had to continue.[50]

When Wilbur failed to change the land allotment policy, Collier gave up all attempts at cooperation. In the spring of 1930 he sent a bitter letter to the Secretary of the Interior which expressed complete disenchantment with his programs. First of all, the Indian Bureau, by yielding to Representative Cramton's budget slashing, had abandoned much of the president's emergency request for food and clothing. It had weakened its educational reform by restoring authority to administer floggings to Indian children in the circular entitled "Student Control." Collier accused Rhoads and Scattergood of a persistent effort to destroy the tribal organization of the Flathead Tribe by forcing these Indians to submit to a superintendent who acted in collusion with the Montana Power Company to develop the valuable power site on terms unfavorable to the Indians.[51]

Other problems omitted from this letter caused Collier to lose patience with the Hoover administration. He was especially upset with the Indian Bureau for abandoning earlier attempts to pass the Defense Association's Indian Arts and Crafts bill on account of opposition from the director of the budget and because of complaints from an influential group of artists who belonged to the Indian Art Fund located at the Laboratory Museum in Santa Fe, New Mexico.[52]

Led by Mary Austin, a writer and friend of the American Indian, these artists opposed Collier's Arts and Crafts bill because they doubted whether the Indians needed an expanded market for their arts.* More important than establishing a wide market was developing a method of persuading the Indians to produce art. It would be folly to spend money that compelled the Indians to engage in quantity production of something they could not make. The artists' position stressed that the bill met a nonexistent situation.[53]

Upset with Austin, Collier wrote her a letter which indicated that the Arts and Crafts bill, contrary to her belief, would promote efforts to develop the skills of Indian craftsmen. He could not visualize how the artist group managed to disregard the subject of an expanded market.[54] Austin replied that he should have paid more attention to the advice of the highly specialized group of people at Santa Fe when planning for legislation to help the Indian. She stated that if he failed to heed this warning, he would face continued resistance on her part.[55]

The inability of the Indian Bureau to obtain the enactment of the Swing-Johnson bill concerned Collier. Both the Defense Association and the Department of the Interior had approved of this measure, but like other reforms it died in the House due to the opposition of Louis C. Cramton, who refused to cooperate with the leaders of his own party. Cramton rejected the notion that the states should assume responsibility for the health and education of thousands of scattered Indians beyond the reach of federal agencies.[56] He warned that the bill would make only limited provisions for their health and education and predicted that if the federal government furnished the money to the states for aiding the Indians the country would "speedily have a demoralized system with politics running riot, extravagance encouraged, and the interests of the Indians suffering accordingly."[57]

When Cramton lost his bid for reelection in 1930, Collier wanted to push for the enactment of the Swing-Johnson bill, but Commissioner Rhoads told him that if the bureau brought the bill to a vote, Cramton's opposition would result in adverse action by the House. They decided to wait until his absence during the spring of 1932 to secure passage of

---

*Mary Austin was born in 1868 and died in Santa Fe, New Mexico, in 1934. Her many books included, *The Land of Little Rain* (1902), *The Basket Women* (1904), *Lost Borders* (1909), *The Arrow Maker* (1911), and *A Woman of Genius* (1912). *Who Was Who in America, 1897–1942*, Vol. 1 (Chicago: A. N. Marquis Co., 1942), p. 37.

this legislation.[58] The hurried events during the end of the congressional session resulted in the bill never being acted upon, but it would pass quickly with the advent of the New Deal.

The inability of the Department of the Interior to get its reform program through Congress brought about an intensified attack, not only from Collier, but from the Senate Indian Investigating Subcommittee, which had been created in 1927 to lay the foundation for a new Indian legislative program. This opposition took the form of exposing the public record of Herbert J. Hagerman, an appointee of former Secretary of the Interior Albert B. Fall and still employed by the Indian Bureau as special commissioner to the Navajos.

Herbert J. Hagerman was the son of James Hagerman, a millionaire who made a fortune in land speculation, railroad development, and mining operations. Through his father's influence Hagerman became second secretary at the United States embassy in Russia. During the first part of 1906 President Theodore Roosevelt had appointed him territorial governor of New Mexico, but Hagerman's failure to unite the Republican party caused the president to force his resignation during April 1907. When he received his appointment as special commissioner to the Navajos in 1923, Hagerman was supervising his Southwestern Land and Cattle Company and serving as president of the New Mexico Taxpayers Association.[59]

A colorful group of progressive politicians led the Senate Indian Investigating Subcommittee, and they were probably more interested in using Hagerman's record to embarrass the Hoover administration for political reasons than in reforming Indian affairs. Lynn Frazier, its chairman and a Republican from North Dakota, was a large balding man whose facial expressions remained "so unmoving that one could not tell when he spoke." Elmer Thomas, a Democrat from Oklahoma, was a quiet and dignified person with a "buttoned up mouth," who spoke "little and then only to learn definite facts" about how to help the Indian. Senator Burton K. Wheeler, a Democrat from Montana, his "fuzzy hair haloed around a bald spot," had the reputation of being a heckler. Wheeler's mobile face expressed "disgust, amusement, and boredom."[60]

During January 1931 Senator Frazier inaugurated the subcommittee's effort to have Hagerman removed from the government payroll. He asked Collier to prepare documents and present damaging evidence about the nature of Hagerman's past record with regard to the American Indian.[61] Collier agreed, because he hoped to expose the reactionary policies, which he believed had long characterized the Indian Bureau, but he had political motives as well and was aware that the Hagerman affair might help elect a liberal Democratic presidential candidate.

The first charge brought before the Senate Indian Investigating Sub-committee concerned Hagerman's poor performance as a member of the Pueblo Lands Board which had been created in 1924 to compensate the Indians for land lost to their neighbors. The board had used the statute of limitation provision provided for under the Pueblo Lands Act and found that the Indians had lost title to over 40,000 acres of land. It employed appraisers who recommended that the fair market value of this land, with its water rights, was $1,892,878.[62]

Hagerman had testified before the U.S. District Court in New Mexico that fellow members of the board left him the task of giving compensation awards. At first in the case of Picuris Pueblo, Hagerman awarded the Indians the full appraised value of their relinquished land. But at Nambe Pueblo, in 1926, he had cut the compensation figure of his own appraisers two-thirds, by not counting Indian water rights, which he claimed the Indians had never lost, and by using a forty-year-old evaluation of Pueblo land as his base.[63] Under pressure from the Bureau of the Budget, Hagerman adhered to this precedent in successive decisions, slashing Indian awards to about $600,000. The board extinguished title to 19,000 acres of Pueblo land without compensation, and it neglected to purchase new property for the Indians as stipulated by the Pueblo Lands Act.

Another controversy revolved around the question of whether the non-Indian settlers could pay delinquent taxes over twenty years old in order to claim title to Indian land under section 4 of the Pueblo Lands Act. The Lands Board had ruled against the settlers, but it was reversed by the U.S. District Court of New Mexico and by the circuit court on April 15, 1930. Discouraged at these decisions, the Department of Justice decided not to appeal the matter to the Supreme Court. This forced the Lands Board to rule against the Indians, which resulted in the loss of more land.[64]

Collier, upset at Hagerman's low awards and the decisions of the federal courts, had attempted to readjust these findings by ordering Defense Association attorneys to appeal the tax question, using Taos Pueblo as a test case. This action proved fruitless, however, because the Department of Justice refused to cooperate and the Lands Board was scheduled to finish its work before the Supreme Court met in the autumn. Consequently, Collier ordered his attorneys to file independent suits of ejection against settlers near the Pueblos of Taos, Picuris, and Sandia. These suits denied the right of white settlers, who had failed to pay their taxes, to acquire title under the 1924 act and asserted the Indians unextinguished Spanish title to disputed lands.[65] Collier thought this action necessary because the Department of the Interior was "endeavoring to accomplish what Fall and Daugherty had tried in 1922" with the promotion of the Bursum bill.[66]

To explore this controversy, Lynn Frazier and the Senate Indian Investigating Subcommittee held hearings during January and February 1931.[67] Collier testified about Hagerman's refusal to give the Pueblos adequate compensation, and the senators agreed that Hagerman had acted improperly.[68] On the other hand, they feared that Collier's suits of ejection, if successful, would destroy seven years of work by the Lands Board. Consequently, they recommended a legislative solution to the crisis.[69]

Soon after this recommendation, Senators Bronson Cutting and Sam Bratton from New Mexico drew up legislation to solve the Pueblo dilemma. Known as the Bratton-Cutting bill, it added $779,636 compensation for the Indians and $232,068 for the Spanish and Anglo settlers for property lost because of the niggardly actions of the Pueblo Lands Board.[70] This bill authorized the Pueblos to use their additional money to purchase needed land and permitted each Pueblo, if it so desired, to set aside 10 percent or less of its increased award to pay for attorneys involved in land litigation.* In August 1932, this legislation received the endorsement of the All Pueblo Council assembled at Santo Domingo.[71]

The Indians' approval of the Bratton-Cutting bill had little impact on the position of the Interior Department, which fought its passage. Secretary Wilbur, in a letter to Senator Frazier, quoted the director of the Budget Bureau, who claimed that the "expenses contemplated by the present legislation would not be in accord with the financial program of the President."[72] Wilbur criticized the section of the bill which compensated Defense Association attorneys, calling it a "lobbyist fee" that Congress should eliminate from the measure.[73] This opposition, plus a threatened veto by President Hoover, killed the bill in the House, but it, too, would be one of the prime pieces of legislation enacted during the New Deal.

At Senate hearings held early in February 1931, Collier continued his attack on the Hoover Indian program by criticizing Hagerman's record as special commissioner to the Navajos. One of Hagerman's chief duties had been, and still was under President Hoover, to consolidate checkerboarded land in the New Mexico part of the Navajo reservation. Some of this land belonged to whites because of land grants owned by the Santa Fe Railroad and two other land companies. Hagerman, acting under a

---

*Starting in 1925 the Defense Association had established a Committee on Pueblo Legal Aid. Charles de Y. Elkus, an attorney from San Francisco was its chairman, and he retained Richard Hanna's law firm in Albuquerque to represent the Indians before the Pueblo Lands Board. These and other lawyers such as Louis Marshall and Nathan Margold, both from New York, were paid only for expenses from contributions to the Defense Association's legal fund. When money ran out they often offered free legal services. John Collier, "Statement Summarizing Section 8 of the amended Pueblo Relief bill," Collier Papers; and John Collier, "Manuscript on the Pueblo Lands Board," Collier Papers.

law passed in 1921, was supposed to expedite exchanges and consolidations of this land mutually advantageous to the Navajos and the whites.[74]

But he made little progress in this matter. Complicated regulations issued by the bureau made compliance difficult, while no provisions had been made to pay for improvements on relinquished land. In 1924, Hagerman again tried to consolidate the New Mexico checkerboarded area and he proposed legislation that would have added over a million acres to the Navajo reservation. These efforts failed, however, because of opposition from the Wool Growers Association and other whites who feared that land exchanges might jeopardize possible oil royalties for New Mexico. The bureau also refused to support Hagerman's suggestion that it continue to provide allotments on the public domain, because of opposition from the New Mexico Cattle Growers Association.[75]

Undeterred by these failures, Hagerman drew up another plan that allowed the Navajo Tribal Council to use part of its oil royalties to buy land. This proposal proved partially successful when Congress passed legislation allowing the Navajos to purchase several small parcels of property. In 1930, Hagerman convinced Senator Carl Hayden to introduce legislation that permitted the relinquishment of private lands in Arizona to the Navajo tribe; in return, the Indians had to give up their right to future allotments on the public domain.[76]

Collier showed little sympathy for Hagerman's problems when he appeared before the Senate Indian Investigating Subcommittee. He claimed that Hagerman had idled through seven years under complicated regulations which made his task impossible. He insisted that the special commissioner's first duty, which could have been performed at any time, was to secure amended regulations to make possible the transfer of land for which the Navajos had paid him out of their tribal funds. Collier pointed out that Hagerman had been obligated to increase Navajo land allotments on the public domain under section 4 of the Dawes General Allotment Act. Instead, he supported the Hayden bill, which provided for the exchange and consolidation of land in Arizona. This offered "distinct advantages," but he doubted if they were great enough to deprive the Navajos, especially those living in New Mexico, of their original right to allotment on the public domain.[77]

Suspicious of the Hayden bill, Collier urged the senators to delay action on this legislation until they could inquire further into the subject. This was necessary because Hagerman had neglected to present the bill to the Navajo Tribal Council, while the Indian Bureau had given conflicting information to the House and Senate over the number of Indians qualified for allotment on the public domain.[78] Collier's opposition prevented a solution to this dilemma.

The most interesting and politically explosive of the various charges brought against Hagerman consisted of the implication that he had associated with Albert B. Fall in an oil scandal that sounded more ominous than the Teapot Dome affair. Like its predecessor, the Hoover administration never completely rid itself of Fall's oil-splattered heritage. This controversy revolved around the Rattlesnake Dome reserve, near Shiprock, in the northeastern corner of the Navajo reservation, and, raised the question of why President Hoover continued to allow Hagerman to hold important positions in the Department of the Interior. Hagerman became the symbol for all the evils that existed in the Indian Service during the previous decade and for the limitations of current reform efforts.

The Senate hearings on the Rattlesnake Dome oil affair revealed that in 1923 Hagerman had been brought out of retirement by Secretary Fall and appointed special commissioner to the Navajos for the purpose of negotiating leases to exploit their large oil properties. Fall wrote Hagerman that he anticipated oil development on the Navajo reservation with both pipeline and railroad construction to follow, and suggested that the $3,600 salary "was no inducement" for the position.[79] Little evidence exists to suggest why Hagerman accepted this appointment except that his primary interest as a large rancher and president of the New Mexico Taxpayers Association concerned the economic development of the Southwest. Essentially an entrepreneur, he wanted to bring property such as oil, railroads, and pipelines onto the taxrolls of New Mexico.[80]

Coinciding with Hagerman's appointment, Secretary Fall issued regulations abolishing the existing Navajo tribal organization, which consisted of five subagencies. Instead of separate tribal councils, the Navajos in the future would meet together in a new, unified, deliberative body. The regulations for this new council provided that in the event of the Indians' refusal to abolish their separate councils the secretary of the interior would appoint delegates to act for them. They directed that the Navajos should meet only upon the request of Hagerman. Fall had ordered these guidelines because of the reluctance of the San Juan Council to approve oil leases and from his fear that Collier might take over control of the Navajo Tribal Council as he had the All Pueblo Council during the dispute over the Bursum bill.[81]

Early in 1923 Hagerman called the five Navajo superintendents to Albuquerque where they discussed tribal matters. He advised them that the Department of the Interior had decided that all Navajos had an interest in mineral and oil leasing. Hagerman then established an enlarged tribal council with delegates from each jurisdiction.[82] He met with this council on July 7, 1923, at Toadlena, New Mexico, and obtained authority to sign on its behalf all oil and mining leases. The Indians had no alternative but to agree since Fall could appoint new delegates if they objected. They also were cooperative because Hagerman promised them government assistance in securing additional land for their reservation.[83]

On October 15, 1923, under the supervision of Hagerman and Indian Commissioner Charles H. Burke, the Interior Department auctioned twenty-two Navajo oil tracts for $87,000 in bonuses to several private companies.[84] One of the structures called Rattlesnake Dome consisted of 4,080 acres and sold for a $1,000 cash bonus to the Metropolitan Oil Company represented by S. C. Muntz and Neil B. Field, both friends of Hagerman. In less than one year after the validation of this lease, the Continental Oil Company purchased a half interest in 200 acres of this structure for $300,000. Within three years after the auction, Continental Oil bought a half interest in the entire Rattlesnake structure for approximately $3,600,000.[85]

In the January 1924 issue of *Sunset Magazine,* Collier had praised Hagerman's activities on the Navajo reservation. He reported that the special commissioner gained the trust of the Indians through "a good choice of delegates to the Navajo Council."[86] Collier indicated that the size of the oil fields remained undetermined, but the Indians obtained generous bonuses in addition to royalties ranging from 12.5 to 25 percent. After "as careful a study as a layman" could make, he concluded that the oil question had been "handled with businesslike honesty and in the best interests of the Navajos."[87]

Seven years later Collier changed his mind and claimed that the further "he got into the subject" the more he became convinced that his earlier judgment had been wrong.[88] Using evidence compiled by Louis Glavis, the well-known conservationist, who was research assistant for the Senate Indian Investigating Subcommittee, Collier became a "sort of public prosecutor."[89] He told the senators that the low bidding on the Rattlesnake Dome stemmed, not from geological uncertainties as Hagerman claimed, but from the existing overproduction of oil which resulted in depressed prices. He pointed out that it was absurd to auction the Navajo oil reserves at such a period. Collier argued that the leases Hagerman used excluded the independents such as the Midwest Oil Company and delivered the Rattlesnake Dome to large companies or speculators acting on their behalf. This resulted in a phenomenal profit for the Continental Oil Company and the neglect of Indian interests.[90]

One of Collier's main indictments against Hagerman focused around two geological reports made by Kenneth B. Nowells, an engineer employed by the Bureau of Mines. He inferred that Hagerman withheld these reports from the public in order to give his friends special information about the potential of the Rattlesnake Dome.[91] In the first report dated

September 28, 1923, Nowells reported to the Indian Bureau that most interest at the Santa Fe auction in October would revolve around the tracts on the Hogback, Tocito, Table Mesa, and Rattlesnake structures, the first three being the most attractive.[92] The second report, written two days before the auction, suggested that all oil structures were geologically as good as the oil rich Hogback Dome except for the Beautiful Mountain Anticline.[93]

Finally, Collier told the senators that the Navajo "rubber stamp" council had been compelled to accept Hagerman's unjust schemes because regulations drawn up by Albert B. Fall decreed that if they refused to accept it the secretary of the interior would arbitrarily name new council delegates.* He concluded his remarks by telling the senators that his charges against Hagerman did not prove premeditated corruption, but implied "ruthlessness, maladministration, inconsistency, incompetency, and a betrayal of the guardianship obligation."[94]

Hagerman, who testified in his own defense, believed that Collier and the senators had unfairly heckled him, and they cared little about his past record. Instead, they wanted to embarrass Commissioners Rhoads and Scattergood for political reasons.[95] He intended to fight this inquisition as long as necessary in order to protect his reputation.[96]

To prove his innocence in the Rattlesnake Dome affair Hagerman cited several affidavits from his former associates. One of the most important was written by Kenneth B. Nowells, who attacked Collier's and Frazier's unwarranted criticisms of Hagerman. Nowells indicated that before the auction at Santa Fe he had never met personally with Hagerman nor corresponded with him over important matters. His report merely indicated the potential of the Rattlesnake Dome, not that prospectors would discover oil. Because oil had been found at this structure the $1,000 bid seemed an extremely low price, but at the time none of the companies considered the lease very attractive. This stemmed, in part, from their knowledge that a nearby well in the Hogback field had produced water the day before the auction.[97]

Oliver La Farge, director of the Eastern Association of Indian Affairs, also defended Hagerman. He claimed that Fall had appointed

---

*Lawrence Kelly gives a generally critical assessment of Collier's indictment against Hagerman. He claims that the creation of a unified tribal council was not a regressive measure depriving the Navajos of their rights, but a progressive one which, for the first time, bound all Navajos together in one body. Nevertheless, Kelly neglected to mention that Fall abolished the separate councils because the Indians at San Juan Council were reluctant to approve oil leases such as the Rattlesnake Dome, which later proved detrimental to their interests. Lawrence Kelly, *The Navajo Indians and Federal Indian Policy* (Tucson: University of Arizona Press, 1968), pp. 192–93.

him as a reform measure after "the scandals of the Bursum bill and Teapot Dome had been aired, at a time when Fall felt the need for a few
honest gestures."[98] La Farge praised Hagerman for creating the unified
Navajo Council, calling it one "of his finest pieces of work," and stressed
that the senators should put the Rattlesnake Dome lease in perspective.
It had been sold only after wide advertising with six other leases, which
brought the Indians generous royalties in wildcat territory. It was ridicu-
lous to call such an "honest and fearless public official" a "political
fixer."[99]

During the course of its hearings, the Senate Indian Investigating
Subcommittee had offered an amendment to a Department of the Interior
appropriations bill which recommended that Congress remove Hagerman
from the government payroll. The Senate agreed and eliminated his salary,
but on February 15, 1931, at a joint conference committee, his salary
was restored at the insistence of the Indian Bureau and Representative
Louis C. Cramton.[100]

Sick and "harried into exhaustion" during the Senate hearings, Hagerman left Washington to return to Santa Fe, where he received support
from local artists and writers. At Lamy he met a noisy motorcade of
admirers who escorted him to Santa Fe. Willard Nash rode on top of
Hagerman's car dressed like an Indian and "beating a tombé," while
another auto in this retinue carried a life-sized puppet of Collier.[101]

Erna Fergusson recalled later that Witter Bynner, writer and "play-
boy extraordinary," had chanted what he termed Collier's doxology:

> *Praise God from whom all blessings flow;*
> *praise Him for the Indians here below;*
> *no matter who may pay the cost,*
> *without the Indians I'd be lost;*
> *whoever really helps the tribes*
> *receives my curses and my jibes;*
> *and there, for Mr. Hagerman,*
> *I say to hurt you all I can,*
> *if there were many more like you,*
> *I should have nothing left to do;*
> *love for the Indian is my boast;*
> *and yet I love John Collier the most.*

Hagerman escaped this escort as soon as he arrived in Santa Fe. The
demonstration ended by hanging Collier in effigy from a cottonwood tree
in front of the old Palace of Governors on the Santa Fe plaza.[102]

This support for Hagerman and opposition to Collier at Santa Fe
came from people who believed that Hagerman had been treated unfairly.
Writers such as Witter Bynner, who worked closely with the New Mexico

Association on Indian Affairs, disliked Collier because he made the Pueblos distrust all assistance outside the American Indian Defense Association. He criticized Collier for dominating their meetings and making the Indians hostile toward Indian Bureau employees. Bynner thought that Collier's general influence among the Pueblos was to alienate them from their Spanish-American neighbors.[103]

This analysis touched upon the essence of the resentment of many people in New Mexico against Collier. The passage of the Pueblo Lands Act had caused a great amount of dissatisfaction from both Anglo and Spanish-American settlers, who had lost land and improvements inherited from their forefathers. These settlers had been forced to spend their savings paying attorneys to defend the titles to their lands, and they supported Hagerman's low awards to the Indians. Collier's attempt to readjust what they considered the already generous compensation of the Pueblo Lands Board only inflamed a tense situation. Real estate owners at Taos, for example, had become enraged against the ejection suits instigated by Collier because these suits had paralyzed the selling, purchasing, and improvements of property.[104]

The episode at Santa Fe had little impact on the Senate Indian Investigating Subcommittee. In 1932, after further hearings, it recommended and Congress agreed to remove Hagerman's position from the government payroll.[105] As Collier had predicted earlier, this type of "critical and muckraking publicity" resulted in negative consequences.[106] It destroyed all semblance of cooperation between the more militant Indian reformers and the Department of the Interior.

Events reached a climax on March 9, 1932, when Senator William King, a Democrat from Utah, presented a petition before the Senate signed by several Indians and important members of the American Indian Defense Association. Prepared by Collier, it criticized Secretary Wilbur for keeping Hagerman in the Indian Service, despite the Senate's elimination of his position, "as an insult flaunted in the face of all Indians." This petition accused the Indian Bureau of abandoning the legislative program it had pledged to support during 1929. Instead of enacting far-reaching reforms, it had forsaken existing programs, broken promises, and established new evils.[107]

The Department of the Interior refuted these charges in a lengthy article inserted in the *Congressional Record* on March 10, 1932. In this statement Secretary Wilbur claimed that the Senate hearings had produced no evidence justifying Hagerman's removal. He pointed out that the legislation endorsed in 1929 in the form of four letters sent to Senator Frazier was the responsibility of Congress, rather than the secretary of the interior or commissioner of Indian affairs. Wilbur called Collier's accusations "a series of misrepresentations almost approaching blackmail," and he found the major obstacle to Indian reform, not the inadequacies of the Indian Bureau, but "the interference with tribal affairs by self-appointed groups making a profession of exploiting Indian grievances."[108]

This total breakdown of communication made the Hoover administration an ad interim regime committed to humanitarian programs, but unable to fundamentally alter Indian affairs. Despite their obvious good intentions, Wilbur, Rhoads, and Scattergood lacked the political clout to push necessary legislation through Congress. Their belief in the validity of the previous policy of assimilation prevented them from taking decisive action to stop land allotment, which threatened the Indians with ultimate disaster, and they mistakenly tied their reputation to the cause of Hagerman, who symbolized past mistakes. Furthermore, Collier and members of the Senate Indian Investigating Subcommittee were often intemperate, and they seemed more concerned with the negative objective of discrediting the Republicans than in the positive task of reform. The result was a false dawn for the American Indian.[109]

Yet, by March 1933, the basic changes required for a new Indian policy had been formulated. Secretary Wilbur and his staff contributed to this effort when they convinced Congress to increase appropriations for the Indian Service, implemented many of the educational recommendations of the Meriam Report, and reorganized the bureau. Collier and his colleagues also deserved credit because they offered alternatives to stop the loss of Indian land holdings, stressed the importance of preserving tribal institutions, and helped formulate legislation such as the Swing-Johnson, Bratton-Cutting, and the Indian Arts and Crafts bills. These innovations would all come to fruition with Franklin D. Roosevelt's appointment of Collier as Indian commissioner.

P113-134

6. The Indian New Deal Begins

Pleased that the Hagerman episode had negative political consequences for the Republicans, Collier favored the election of Franklin D. Roosevelt in November 1932. He believed that the president-elect, "a liberal in thought and heart" and an advocate of "scientific government," would be sympathetic to a fundamental reorganization of Indian affairs.[1]

But to make sure that the Democrats understood what reforms needed implementation, Collier suggested in the January issue of *American Indian Life* that the new administration end the land allotment policy in order to begin collective and corporate use of Indian property. He indicated that the government should provide the Indians with financial credit, replace boarding schools with day schools, enlist the aid of the Department of Agriculture to assist the Indians, employ more natives, and repeal several archaic espionage laws adversely affecting their civil liberties.[2]

While Collier searched for a safer and "politically stronger" candidate for Indian commissioner than himself, other pressure groups made a strong bid for their nominees. The Indian Rights Association favored the continuance of the present commissioners, Charles J. Rhoads and J. Henry Scattergood, while Senator Joseph T. Robinson of Arkansas supported Edgar B. Meritt, a native son from Fayetteville, who had been assistant commissioner during the Harding and Coolidge years.[3] The Board of Indian Commissioners indirectly endorsed these candidates when it passed a resolution which called for the appointment of a person with Indian Service experience rather than "party-men."[4] According to Collier, the possibility existed that Senators Sam G. Bratton and Burton K.

Wheeler had made a trade by which Bratton would support Harry Mitchell from Montana, who was Wheeler's man for the commissionership, if Wheeler would advance Reuben Perry, Meritt's campaign manager, for assistant commissioner.[5]

All of these candidates were distasteful to Collier because of their previous association with Republican administrations. In order to assure the nomination of a commissioner committed to fundamental reform, he contacted Lewis Meriam from the Institute for Government Research and Nathan Margold, a New York lawyer, who had served as legal advisor to the Pueblos. They agreed that if Roosevelt favored one of them, the other two men should close ranks to insure his victory. Collier then sent an open letter to several personal friends which asked them to actively support Meriam, Margold, or himself for the commissionership. He told his associates that they should send recommendations immediately to President-elect Roosevelt, his advisors, and the senators of the candidates' states, urging them to nominate one of the three men.[6]

Collier also mailed letters to the governors of the various Pueblos requesting that they assist in the selection of a new commissioner. He suggested that it "might be extremely useful if a delegation from the All Pueblo Council would come to the East and talk with Governor Roosevelt and with Mrs. Roosevelt."[7] This delegation might stop at Washington and impress on Congress the need for adopting the Pueblo Relief bill, as well as supporting either Meriam, Margold, or himself, for commissioner.[8] The All Pueblo Council responded to this plea at a meeting held at Santo Domingo on January 12, 1933, by adopting a resolution, addressed to Roosevelt, which favored the appointment of Collier. If this proved impossible, the council indicated a preference for either Meriam or Margold.[9]

This type of pressure grew when 600 of the nation's leading educators, physicians, churchmen, social workers, and Indian reformers sent Roosevelt a petition on January 28, 1933. Signed by Collier and many of his colleagues, it warned the president-elect that he must take immediate action to save the Indians from complete cultural, political, and economic disintegration. Because the Dawes General Allotment Act had caused the "rapid shrinkage" of Indian property, this petition maintained, the Roosevelt administration represented "almost a last chance for the Indians."[10]

One month later, the Board of Directors of the American Indian Defense Association issued the most persuasive statement endorsing Collier for commissioner. They reviewed and praised his legislative and legal battle for Indian rights during the past decade — a struggle that had preserved Pueblo property rights, blocked the effort to destroy the Indian title to executive-order reservations, prevented the confiscation of the Flathead water power site, and worked to establish religious freedom for the Indians. According to the Defense Association, Collier had "altered the whole perspective of Indian affairs" and given the red man a "new and realistic hope."[11]

Roosevelt realized that he needed new policies to assist the Native American population, but having few ideas of his own, he referred the subject of Indian Bureau appointments to Professor Raymond Moley from Columbia University.[12] At the request of Senator Bronson Cutting from New Mexico, the president-elect also asked Felix Frankfurter, the dean of the Harvard Law School, to examine the Indian situation and make recommendations. Cutting favored Collier but Frankfurter leaned toward the candidacy of Margold, a fellow attorney. Because they hoped to get an answer over who would head up the Indian Bureau, Collier, Meriam, and Margold met with Moley to discuss this matter, but they came to the conclusion that a final decision depended upon the appointment of a secretary of the interior.[13]

Roosevelt's selection of Harold L. Ickes for this cabinet post marked the beginning of the Indian New Deal.* Both Ickes and his wife had become deeply interested in the Indian welfare cause while living at their summer home near Coolidge, Arizona.[14] Among the first members to join the Indian Defense Association during 1923, Ickes had suggested in a journal article that one of the worst aspects of American history concerned "our treatment of the American Indians."[15] He indicated that there existed "no more blush-raising record on this shameful page than the administration of the Bureau of Indian Affairs by Messrs. Burke and Meritt."[16] Anna W. Ickes demonstrated even more interest in the Indian than her husband; she spoke Navajo and her book, *Mesa Land,* made her a recognized authority on the life and history of Indians in the Southwest.[17]

Shortly after taking office, Ickes picked Collier for the position of Indian commissioner with a public warning that he would refuse to submit further nominations until the Senate took action. According to Lemuel

---

*Born on March 15, 1874, Harold L. Ickes received his B.A. and law degree from the University of Chicago. A delegate-at-large in the Republican convention of 1920, he helped block the attempt to unanimously nominate Warren G. Harding and eventually bolted the party to work for the Democratic candidate. In between his political activities, he accepted civil liberty cases without pay, taught classes at Hull House, fought against Samuel Insull's utility company, and joined the American Indian Defense Association. In 1933, President Franklin D. Roosevelt chose Ickes as secretary of the interior because of his liberal reputation, interest in conservation, and political assistance in swinging liberal midwestern Republicans to the Democratic party. Maxine Block, ed., *Current Biography* (New York: H. W. Wilson Co., 1941), pp. 426–28.

Harold L. Ickes,
secretary of the interior
from 1933 to 1946.

National Archives

Parton, an editor for the *New York Sun,* the issue of Collier's confirmation in the Senate had started a modern day "Battle of the Big Horn" because "all the winds of patronage" opposed his appointment.[18] This included the enmity of such powerful senators as Joseph T. Robinson, the majority leader, and Elmer Thomas from Oklahoma. They were joined by land, oil, and water power companies who "did everything but offer a bounty for his skin." Despite this hostility, Parton believed that Collier, who had made Albert B. Fall, a former secretary of the interior, "bark like a coyote at the mention of his name," would slip "under the tepee, politically speaking."[19]

This reluctance of many politicians to accept Collier's nomination caused President Roosevelt to call Ickes and Senator Robinson to his office for a "showdown conference." When the secretary arrived at the White House at 5:30 P.M. on April 11, 1933, he discovered that Robinson had preceded him to support his brother-in-law, Edgar B. Meritt, as Indian commissioner. The president started the conversation by indicating that he had received many protests against Meritt, but Robinson remained adamant and made a short statement in behalf of his candidate. Roosevelt asked Ickes for his opinion, and the secretary reported that he had documentary proof showing that Meritt was totally unqualified for the job. After Ickes finished his presentation the president turned to Robinson and said, "Well Joe, you see what I am up against. Every highbrow organization in the country is opposed to Meritt, and Secretary Ickes, under whom he would have to work does not want him."[20]

Nine days later the Senate confirmed the appointment of Collier after Robinson withdrew his support for Meritt at the request of Roosevelt. Ickes believed that Collier was "the best equipped man who ever occupied the office," and he appointed an old family friend, William Zimmerman, a liberal Indianapolis businessman who had advocated the ownership of corporations by workers, as assistant commissioner.[21] To help Collier and Zimmerman in their task of promoting Indian reform, the secretary appointed three Defense Association attorneys, who had aided the Pueblo Indians during the past decade, to positions in the Interior Department. Nathan Margold became solicitor, while Charles Fahy and Felix Cohen were selected as his assistants. Another appointment beneficial to the Indians was Louis Glavis, the former investigator for the Senate Indian Investigating Subcommittee, who headed the department's inspection division.[22]

One of the most colorful of the New Dealers, Collier was a small stooped-shouldered man who wore glasses and kept his hair untidy.[23] A "long-legged, somewhat humorless Savonarola," who blazed "with zeal for the Red Man," he had the reputation of being a dreamer, which soon aroused the suspicions of Congress.[24] At the office Collier often sat in his swivel chair "coiling his legs into a kind of nest" and he frequently smoked a corncob pipe, which he kept in an empty water glass on his desk.[25] Instead of wearing a suit, Collier usually came to work in a baggy old long-sleeved green sweater. Gossips in Washington rumored that the commissioner sometimes kept a pet frog in his pocket.[26]

After being sworn in as Indian commissioner on April 21, 1933, Collier explained the policies he planned to follow. He praised the "solid foundation" laid by his predecessors, Rhoads and Scattergood, and promised to continue their progressive programs in the areas of health, education, and industrial extension work. But the commissioner indicated that he would seek the assistance of other federal agencies to provide the Indians with agricultural and reclamation assistance, as well as rural credit facilities. Collier hoped that he could make available the social services of the states to the tribes "while preserving the guardianship which the United States owed to the Indians."[27]

Collier proposed that the government follow a colonial policy known as "indirect administration" that had worked previously with the Cherokee tribe and the Pueblo Indians. The commissioner believed that the bureau would have to decrease its paternalism and extend both civil rights and modern business enterprise to the Native American population. This meant that those Indians who still had a strong cultural and institutional life should be encouraged "to develop their own life in their own patterns, not as segregated minorities but as noble elements in our common life."[28]

A few months later Collier spoke to the Navajo students at Fort Wingate, New Mexico, where he elaborated on the purpose of his Indian New Deal. First, he said that the government had the duty to bring education and modern scientific knowledge within the reach of every Indian. And, at the same time, the government should reawaken in the soul of the Indian not only pride in being an Indian, but hope for the future as an Indian. It had the obligation to preserve the Indian's love and ardor toward the rich values of Indian life as expressed in their arts, rituals, and cooperative institutions. Collier warned the Navajos that if they turned away in scorn and shame from their heritage, they would throw away that part of their being which made them powerful and interesting as individuals, and cancel the great spiritual contributions required in the future by American civilization.[29]

Once in office, Collier pushed for the passage of the Pueblo Relief bill, which became law on May 31, 1933. The successful conclusion to over a decade of reform, it made an additional appropriation of $761,958 to the Pueblos, who agreed to drop their independent suits of ejection against non-Indians, while the settlers received $232,086 to make up for inadequate compensation ordered by the Pueblo Lands Board. The Indians received a veto power over the use of these funds which they had to spend for the purchase of needed land, water rights, and other permanent economic advantages. If they desired, the Pueblo Indians could pay Defense Association attorneys fees in any amount up to 10 percent of the increased compensation. Finally, the Taos Indians received from the Department of Agriculture a fifty-year renewable permit to use government land surrounding their Sacred Blue Lake for economic and religious purposes.[30]

Satisfied with the conclusion of his struggle to assist the Pueblo Indians, Collier continued his reform activities by executive power. On May 25, 1933, President Roosevelt, at the request of Secretary Ickes and Collier, issued an executive order abolishing the Board of Indian Commissioners "to reduce expenditures" and "increase the efficiency" of government operations.[31] This justification, however, was merely a

Commissioner Collier shed his baggy sweater and
corncob pipe for this formal portrait.

smokescreen because the board, which had never been adequately funded,
operated on a small budget of about $13,000 a year.[32] Collier and Ickes
wanted to end the board's existence for political reasons, because it was
controlled by Republicans and conservatives who favored the assimilation
policies associated with the Dawes General Allotment Act. Many of the
board's members had worked closely with missionaries and Christian welfare groups, giving them a free hand in the bureau's schools. They represented an obstacle to Collier's plans for the preservation of Indian heritage
and the collective use of tribal lands.

Secretary Ickes planned to replace the board with a "small advisory
committee of outstanding men and women who were really intelligently
interested in the Indians and knew something about them."[33] But Collier
rejected this idea of creating a formal advisory committee because he felt
that any body with functions identical to those of the Board of Indian

Commissioners might result in increased antagonism on the part of former board members and reveal poor political judgment.* Collier recommended and Ickes accepted the principle that they form a consultant group of social scientists who were experts concerning Indian arts and crafts, cultural anthropology, education, the use of natural resources, regional planning, health, and Indian law.†

This action led to positive results after Secretary Ickes appointed Felix Cohen to the position of assistant solicitor in the Interior Department. Cohen helped draft legislative bills until 1939 when Collier loaned him to the Justice Department to head an Indian Law Survey. With the assistance of Theodore H. Haas, another lawyer, Cohen compiled a forty-six volume collection of federal laws and treaties and wrote a scholarly book called the *Handbook of Federal Indian Law*. It presented legal and moral arguments which demonstrated that Indians had certain sovereign rights. They included the political equality of races, the right to tribal self-government, federal jurisdiction in Indian affairs, and the government's duty to pass legislation protecting natives in their relations with non-Indians.[34]

Collier kept his promise to enlist the support of other federal agencies to help the Indians by continuing the policies of Commissioner Rhoads, who had persuaded Robert Fechner to include the Indians in the Civilian Conservation Corps. Immediately after he assumed office, Collier prepared a memo for Secretary Ickes stressing that the CCC establish a separate program for Indians. He feared that they would resent the importation of whites, and several federal laws indicated that the Indians should receive preference for reservation employment. Collier believed that Indians were accustomed to working in family groups and their employment, preferable to issuing rations, avoided expensive transportation costs.[35]

President Roosevelt approved of a plan for Indian Emergency Conservation Work during the last part of April. Three months later, Congress

---

*Despite Collier's caution, two members of the board, Flora Warren Seymour, an author from Chicago, Illinois, and G. E. E. Lindquist, a missionary from Lawrence, Kansas, would become severe critics of the Indian New Deal. John Collier, "Memorandum for Secretary Ickes, September 21 and 22, 1933," Collier Papers.

†Emphasizing the desirability of bringing government and science together, Collier formed an Indian Bureau brain trust. The most important members of this advisory group were Robert Marshall, director of Indian forestry; Ward Shepard, principal planning specialist; H. L. Shapiro, assistant curator at the Museum of Natural History; J. G. Townsend, chief of the development of industrial hygiene at the Public Health Service; Ralph Linton, professor of anthropology at Columbia University; Edward Kinnard, specialist on Indian languages; and Jay Nash, emergency unemployment. Oliver La Farge, ed., *The Changing Indian* (Norman: University of Oklahoma Press, 1942), pp. vii–x.

National Archives

Workers enjoy a respite at the Indian Emergency Conservation Work Camp on the Yakima reservation, 1938.

appropriated $5,875,000 for the first six months of Indian conservation programs at seventy-two camps on thirty-three reservations. The three types of facilities established included a permanent camp for single men, a camp where Indians lived in their homes and commuted to work, and family camps where Indians such as the Navajos resided at their summer hogans.[36]

Most Indian conservation activity was planned for the states of Arizona, Oklahoma, Montana, New Mexico, South Dakota, and Washington. The benefits obtained from these projects included the placing of roads in reservation forests for fire control, the building of storage dams to prevent erosion, and the construction of fences and wells. The Indians received a salary of thirty dollars a month, and they attended weekend leadership conferences to help them learn skills such as the operation of mechanized equipment and the principles of land management.[37]

Approximately 85,000 Indians worked for the IECW between 1933 and 1942.*

On August 1, 1933, Collier publicized these activities by starting a biweekly magazine called *Indians at Work*. Financed by CCC and bureau funds, it was edited by Mary Heaton Vorse, a writer whom Collier had known in New York City during the Progressive Era.† This magazine tried to stimulate Indian interest in conservation by providing photographs of camp life and by discussing human interest stories and topics such as the prevention of soil erosion and the control of forest fires. Collier began each issue with editorials that discussed a variety of topics dealing with Indian affairs. As the magazine grew in popularity, the commissioner broadened its scope to include articles from anthropologists, conservationists, lawyers, and Indian Service personnel dealing with all aspects of Indian life. Extremely popular, *Indians at Work* had a circulation of 12,000.[38]

Pleased that the CCC had cooperated with the bureau, Collier asked Henry A. Wallace, the secretary of agriculture, to help the Indians. Wallace agreed and he spent many hours with Collier at the Cosmos Club in Washington, D.C., where they discussed such topics as how the Indians were our "true subsistence farmers."[39] These talks led to a visit by both men during the spring of 1934 to New Mexico and Arizona, in search of additional submarginal land for the Pueblos and Navajos.[40] Assistant Secretary Rexford Tugwell, who had appointed a former student to represent him in matters connected with the Indian Bureau, also supported Collier. He told him to let "me know whenever the Department of Agriculture can be of any assistance in solving those questions of Indian development and progress in which we are both so interested."[41]

Both Tugwell and Wallace used their influence to aid the Indians on several occasions. The Agricultural Adjustment Administration gave the Indian cattle industry an impetus through the allocation of $800,000 for the purchase of pure-bred stock from drought-stricken white ranchers

---

*In 1942, when the IECW ended because of World War II, substantial improvements had been made in the area of conservation. The IECW constructed 9,737 miles of truck trails, built 91 lookout towers, and placed 1,315,870 acres of land under pest control. Indian grazing and farm lands were aided by projects such as 263,129 acres of poisonous weed eradication, 12,230 miles of fencing, and 1,742 large dams and reservoirs. Donald Parman, "The Indian and the Civilian Conservation Corps," *Pacific Historical Review* 40 (February 1971): 46–54.

†Mary Heaton Vorse was a liberal author from Provincetown, Massachusetts. She sympathized with radical labor causes in her books such as *Men And Steel* (1921), *Strike* (1930), and *Labor's New Millions* (1938). Durward Howes, ed., *American Women: The Official Who's Who Among the Women of the Nation 1935–36* (Los Angeles: Richard Blank Publishing Co., 1935), p. 568.

to establish foundation herds on various reservations.* In order to reduce the problem of overgrazing on Indian land, the AAA purchased surplus goats and sheep from the Navajos, while experts at the Bureau of Animal Husbandry organized a sheep breeding station at Fort Wingate, New Mexico, to assist in obtaining the right kind of wool for Navajo blankets and rugs.[42] And the Indians continued to benefit from the efforts of the Soil Erosion Service after it was transferred from the Interior to the Agriculture Department. Collier believed that this cooperation was "epoch making, for many tribes, and of practical help to Indians everywhere."[43]

The commissioner successfully included the Indians under the New Deal's several relief agencies. On May 12, 1933, Congress created the Federal Emergency Relief Administration which channeled a half-billion dollars in relief money to state and local governments.† At first the Indians did not participate in this program, but at Collier's insistence, Harry Hopkins, the director of FERA, addressed a letter on November 7, 1934, to all state relief administrators with orders that "the Indians should be eligible on the same basis as whites for any phase of your program."[44] This aided Oklahoma Indians, who were paid by FERA funds to build roads and bridges, while other tribesmen made surveys to evaluate economic and social conditions on their reservations.[45]

In addition to state and local relief, FERA developed new programs of its own. One such experiment was the Federal Surplus Relief Corporation, which purchased surplus commodities to meet relief needs. The Navajos came under this program and sold 49,052 sheep and 147,787 goats to the FSRC for $250,000. The meat was distributed to needy Indians in the northern plains states.[46]

Many Indians received salaries directly from the federal payroll when President Roosevelt authorized Harry Hopkins, on November 23, 1933, to establish the Civil Works Administration. The CWA employed

---

*The New Deal fostered a great expansion of the Indian beef cattle industry although it reduced the number of sheep and goats. Between 1933 and 1939 the number of Indians owning cattle increased from 8,627 to 16,624, the size of the herds jumped from 167,373 to 267,551, the money income derived from these cattle expanded from $263,095 to $3,125,326, while the income from all Indian livestock jumped from $2,087,000 to $5,859,000. *Annual Report of the Secretary of the Interior: Report of the Commissioner of Indian Affairs* (Washington: Government Printing Office, 1935), p. 119, and Ibid., 1940, p. 375.

†Collier also worked with the War Department to secure surplus items for needy Indians. They included 35,000 pants, 123,000 suits of woolen underwear, 40,000 overcoats, 33,000 shirts, 24,000 pair of shoes, 176,000 pair of socks, 25,000 caps, and 10,000 pair of leggins. Furthermore, the Red Cross assisted the Indians by providing them with five million pounds of flour, blankets, and clothing. *Annual Report of the Secretary of the Interior: Report of the Commissioner of Indian Affairs* (Washington: Government Printing Office, 1933), pp. 106–7.

Woodrow Crumbo adds finishing touches to his mural, "Wild Horses," for the Department of the Interior building.

4,423 Indians through the winter of 1934 to repair government and tribal buildings. Other tasks included road construction, the digging of wells, clerical work, and the making of clothes.[47] The CWA stimulated Native American culture when it hired fifteen Indian artists to paint murals on government buildings and twenty-five craftsmen to manufacture rugs, pottery, and jewelry, which Collier placed in Indian Service facilities.[48]

Another relief agency, the Public Works Administration, was established in June 1933 with appropriation of $3.3 billion, under Title II of the National Industrial Recovery Act. Directed by Harold L. Ickes, it improved the physical conditions at several reservations by building day schools, hospitals, roads, irrigation projects, and sewer systems.[49] This recovery program promoted Indian arts and crafts by constructing several museums for the demonstration and marketing of Indian products.[50] Indian artists employed by PWA, such as Woodrow Crumbo, a Potawatomie from Oklahoma, added to this effort by painting murals on several Department of the Interior buildings.[51] Furthermore, Secretary Ickes engaged the architectural firm of Mayers, Murray, and Phillip from New York to design buildings in the Pueblo and mission styles of the Southwest. One example consisted of an adobe-type community center which made up part of the new Navajo capital under construction at Window Rock, Arizona.[52]

Funds provided by Title II of the NIRA enabled Ickes to establish a Subsistence Homestead Division in the Interior Department. At the request of Collier, he earmarked over $400,000 for five subsistence Indian homesteads at Burns, Oregon; Great Falls, Montana; Chilocco, Oklahoma; Rosebud, South Dakota; and at the Sacramento Agency in northern California.[53] These villages were set up for landless people such as the Hill Indians, who formerly worked in the smelters at Great Falls, Montana. Since the start of the depression they had lived on the verge of starvation in huts made of poles and flattened tin cans.[54]

When the depression continued, Congress passed the Emergency Relief Appropriations Act which permitted President Roosevelt to spend $5 billion in additional relief funds.[55] Collier immediately went before the Emergency Relief Council and requested $15 million for Indian rehabilitation.[56] This intervention proved successful because the Indians were included in both the Works Progress Administration and the National Youth Administration.* The WPA employed over 10,700 Indians annually on projects such as indexing and filing documents for the bureau.[57] Young Indians who participated in the NYA were allowed six dollars a month to help provide for clothing, supplies, and lunches at day schools. In New York, the NYA trained Onondaga Indians to act as counselors for city children during summer vacation.[58]

Rexford Tugwell, after a series of discussions with Collier, agreed to allow the Indians to use the Resettlement Administration's program of crop loans, drought relief, and subsistence grants. Tugwell visited drought stricken areas in the West during 1936 where he learned that Indians had started to drink water from green stagnant pools left in river-

---

*Expressing their thanks for relief aid, the Indians on the Swinomish Reservation, in Washington, used WPA funds to carve the portrait of President Franklin D. Roosevelt on a totem pole. New York Times, August 22, 1938, p. 15.

beds. Shocked at these miserable conditions, he ordered the Resettlement Administration to release funds for the purpose of digging new wells on reservations in North and South Dakota.[59] He also purchased over 993,673 acres of additional land for the Indians, most of it being grazing land for the Pueblos and Navajos living near the Rio Grande watershed in New Mexico.[60]

In February 1936, the Resettlement Administration further assisted the Indians by spending over $1.3 million for self-help projects. They included the development of canning kitchens, root cellars, sewing centers, and low-cost housing.[61] The Resettlement Administration placed special emphasis on creating subsistence homestead communities and clusters of white frame homes with communal garden tracts soon appeared on reservations in California, North and South Dakota, Washington, Oklahoma, and Arizona. Between 1936–1937 the number of units of fruits, vegetables, and meat canned increased from 765,051 to 1,898,579, while the pieces of clothing made jumped from 142,710 to 182,415.[62]

Secretary Ickes and Commissioner Collier were proud of their accomplishments in the area of conservation and public relief. Collier believed that the Indians had "best proved the efficacy of public works in a depression," and Ickes wrote a letter to President Roosevelt which pointed out "that he had been a real White Father to the Indians and they appreciated it deeply."[63] The secretary prophesized that "your administration will go down in history as the most humane and far seeing with respect to the Indians that this country ever had."[64]

This euphoria, however, did not alter the reality that the Indian New Deal conservation and public relief programs had many shortcomings. In Oklahoma, the Indian Civilian Conservation Corps program proved ineffective because Indian owned lands were widely scattered.[65] On the Klamath reservation in Oregon, an inexperienced all-Indian crew cut green timber in a beetle control project, causing the tribe to lose several hundred dollars.[66] Jacob Morgan, a member of the Navajo Tribal Council, believed that the government had wasted money on unnecessary personnel and useless equipment. He claimed that public relief money had resulted in groups of men "going to Gallup and other towns to buy booze."[67] In a more serious analysis, William Endersbee, a bureau employee, suggested that, except for a few reservations in the Southwest and plains states, land conservation had been "meager and spotty" because of inadequate funds.[68]

Many Indian relief programs which proved beneficial in the short run had little long range effect. Charles Young, supervisor of Indian Rehabilitation, concluded that the Resettlement Administration had enabled over 900 Indian families to construct new homes and farm buildings on land previously leased to whites. Nevertheless, this home improvement program proved ineffective because most reservation Indians continued to live in tents and shacks. Young estimated that 73 percent of Indian families still needed new or improved housing.[69] The same analysis applied to Indian relief under WPA, CWA, and NYA. These programs provided money to feed hungry families but failed to effect permanent changes in Indian poverty.

Collier paralleled his efforts to conserve Indian land and to provide public relief with an assault on the land allotment system. He rejected the idea that the Dawes Act had turned the Indians "into responsible self-supporting citizens" or enabled them "to enter urban industrial pursuits."[70] Instead, it had deprived them of vast quantities of property and created a class of landless paupers who depended upon the federal government. To solve this problem partially, he wrote a letter on August 12, 1933, to all of his superintendents to prohibit the sale of Indian trust land until further notice. The commissioner ordered the superintendents not to submit certificates of competency, patents in fee, or requests for the removal of restrictions on Indian property to the Indian Office. However, he did agree to make exceptions "in individual cases of great distress."[71]

Collier took this drastic action because he thought that the most pressing problem facing the bureau was lifting the Indians out of their "spiritual dependency and hopelessness," instead of absorbing them into the white population. If the Indians failed at the relatively simple task of farming, he doubted whether they could adopt to "the more exacting technology of urban industry." Collier believed that the depression demonstrated that the country had far too many industrial workers and a great surplus of land. The government, therefore, should pursue a policy of acquiring real estate to provide subsistence living for 90,000 landless Indians, who would not compete with white industrial labor or commercial agriculture. He advocated government loans to help established Indian farmers and suggested that the tribes undertake community ownership of existing forest, range, and agricultural lands to prevent these resources from being "exploited by whites."[72]

The commissioner continued his reform activities by persuading Secretary Ickes to implement a policy advocated by the Indian Defense Association during the previous decade. Ickes used a piece of legislation passed by Congress on July 1, 1932, which authorized him "to adjust or eliminate reimbursable charges," to cancel over $3,000,000 worth of Indian debts during the first year of the Indian New Deal.[73] By 1936, over $12,000,000 in debts for roads, bridges, tribal herds, and irrigation projects had been cancelled, including the $100,000 charge to the Navajos for the Lee's Ferry tourist bridge.[74]

Collier kept his promise to follow the educational program started during the Hoover administration, when he retained Will Carson Ryan as director of Indian education and accelerated the policy of replacing boarding schools with day schools.[75] Aided by reductions in regular appropriations during the depression, Collier closed six boarding schools on July 1, 1933, and reduced the enrollment at Haskell Institute in Lawrence, Kansas, from 900 to 600 students.* The commissioner then took advantage of PWA funds totaling $3,613,000 to construct 100 day schools.[76] He hoped that these schools would become the focal point for local administration and "community activities."[77]

The commissioner's educational reforms, however, occasionally met resistance from Indians. On the Navajo reservation, the government used PWA funds for the construction of day schools to accommodate 3,000 Indian children. Built with native materials by the Navajos under the supervision of white architects, these schools resembled large hogans.[78] According to Flora Warren Seymour, a former member of the Board of Indian Commissioners, and a critic of Collier's programs, many Navajos did "not want to revert to their old customs;" instead they favored continuing the boarding schools. She pointed out that many Indians viewed "with alternate amusement and disgust . . . the hogan schools with their low ceilings and dirt floors" that needed constant repair, and their hostile attitude had resulted in low attendance at the day schools and the overcrowding of missionary boarding facilities.[79]

Although some Indians resisted his educational reform, which eventually included the closing of twenty boarding schools, Collier pushed for greater experimentation when he appointed Willard W. Beatty, in 1936, to replace Ryan as director of Indian education. A progressive educator from Winnetka, Illinois, Beatty rejected the notion that the bureau should train Indians for non-existent urban jobs such as auto mechanics and masonry, so he altered Indian curriculum to help solve rural problems on the reservations.[80] Under his guidance, Indian children were taught to plant community gardens, care for livestock, and learn modern methods of conservation.[81] Day schools became centers for a variety of community activities where children and adults learned homemaking skills, attended health clinics, and perpetuated their native crafts and dances.[82]

---

*The six boarding schools closed were those at Genoa, Nebraska; Mt. Pleasant, Michigan; Hayward, Wisconsin; Rapid City, South Dakota; Theodore Roosevelt, Arizona; and Salem, Oregon. "Minutes of the Annual Meeting of the Board of Indian Commissioners, May 20, 1933, Washington, D.C.," NA, RG 75, Records of the Board of Indian Commissioners.

Beatty also tried to improve the professional standards of the bureau's teaching staff. He organized several summer school sessions at various boarding schools to offer classes in anthropology, home economics, rural sociology, arts and crafts, health education, and native languages.[83] Especially interested in bilingual education because he believed it would encourage Indian literacy, Beatty ordered many schools to use bilingual textbooks, dictionaries, and motion pictures.[84] He persuaded officials at the University of Oklahoma to offer courses in Indian languages, but according to Collier, they came "too late to resurrect Oklahoma Indian languages in teachable form."[85]

Other problems that Collier failed to mention continued to plague Indian education. The bureau's budget, excluding relief funds, diminished during the New Deal from an all time high in 1932 of $11,224,000 to $10,523,475 by 1940. This prevented the commissioner from providing adequate facilities for thousands of Indian children who remained out of school. And he added to this misfortune by making budget miscalculations. On the Navajo reservation his appropriation requests in 1937 allowed only thirteen cents per day for noon meals at day schools, a figure far below the minimum recommended by the Meriam Report. This mistake forced the bureau to divert funds authorized for children's clothing in order to supply adequate food.[86]

Unfortunately, the day school program was a failure among the Navajos. These Indians opposed this innovation because they received fewer meals at day schools than at boarding facilities, and they disliked the government's decision to discontinue clothing allotments because of budgetary restrictions. Other difficulties included bad roads causing low attendance, the shortage of fresh water for children, and the migratory habits of the Navajos.[87]

Furthermore, the bureau's progressive education policies led to the neglect of boarding schools, which remained in a dilapidated condition. They also faltered because of the shortage of properly trained teachers. According to Ben Reifel, a Brule Sioux, the older instructors never adjusted to the John Dewey method. These "poor teachers were just going around because they had never been taught to handle the situation." Reifel claimed that while Indian children benefited from knowing how to raise rabbits and chickens, they often failed to learn how to read and write properly.[88]

The commissioner paralleled his educational innovations with an effort to improve Indian health conditions. In 1933 he obtained $1,735,000 from the Public Works Administration to begin construction of eleven Indian hospitals and to improve ten existing facilities.[89] An increase in general health appropriations of almost half a million dollars allowed Collier to hire more part-time physicians, dentists, and nurses.[90] Furthermore, trachoma cases diminished significantly because of a new sulfanilamide medication, and many Indians participated in a tuberculosis vaccination program.* In addition, the bureau opened a TB sanitorium at Albuquerque and a trachoma hospital at Toadlena, New Mexico.[91]

The most dramatic example of Collier's concern about Indian health focused around an episode which involved the Hiawatha Insane Asylum for Indians at Canton, South Dakota. In 1929, Dr. Samuel Silk, the medical director at Saint Elizabeth's Hospital in Washington, D.C., had made a full investigation at Canton where he found such intolerable conditions as antiquated plant equipment, filthy living quarters, untrained employees, and abused inmates.[92] Concerned about this report, bureau officials hoped to improve the medical care for these Indians, but they found it impossible to obtain appropriations from Congress because of the depression.

This inability to improve conditions at Canton worried Charles Lowndes, a member of the Board of Indian Commissioners, who visited the Hiawatha Asylum during October 1932. He found that little had changed during four years and blamed Congress for refusing to appropriate funds that would allow the transfer of these Indians to St. Elizabeth's Hospital.[93] But he was rebuffed by Flora Warren Seymour, another member of the board, who defended the inaction of the bureau. She traveled to Canton during the following spring and found little wrong with the conditions at the asylum. Seymour reported that the Indians were adequately fed and sheltered, although she admitted that something might be done to encourage occupational therapy.[94]

While visiting Santa Clara Pueblo during the summer of 1933, Collier had promised the wife of an inmate at the Hiawatha Asylum that he would investigate the possibility of securing the release of her husband. When the commissioner looked into the matter he found that the bureau conducted what he called "an institution so outrageously cruel and injurious that we would deserve to be blown out of the water if we continued it."[95] Immediately, Collier asked Dr. Silk to make another investigation at Canton and he reported that conditions remained unimproved and that inmates were still "kept shackled to beds or water pipes." Silk made the grave charge that a few patients had been placed at the asylum "after some slight difficulty at school or on the reservation."[96]

---

*Between 1939 and 1943 trachoma cases fell from 20.2 percent to 7.2 percent of the Indian population. But Collier admitted before congressional hearings that Indian Medical Service appropriations remained "tragically inadequate" because of continued budgetary restrictions. U.S., Congress, House, Committee on Indian Affairs, *Hearings, on H.R. 7781, Indian Conditions and Affairs,* 74th Cong., 1st Sess., 1935, p. 744.

His worse suspicions confirmed, Collier wrote to Secretary Ickes explaining the adverse report made by Dr. Silk with the recommendation that "Canton should be abolished entirely and its personnel discharged." The commissioner suggested that they use Public Works Administration funds to build an extension on Saint Elizabeth's Hospital in order to facilitate the transfer of the Canton Indians.[97] The secretary agreed with these proposals and supported Collier, who then wrote a letter of dismissal to Dr. Harry Hummer, the superintendent at Canton for twenty-five years.[98]

Collier told Dr. Hummer that he was discharged, not because of failure due to limitations in plant and equipment, but because he had permitted "acts of needless cruelty" such as the chaining of Indians to beds. His policy of locking Indians in rooms and dormitories without an attendant could have led to extermination in case of fire. The commissioner criticized Dr. Hummer for allowing unsanitary conditions to exist and for being careless in the keeping of case records. He reminded the superintendent that he had held at least ten Indians who were unaffected by psychoses. Collier saw in this picture "misfeasance and malfeasance of extreme character . . . and of practically complete failure of medical administration."[99]

Dr. Hummer responded to Collier by calling the government's charges "lies, all lies."[100] He received support from some whites and Indians living at Canton, who persuaded the federal district court in Washington, D.C. to issue a temporary injunction preventing the removal of insane Indians to St. Elizabeth's Hospital. An article in the *New York Times* indicated that this action stemmed from a desire by local residents to preserve their $40,000 annual revenue from the institution. This allegation contained some truth, but several Indians opposed relocating the asylum because they disliked the idea of having their friends and relatives moved to far-away Washington. Unimpressed by these objections, Collier successfully transferred the Indians to the nation's capital.[101]

The most controversial executive reforms instigated by Collier consisted of two executive orders. They limited the influence of missionaries over Indian education and symbolized the anticlerical thinking permeating much of the Indian New Deal. The first order, dated January 3, 1934, was entitled "Indian Religious Freedom and Indian Culture." It demanded that "the fullest constitutional liberty, in all matters affecting religion, conscience, and culture exist for all Indians," and, furthermore, that an "affirmative, appreciative attitude" toward native heritage was desired in the Indian Service.[102]

The second order, dated January 15, 1934, curtailed missionary activity at Indian boarding and day schools. It prohibited compulsory attendance at religious services, but allowed ("as a privilege but not as a right") any denomination, including representatives of a native Indian religion, to use the facilities at boarding schools for religious instruction on the condition that the children's attendance was by personal or parental choice. This second order also limited religious exercises at Indian day schools. Any child, however, upon the written request of his parents, might be excused for religious training, including instruction in a native Indian religion, for one hour each week. The government would loan day school facilities to denominational bodies only when not in use by the Indian Service or the community.[103]

These orders struck at the heart of missionary work on the reservations and brought a protest from both Indians and whites. Upset at Collier's two orders, 962 parents of approximately 3,000 Sioux children at the Pine Ridge reservation in South Dakota sent a petition to Mrs. Eleanor Roosevelt. Enclosed in a buckskin case bordered with red, white, and blue beads around a gold cross, it accused Collier of planning to close both their missionary and boarding schools for day schools. Demonstrating little interest in preserving their native religion, these Indians wanted to continue Christian education on the reservation.[104]

Activities in Oklahoma offered another example of the hostility manifested by many clergymen and Indians toward Collier's policy of religious freedom. Fearing that the government might prohibit their religious work among the Indians, two ministers called a protest meeting on November 1, 1934, at Oklahoma City. Over twenty missionaries representing twelve denominations assembled at the Oklahoma capital, and they adopted a resolution suggesting that Collier study the pagan religions to which he encouraged the Indians to return.* In a separate statement, the Baptist General Convention, which represented 185,000 white and Indian Baptists, criticized any policy that interfered with their work in the government schools and supported the revival of demoralizing ceremonial expressions such as the use of peyote by the Native American Church.[105]

One day later, in an interview reported by the Associated Press, Collier criticized the "small minority" among the missionaries who agitated for the denial of liberty of conscience to the Indians. He rejected the missionaries' demand that the Indian Bureau use official coercion to place Indian children in denominational classes even when their parents belonged to other faiths. He called such a policy "an outrage upon human nature as well as an express violation of the Constitution."[106]

---

*The leaders of this protest were G. Lee Phelps, a member of the Baptist Home Mission Board from Wetumka, Oklahoma; and Dr. G. E. E. Lindquist, a former member of the Board of Indian Commissioners, from Lawrence, Kansas, who had directed missionary work for the YMCA. John Collier, "Memo for Secretary Ickes, November 2, 1934," NA, RG 75, File on Adverse Propaganda.

When this reply failed to stifle criticism, the commissioner sent a lengthy letter to the Oklahoma *Tushkahomman,* which rejected the accusation that he was an infidel and atheist, hostile to the Christian religion. He reminded the missionaries that liberty of conscience in America was never meant only for those who professed Christianity. Collier pointed out that the bureau favored a protective attitude toward native Indian religions because they "had been forged out through thousands of years of striving and endurance, and search for truth," and because they contained "deep beauty, spiritual guidance, consolation, and disciplinary power."[107]

The missionaries who saw Collier as antireligious were misinformed. The commissioner expressed his interest in the spiritual rejuvenation of America when he told the Christianized Indian students at Bacone College near Muskogee, Oklahoma, that "the light which streams from 2,000 years ago" was now kindled for Indians as well as for many other Americans. Collier called upon these students to bring their "native endowment to the renewal of religion" in the United States. He told them that "religious-mindedness" — one of the most universal and emphasized traits of the Indian race — was needed, because religion has come to run thin "in the present day white world."[108]

The commissioner followed his departmental orders on Indian religious freedom with a successful attempt to secure the passage of several important pieces of legislation. In January 1934, he transmitted to Senator Burton K. Wheeler the draft of a bill to abolish twelve archaic espionage and gag rules affecting Indians.[109] Enacted in May, this act repealed statutes which had authorized military activities on the reservations, required foreigners entering Indian country to secure passports from the Department of the Interior, and prohibited the sending of seditious messages to Indians. It also cancelled the power of the commissioner to remove from Indian land persons whose presence he considered detrimental to the peace and welfare of the Indians.*

Collier then threw "whole hearted" administration support behind the Johnson-O'Malley bill, a measure similar to the Swing-Johnson proposal that had faltered in Congress during the last days of the Hoover presidency.[110] Passed during April 1934, it allowed the secretary of the interior to provide money for local assistance in the areas of Indian health, education, agriculture, and social welfare.[111] Collier had great

---

*In 1935, Secretary Harold L. Ickes requested the repeal of 36 additional obsolete sections of the U.S. Code dealing with Indians but Congress refused to act on this matter. Felix Cohen, *Handbook of Federal Indian Law* (Washington: Government Printing Office, 1942), pp. 174–75.

hope for the Johnson-O'Malley measure, but the impact of this reform was minimal, especially in the area of education, for three reasons: 1. the bureau failed to retain control over its funds; 2. animosity developed between federal and state administrators; and 3. the public schools refused to establish special Indian programs.[112]

Finally, Collier completed plans started by President Herbert Hoover for the expansion of the Navajo reservation. Early in 1934, the Interior Department endorsed two bills authorizing $481,879 for Arizona, and $482,186 for New Mexico, reimbursable from the Navajo treasury, to consolidate Navajo land on the public domain. This legislation allowed whites, who owned land in the checkerboarded area, to select other public lands outside the enlarged reservation, and permitted the Indians to purchase the remaining privately owned lands from the Santa Fe Railroad. The Arizona bill passed during June and added approximately one million acres to the Navajo reservation in that state. But the House killed the New Mexico bill after it passed the Senate.[113]

Dr. Haven Emerson, president of the American Indian Defense Association, believed that Collier had finished a remarkable initial year in office. The commissioner justified his appointment when he implemented a policy of religious liberty and cultural freedom for all Indians, stopped the further sale of tribal land, supported the Swing-Johnson bill, used PWA funds to build new day schools and hospitals, exposed the notorious Canton Insane Asylum, and helped establish an Indian CCC. On the debit side, Emerson warned that Collier needed to cut "bureaucratic red tape" and implement more of the Meriam Report's recommendations, such as the improvement of bureau personnel.[114]

Collier agreed that he needed to expand his reform program. He believed that all of his previous achievements would be "temporary structures built on sand" unless he altered the Dawes General Allotment Act.[115] Consequently, he drew up legislation to restore tribal self-government and communal ownership of land.

7. Failure To Create a Red Atlantis

Because of his interest in reversing the land allotment policy, Commissioner Collier called a conference on January 7, 1934, at the Cosmos Club in Washington, D.C., to unite various groups such as the American Indian Defense Association, the Indian Rights Association, and the National Association on Indian Affairs behind a program of legislation to replace the Dawes General Allotment Act.* Lewis Meriam, who had directed a private investigation of the bureau during 1926, under the auspices of the Institute for Government Research, chaired this session. Other notable guests included Anna W. Ickes, wife of the secretary of the interior; J. Henry Scattergood, former assistant commissioner; and Dr. Moises Saenz, educator and scholar on Indian life from Mexico.[1]

The delegates at the Cosmos Club followed many of the suggestions in Meriam's published report, *The Problem of Indian Administration,* and they reached a "unanimous conclusion" concerning what reforms Congress should enact. They wanted to repeal the land allotment law, consolidate Indian heirship and trust lands for agricultural purposes, promote tribal ownership of grazing and forest lands, and acquire additional land

---

*Other welfare groups attending this conference included the American Civil Liberties Union, the National Council of American Indians, and the General Federation of Women's Clubs. In 1933 the Eastern Association on Indian Affairs changed its name to the National Association on Indian Affairs to get away from implied sectionalism. D'Arcy McNickle, *Indian Man: A Life of Oliver La Farge* (Bloomington: Indiana University Press, 1971), pp. 90–91.

Collier as caricaturized
in the *Washington Post.*

Yale University Library

for landless Indians. Another proposal suggested that the government
provide a system of credit to further Indian economic development; this
would allow the bureau to gradually transfer its powers into organized
Indian communities. Finally, the delegates indicated that Congress should
return the Five Civilized Tribes in Oklahoma to federal control and settle
all claims arising from broken treaties.[2]

Delighted with the suggestions offered at this conference, Collier
pushed forward with his plans to end the land allotment system. He had
already sent a questionnaire to various superintendents and anthropologists to survey the economic and political conditions on various reservations. The commissioner was particularly interested in finding the
potential for cooperative economic activity that existed in tribal social
structures because he wanted to enlarge "tribal ownership of land in lieu
of the present system of allotments."[3]

The response to this "questionnaire" varied from extreme pessimism to guarded optimism. Ralph Linton, an anthropologist from the University of Wisconsin who had studied the Commanches in southwestern Oklahoma, warned Collier that any plans to resurrect tribal political and economic life among these Indians would meet with failure because they seemed quite content with their individual land allotments and feared only the loss of land to white real estate interests. Linton concluded that the Commanches were adjusting well to white culture and if the government protected their land rights for another fifteen years, they would be as self-reliant as their white neighbors.[4]

Oliver La Farge, the president of the National Association on Indian Affairs and an expert on Indians in the southwestern part of the United States, also answered Collier's "questionnaire" with candor. He pointed out that many Navajos favored individual ownership of property such as sheep and allotments on the public domain, but they needed large blocks of communal land for grazing purposes. La Farge indicated that the Navajo Tribal Council was effective and well established, but sectionalism might develop in the future between older conservatives and the younger progressives. As far as the Hopi were concerned, they approved of collective ownership of land, but he doubted whether these Indians could develop a viable tribal government because authority rested in separate villages.[5]

Finally, La Farge commented on the economic and political situation among the New Mexico Pueblos. He believed that they favored any plan concerning the collective ownership of land because the ultimate title to their property already rested with the tribe. Nevertheless, La Farge had qualms about the viability of Pueblo self-government. These Indians had traditionally run their own affairs, but their government consisted of an unusual blend of democracy and absolutism which often worked very badly. Ultimate authority in each Pueblo rested with a priest called a cacique, while the people elected a governor and counsellors who handled civil matters. In theory, the governors and their advisors were selected alternately from two groups called Summer and Winter People. If a dispute started between these two moieties, the Indians supposedly thrashed the matter out in a meeting of the whole Pueblo. What had happened in practice, however, was the growth of factionalism and hostility, which led to the breakdown of Pueblo self-government. At Santa Clara, for example, the alternating system of government had disintegrated to the point where each moiety simultaneously elected its own governor.[6]

Despite these warnings that his plans for a revival of tribal authority might prove difficult, Collier sent a lengthy circular entitled "Indian Self-Government" to superintendents, tribal councils, and individual Indians.[7] Dated January 20, 1934, it stressed that the government planned to reorganize Indian administration and suggested that the superintendents and tribal councils engage in a "free and frank" discussion of alternatives to the land allotment policy and consider plans for enlarged self-government. Within three weeks they were to send their recommendations to the bureau so that it could draw up appropriate legislation.[8]

Collier offered a guideline of the changes that he wanted. First, the Indians needed to alter their system of land tenure to "assure to all Indians born on the reservation a fair share of land." Tribes could accomplish this by transferring individual control over their property to a corporation; in return, they would receive "a proportionate interest in the entire land holdings of the community." Such a system would permit them to establish proper timber, grazing, and farm units. Collier pointed out that the Indians should discuss the possibility of increasing their powers of self-government by organizing chartered municipal corporations with the powers of "a village or county government." Gradually assuming the powers exercised by the Indian Bureau, these autonomous Indian communities would elect their own officers, control the expenditure of tribal funds, assume responsibility for law and order, and engage in "cooperative marketing and purchasing." It might be necessary for an Indian community to "require all its members to take part in common labor such as irrigation and the construction of homes."[9]

Expecting general approval of his plan for "Indian Self-Government," Collier must have been dismayed by the negative response from many Indian tribes and their superintendents. Opposition proved strong on reservations where land allotment had broken down tribal life. Americanized Indians, who had become assimilated, were especially hostile to his circular. They objected to relinquishing individual allotments for community ownership and feared that the creation of self-governing communities would restore outdated traditions. Many superintendents also opposed the measure because it might eliminate their jobs.

W. O. Roberts, superintendent of the Rosebud Indian Agency, told Collier that his circular had created a tumultuous situation among the Sioux. Roberts indicated that it was a fatal error to treat the Sioux in the same manner as the southwestern Indians, and he suggested that the restoration of self-governing tribal communities might apply to the Navajo but not to the Sioux, because jealousy and hatred existed between the full and mixed-bloods. The superintendent warned that the possibility of returning restricted alloted land to tribal ownership upset the full-bloods who had kept their land. They believed that he favored the mixed-bloods, who had lost their property to the whites. Roberts pointed out that the preservation of Sioux culture would prove difficult because these Indians had forgotten most of their cultural heritage, and they looked to the missionaries for guidance.[10]

Two other superintendents who wrote Collier also doubted whether his plan would work in their jurisdiction: O. H. Lipps, superintendent at the Sacramento Indian Agency in California, pointed out that the California Indians lived in small groups on rancherias, public domain homesteads, and allotments in over forty counties. Never a united people, these Indians constantly engaged in family feuds, petty jealousies, and tribal factions that would make it difficult for them to work together for their common welfare.[11] In a similar vein, Superintendent P. W. Danielson warned Collier that the tribal business committees representing the Five Civilized Tribes in eastern Oklahoma, who owned land, had rejected his proposal because they had little interest in sharing property with those who had dissipated their holdings.[12]

Many tribes wrote him directly and voiced conflicting opinions over his plan for "Indian Self-Government." Carpio Martinez, the governor of San Juan Pueblo, reported that his tribe favored the proposed changes as long as they did not interfere with their traditional form of self-government.[13] The Eastern Band of Cherokees in North Carolina offered a more sophisticated reply. They agreed in principle to a larger degree of self-government and control of their land but reminded the commissioner that they had already managed their own affairs by incorporation under the laws of the State of North Carolina. The Cherokees saw little need to modify this arrangement which had worked satisfactorily, but they believed that it would be advantageous to operate in the future under a federal charter because most of their business was concentrated at the national level.[14] However, they offered several objections to Collier's reform program. They favored continued enforcement of law and order by the state and stressed that voluntary organizations, such as their handicraft guild, undertake the purchasing and selling of community products. They also recommended that individual members keep their heirship rights even though the land ultimately belonged to the tribe, and they saw little reason for changing the present method of controlling the expenditures of tribal funds which depended upon a congressional authorization.[15]

Other Indians who had undergone land allotment offered more opposition. Fifty-two members of the Arapaho tribe on the Wind River reservation in Wyoming indicated that the time was not ripe for extreme change. They called the idea of community government foreign to the Plains Indians and opposed communal ownership of property as unsuited to their tribe.[16] They were joined by several Sioux at the Cheyenne Agency in South Dakota, who claimed the era for community organization had passed, and they worried about being segregated from the state and local government.[17] The Assiniboine and Atsina Indians at the Fort Belknap reservation in Montana stated that they would refuse to relinquish their allotments without suitable financial reimbursement but favored the establishment of some form of community government.[18] Tribes such as the Blackfeet in Montana, the Shawnee in Oklahoma, the Southern Utes in Colorado, and the natives living on the Colville reservation in Washington also registered various objections to Collier's circular.[19]

These warnings worried Collier, but he remained convinced that the Indians could become "pioneers" in President Roosevelt's effort to substitute "conscious planning" for aimless drift.[20] Consequently, he united the recommendations made at the Cosmos Club with some of his own ideas and ordered the solicitor's office to draw up an omnibus bill incorporating a new Indian policy to replace the land allotment system.* Collier knew that the Indians were "unacquainted with its most essential provisions," but he hoped that a single legislative measure "would have a massive and dramatic nature, commanding the imagination of Indians and Congressmen alike."[21]

Introduced in mid-February 1934 by Edgar Howard of Nebraska and Senator Burton K. Wheeler of Montana, as an administration measure, this bill made up a forty-eight page document containing four major sections. It reflected Collier's ideas concerning democratic colonial administration. Deeply influenced by Julian Huxley's *African View,* the commissioner rejected the existing policy of "direct rule," where the central government imposed its will through a large bureaucracy. He favored Huxley's concept of "indirect rule" as the way into the future for the American Indian.† Collier believed that the federal government should use native institutions as the vehicle for progressive social change. He hoped that the bill would encourage local pride and initiative while blocking white "predatory exploitation" through the technique of "democratic communal organization."[22]

Collier wanted to follow the example of the Friar Bartolomé de Las Casas, who had attacked Spanish colonialism in the New World. Famous for his book, *History of the Indies,* Las Casas believed that the Indians lived in a golden age untainted by the corruptions of civilization. He thought that their social, economic, and religious institutions were "not only good but excellent and far superior to those of many other nations."[23]

---

*Nathan Margold, solicitor for the Interior Department, and his assistants Felix Cohen and Charles Fahy, helped formulate the Wheeler-Howard bill. John Collier, "The Purposes and Operations of the Wheeler-Howard Indian Rights Bill, February 19, 1934," Library of Congress, Bronson Cutting Papers, Box 30.

†Collier was also influenced by the writing of Sir Edward Maine, a British author, who wrote about village life in India, and Lester Frank Ward, the American sociologist, who called for "attractive legislation" in his book *The Psychic Factors of Civilization.* John Collier, *American Indian Life,* July 1931, pp. 32–38; and John Collier, "Sir Henry Maine and the Primitive Communities of British India and the Suggestion for American Indian Policy," NA, RG 316, Series 1, Item 43.

Collier agreed and hoped that the Wheeler-Howard bill would establish Las Casas' "utopian dream" of a "free co-operative commonwealth" which the Jesuits had created in Paraguay early in the seventeenth century.[24]

Title I of the Wheeler-Howard bill, called "Indian Self-Government," provided for the renewal of Indian political and social structures destroyed by the Dawes General Allotment Act. It reaffirmed the right of tribal societies to control their lives and property by establishing a system of home rule under federal guidance. When twenty-five percent of the adult population on any reservation asked for home rule, subject to ratification by three-fifths of the adult population that participated in the election, tribal communities would receive charters of incorporation. These charters allowed tribal societies to establish federal corporations, exempt from taxation, with the powers to operate property of every description. They could borrow money for economic development from a revolving five million dollar credit fund and exercise all powers consistent "with the Constitution of the United States."[25]

According to Collier, Indian communities would eventually assume the powers of the Interior Department relating to Indians. He pointed out that the bill authorized the government to turn over to chartered communities the lands, buildings, and equipment of the Indian Service, and to spend an annual sum of $500,000 for the construction of new municipal facilities. These chartered communities had the authority to compel the transfer of undesirable federal employees after receiving approval from the commissioner. In order to prevent the construction of useless irrigation and other public projects, the government could not impose on chartered tribes a reimbursable debt without their consent or have tribal funds spent without authorization from a community official. The Indians were to receive copies of all bills affecting them, and they could offer suggestions concerning Interior Department appropriation requests sent to Congress and the Bureau of the Budget. If any person left a chartered community, he would receive compensation for his assets.[26]

Title II of the Wheeler-Howard bill, entitled "Special Education for Indians," reflected Collier's view that the government must preserve the rich values of Indian life.* Stating that Congress intended "to promote the study of Indian civilization," Title II directed the commissioner

---

*The Wheeler-Howard bill exempted the Indians of New York from all of its provisions except Title II concerning education. It did not prevent the removal of restrictions on taxable lands of members of the Five Civilized Tribes or change current laws relating to the guardianship of minor and incompetent members of the Osage or Five Civilized Tribes. H.R. 7902, February 12, 1934, NA, RG 75, Records Concerning the Wheeler-Howard Act.

to use the staffs of existing boarding schools to prepare courses in Indian history, arts and crafts, including the problems of Indian administration. It provided chartered communities with an annual $50,000 appropriation for training in their peculiar social and economic problems such as public health, management of forests, law enforcement, and the keeping of financial records. If Indian students lacked money for this special education, the government paid all expenses with half the tuition becoming a non-interest reimbursable debt, except during periods of unemployment. Indians of exceptional ability might receive free tuition from a $15,000 annual scholarship fund.[27]

Title III, the most controversial part of the bill, proposed to establish an agricultural revolution on Indian land. Influenced by Mexico's *ejido* program, which restored land under communal title to Indian villages, Collier believed that the government could do little of lasting consequence to assist the Indians without basic "land reform."[28] Title III prohibited future land allotment, restored to tribal ownership existing surplus lands created by the Dawes General Allotment Act, extended restrictions on the alienation of allotted land, and prevented the future sale of community property to non-Indians. In order to assist landless Indians, it authorized an annual appropriation of two million dollars to purchase new land for existing reservations or to establish new colonies for scattered groups of Indians.[29]

The most radical sections of Title III concerned procedures to consolidate allotted and heirship lands into viable economic units for community use. Compulsory in nature, these sections directed the secretary of the interior to acquire restricted allotted land through "purchase, relinquishment, gift, exchange, or assignment," for the purpose of providing community land for landless Indians and for consolidating checkerboard reservations. In exchange, the allottee received a non-transferable descendible certificate evidencing a proportionate interest in tribal lands of similar quality. As well as abolishing inheritance among Indians, Title III directed that all restricted property revert to tribal ownership after the death of the allottee. In return, the heirs obtained equivalent interest in tribal lands. To solve the problem of existing heirship lands, the bill authorized the secretary of the interior to sell this land to Indian communities, who would pay the heirs money equal to the annual rental of the land or the equivalent right to use tribal property. If a fee patent had been issued, the Indian could either keep his land or voluntarily return it for equal rights in community property.[30]

Title IV, the last part of the Wheeler-Howard bill, established a federal court of Indian affairs to provide a just, speedy, and inexpensive determination of legal controversies affecting chartered Indian communities. Consisting of a chief judge and six associate judges appointed by the president with the consent of the Senate, this court could exercise its authority either in full session or through one of its judges assigned to an Indian circuit court in a particular locality. Although holding office for ten years, the judges could be removed by the president "for any cause," with the approval of the Senate.[31]

The court's jurisdiction extended over all matters affecting Indian chartered communities, such as the right of individual Indians to allotments and the question of heirship rights. The court had authority over cases involving crimes committed on reservations and litigation where an Indian was at least one party. Local Indian courts had power to impose fines of up to $500 and jail sentences of six months, but defendants could appeal most of their decisions to the federal court of Indian affairs. To assist the Indians in these legal matters, Title IV gave the secretary of the interior the power to appoint ten special attorneys to help interpret Indian law and take over the function of existing probate attorneys. Individuals could challenge all decisions of the Indian court either in the circuit court of appeals or eventually before the Supreme Court.[32]

Collier favored establishing this federal Indian court for several reasons. He pointed out that existing federal courts only had jurisdiction over a few major crimes such as murder, arson, rape, and incest. In other matters Congress had neglected to create judicial machinery that handled the problem of law and order. Consequently, most legal problems on the reservations were settled in arbitrary administrative tribunals operated by the Indian Service. These tribunals did not provide attorneys or jury trials; instead, the superintendent and his appointed Indian judges made decisions that could be appealed only to the secretary of the interior.[33] Collier feared that if controversies involving chartered communities were litigated in existing federal courts delays would put endless obstacles in the way of self-government and the return of land to communal ownership. He wanted an Indian court because the Indians used the services of the nearest district court, often hundreds of miles away, only with great expense and difficulty. Collier doubted whether the state courts could deal with these matters because the proposed chartered communities existed as agencies of the federal government.[34]

When the Wheeler-Howard bill passed through Congress during February 1934, it met resistance from members of the House and Senate Indian Affairs Committees, who feared a policy of segregation and doubted the wisdom of communal ownership of property. Theodore Werner, a representative from South Dakota, told Collier that he disliked the measure because it isolated the Indian "and made it impossible for him to ever become an assimilated part of the citizenship of the country."[35] The commissioner replied by citing the Mormons as an example of unique citizens who had the "advantages of cooperative living," but Werner still feared that the Indians would remain under the thumb of an unresponsive federal bureaucracy.[36] He opposed the bill because it contained unconstitutional sections depriving the Indians of their vested rights.

In the Senate Indian Affairs Committee, Collier faced the hostility of Senator Henry F. Ashurst from Arizona, who thought that the Wheeler-Howard bill would give the secretary of the interior the power to extend the exterior boundary of the Papago reservation. This proved a mistaken assumption, but Ashurst blocked further discussion of the legislation until he aired a problem that existed between the Papagos and whites in Arizona. The senator was particularly upset at a decision made by former Secretary of the Interior Ray Lyman Wilbur to temporarily withdraw certain Papago lands from mineral entry. Wilbur had taken this action on October 12, 1932, to prevent further harm to the Indian livestock industry and to give Congress a chance "to consider the claim of the Indians to the mineral rights within those lands."[37]

This executive order stirred up controversy because most whites in Arizona insisted that the Papagos did not own the subsurface rights to their land. Ashurst pointed out that under the Gadsden Purchase Treaty of December 30, 1853, the Papagos relinquished legal title to land in his state unless they had land grants recorded in the archives of Mexico. He indicated that the whites had agreed to President Woodrow Wilson's executive order in 1917, adding over 2,000,000 acres to existing Papago land, because it was expressly stipulated that subsurface mineral rights remain under government control and "subject to the existing mining laws of the United States." This had resulted in 122 claims for gold, copper, and silver mines, covering approximately 2,400 acres.[38]

These precedents, however, had been challenged by the Hunter-Martin claims. In 1880 several Papago Indians drew up sixteen deeds to land in certain of their villages; one deed included 16 million acres in the southwestern portion of Arizona. The Indians gave one-half interest in these lands to Colonel Robert F. Hunter, a Washington attorney, who worked to validate their title. For some unknown reason Hunter refused to record these deeds, but in 1911, he entered into a contract with another attorney named Martin who attempted to establish Indian ownership in return for a three-fourths interest from Hunter. Three years later, Martin instituted a suit in the Supreme Court on one of the deeds covering the village of Santa Rosa in order to prove Papago title under Mexican land grants. The Interior Department had fought this case and the Court declared the deed void because it failed to follow the guidelines required by federal statutes. But the Court left the door open for further litigation by claiming that its decision should not prejudice the "bringing of any other suit" to recover Papago property.[39]

Ashurst told the Senate committee that this loophole had enabled

Secretary Wilbur to hire the law firm of Graves, Slemp, and Calhoun on a 10 percent fee basis to determine the validity of the Hunter claims. The senator then asked Collier if he approved of this contract.[40] The commissioner, who had been a militant concerning Indian mineral rights during the twenties, gave a moderate reply. Worried about the passage of the Wheeler-Howard bill and convinced that the Papagos lacked evidence concerning Mexican grants, he doubted whether they owned the minerals. But he refused to withdraw Wilbur's order preventing further mining because nobody could forbid these Indians "their day in court."[41] The hearings ended on this note with little progress made toward discussing the Wheeler-Howard proposal.

In response to the hostility he found in Congress and because of the opposition of several tribes to his earlier circular, "Indian Self-Government," Collier took an unprecedented step. He decided to call a series of Indian congresses to discuss the controversial features of the Wheeler-Howard bill and gain Indian support before returning to Congress. Announcing his decision in a press release, the commissioner cited a recent dispatch from the Umatilla reservation at Pendleton, Oregon, as an example of misunderstanding concerning the bill. Victimized by white "leasing and land grabbing interests," these Indians had written him a letter of protest stating "thumbs down on Socialization and Communism."[42]

Collier hoped that the Indian congresses would dispel such unfounded anxiety. He believed that once the Indians realized the bill safeguarded their "vested rights" to allotted and inherited land they would support the administration. The commissioner thought that he could convince the tribes that municipal home rule, cooperative merchandizing, cattle users associations, and corporations were not "socialistic devices, but commonplace necessities of modern life."[43]

Eventually ten congresses were held in various parts of the country, and Collier personally attended most of these meetings. He opened the sessions with a general discussion concerning the evils of the Dawes General Allotment Act and asked for written questions concerning the Wheeler-Howard bill. Many natives supported the commissioner, but frequently he faced hostility from those who viewed the reservation as a prison, where they were held captives, instead of a viable community. They disliked the bill because it destroyed their heirship rights and confiscated their allotted land to give to poor Indians.*

---

*Indian Congresses were held at Rapid City, South Dakota, March 2–5, 1934; Chemawa, Oregon, March 8–9; Fort Defiance, Arizona, March 12–13; Santo Domingo, New Mexico, March 15; Phoenix, Arizona, March 16; Riverside, California, March 17–18; Anadarko, Oklahoma, March 20; Muskogee, Oklahoma, March 22–23; Miami, Oklahoma, March 24; and Hayward, Wisconsin, April 23–24.

Mrs. John Collier, Sr.

Blackfoot Indians and John Collier, at the Rapid City Indian Congress, March 3, 1934.

When the Plains Indian Congress met at Rapid City, South Dakota, on March 2, 1934, for a four-day conference, Collier spoke before 200 delegates from 40 tribes representing a population of 60,000. At this first meeting he confronted "a horde of resentful redmen who glowered in the background," afraid that the bill inaugurated a "back to the blanket movement," and they immediately rejected his suggestion that an Indian preside over the meeting.[44] Aware that he faced a hostile crowd, Collier asked the delegates to reject any fixed ideas about the legislation and "have open minds" because the proceedings of the conference would be read by members of the House and Senate Committees on Indian Affairs.[45]

In an attempt to allay their fears, Collier told them that the bureau could have pushed the Wheeler-Howard bill "quickly and quietly" through Congress, but it wanted their advice on this important matter. Once they understood the bill, he maintained they would back him "practically one-hundred percent." He then proceeded to launch into a lengthy attack against the evils of the allotment system, using maps and charts of allotted reservations to clarify his arguments. According to Collier, this policy had resulted in the loss of 80 percent of their land. The Oklahoma Indians, for example, had twenty-three million acres before allotment, and all of this property had "melted away" except three million acres. The problem of heirship lands had brought economic disaster because once the allottee died his estate was probated and passed into heirship status. It became necessary under law to sell the land and divide the proceeds among the heirs or lease it and distribute the rental in a similar manner. Because of the large number of descendants, this had resulted in cases where individuals received as little as two and one-half cents a year for their interests in an allotment.[46]

Collier stressed that the Wheeler-Howard bill solved these problems by ending the allotment policy and returning heirship lands to communal ownership. This legislation allowed Indians "to organize for mutual benefit, for local self-government, and for doing business in the modern organized way." Tribes could use the bill's credit system to establish cattlemen's associations and cooperative societies, such as creameries, in order to "cut out the middleman's profits." He rejected the notion that his plans were Communism and argued that both he and President Roosevelt wanted to help the "forgotten man." By allowing them to organize chartered communities and business corporations, the bill helped the Indians, "who were staggering under the burden of the rich." They could use this legislation to get the "blind giant of big business off their back."[47]

This rhetoric failed to satisfy many Indians who were "boiling over with questions," so Collier opened the floor to discussion when the second session of the Rapid City Congress convened on March 3.* Most of the Indians' uncertainty concerned the section of the bill which gave the secretary of the interior the arbitrary power to transfer the title of allotted land to community ownership. Collier pointed out that this provision protected Indian rights because they received a proportionate interest in tribal lands of similar quality. But he agreed to amend this "relatively unimportant point" and make all land exchange voluntary after most delegates indicated that they disliked this part of the bill. He promised that they would retain all subsurface rights to oil and other minerals on their land, even if the government returned it to community ownership.[48]

Several Sioux also objected to the provision of the Wheeler-Howard bill that gave the Indians a veto power over the expenditure of tribal money. They feared that some of their leaders might stop paying the tuition of children attending mission schools with money from "treaty

---

*Dr. Henry Roe Cloud, a Winnebago educator at Haskell Institute, spoke at this and other Indian congresses in support of the Wheeler-Howard bill. "Minutes of the Indian Congress, Rapid City, South Dakota, March 2, 1934," NA, RG 75, pp. 15–18.

funds." Collier responded that this objection stemmed from a misunderstanding. The government's appropriations in this matter were authorized by previous legislation which had expired. It was practically certain that these particular funds from which the government paid tuitions to church schools were not tribal funds, and he doubted if they would come under the control of chartered communities. But if a court in the future decreed that they were tribal trust funds, they would come under community control.[49]

This question had arisen because of Collier's testimony before the House Appropriations Committee during December 1933. Due to a previous arrangement between the Sioux and the United States, some Catholic educational institutions such as the Holy Rosary Mission in South Dakota had acquired an 80 percent monopoly of the total government grant for religious schools. Because this agreement had lapsed, Collier took the position at these hearings that the government should pay only for the physical maintenance at Catholic schools but not for the tuition of Indian students. He proposed to use the money saved to pay for the physical care of Indian children attending mission schools in all parts of the country, greatly aiding the Protestant establishments.[50]

Resentment by Roman Catholic Jesuits and their Indian parishioners in South Dakota over this testimony had turned into a defamatory campaign, in the form of chain letters and attacks in the Catholic press, against Collier and the Wheeler-Howard bill. The *Catholic Daily Tribune* mistakenly warned its readers that the bill endangered the status of their mission schools and suggested that Collier showed little interest in "religious influences." *The Little Bronzed Angel,* a Catholic periodical published by the fathers at Marty, South Dakota, also carried this type of innuendo.[51]

Because he knew that many Sioux remained hostile toward his program, Collier held a special meeting on the evening of March 3 with the delegations from Pine Ridge, Rosebud, Crow Creek, Brule, Cheyenne River, Santee, and the Sioux of Fort Peck, Montana. George White Bull from Standing Rock spoke first, and he indicated that many fullbloods were just "getting accustomed to the allotment system" and they distrusted the landless mixed-bloods who favored passage of the bill. He also disliked this legislation because it contained no provision for Indian claims against the government. Collier replied that he planned to introduce a claims bill in Congress "to enable all Indian tribes to get their day in court without delay." But it was politically inexpedient to attach such a measure to the already expensive Wheeler-Howard bill. It cost so much that Lewis Douglas, the director of the budget, "would faint."[52]

Fire Thunder from Pine Ridge raised another question that concerned many delegates: he wanted to know what would happen to the Sioux Benefits if the Wheeler-Howard bill passed. Under legislation passed in 1889 and successive congressional acts, certain Sioux had received cash payments when they acquired a land allotment. Fire Thunder and others worried that this money would disappear when allotted land returned to tribal ownership. Collier agreed that this question deserved consideration, and he favored an amendment to "protect these Sioux Benefits."[53]

During the last two days of the Rapid City Congress representatives from each delegation rose to comment on the Wheeler-Howard bill. In a standing vote thirteen delegations approved of the proposal with amendments while four opposed it. Max Bigman from the Crow Agency spoke for many of the hostile Indians when he warned that it took "competition and big knocks to make a man" and criticized the bill because it promoted segregation "from my white friends." He received support from Joe Irving of Crow Creek, who called Collier a "socialist" and indicated that he had little taste for community life. Jacob White Cow Killer of Pine Ridge cautioned that the Republicans would oppose Collier and might modify the bill beyond recognition.[54]

Most delegations, however, swung from an earlier position of open defiance to support Collier's program. The Fort Belknap spokesman explained the success of their cattle association and urged all Indians to consolidate their grazing lands. George Yellow from the Lower Brule praised Collier's plans to end the allotment system which had allowed white men to reach into his pockets and rob him "of everything except the soles of my shoes." This sentiment continued when Sam La Pointe from Rosebud suggested that the Indians call the commissioner "iron man" because he had "worn out every interpreter we have got." The Blackfeet demonstrated their support by adopting Collier into the tribe. They gave him the name "Spotted Eagle" because the Wheeler-Howard bill would rub off the checkerboarded spots on every Indian reservation.[55]

Collier had planned on addressing the Northwest Indian Congress held on March 8 and 9 at Chemawa, Oregon, but he failed to attend this meeting because he had lost his voice and suffered physical exhaustion after the lengthy discussions at Rapid City.* Consequently, Assistant

---

*After the Chemawa Congress, Elwood A. Towner, an Indian attorney from Portland, wrote Collier that his people disliked the bill because it was too communistic and would not develop initiative and self-reliance. Towner claimed that the Northwest Indians opposed the commissioner's attempt to experiment with them like guinea pigs and suggested that the plan be tried on the whites first. If it killed them, the Indians would be safe for awhile. Elwood A. Towner to John Collier, March 14, 1934, NA, RG 75, Part 10–A, Records Concerning the Wheeler-Howard Act.

Commissioner William Zimmerman and other Indian Bureau officials explained the various sections of the Wheeler-Howard proposal, including the amendment which provided for the voluntary exchange of allotted land to tribal ownership. Zimmerman stressed that for two generations the Indians had steadily lost their property because of the "wicked and stupid" allotment laws. He pointed out that Collier's reform measure would change this evil system and help the Indians organize chartered communities to control their own destiny. But many of the "old timers" did not understand "what a community meant."[56]

Representatives from the Ft. Hall, Flathead, and Sacramento agencies supported Zimmerman, but most of the delegates at Chemawa were suspicious of any change in policy. Chief Peter Mocktum, from the Coeur d'Alene reservation, said the whites had "broken all of the prosperity I ever had," but he wanted to keep his remaining allotments and heirship lands. Chief Ishadore, a Kootenai, affirmed this fear of change when he indicated that without a superintendent's guidance he "would feel like a child who would get lost when his guide left him." He was joined by Harry Shale from the Quinaielt reservation, who stated that his tribe was "getting along nicely" with their fishing and it did not need the bill, but they might accept some form of self-government if nearby Indians made a success of it.[57]

Several other delegations offered objections to the Wheeler-Howard measure. John Wilson, a Nez Percé, claimed that his tribe opposed the bill because it might interfere with their $18 million claim against the State of Montana for ceded hunting grounds. The Umatillas, under the leadership of Jim Kanine, added to this protest, by stressing that they were "happy and contented" and liked their superintendent. Kanine claimed that most of the Umatillas owned land and the bill only disturbed them and made them fearful. Thomas Sam, a Yakima, agreed, maintaining that his tribe had "plenty of land" which they wanted to keep. If the government planned on purchasing property for landless Indians, it should be outside the reservation. Joe Buck, a Flathead, summed up the sentiment at Chemawa, when he pointed out that if you put "a bunch of twenty dollar bills on the table" the Indian would be afraid to "go and get them." He had learned to be "suspicious, but you can't blame him."[58]

On March 12, 1934, Collier met with a special session of the Navajo Tribal Council at Ft. Defiance, Arizona. He explained that the Wheeler-Howard bill repealed the land allotment law of 1887 and warned that they should support his measure because some future administration might decide to divide their reservation despite the treaty of 1868. He pointed to the example of the Five Civilized Tribes who had treaties guaranteeing the ownership of the best farm land in Oklahoma. They felt secure, but the whites wanted the land for farming and tax revenue, so the allotment law was brought into action, resulting in a loss of 13 million acres and 72,000 landless Indians. Several Navajo delegates responded to Collier's statement by asking whether the Wheeler-Howard bill would affect six thousand allotments on the public domain. Relieved of their anxiety when he said no, these Indians showed little desire to return their allotments to communal ownership or lose the right to pass it on to their heirs.[59]

Collier also discussed his unpopular stock reduction program at the Ft. Defiance Tribal Meeting. In doing so, the commissioner made a strategic error, for many Indians confused this controversial issue with the Wheeler-Howard bill.* During the previous year, Collier had told the Navajos that to save their land from further erosion the tribe would have to kill 400,000 head of sheep, goats, and horses. By reducing the Navajo stock on a flat rather than graduated scale, he ignored the minimum number of animals the Indians needed for subsistence. While the wealthy Navajos culled their herds and eliminated worthless stock, many small owners found their livelihood threatened. When Collier called for a reduction of 150,000 goats at Ft. Defiance, many Indians demonstrated their hostility by criticizing his proposal.[60]

Missionaries and traders who attended the meeting at Ft. Defiance added to this turmoil by opposing the Wheeler-Howard bill. On March 13, 1934, a group of missionaries passed a series of resolutions which warned that the Navajo "must be saved by a process of Christian assimilation of American life, not by carefully guarded and subsidized segregation."† They feared a "revival of tribalism" and believed that the bill "would put the clock of Indian progress back at least fifty years."[61] The missionaries received support from members of the United Traders Association, who feared that Indian cooperatives might put them out of business.[62] Upset by this conflicting advice from local whites and government officials, the Navajos decided to postpone consideration of the bill until April 10, when the tribal council despite internal dissension voted in favor of its passage.[63]

Collier left the confusion at Ft. Defiance behind him and looked forward to meeting with some of his old friends on the All Pueblo Coun-

---

*Many of the Navajos disliked section 15 of Title II which authorized the secretary of the interior to restrict the number of livestock grazed on Indian land to prevent soil erosion.

†The greatest opposition stemmed from the Christian Reformed Church, Presbyterians, Baptists, and an Independent Hopi Mission. "The Missionaries' View on the Wheeler-Howard bill, Resolutions Adopted by a Group of Missionaries at Ft. Defiance, Arizona, March 13, 1934," NA, RG 75, Part 6-BB, Records Concerning the Wheeler-Howard Act.

cil. On March 15, 1934, 117 delegates from nineteen pueblos met at Santo Domingo to hear Collier explain why they should support the Wheeler-Howard measure. He warned that the status of their lands might be endangered by some future administration unless they endorsed his bill.* Most of the Indians backed Collier because this reform did not threaten their traditional form of self-government, but after further consideration two Pueblos offered objections. The governor of San Ildefonso opposed the section allowing a member of a chartered community to withdraw for a cash compensation, while Indians from Santa Clara suggested that they have the right to appeal from all decisions of local Indian courts. Split into factions, they were apprehensive that Indian judges selected by "majority groups" would try to ruin their political opponents "by fines and imprisonment."[64]

Unable to attend the next two Indian congresses, Collier departed for Washington, D.C., to prepare for congressional hearings on the Wheeler-Howard bill. When the Phoenix Congress met on March 16, 1934, A. C. Monohan, assistant to the commissioner, and Walter Woehlke, a bureau field representative, spoke for the government. They described the various sections of the bill and asked the Indians to submit written questions. The Papagos responded by doubting whether self-government would work on their reservation, consisting as it did of "independent ranching and farming communities, with no union between the villages." They rejected the government's attempt to abrogate their old laws regarding inheritance; more important, the government should protect their title to Mexican land grants before it tried new forms of land ownership.[65]

The Pimas and San Carlos Apaches also had qualms about the Wheeler-Howard proposal but other tribes supported the measure. The Pimas indicated a desire to continue their restricted individual ownership of property, including mineral rights, without a "communistic land basis." They criticized the bill because it failed to guarantee Indian water rights. The San Carlos Apaches joined the Pimas, falsely believing that the legislation would expropriate their cattle herd and put it under community control. But the Apache delegates from Fort McDowell favored the bill because it protected their reservation, which God had given them, and it ended the government paternalism which "told us not to say anything and just put your head down." The Mohave and other Colorado River delegates joined the Apaches and called for the passage of the bill.[66]

---

*Collier argued that unless the Pueblos supported the Wheeler-Howard bill some government official in the future might try to apply land allotment against the executive-order part of their reservations. He indicated that the bill would protect their ancient land grants which might eventually face allotment because the Supreme Court had neglected to determine the status of the grants. "Minutes of the All Pueblo Council at Santo Domingo, New Mexico, March 15, 1934," NA, RG 75, Part 2-A, Records Concerning the Wheeler-Howard Act.

When the Indian Bureau officials convened the Indian congress at Riverside on March 17, 1934, they discovered that the Indians of southern California, like those in Phoenix, had mixed feelings about the Wheeler-Howard proposal. Several Mission Indians, led by Rupert Costo, agreed with an unsigned three-page circular sent around the reservations which claimed that Collier's ideas were "communistic and socialistic." Concerned about "the pot at the end of the rainbow" or their claims for land ceded to whites, they believed the bill would reverse the policy of civilizing the Indian and force "him to revert to old conditions." Nevertheless, delegates from the Santa Rosa, Fort Yuma, and Pyramid Lake reservations supported the bill, but they believed that its section providing for a $2 million appropriation to acquire new land inadequate — a mere "drop in the bucket."[67]

The final series of Indian congresses took place in Oklahoma and Collier left Washington to attend these meetings. When the commissioner met with the Indians from western Oklahoma at Anadarko, on March 20, 1934, and with delegates from the Osage and Quapaw jurisdiction at Miami, four days later, he faced open hostility. At Anadarko, Jasper Saunkeah expressed the opposition of the Kiowa tribe, while James Otippoby, a Comanche, pointed out that "we love our allotments . . . and don't want to be segregated."[68] Representatives from the Arapaho and Cheyenne tribes supported him when they introduced a resolution rejecting "the plan of abolishing the allotment act." The tribal business committees representing the Pawnee, Ponca, Kaw, Otoe, and Tonkawa tribes also criticized the Wheeler-Howard bill.[69] At Miami, Ray McNaughton, a Peoria Indian, expressed the sentiment of many natives from Ottawa County when he warned that they had little interest in "returning to the hunting class." More opposition, however, focused around the fear of several Quapaws that the bill might destroy their rights to allotments containing lead and zinc mines.[70]

On March 22, 1934, the commissioner met with at least 2,000 members of the Five Civilized Tribes at the city hall and federal courtroom in Muskogee, Oklahoma. The congress opened on a positive note with spokesmen for each of the Five Tribes welcoming Collier.[71] But an undercurrent of hostility remained because of the activities of Joseph Bruner, a Creek Indian, and chief of the National Indian Confederacy, located at Sapulpa, Oklahoma. Bruner, representing the assimilated members of the Five Tribes, led the opposition at Muskogee against Collier's efforts to return these Indians to a disintegrating tribal heritage. Bruner and his followers feared that the Wheeler-Howard bill would segregate them, eliminate the beneficial influence of missionaries, confiscate their oil and mineral rights, and take away their allotted land.[72] They received assistance from G. E. E. Lindquist, a former member of the Board of Indian

Commissioners, who asked his fellow missionaries and their Indian friends to oppose the bill because it would send the natives back to the blanket.[73]

Concerned about this negative reaction to his program, Collier told the Five Tribes to disregard rumors that the bill was connected with "communism, socialism, and paganism." Contrary to many rumors, it did not destroy their property rights or compel them to organize into communities. Collier indicated that he realized the government had "crushed" their tribal organizations, but he warned that "organization in the modern world was the key to all power." In Oklahoma, the Indians could form colonies and use the concept of the business corporation which came not "from Russia or Karl Marx" but was strictly an American product. If the Choctaws, for example, desired to become a chartered community they could form a coal company to operate their mines, while other Indians could establish cattle cooperatives. Collier suggested that his legislation was no more communism "than the Empire State Building," which existed because "a great many people had pooled their investments."[74]

These arguments, however, failed to deter several delegates who asked Collier "a thousand and one questions" concerning segregation and possible loss of their property rights. His face turned "red," but one sympathetic observer believed that the commissioner answered all questions "to the satisfaction of practically all present," and his "steel blue eyes and winning smile" captivated the audience.[75] Impressed with Collier's obvious good faith, the Eastern Emigrant and Western Cherokees passed a resolution favoring the "immediate enactment of the Wheeler-Howard bill." The 6,000 full-blood Cherokees who made up the Night Hawk Keetoowah Society also "heartily approved the contents" of the bill. Joseph W. Hayes, the Chickasaw spokesman, added his endorsement because "every morning our children will be Indians." Hayes claimed his tribe favored the measure because they believed that Collier was "one white man with a red man's heart." The Creek and Choctaws refused to officially act at Muskogee, but they endorsed the bill later at separate council meetings.[76]

Collier returned to Washington, D.C., on March 29, 1934, with his hopes high, but he discovered that the unity demonstrated by the Indian welfare associations at the Cosmos Club in January had disintegrated because of the controversy concerning the Wheeler-Howard bill.* M. K.

---

*The National Association on Indian Affairs, under the leadership of Oliver La Farge, and the American Indian Defense Association, directed by Allan Harper, favored the principles embodied in the Wheeler-Howard bill with only minor reservations. U.S., Congress, Senate, Committee on Indian Affairs, *Hearings, on S. 2755, To Grant Indians the Freedom to Organize,* 73rd Cong., 2nd Sess., 1934, pp. 325–28.

Sniffen, editor of the Indian Rights Association's journal, *Indian Truth*, opposed Collier's reform in an article entitled "Stop, Look, and Consider."* Sniffen warned that the bill proposed "revolutionary departures" in Indian policy by perpetuating segregation under the guise of self-government and by "reversing the incentive which the authors of the allotment law had in mind for individual ownership of property leading toward citizenship."[77] Upset at this hostile attitude, Collier wrote the association's president, Jonathan Steere, that he was "momentarily bewildered" to find what amounted to "a denunciation of the bill they had agreed on only two and one-half months ago."[78]

Sniffen and Steere paid little attention to Collier's protest; instead, they offered more extensive criticism of the bill in the May issue of *Indian Truth*. Referring to decisions made at a special meeting of the association's board of directors, Sniffen suggested that Collier rewrite or discard Titles I and IV of the bill which established self-governing communities and a separate Indian court. He called these proposals "artificial and impractical" for allotted reservations where Indians had amalgamated with the white race. Sniffen rejected the idea of permanent Indian freedom from taxation, credit facilities that applied to only chartered communities, and the provisions for taking Indian appointments out from under civil service requirements. He suggested that Congress draw up four or five separate bills in preference to the lengthy and imprecise Wheeler-Howard proposal.[79]

Two former members of the Board of Indian Commissioners joined this protest by publicly denouncing the Wheeler-Howard bill. G. E. E. Lindquist claimed that Collier's "schemes" for reviving tribalism would wipe out "most of the gains of the last fifty years." He thought that reports from the Indians clearly indicated that they disapproved of "the communization of land."[80] Flora Warren Seymour agreed with her colleague, calling the bill a "unique program of regimentation" and the most extreme gesture yet made by the Roosevelt administration "toward a Communist experiment." Fortunately, several Indians at Rapid City and other congresses had opposed Collier's effort to destroy individual ownership of property. They had courageously called "a spade a spade and a Democrat, a Communist."[81]

Collier responded to these criticisms and suggestions offered at the Indian congresses, including the favorable meeting held at Hayward, Wis-

---

*The New Mexico Association on Indian Affairs, under the influence of Herbert Hagerman, a former governor of New Mexico and special commissioner to the Navajos during the Hoover administration, supported the Indian Rights Association. Herbert Hagerman to Charles Rhoads, March 22, 1934, NA, RG 316, Series 1, Item 49.

consin, on April 23-24, 1934, by preparing more than thirty amendments to the Wheeler-Howard bill.* The most important ones proposed the following actions: 1. preventing the secretary of the interior from transferring the title of allotted land into community ownership without the Indian's consent; 2. continuing the system of partitioning farm lands among heirs upon the death of the owner as long as the land could be used as an economic unit; and 3. prohibiting individual title to minerals such as gas and oil from being transferred from individual to communal ownership. Other significant amendments protected the Sioux Benefits, stated that the claims of Indian tribes would remain unaffected by the bill, and maintained the right of every tribe to exclude itself from all provisions of the bill at a referendum held within four months after its passage.[82]

Much to Collier's dismay even this amended version met opposition during hearings before the Senate Indian Affairs Committee in April and May 1934. Burton K. Wheeler, chairman of the committee, admitted that the bill might work in the Southwest but for the assimilated Montana Indians "it would be a step backward." Wheeler believed that instead of separating the Indians into self-governing communities, Congress should help them "as nearly as possible adopt the white man's ways and laws." As soon as they proved capable of handling their own affairs, the government should end its supervision and give the Indians their property. Wheeler warned Collier that the Bureau of the Budget might refuse to approve this expensive bill and even if it did, Congress would never appropriate money and "turn it over to a tribe" for self-government. Finally, Wheeler expressed hostility to a separate Indian court because it duplicated the jurisdiction of federal and state courts.[83]

Elmer Thomas, a Democrat from Oklahoma, joined Wheeler in his fight against the amended Wheeler-Howard bill. He told Collier that assimilation had worked in his state, and he resisted any attempt to change that policy by putting the Indians back on reservations where they could "perpetuate their ancient tribal ways indefinitely." Thomas pointed out that for the Oklahoma Indians the bill reversed the "trend of one-hundred years" and created an "Indian zoo." Like Wheeler, he questioned whether Congress would indefinitely appropriate money for chartered Indian communities. Thomas believed that to assist the Oklahoma Indians the government needed only to start a land acquisition program

---

*At the Hayward Congress the delegates from the Bad River and Lac du Flambeau reservations feared that the bill might destroy their hunting and fishing rights. But the overwhelming majority of tribes supported the measure. They included the Chippewas from Grand Portage, Red Lake, White Earth, Red Cliff, and L'Anse. The Wisconsin Menominees, Winnebagos, and the Oneidas favored the bill, as well as the Mount Pleasant Potawatomies from Michigan. "Testimony Taken at Hayward, Wisconsin, April 23–24, 1934," NA, RG 75, pp. 1–74.

for helpless natives, stop issuing fee patents, and extend the trust period on allotted land. He refused to allow Oklahoma to come under the bill until its provisions were worked out in "a more businesslike manner."[84]

Collier's amended bill faced even tougher opposition in hearings before the House Indian Affairs Committee. When the commissioner appeared before these hearings he pointed out that most Indians favored its passage. In votes taken during and after the Indian congresses, fifty-four tribes representing a population of 141,881, had expressed approval of the Wheeler-Howard bill, while twelve tribes with a population of 15,106 had voted against it.* Despite these figures, Will Rogers, a representative from Oklahoma, doubted support for the measure. He stated that members of the House could not figure out what it was "going to do," thus how could the Indians understand the bill.[85] Representative Thomas O'Malley from Wisconsin also doubted whether this experiment in Soviet-type "collectivism" would prove successful. Such skepticism caused many members of the committee to boycott the hearings during the first two weeks of May. Without their cooperation, the committee's chairman, Edgar Howard, found it difficult to formulate a compromise measure or obtain a quorum to report the bill to the floor of the House.[86]

Frustrated because Congress blocked his measure, Collier tried to insure its passage by impugning the motives of non-Indians who opposed it. In an article written for the Washington *Daily News,* he classified cattlemen, job seekers, real estate interests, attorneys, and missionaries as the major critics of his reform program. White cattle interests fought the bill, he argued, because they would gradually lose control of millions of acres of grazing lands rented to them by Indians. Several missionaries had embittered the Indians against the bill because they falsely believed that it would "return them to the blanket."[87] The commissioner accused a group of Oklahoma attorneys of discrediting the measure because they would lose Indians as clients in land litigation. He pointed out that many Indian Service employees had criticized the bill because they feared losing their positions once the Indians started the process of self-government.†

Secretary Ickes assisted Collier by attempting to stifle criticism of the bill within the Interior Department. On April 30, 1934, he sent a lengthy memo to "All Employees of the Indian Service," which pointed

---

*Tribes voting against the bill as of May 7, 1934, included: those on the Rincon reservation, in California; the Montana Crow; the Yankton Sioux of South Dakota; the Klamath of Oregon; the natives on the Colville and Spokane reservation in Washington; and the Arapaho and Shoshone of Wyoming. U.S., Congress, House, Committee on Indian Affairs, *Hearings, on H.R. 7902, Readjustment of Indian Affairs,* 73rd Cong., 2nd Sess., 1934, pp. 422–25.

†Collier had already abolished more than 600 jobs held by whites. Vera Connolly, "The End of a Long, Long Trail," *Good Housekeeping* 98 (April 1934): 249. The commissioner followed this assault with two feature articles, on May 6, 1934 in the *Washington Post* and *New York Times,* demonstrating the evils of the allotment system and explaining the reforms proposed by the New Deal.

out that it was not expected that personnel in the bureau would deliberately attempt to obstruct the new Indian policy. Ickes ridiculed the
"subtle, misleading propaganda against the new Indian program emanat-
ing from a minority of employees within the Indian Service." He warned
the Indian Bureau staff that any person engaged "in this scheme to defeat
our program" would face the "penalty of dismissal."[88] This action seemed
reminiscent of the arbitrary decrees issued by the bureau during the
twenties.

In order to weaken congressional opposition to his program, Collier
decided to ask for White House support. Earlier President Roosevelt had
favored the bill, noting in a memo that "it was great stuff," but he had
neglected to put it on the administration's priority list.[89] Now at Collier's
instigation, both Secretary of the Interior Harold L. Ickes and Secretary
of Agriculture Henry A. Wallace spoke with Roosevelt about this matter.
After meeting with the chief executive, they assured Collier that he would
give the legislation preferred status.[90]

On April 28, 1934, the president came to Collier's defense by endorsing the amended Wheeler-Howard bill in identical letters sent to Representative Edgar Howard and Senator Burton K. Wheeler. Roosevelt indicated that the government must terminate the land allotment system
because it had caused the Indians to lose more than two-thirds of their
land. He called the proposed legislation a measure of justice long over-
due and suggested that Congress immediately extend to the Indians the
fundamental rights of political liberty and local self-government.[91]

Under pressure from the White House, members of the House Indian
Affairs Committee met for an evening session on May 21 and completely
redrafted the Wheeler-Howard bill. According to Representative William
Hastings, a Cherokee from Oklahoma, they changed "every provision
except the title."[92] Missing from the bill were Title I, which had established tribal communities with the powers of municipalities, and Title IV,
which provided for the creation of a special federal Indian court.

The Senate further amended this weakened version before it passed.
Senator Henry Ashurst added an unrelated section which revoked Ray
Lyman Wilbur's previous order withdrawing Papago lands from mineral
entry or claims under the public land mining laws.* Senator Elmer Thomas

---

*At the insistence of Collier and Senator Burton K. Wheeler, who opposed
Henry Ashurst on the floor of the Senate, the Indian Reorganization Act did protect
the Papagos' surface rights. Whites had to pay the Papago tribe damages for loss
of improvement on their land opened to mining and an inadequate yearly rental not
exceeding five cents an acre for the loss of land withdrawn for mining operations.
Finally, any party desiring a mining patent had to pay the Papagos a token one
dollar per year fee in lieu of annual rental. See John Collier, "The Papago Mineral
Question in Relation to the Wheeler-Howard Indian bill," May 31, 1934, NA, RG 75;
and *Congressional Record*, 73rd Cong., 2nd Sess., June 12, 1934, 78, Part 10:
11122–37.

FAILURE TO CREATE A RED ATLANTIS 159

also inserted an amendment excluding the Indians of his state from most of the bill's provisions.[93]

Signed by President Roosevelt on June 18, 1934, this legislation became known as the Indian Reorganization Act. Although it bore little resemblance to Collier's original proposal, the IRA established a turning point in Indian history by abandoning future land allotment. It extended the trust period on restricted land, allowed for the voluntary exchange of allotments to consolidate checkerboard reservations, continued existing practices of inheritance, and restored to tribal ownership remaining surplus lands created by the Dawes General Allotment Act.* The IRA empowered the secretary of the interior to initiate conservation measures on Indian land and authorized an annual appropriation of two million dollars for the acquisition of real estate at several reservations. Special civil service requirements allowed Indians to hold more positions in the Indian Service, while an annual appropriation of $250,000 provided tuition and scholarships for promising Indian students.†

Provision for the partial renewal of Indian political and social structures destroyed by the land allotment policy paralleled this restoration of land. The IRA authorized Congress to spend $250,000 annually for the expense of organizing chartered corporations. Operated by tribal councils that established a constitution and by-laws, these corporations could employ legal council, prevent the leasing or sale of land without tribal consent, negotiate with federal or state governments for public services, and borrow money from a ten million dollar credit fund to promote tribal economic development.[94]

The year 1934 had been a time of optimism for Indian reformers who looked forward to correcting many of the abuses associated with the land allotment policy. But dissension appeared when Collier drew up the Wheeler-Howard bill, despite objections from anthropologists and Indians who feared that his proposal would prove difficult to accomplish. The commissioner failed to heed these warnings because he wanted the Indians to offer an alternate way of living for individualistic-oriented white America. His previous experience with the New Mexico Pueblos convinced him that Indian reservations contained viable communities

---

*The Klamath Indians of Oregon were exempt from section 4, which prevented the sale of restricted land to whites. U.S., *Statutes at Large,* Vol. 68, June 18, 1934, pp. 984–88.

† Under special civil service requirements specified by the IRA, the employment of Indians to permanent positions in the bureau increased from 1,785 in 1934 to over 5,000 by 1940. U.S., Department of the Interior, *Annual Report of the Secretary of the Interior: Report of the Commissioner of Indian Affairs,* (Washington: Government Printing Office, 1941), p. 439.

where Indians could establish cooperative commonwealths similar to the Red Atlantis he found at Taos.

These romantic ideas, however, faced opposition from the Indians who favored assimilation, as well as from congressmen, missionaries, bureau personnel, and the Indian Rights Association. Their concept of Indian progress originated from a different reform tradition which stressed the desirability of the melting pot concept.[95] They viewed the reservation either as a backwater where segregation and poverty flourished or as a temporary way station for full-bloods, but not as a base for social achievement.[96]

These groups successfully opposed Collier and forced Congress to pass the IRA, a compromise measure that protected the Indians' land while providing them with credit and limited self-government. They hoped this legislation, with its provision for educational training, would promote assimilation, but Collier used it to impose on the Indians many of his own ideas, thus opening the door for future conflict.

8. A Partial Restoration of Tribal Sovereignty

Disappointed that the IRA failed to incorporate all of the reforms he wanted, Collier still believed that with "undeviating" administrative will he could use it to forge "new collective advantages" for the Indians.[1] The commissioner thought that their revived group life would recognize the important sociological principle that society "must be a collaboration of local and unique groups cooperating in order to intensify their significant individualities." This would provide an example for the "directionless" white race, which had become "psychically, religiously, socially and esthetically shattered" during the twentieth century.[2]

Collier elaborated on this theme at an address given before Haskell Institute, at Lawrence, Kansas, where he warned young Indians to discard the "shallow and unsophisticated individualism" that limited the life ambition of the "Babbitts of twenty years ago." He indicated that they must avoid being indoctrinated with values that measured success in terms of profit, because they would not be "the views of the modern white world in the years to come." They needed to help "the tribe, the nation and the race — their fulfillment would come by holding to ideas and passions that mattered."[3]

In order to implement his goal of restoring tribal life, Collier turned to anthropologists who replaced missionaries as the dominant influence on the Indian Bureau. At a meeting in Pittsburgh during December 1934, the commissioner and members of his staff asked anthropologists how to utilize their discipline in organizing Indian self-government under the IRA, especially the task of establishing tribal constitutions. They suggested that the government take a census of their profession in order to find people acquainted with Indian needs.* A general feeling prevailed that Collier appoint a consultant to help contact anthropological groups in various sections of the country. This recommendation caused the Bureau of Ethnology to loan Collier the services of Dr. Duncan Strong, who helped make studies of how to use tribal institutions as vehicles for social change.[4]

In a similar move, Collier brought to Washington experts who met with Indian Service personnel and discussed ideas about self-government and cooperative economic enterprise. During the first part of January 1935, George Russell ("A. E."), a poet and editor of the *Irish Homestead,* a journal of rural economics, presented a talk on the Irish folk-revival. He discussed technical information about the Irish community effort, such as the organization of cooperative dairies, credit unions, and schools. Russell explained how the Irish folk-revival had resulted in the biological and spiritual regeneration of his country after centuries of colonial rule.[5] A short time later, Dr. James P. Warbasse from the Cooperative League discussed the consumer movement in the United States.†

But Collier's zeal for reestablishing communal life still required Indian approval. Because of an amendment added to the IRA by Edgar Howard of Nebraska, all tribes had the opportunity either to accept or reject this legislation in a referendum. Section 18 made the act inapplicable on any reservation where a majority of the adult Indians held a special election and voted against it. This caused the solicitor's office to issue a special ruling which counted in favor of the measure all eligible voters who failed to cast a ballot. Seventeen tribes with a population of 5,334 were affected by this decree. They rejected the act by a vote of 1,411 to 877 but came under its provisions.[6]

This brought a justifiable charge from the California Mission Indians that the bureau had rammed the IRA down their throats. On the Santa Ysabel reservation near Riverside, for example, forty-three Indians voted against the act and nine for it, but they came under its provisions because

---

*Anthropologists who attended the Pittsburgh Conference included E. Sapir, Yale University; Ralph Linton, University of Wisconsin; Reverend Berard Haile, Gallup, New Mexico; Robert Redfield, University of Chicago; Margaret Mead, Museum of Natural History, New York City; Herbert Spinden, Brooklyn Museum; and Leslie A. White, University of Michigan. For a complete list consult "Anthropologists and the Federal Indian Program," *Science* 81 (February 15, 1935): 170–71.
†Collier first became acquainted with Dr. James Warbasse at the People's Institute. A surgeon from Brooklyn, Dr. Warbasse was one of the pioneer advocates of cooperative medicine. He founded the distributive cooperative movement in the United States and wanted to continue the experiments started by Robert Owen and the Rochdale spinners. According to Collier, Dr. Warbasse "contributed momentously to the Indian New Deal." John Collier, *From Every Zenith* (Denver: Sage Books, 1963), pp. 104–5; and John Collier, "All for Each and Each for All," *Indians at Work,* February 1, 1935, pp. 1–5.

the bureau counted in favor of the measure sixty-two people who refused to come to the polls. The controversy aroused over this ruling forced Collier to agree that the government should amend the IRA.[7] In 1935, Congress passed special legislation which required that a majority of Indians actually voting would determine whether a tribe accepted or rejected the act.[8]

Eventually 181 tribes which contained a population of 129,750 approved of the IRA, while 86,365 repudiated it, including the important Navajos who associated it with Collier's unpopular stock reduction program.[9] The Navajos turned down this legislation on June 15, 1935, by a margin of 8,214 to 7,795. According to Roman Hubbell, a trader, the western Navajos accepted it on account of their isolation from white interference. The northern and eastern Navajos, however, disliked it because they came under the influence of Jacob C. Morgan, an Indian missionary, who told them that livestock reduction would continue if they voted yes.[10] But Hubbell neglected to explain that many Indians in the eastern jurisdiction opposed the act because it was the area most affected by Collier's earlier failure to secure passage of the New Mexico boundary bill, which would have provided them with land on the public domain.*

Upset over the Navajo rejection, Collier sent the tribe a message on July 21, 1935, informing them that he regretted their mistaken assumption that voting against the act would stop further stock reduction. The commissioner promised to help the Indians in every possible way, but he warned that they had deprived themselves of an important source of income. Collier calculated that a favorable vote would have entitled the tribe during the 1936 fiscal year to a million dollars in grants and loans: $648,000 from the revolving credit fund, $37,770 for tribal organization, $259,200 for land purchase, and $49,050 from the student loan fund. Unfortunately, many Navajos interpreted this message as a threat and it only increased their hostility.[11]

More disappointing than this defection was the smaller number of tribes who adopted constitutions and charters after they accepted the IRA. During the New Deal only ninety-three tribes wrote constitutions, while seventy-three set up charters of incorporation allowing them to borrow money from the revolving credit fund. Nevertheless, the principle of self-government became firmly established because the Interior

---

*The Navajo boundary bill passed the Senate on May 28, 1935, but was restored to the calendar at the request of Senator Dennis Chavez from New Mexico on the grounds that he have an opportunity to familiarize himself with its contents. Chavez had just replaced Bronson Cutting, who favored passage of the bill. Cutting died in an airplane crash on May 10, 1935. Chee Dodge to Harold Ickes, April 26, 1935, NA, RG 75, Records Concerning the Wheeler-Howard Act.

Department in subsequent years authorized the creation of numerous constitutions modeled after the IRA.[12]

Scudder Mekeel, the director of the bureau's applied anthropology unit, claimed that this feeble response stemmed from a conceptual flaw in the act; it tried to impose rigid white political and economic concepts in a situation which called for flexibility. Tribes varied in their acculturation and many Indians failed to understand "foreign terms" such as constitutions, charters, and the keeping of financial records.[13]

Mekeel's analysis certainly held some validity. Although Indian constitutions varied, they were patterned after the United States Constitution rather than tribal custom. Most of them contained a preamble stating that the tribes had the power to establish certain rights of home rule consistent with federal laws. A series of "articles" then set forth powers such as the right to employ legal counsel, to negotiate with federal, state, or local governments, and to regulate the use of tribal land. These constitutions also provided for progressive election procedures such as the recall and referendum, while many contained a "Bill of Rights."[14]

Corporate charters, with their legal jargon, proved confusing. Most Indians lacked a high school education or sophisticated legal background. Often their only business experience consisted of trying to prevent land allotments from falling into white hands. Consequently, they found it difficult to contemplate federal incorporation so their tribes could operate "property of every description," borrow money from the revolving credit fund, sue in United States courts, and request the termination of supervisory powers reserved for the secretary of the interior.[15] Representative Francis Case from South Dakota believed that the problem of corporate charters was further complicated when Indians such as the Sioux had to use interpreters.[16]

Many tribes remained suspicious of the constitutions and charters because Collier used them to resurrect certain features of the original Wheeler-Howard bill. The preambles implied a restoration of tribal sovereignty and possible segregation from white society. Several constitutions established separate Indian courts, and gave tribal councils power to "cultivate native arts, crafts, and culture" and to regulate the inheritance of property other than allotted lands.* Many Indians who had kept their

---

*After the defeat of his federal Indian court plan found in the original Wheeler-Howard bill, Collier reformed the reservation courts of Indian offenses by executive decree. On November 24, 1935, he replaced the old "Code of Indian Offenses" with new law and order regulations. They prohibited bureau officials from interfering with the functions of reservation courts and allowed the Indians to confirm the appointment or removal of their judges. These regulations gave Indian defendants the benefit of formal charges, the power to summon witnesses, the privilege of bail, and the right to trial by jury in all important cases. Jay B. Nash, ed., *The New Day for the Indians: A Survey of the Working of the IRA of 1934* (New York: Academy Press, 1938), p. 27.

allotments disliked the constitutions because they allowed landless Indians to have a preference in the assignment of tribal real estate.[17]

The plight of the Indians on the Pine Ridge reservation in South Dakota revealed some of the difficulties encountered in adopting charters and constitutions. At Pine Ridge, the tribe voted to accept a constitution, but severe economic conditions caused them to reject a charter and made it hard to concentrate on self-government. The depression had forced white homesteaders who lived on the reservation to default on payments owed the Sioux; furthermore, a severe drought and harsh winter during 1935 and 1936 made this situation worse. Because of a fuel shortage, Indian women had to hand their children back and forth to keep them from freezing; several families hunted for food in dump grounds; and at Bull Head, South Dakota, a woman crawled into a clump of bushes to die from starvation.[18]

Chief Bad Wound, an Oglala, told members of the House Indian Affairs Committee that these "pathetic" conditions meant that over 1,000 out of 8,000 people had to live on an inadequate bi-monthly eighty-three cent ration.[19] When Collier testified, he agreed that the Sioux were "one of the most depressed populations in the country," but rejected the notion that he had been inattentive to their needs. Since 1933, the government had helped them by spending over $3 million on the Indian Conservation Corps in South Dakota, while the Public Works Administration had expended over $5 million on roads, hospitals, and schools. Direct relief had been provided by the CWA and FERA, but Collier admitted that he needed more money, and if relief funds ended "acute and terrifying conditions would haunt the Sioux."[20]

Other issues diverted the Pine Ridge Sioux from implementing their constitution. This large reservation covered four counties and the long distances, bad roads, and small number of horses made it hard for the Indians to meet regularly. Their tribal organization, which had been dismantled with the advent of the allotment system, offered little foundation for self-government and economic activity. Ben American Horse dramatized this dilemma when he explained that the IRA had only caused confusion "amongst ourselves" by dividing the reservation into two equal factions: a "treaty council," which wanted to restore treaty rights and collect cash settlements before it engaged in self-government, and a "tribal council," which cooperated with the bureau.[21]

Collier's insistence that all Indians develop a closely knit communal existence similar to the New Mexico Pueblos proved impractical in other states besides South Dakota. The Montana Blackfeet adopted a constitution which created a new tribal law code, including comprehensive game laws designed to conserve the reservation's wildlife. But the constitution's provision for a business council based on "proportionate representation" from four districts caused resentment from the full-bloods. A minority consisting of only 22 percent of the tribe, they were not concentrated in any single electoral district and this led to a disproportionately small representation on the first council. Therefore, 164 full-bloods sent Secretary Ickes a petition requesting that he withhold approval of the newly adopted charter. They claimed the council would give the mixed-bloods, who owned modern equipment such as trucks, preference concerning loans.[22]

Another tribe, the Hopi of Arizona, found it difficult to understand white concepts of self-government. Shortly after Congress passed the IRA, Collier visited the Hopi villages to emphasize that this legislation would protect their institutions and customs against a possible future attack by unsympathetic bureau officials. Because many Hopis trusted Collier and remembered his earlier fight to help the Rio Grande Pueblos defeat the Bursum bill, they voted to accept the IRA by a vote of 519 to 299.[23] Although pleased with this favorable reaction, Collier knew that the Hopis had a complex culture and remained suspicious of the bureau. Consequently, he asked Oliver La Farge, president of the National Association on Indian Affairs, to help establish a tribal government and coordinate the activities of eleven separate villages.[24]

La Farge arrived in Arizona during the summer of 1936 and spent three months with the Hopi tribe. He quickly realized that local officials knew little about Hopi customs when they introduced him at several meetings without proper advance notice and held sessions in places "obnoxious to conservatives." More important, no white person who lived on the reservation could name the kikmongwi, the important religious leaders of the villages. These obstacles, however, did not deter La Farge, who held several meetings where only 10 percent of the voting population attended, to help the Hopis draw up a constitution. By tradition, the First Mesa experimented with new ideas, so its leaders drafted this document.[25]

A blend of native tradition and white legal concepts, the Hopi constitution created a tribal council whose delegates were chosen according to population. In each village, the kikmongwi "certified" councilmen, except in predominantly Christian villages where the Indians could elect representatives. The council had the power to negotiate with the federal, state, and local governments, employ attorneys, regulate the disposition of tribal property, and convene as a court to settle disputes between villages. But the villages maintained a certain degree of autonomy because they could appoint guardians for orphan children, adjust family disputes, regulate the inheritance of property, and assign farming land.[26]

On October 26, 1936, the Hopis adopted this constitution by a vote of 651 to 104; nevertheless, tribal self-government remained weak.[27] La

Farge warned Collier that he should interpret the large abstention among 2,800 eligible voters "as a heavy opposition vote." He indicated that many Indians abstained or voted against the constitution because they feared the council delegates would undergo public criticism, a "dreadful thing" in Hopi society. Other Indians, such as Jaob Kivahema, a kachina chief, had voted no for irrational reasons. Kivahema had rejected the constitution because a favorable vote was indicated by an X, which resembled a cross drawn at an angle, and the cross symbolized the Spaniards.[28]

The Hopi tribal government immediately faced several problems. A rivalry started between the villages of Shongopovi, Old Oraibi, Hotevilla, and Walpi, each claiming the right of decision in all important matters.[29] According to La Farge, the Hopis split into two hostile groups, the "true conservatives" and the "smarties."[30] The latter consisted of Christians and "social misfits" led by Colonel M. W. Billingsley, a local white.* When the "smarties" managed to get themselves elected to the council, they increased distrust of the government by the traditionalists who often boycotted council meetings. Hopi religious beliefs which stressed the notion of the "Hopi Path" and an ensuing millennium also prevented many Indians from trying to solve current social problems.[31]

Collier admitted that the bureau had "simply muffed the Hopi job."[32] Their constitution "never worked," but he refused to blame La Farge, who had completed his task with sensitivity and intelligence. The commissioner believed that the constitution conformed to the tribe's institutional structure, but it made the "unavoidable assumption" that the Hopis would use an "Occidental rationality." Unfortunately, the bureau's staff lacked the sophistication to provide channels of expression for the "conscious and unconscious motivations" that led to the resistance of these diverse people.[33]

Although Collier found the IRA hard to implement, he successfully helped several tribes develop viable self-government and cooperative economic enterprise. The Flathead Indians, for example, whose cause Collier had championed during the twenties, benefited from the act. Back in 1930, the right to develop the Flathead power site had been contracted to the Montana Power Company. Because of the depression, construction of the dam stopped and the company proposed to pay the Indians a minimal rental to keep the site under its control. When the Justice Department failed to resolve this matter in favor of the Indians, Collier

---

*Oliver La Farge disliked Colonel M. W. Billingsley, whom he called a "circus impressario," because Billingsley had convinced the Hopis of the Second Mesa that the Masons were their blood brothers who would help them with all their problems. For an opposite interpretation consult M. W. Billingsley, *Behind the Scenes in Hopi Land* (Kennesaw, Georgia: Phoenix Press, 1971).

National Archives

Secretary of the Interior Ickes signs the constitution and by-laws of the Flathead Indians.

obtained an interview with Attorney General Homer Cummings and demanded action.[34]

After an investigation the attorney general cancelled the company's lease, while Collier pushed for public ownership of the facility. A short time later he received a negative response from the Federal Power Commission, which pointed out that the Flathead site existed in the midst of a primitive wilderness, making it difficult to sell electricity. The commission indicated that the administration had already committed itself to the Bonneville and Grand Coulee dam projects without assurance of creating enough purchasers for the power.[35]

Collier lost on the question of public ownership, but he used the IRA to help the Flathead Indians. On April 25, 1936, the tribe ratified a charter of incorporation which gave it the right to bring lawsuits and to make contracts on its own initiative. With the commissioner's assistance they drew up plans to start a seven million dollar lawsuit against the Montana Power Company for failing to fulfill its previous obligations. Facing this prospect, the company agreed to resume work on the dam and pay the Flatheads the amount in rentals they would have received if the construction had been completed on time. It promised to give members of the tribe preference in employment which meant that 90 percent of the work force would consist of Indians.[36]

Two other tribes that took advantage of the IRA included the Mescalero and Jicarilla Apaches in New Mexico. The Mescalero Apaches adopted a constitution after tribal leaders organized a series of popular plays to illustrate its various sections. They drew up a charter that enabled them to borrow $242,000 from the credit fund to abandon a slum camp of brush tepees and board shacks around the agency headquarters in Tularosa Canyon. They also used this money to increase farm production eightfold, expand their cooperative cattle industry, close out leases to whites, and start a tribal warehouse.*

Just as impressive, the Jicarilla Apaches listened attentively to Collier when he told the tribal council about the English consumer movement and suggested that they form a "cooperative commonwealth."[37] The Jicarillas accepted this advice and adopted a constitution containing the unique provision that the tribe maintain a flock of sheep "to care for the aged and incapacitated."[38] They voluntarily returned their allotments to communal control, including individual oil rights, and they procured a loan from the revolving credit fund to buy out Emmit Wirt, a white trader, in order to start the first Indian-operated "Tribal General Store." Collier believed that they had set up this trading post along the classic cooperative line of "all for each and each for all."[39]

Several other tribes established cooperative economic enterprise under the IRA. The Chippewa on the Lac du Flambeau reservation in Wisconsin constructed tourist cabins, the Native Americans on the Swinomish reservation in Washington planted Japanese oysters in a fishing project, and the Manchester Band of Pomo Indians at Point Arena, California, created a dairy and farming enterprise. In Montana, the Chippewa Cree of the Rocky Boy band and the Northern Cheyenne borrowed

---

*In 1935, the cattle income received by the Mescaleros was $18,000, by 1937 it grew to $101,000. Value of feed produced by these Indians was $5,000 in 1935 and it reached $40,000 by 1937. Jay B. Nash, ed., *The New Day for the Indians: A Survey of the Working of the IRA of 1934* (New York: Academy Press, 1938), pp. 18–19; John Collier, "Indians Come Alive," *Atlantic Monthly* 170 (September 1942): 78–79; and John Collier, *From Every Zenith*, (Denver: Sage Books, 1963), p. 181.

money to purchase hay and cattle for their tribal herds. Most loans, however, went to individuals through tribal corporations for the purchase of livestock, machinery, seed, and permanent improvements.[40]

Finally, most of the New Mexico Pueblos voted to accept the IRA but this action proved meaningless. While Santa Clara, Zuni, Isleta, and Laguna eventually adopted constitutions, most of the other Pueblos made no effort to implement Collier's reform because of their cultural conservatism favoring the status quo. Yet, by the early 1970s, Pojoaque had modified its traditional government to conform with the IRA.[41]

The constitution adopted by Santa Clara demonstrated how this legislation helped solve internal problems. Divided into conservative and progressive factions, the Indians at Santa Clara had become so bitter toward each other that they simultaneously elected two governors. To solve this problem they drew up a constitution creating a fourteen-member tribal council, which had the power to employ attorneys, prevent the disposition of Pueblo land, and negotiate with federal, state, and local governments. It could decide internal disagreements by a majority vote and all members of Santa Clara had to fence their land within three years to prevent property disputes. Their constitution authorized a tribal sheriff to stop trouble immediately without special permission from the governor. On the other hand, it protected traditionalist values by requiring that each council delegate speak the Tewa language fluently.[42]

But Collier's dream of creating communal organizations that would "conquer the modern world" not only met a mixed response from the Indians, it crashed against the reality of an unsympathetic Congress. Under the direction of Representative Abe Murdock from Utah, the House Indian Affairs Committee became the focus of anti-New Deal sentiment. Members of this committee preferred the abolition of the bureau and the Indian's rapid assimilation into the white community.* Their hearings became a forum for a series of emotional charges against the commissioner, making it difficult for him to concentrate on implementing the IRA.[43]

Between February and April 1935, Murdock and his colleagues listened to hostile testimony from the American Indian Federation. Organized on August 27, 1934, at Gallup, New Mexico, by Indians from all parts of the country who disliked Collier's policies, the federation had a membership of approximately 4,000 persons. Its constitution stressed

---

*Committee members hostile to Collier's program included Representatives Roy Ayres from Montana, Usher Burdick from North Dakota, Mrs. Isabella Greenway from Arizona, John McGroarty from California, and Theodore Werner from South Dakota. U.S., Congress, House, Committee on Indian Affairs, *Hearings, on H.R. 7781, Indian Conditions and Affairs,* 74th Cong., 1st Sess., 1935, pp. 1–2.

Joseph Bruner,
president of the
American Indian
Federation.

National Archives

intertribal cooperation and the need to uphold "American civilization and citizenship." At Gallup the leaders of the federation had drawn up a resolution which requested Collier's removal from office because he had "insulted Indians in magazine articles, misrepresented their attitude toward the Wheeler-Howard bill, retained incompetent superintendents, and consistently advocated measures which created tribal division."[44]

The president and driving force behind the AIF was Joseph Bruner, a full-blood Creek from Sapulpa, Oklahoma. A successful product of the assimilationist program associated with land allotment, Bruner had attended the tribal schools of the Creek Nation and after spending his youth as a cowboy he became a successful businessman. While engaged in the oil and real estate business, Bruner also owned a farm and wrote "insurance of a general character." During the twenties he had helped select a lawyer to prosecute Creek tribal claims and opposed Commissioner Charles H. Burke's handling of the Jackson Barnett case. Impressed by Collier's crusade to stop construction of the Lee's Ferry bridge and exposure of the Navajo oil lease bill, Bruner had favored his appointment to head the bureau.[45]

Shortly after Collier took office, several "prominent" Oklahoma Indians called a meeting of the Five Civilized Tribes, which led to the formation of the National Indian Confederacy with Bruner elected as its chief. But he soon realized, after reading a copy of the Wheeler-Howard bill, that his notion of voluntary tribal associations did not match Collier's idea of self-government. Bruner believed that the bill would segregate the Indians and continue existing racial prejudice. He wanted to continue the work of Dr. Carlos Montezuma, an Indian who stressed the desirability of adopting white civilization. Because he disliked Collier's program, Bruner used the National Indian Confederacy to launch a statewide campaign to persuade Oklahoma Indians to oppose the Wheeler-Howard bill at the Muskogee Indian Congress. Bruner claimed that without his opposition this legislation would have been "approved without a dissenting vote."[46]

When Collier failed to listen to his objections at Muskogee, Bruner decided to form a national organization called the American Indian Federation. Working out of Washington, D.C., as a lobbyist, Bruner issued a "Memorial by American Indians" on December 21, 1934, copies of which he sent to President Roosevelt and members of Congress. It pointed out that Indians had become citizens in 1924 and criticized the "notorious" Wheeler-Howard Act for dispensing "Russian communistic life in the United States." This memorial demanded the removal of Collier and his appointees from the bureau. In their place, Bruner wanted personnel who would free the Indians from federal wardship; provide state-controlled health, educational and legal services; and "untangle the Indian property mess."[47]

As one of the first witnesses to testify before the House Indian Affairs Committee Bruner tried to discredit Collier by implying that his ideas tended toward "Communism instead of Americanism." He indicated that the commissioner favored atheism because he had written poems which praised Isadora Duncan, an "avowed atheist," and Francisco Ferrer, a Spanish anarchist. Bruner suggested that Collier had introduced these ideas in the government when he encouraged an alien, Dr. Esherf Shevky, a well-known Turkish biologist, to take out first citizenship papers so he could join the bureau. In a similar vein, he argued that Collier had brought Dr. Moises Saenz, a Mexican educator, to Washington to discuss his socialist programs which included an oath taken by school teachers declaring that they were atheists and opponents of the Roman Catholic church.[48]

This attack continued when Mrs. Alice Lee Jemison, a mixed-blood Seneca, and district president of the AIF, took the stand. Proudly admitting that she was a product of the American "melting pot," Jemison stated that the Indians would make progress if Congress abolished the bureau and turned them "loose." She pointed out that the Senecas had opposed Collier's appointment because they believed his Defense Association had solicited funds from "ignorant Indians" to keep them in a "primitive state." Jemison told the committee members that her people disapproved of the Wheeler-Howard Act because it violated their treaty of 1794, which guaranteed Seneca sovereignty and "exemption from all blanket legislation." They opposed the act because it consisted of "special class legislation," and its election procedures allowed transient Indians who lived on their reservation to hold land and participate in tribal affairs illegally. Jemison questioned Collier's fitness to hold office, warning that he belonged to the American Civil Liberties Union, an organization which had defended the two Italian anarchists Sacco and Vanzetti.[49]

Jacob C. Morgan, a member of the Navajo Tribal Council and first vice-president of the AIF, followed Mrs. Jemison. Morgan wanted the Indians to repudiate their cultural heritage and adopt white civilization. A zealous Christian convert, he became involved in missionary work for the Christian Reformed church.[50] Morgan, who had previously opposed Collier, told members of the committee that the Navajos in the northern part of New Mexico had never understood the Wheeler-Howard bill, and they demonstrated little interest in organizing into a separate nation. He criticized Collier's program of closing boarding schools, where children received proper food and adequate classrooms and dormitories, for hogan day schools constructed of "rock walls and flat dirt roofs." He thought that these schools promoted "the old traditional life of our people," instead of allowing them to acquire a good education and live like "other American citizens."[51]

When Collier appeared before the committee he called the federation "an audacious humbug" which falsely claimed the right to speak for forty Indian tribes which had never authorized the use of their names. According to Collier, its membership came substantially from the California Mission Indians and the New York Senecas. He pointed out that Bruner, an individual "acting upon his own," did not represent the Creek Nation "in any way, shape, or form." He admitted that Mrs. Jemison probably had "undisclosed authority" to represent the Senecas, but he introduced a letter from Thomas H. Dodge, the chairman of the Navajo Tribal Council, which denied Morgan's authority to speak for the entire Navajo tribe. Dodge claimed that Morgan had become a "tool and associate of unscrupulous white parasites" and a small group of their Indian victims.[52]

After a lengthy rebuttal of the federation's charges, Collier expressed concern about the hostile attitude of the Indian Affairs Committee. He suggested that normally it heard a complaint and then gave the accused official an immediate chance to reply. Instead, the committee had changed its procedure and adopted a rule allowing all complaining witnesses to testify "one after another."[53] Collier believed that this had resulted in the accumulation of a vast amount of critical material which his enemies exploited outside the committee room. This analysis was accurate because the federation's leaders pulled their charges out of context and sent them to members of Congress in a memorial entitled "To the American Citizenship of the United States."[54]

Angry over the commissioner's statement, several committee members attacked his program. John McGroarty from California told Collier that he wanted to give the Indians individual ownership of property, "if only a small patch," and then abolish the bureau because it served "no earthly use."[55] McGroarty believed that young educated Indians could take care of themselves and if they lost their land, "that was their lookout."[56] Usher Burdick from North Dakota told the commissioner that the IRA was unconstitutional because it had prevented future land allotments "without due process of law," and he opposed any return to "tepee days."[57] Roy Ayres from Montana agreed with Burdick and suggested that the act had been run "on the theory of communistic administration" by creating "governments within governments."[58] Theodore Werner from South Dakota indicated that if he were commissioner he would attempt to lead the Indians "out of the wilderness instead of trying to put them back in it."[59]

Because they sympathized with many of the federation's criticisms, these congressmen probed the question of whether Collier wanted to impose his radical social theories on the Indians. They accused him of being a member of American Civil Liberties Union, which had protected individuals who advocated violent revolution, and asked whether he associated with Roger Baldwin, its director. Collier replied that Baldwin was a very close friend and praised his defense of the constitutional right to freedom of belief and speech. The commissioner could not remember whether he belonged to the ACLU but admitted "sympathy" for its attempts to organize itinerant labor in California's Imperial Valley and defended its crusade against "criminal syndicalist laws."[60]

Satisfied that Collier had revealed "his high regard for extremists in radicalism," Representative Werner and other committee members continued their cross-examination by asking why he had abandoned reform measures advocated during the twenties.[61] They wanted to know if he still used tribal funds for the bureau's operation and wondered why he refused to consolidate the Indian Health Service with the United States Public Health Service, and transfer the Indian Forestry Service to the

Agriculture Department and the Indian irrigation program to the United States Reclamation Service.[62]

Collier replied that he had favored these policies in the past but budgetary restrictions prevented their implementation. He pointed out that the bureau still used over one million dollars in tribal money for Indian hospitals, schools, and agency personnel because his efforts to curtail these funds had met resistance before the Bureau of the Budget and congressional appropriation committees. This niggardly attitude made it impossible to transfer Indian health care to the United States Public Health Service — that would cost an extra million dollars in salaries alone. These setbacks, however, had not prevented him from successfully using the Johnson O'Malley Act to make contractual arrangements with several states to provide health care for their Indians.[63]

Collier suggested that new conditions made the transfer of the bureau's Irrigation and Forestry Service impractical. The United States Reclamation Service found it impossible to handle Indian irrigation because it had become "completely swamped" by public work assignments such as Boulder Dam. Nevertheless, he had followed the recommendations of a 1933 report by the Senate Indian Investigating Subcommittee which recommended that Congress spend irrigation money on lands controlled by the Indians themselves, rather than on property leased to whites. With the assistance of PWA funds he had started more than one hundred new irrigation projects and the Indian Conservation Corps made possible the use of Indian labor. The commissioner doubted the wisdom of transferring the bureau's forestry division because the administration had ended the system of contract cutting in favor of marketing Indian timber through tribal-owned sawmills.[64]

When members of the committee continued their hostility and pressed their ideas about abolishing the bureau, Collier questioned whether this notion was "politically or legally practicable."[65] He favored the present program establishing a maximum of responsibility and power for Indian tribes with the privileges that came with federal wardship. He stressed that the hearings had drawn a clear issue: whether the government should abandon its guardianship or continue the policy which protected Indian real estate and provided for self-government. The commissioner warned that the advocates of a total abolition of protection for the Indians had already won "a preliminary victory" in the Bureau of the Budget and the House Appropriations Committee. These groups had slashed funds needed by the bureau and the Indian's cause was "in peril."[66]

Despite Collier's pleading, the drive to curtail the effectiveness of the IRA proved successful. This became apparent at hearings before the House Subcommittee on Interior Department Appropriations during

April 1935. Led by Jed Johnson, a Democrat from Oklahoma who considered Collier a subversive and was unimpressed with the small number of tribes who adopted constitutions and charters, it cut even further Bureau of the Budget recommendations that Congress fund only half of the money authorized by the IRA.* Johnson slashed the credit fund to $2.5 million, the annual land purchase fund to $1 million, the sum for organizing tribes to $100,000, and education loans to $175,000.[67]

Collier pointed out in a memo to Secretary Ickes the practical effect of cutting these appropriations. It forced the Indians to let white men use their resources, while the problem of landless Indians remained unsolved. Collier's analysis proved correct because Indian real estate increased during the New Deal by only four million acres, which amounted to one-sixth of Indian property requirements as estimated by the National Resources Board.[68] Nevertheless, Indian real estate grew instead of shrinking, and many Indians used the revolving credit fund to buy livestock and equipment.† They also received assistance from bureau agricultural agents who helped them regain control of 400,000 acres of farming land and 7 million acres of grazing land previously leased to whites.[69]

Collier lamented these budgetary cuts, but found some consolation when Congress passed the Oklahoma Welfare Act. This achievement came after a prolonged controversy similar to the one that plagued the Wheeler-Howard bill. The Indians of Oklahoma needed new legislation due to action taken by Senator Elmer Thomas. He had exempted them from six important sections of the IRA, believing they were fashioned for "reservation Indians in the far west."[70] These sections had extended existing trust periods, limited the alienation of restricted land, authorized the establishment of new reservations, and provided for tribal incorporation.

---

*The Bureau of the Budget cut the land purchase fund because it wanted to see what the Indian Bureau could accomplish under the Federal Emergency Relief Administration's submarginal land program. But it supported Collier by proposing that Congress spend $250,000, the original authorization, for tribal organization. M. K. Sniffen, ed., "Restore Budget Estimates," *Indian Truth* 12 (March 1935): p. 1.

†By 1941, when IRA appropriations ceased due to budgetary restrictions imposed by World War II, Congress had spent $5,500,000 for 400,000 acres of land and returned almost one million acres of ceded surplus land to the tribes. In addition, special legislation such as the Taylor Grazing Act procured 875,000 acres for various reservations and the government turned over more than one million acres of public domain for Indian use. The Resettlement Administration also purchased submarginal land and several tribes used their own funds to acquire 390,000 acres at a cost of more than $2 million. By 1945, Congress had rehabilitated 12,000 Indians on their own land by loaning money from the $4,250,000 revolving credit fund. The repayment of this money was almost 100 percent, making the Indians one of the best credit risks in the United States. "MSS., Credit Operations," Collier Papers; and Angie Debo, *A History of the Indians of the United States* (Norman: University of Oklahoma Press, 1970) p. 294.

Consequently, Oklahoma Indians found it impossible to borrow money from the revolving credit fund.[71]

Thomas knew that he had acted without the Indians' consent, so he decided to visit Oklahoma to see whether they wanted to come under the six omitted sections. Aware that he could accomplish little without the bureau's cooperation, Thomas asked Collier to accompany him on his tour.[72] This second series of Indian congresses, which took place during the last part of October 1934, resembled the debates over the original Wheeler-Howard bill. They showed a mixed Indian response to Collier's policies but demonstrated that most tribes desired some kind of legislation to solve their particular problems.

The first Indian congress met at the Muskogee City Hall to determine the attitude of the Five Civilized Tribes. Senator Thomas opened the discussion by explaining why he had exempted the Indians from certain sections of the IRA. Thomas told the Indians that he realized most of them wanted their land restrictions extended, but warned that assimilated individuals such as former Vice-President Charles Curtis, a Kaw, needed protection. Under the present law they were prohibited from selling restricted land even if farming no longer occupied their attention. Thomas indicated that he opposed that part of the IRA providing for tribal incorporation because it authorized loans only for chartered Indians who lived on a reservation. The senator pointed out that members of the Five Civilized Tribes lived on separate allotments; therefore, they needed special credit facilities. He proposed an amendment which provided for individual loans for the purchase of farm machinery, cattle, and other livestock. Thomas stated that he opposed the section permitting the creation of new reservations because he doubted whether the Indians desired to "surrender their present lands and move on to community property."[73]

Collier followed Thomas and he stressed consensus rather than conflict by praising the senator for being a "progressive" who concerned himself with the "human element of life." The commissioner told the Indians that he appreciated their earlier support of the Wheeler-Howard bill, although he knew that this action was not based on a "close analysis" of the measure but faith that President Roosevelt wanted "to do the right thing." Collier agreed with Thomas that Congress should amend the IRA so the government could get on with its duty of helping the Oklahoma Indians obtain credit and purchase the needed two million acres of land necessary for their economic independence.[74]

After the commissioner's brief address, delegates from the Five Civilized Tribes spoke and most of them favored the IRA with certain modifications. W. A. Durant, a Choctaw, claimed that his people wanted to come under the New Deal programs, and they appreciated the efforts of Collier and Thomas, who cared for more than the "god" of "material wealth." Joseph W. Hayes, a Chickasaw, agreed and indicated that the full-bloods of his tribe favored all of the provisions found in the IRA. If the self-government part of this legislation was made optional for mixed-bloods such as himself, he would never oppose the desire of the full-bloods to live in their own communities. John Smith, a Cherokee, supported this position by presenting a petition from 297 full-blood Keetoowahs who asked for assistance in "forming a reservation or colony" where they could hold lands in common. But Blue Murphy, from Kenwood, Oklahoma, spoke for 300 assimilated Cherokees when he argued against any return to a reservation. Similar doubts were expressed by Charles Grounds, a delegate for the Seminoles, who indicated that his tribe desired to continue the "rights and privileges they enjoyed as citizens of Oklahoma," while a white attorney for the full-blood Creeks stated that these Indians were in "almost absolute agreement with Thomas."[75]

The next day Collier and Thomas traveled to Miami where they learned that the Indians in northeastern Oklahoma desperately needed federal aid. Lucien Daseney, an Ottawa, indicated that his tribe had lost all of its land under the allotment system except for a five-acre graveyard that was "awaiting us all." He asked for 1,300 acres so his people could have "a chance to make a living for ourselves." Moody Palmer, a Miami, stressed that his tribe faced a similar dilemma. "Discriminated against everywhere," they found it impossible to obtain jobs or purchase life insurance. Thomas Armstrong, a Seneca, added to this gloom by pointing out that his people lived in "shacks" on forty-acre plots in the rough hill country. They wanted property for landless Indians and better educational facilities. Allen Johnson, a Wyandotte, agreed that they needed economic assistance but warned that most of his tribe feared community government. They favored a claims settlement for lost land and hoped to make individual loans from the revolving credit fund. He was followed by Vern Thompson, an attorney, who indicated that the Quapaws favored the status quo.*

When Collier and Thomas attended the Indian congress at Pawnee two days later, they found little support for the IRA. James Williams, a Ponca, stressed the need for a court of claims, while Adell Dennison, a Kaw, stated that his tribe opposed this legislation because many indi-

---

* The annual income of the Ottawa, Wyandottes and Eastern Shawnees ranged from $110 to $190, far below the $300 subsistence level recognized by the National Resources Board. "Meeting Held at Miami, Oklahoma, October 16, 1934," Elmer Thomas Papers.

viduals had lost interest in farming, but they favored "having a voice" in government policy. The Pawnees were divided over the act, and Good Eagle expressed their resentment toward the previous allotment system when he defined a reservation as "a body of land occupied by whites surrounded by Indian thieves."[76]

The meeting at the Shawnee Agency was in marked contrast to previous congresses and many delegates criticized Senator Thomas for removing them from important parts of the IRA. Frank James, representing the Sac and Fox, stated that they wanted to continue the restrictions on their land and resented the exclusion of their business council from the act's incorporation provisions. Thomas Sloan, a Shawnee, regretted being omitted from legislation his people favored and warned Thomas that land allotment had been the "reverse of our best interests." Robert Small, from the Iowa tribe, supported this protest because only eighteen out of 108 Iowa allottees still owned land. But W. W. Gilbert, a Potawatomie, indicated that his tribe no longer had any interest in self-government or living on a reservation, since over half the members had less than quarter-blood and feared the idea of "Jim Crowing" themselves. On the other hand the Potawatomies did favor individual loans and business incorporation because they "had everything to gain and nothing to lose."[77]

The final congress assembled at Anadarko and the delegates expressed a variety of opinions concerning the IRA. Delos Lonewolf, a Kiowa, strongly opposed the measure because it put Indian progress "back sixty years." He claimed that he would rather "pay taxes and be a man among men than a useless Indian forever." Any further amendments to the IRA would only get the Indians into "deeper water." Robert Coffey, a delegate for the Comanches, spoke next and pointed out that his tribe wanted to continue the trust period on allotted land but opposed the consolidation of property and the establishment of a reservation. Instead, they hoped to borrow money on an individual basis from the revolving credit fund. The next speaker, John Loco, a Fort Sill Apache, who had been captured with Geronimo, asked why the government wanted "to bring us up like white people and then we come up like white people they don't like it." Loco desired that the government treat him like a "human" and provide his children with a "house and team and everything to work with."[78]

After he returned to Washington, D.C., Collier responded to these conferences by drawing up legislation known as the Thomas-Rogers bill. It reaffirmed federal guardianship for Oklahoma Indians with the purpose of allowing them to "eventually assume full responsibility as citizens." Section 2 reflected this mixed mandate by extending restrictions on land owned by persons having one-half or more Indian blood, while Indians with less than one-half Indian blood would be "relieved of all restrictions" when the secretary of the interior determined it was "in their best interest." To facilitate the latter, the bill required the creation of a competency commission once every four years to examine each Indian with less than one-half blood to determine whether the government should remove restrictions on his property.[79]

Sections 8 through 10 established similar procedures for the administration of Indian wills and heirship lands. They reflected government concern about previous corruption by state courts in probate matters and gave the secretary of the interior "exclusive jurisdiction" over the estates of deceased members of the Osage and Five Civilized Tribes who had one-half or more Indian blood. No guardian could be appointed for these Indians except on a petition approved by the secretary of the interior. Indians with less than one-half blood came under the jurisdiction of the Oklahoma probate courts, but the secretary of the interior still had the authority to investigate state guardians and appear in local courts to protect Indian interests.*

This legislation provided for Indian self-government and communal ownership of land similar to the original Wheeler-Howard bill. Section 6 empowered the secretary of the interior to acquire through "purchase, relinquishment, gift, exchange, or assignment" any restricted land for the purpose of creating new reservations. This land would remain "free from any and all taxes." Any group of Indians living on this tribal property could adopt a constitution and charter which empowered them to borrow money from a two million dollar fund administered by an Oklahoma Indian Credit Corporation. The bill also extended these facilities to ten or more Indians living "in convenient proximity to each other" who wanted to create cooperative marketing and land management associations.[80]

Finally, the Thomas-Rogers bill stated that Congress intended to provide adequate health and educational care for the Indian population

---

*The following probate cases offer an example of the abuses found in Oklahoma state courts. In 1924, Judge William Seawell, from Okfuskee County, approved a contract that allowed white lawyers to collect $1 million from the $5 million estate of John Lewis, a restricted Indian. In addition, the judge appointed eight guardians for the five heirs of John Lewis. In another episode, Ledci Stechi, a full-blood minor Choctaw Indian, inherited twenty acres of valuable oil land from her deceased mother. A guardian was appointed by the local county court, but he paid little attention to the well-being of his ward, who died because of poor health and starvation. After her death, this $131,858 estate was inherited by two Indians, who received only $15,929 each after paying attorney's fees. U.S., Congress, House, Committee on Indian Affairs, *Hearings, on H.R. 6234, General Welfare of the Indians of Oklahoma*, 74th Cong., 1st Sess., 1935, pp. 75, 197.

residing in Oklahoma. It directed the continued operation of existing boarding schools with preference given to poor, retarded, and orphaned children. The bill required Congress to provide funds for the construction of additional day schools, hospitals, and sanatoria. The Indians needed this assistance because 3,700 children in the hills of eastern Oklahoma lacked classrooms, while the government had built only eight hospitals with 521 beds for approximately 50,000 Indians.[81]

This bill came before the Senate and House Indian Affairs Committees during April 1935, and it met opposition from both Indians and whites. Several Indians from western Oklahoma proved especially hostile to the creation of competency commissions when they appeared before the Senate committee. Remembering the work of competency commissions under Commissioner Cato Sells between 1913 and 1921, which had indiscriminately issued fee patents, these Indians feared that the removal of restrictions would result in the loss of their property. Thomas Alfred, an elderly Shawnee, expressed this anxiety when he recalled that agents had come to him and said "please apply for your patent." He refused, but the government sent him one in three months without his consent.[82]

White resistance to the Thomas-Rogers bill proved especially intense at hearings before the House Committee on Indian Affairs. Three members of the committee — Usher Burdick, Thomas O'Malley, and John McGroarty — led the attack against its passage. Burdick warned that it attempted to "shove" the discredited provisions of the Wheeler-Howard bill back on the Indians, while O'Malley praised the Oklahoma delegation for excluding its Indians from "experimental legislation" which treated them like "guinea pigs."[83] McGroarty expressed the mood of the committee by asking what the purpose was of "monkeying" with the Thomas-Rogers bill, instead of killing it.[84]

In order to strengthen their position, these committee members allowed two hostile Oklahoma representatives to testify against the bill. Jack Nichols, whose district was located in the eastern part of the state, claimed that the bill would "drive a wedge" between the Indians and their white neighbors. He disliked the section which struck at the heart of Oklahoma's "sovereignty" by allowing an "autocratic" Interior Department to take over the power of state courts.[85] Nichols indicated that an increase in tax exempt land would make it difficult to maintain adequate school facilities and county government. He pointed out that these objections had caused the Oklahoma House and Senate to pass resolutions opposing the passage of the Thomas-Rogers bill. Wesley Disney of Osage County added his voice of protest by stating that nineteen bar associations had objected to this measure because it clouded land titles and discouraged investments. Disney maintained that the bill would destroy "fifty years' effort" to assimilate the Indians with the white population.[86]

These objections caused Senator Thomas to draft a completely new piece of legislation which Congress passed during June 1936. Known as the Oklahoma Welfare Act, it bore little resemblance to Collier's original proposal. Missing were the sections lifting restrictions on Indian land, authorizing the secretary of the interior to handle certain probate cases, and declaring it the intent of Congress to provide adequate health and educational facilities for Indians. But this act did give the secretary of the interior the power to "acquire by purchase, relinquishment, gift, exchange or assignment" restricted land of "good quality" for the purpose of creating communal ownership of property. This real estate, held in trust by the government, was exempt from all taxes except a state "gross production tax" on oil and gas not in excess of the rate levied upon similar land held in private ownership.[87]

The Oklahoma Indians had the right to engage in self-government and borrow money from a special credit fund. Any recognized tribe or band of Indians except for the Osage, who were excluded from the act, could organize for "its common welfare" and adopt a constitution and charter of incorporation prescribed by the secretary of the interior. Once they adopted a charter by a majority vote, the Indians could borrow money from a two million dollar credit fund. Ten or more Indians who lived in "convenient proximity to each other" could form local cooperative associations and make individual loans.[88]

During Collier's commissionership, nineteen Oklahoma tribes with a total population of 13,241 adopted constitutions, while thirteen ratified charters of incorporation.* Differing from other states, the substantive powers of the tribe were set forth in the charters which allowed the Indians to file law suits, borrow money from the credit fund, own and manage property of every description, negotiate with federal, state, or local governments, and advise the secretary of the interior concerning appropriation estimates. No provision, however, was made for tribal courts. Limited in scope, the constitutions dealt with topics such as tribal membership and organization, while many contained a bill of rights.[89]

The Oklahoma Welfare Act was partially successful, but it did not bring about the realization of Collier's Red Atlantis. All of the Five Civilized Tribes, except for three Creek towns and the Cherokee Keetoowah

---

*The following Oklahoma tribes adopted constitutions: the Cheyenne-Arapaho, Creek (three tribal towns), Caddo, Pawnee, Tonkawa, Eastern Shawnee, Miami, Peoria, Ponca, Seneca, Wyandotte, Iowa, Kickapoo, Potawatomie, Sac and Fox, Absentee-Shawnee, and the United Keetoowah Band. Theodore Haas, *Ten Years of Tribal Government Under IRA* (Washington: U.S. Indian Service, 1947), p. 41.

Band, failed to adopt constitutions and charters because they owned only small amounts of tribal land. The Cherokees, for example, owned 365.87 acres of unsold land, while the Seminoles held title only to the Mekusukey school ground. Nevertheless, at Collier's encouragement most of the Five Tribes revived their tribal governments. The Creek towns sent representatives to a monthly meeting in the old capitol at Okmulgee or at the New Town church northwest of the city to discuss tribal matters. In 1934 these delegates held their first tribal election since 1906, and they selected Roley Canard as chief. In a similar manner, the Seminoles resurrected their tribal organization and elected George Jones as principal chief. Collier also authorized the calling of a Choctaw convention at Goodland which created an advisory council of eleven members and chose W. A. Durant as principal chief. Five years later, Floyd Maytubby was appointed governor of the Chickasaws.[90]

The credit fund was the most successful feature of the Oklahoma Welfare Act. Several chartered tribes such as the Caddo used loans to take their members off direct relief, while the three Creek towns of Thlopthlocco, Alabama-Quassarte, and Kialegee borrowed money to acquire communal land, start business enterprises, and care for indigent members. The government, however, lent most of its money to smaller groups of Indians and by 1939 they had created thirty-nine credit associations which made 193 individual loans worth $138,000. One of these endeavors consisted of giving $2,800 dollars to twelve full-blood Cherokees near Stillwell for the purpose of growing strawberries. They quickly paid off the debt and earned a profit of $600 a year compared to a previous annual income of $54.[91]

The natives of Alaska came under all of the provisions of the IRA when Congress passed the Alaska Reorganization Act in June 1936. An oversight by a congressional conference committee had excluded the Alaska Indians from section 17 of the IRA which provided for tribal incorporation. This resulted in a ruling from the solicitor's office that excluded these Indians from using the revolving credit fund until Congress passed new legislation.[92] The Alaska Reorganization Act corrected this mistake by allowing groups of natives in Alaska to adopt constitutions and charters of incorporation. It authorized the secretary of the interior officially to create reservations on public lands occupied by groups of Indians.[93]

During the New Deal forty-nine villages containing a total population of 10,899 adopted constitutions and charters under the terms of the Alaska Reorganization Act.[94] With the help of bureau officials several communities established trading posts under the authority of the Alaska Native Industries Cooperative Association which borrowed money from the revolving credit fund. Other Indians such as the Haida and Tlingit tribes used the act to form community associations, and they received credit to buy new boats and repair old equipment.[95]

The Department of the Interior also leased a cooperative salmon cannery to the Metlakahtla Indians, who resided on the Annette Islands in southeastern Alaska. This enterprise flourished and the Metlakahtlas built up a large trust fund from their profits. In 1962 the mayor of this village reported that the native-owned cannery and fish traps provided jobs for more than 200 people.[96]

Collier and Ickes used the Alaska Reorganization Act to create six reservations in an attempt to secure native title to public land. Unfortunately, their effort to add others failed because local white interests aroused Indian suspicion by falsely telling them that they would be confined to these areas and lose the citizenship rights acquired in 1924.* One reservation included property on Kodiak Island near the salmon-spawning waters of the Karluck River and the adjoining coast. This angered white commercial fishermen who had to procure licenses to operate in this area, so they filed a lawsuit contesting Ickes' action. In 1949, the Supreme Court ruled in this case that the secretary of the interior lacked statutory authority to convey permanent title to these Indians, thus negating the efforts to secure their property rights.[97]

The limited success of the IRA, the Oklahoma Welfare Act, and the Alaska Reorganization Act disappointed Collier but he pushed for other reforms. With the commissioner's assistance, the Crows in Montana received seventy-seven buffalo from Yellowstone National Park. The Sioux on the Pine Ridge Reservation in South Dakota also obtained fifty-four buffalo, while the bureau offered smaller herds to most of the New Mexico Pueblos.[98] In a similar gesture Collier encouraged the revival of ancient dances that had been previously frowned upon as heathenism. The Gros Ventres in North Dakota held ceremonies to petition the Great Spirit for prosperity; the Assiniboines performed a rain dance; and the Flathead, Blackfeet, and Crows made preparations for Sun Dances.[99]

Collier's daughter-in-law, Mrs. Charles Collier, supported these efforts by successfully promoting the sale of Indian arts and crafts. While working on a PWA project that consisted of compiling a complete directory of native artists and craftsmen, Mrs. Collier developed an interest in expanding the market for Indian products. In 1934, she approached several Navajo and Hopi traders who agreed to send rugs, pottery,

---

*Many Indians in Alaska also became suspicious of the government because of dissatisfaction over the Department of the Interior's failure to protect their reindeer herds from outside competition. M. K. Sniffen, "Eskimo Sentiment," *Indian Truth* 12 (June 1935): 1–2.

blankets, and jewelry to the R. H. Macey store in New York City. Mrs. Collier charged a 10 percent fee for her merchandizing activities and offered to turn this money over to the United Indian Traders Association. Rebuffed when that organization refused (unless she made the percentage considerably higher) Mrs. Collier contacted the American Indian Defense Association, which agreed to cooperate and place these receipts in a special trust fund to encourage future promotion of Indian-made goods.[100]

One year later at Collier's request, Congress passed legislation authorizing the Interior Department to establish an Indian Arts and Crafts Board which consisted of five commissioners appointed for four-year terms. Under the direction of René d'Harnoncourt, the board tried to enlarge the market for Indian arts and crafts and improve methods of production; it also used a government trademark to protect Indian-made goods from imitation.[101] Encouraged when the board established an experimental laboratory at Tesuque, New Mexico, many older Pueblo Indians once more started teaching their children the techniques of pottery making. Other board-sponsored activities included a bead and leatherwork project in Oklahoma, the Navajo Arts and Crafts Guild, an exhibit at the 1939 San Francisco World's Fair, and the publication of a volume entitled *Indian Art of the United States* in cooperation with the Museum of Modern Art in New York.[102] According to Collier, the modest appropriation funding this board limited its effectiveness; nevertheless, the Indian art and craft enterprise increased from $1,000 a year in 1936 to $8,000 a year in 1940.[103]

In another dramatic move, Collier reaffirmed the Indians' close spiritual bond with the land. In 1937, in response to Robert Marshall, the bureau's chief forester, he issued an executive order creating over five million acres of roadless and wilderness areas on several reservations, the largest being the Rainbow Bridge region on the Navajo reservation.* The commissioner hoped that this order would enable the Indians to maintain a retreat where they might escape from the constant "disturbance of the white race" with its "mechanized civilization."[104] An editorial in the *New York Times* approved of this order and it asked white readers: "How would you like to have the Pueblo Indians climb into your house and ask you by the mouth of a girl guide heap damn fool questions?"[105]

These cosmetic reforms, however, failed to alter the reality that Collier had been unable to change "decisively" the Indian affairs system.[106] Several tribes did establish viable self-government, but the IRA

---

*Collier established twelve roadless areas consisting of 4,475,000 acres, and four wild areas aggregating 84,000 acres. For a detailed description of these regions see John Collier, *From Every Zenith* (Denver: Sage Books, 1963), pp. 271–72.

(and subsequent legislation) was flawed because it imposed rigid political and economic ideas on tribes that varied in their cultural orientation. Many Indians such as the Sioux, who lacked tribal solidarity, found it difficult to implement self-government because it created factionalism and grievances. At the other extreme were the Hopis and New Mexico Pueblos, whose cultural conservatism made it hard to adopt white concepts such as majority rule and cooperative economic development. Furthermore, the Senate and House Indian Affairs Committees continued their hostility and this resulted in disastrous budgetary cuts.

While the IRA successfully ended land allotment, restored surplus land at various reservations, and provided funds for purchasing new real estate, it failed to solve the problem of seven million acres of land allotted before 1933.* Most Indians, influenced by two generations of assimilation, refused to return voluntarily their heirship and allotted lands to tribal control, although it meant a reduced standard of living and idleness. This property continued to divide into smaller equities, and the problem became extremely serious on the Great Plains where Indians leased 40 percent of their allotted lands to whites.[107]

But Collier's ideas found some success among closely knit tribes such as the Jicarilla and Mescalero Apaches who used the IRA to promote social and economic progress. They showed that Collier correctly assumed that group life, if given a chance to flower, could become a dynamic force in the evolution of society. Even tribes that encountered difficulty with self-government had the chance to learn through mistakes by running their own affairs. The critics who called Collier a visionary or a sentimentalist had nothing to offer but a return to the old assimilationist policies fostering cultural disorientation and loss of tribal assets.

---

*Tribes that benefited the most from the restoration of surplus land lived on the Grand Portage reservation in Minnesota, the Kiowa, Commanche and Apache reservation in Oklahoma, the Pine Ridge reservation in South Dakota, the Standing Rock reservation in both North and South Dakota, the Colorado River reservation in Arizona, and the Flathead reservation in Montana. "Report of the Secretary of the Interior on Senate bill 1736 to repeal the Indian Reorganization Act," NA, RG 75, Fort Worth Federal Records Center.

9. Thunder Over the Southwest

As an active promoter of social change, Collier wanted to implement the goals of the conservation movement that had flourished during the Progressive era. He worried about waste, exploitation, and the unproductive use of Indian natural resources. Favoring "the gospel of efficiency" and scientific planning, Collier thought that the reservations offered an excellent testing ground for programs such as the prevention of soil erosion, subsistence farming, and the development of community life. The Indians and their lands could thus become "pioneers and laboratories in the supreme new American adventure now being tried under the leadership of the President."[1]

Because he was interested in the managerial reorganization of American society, Collier used the Soil Conservation Service and the National Resources Board to start a series of surveys to help bureau employees introduce grazing control and land management on several reservations.[2] However, Collier stated pointedly that the method of these agencies was more important than the information they compiled. Such reorganizational policies drove home the reality that the United States had to order its future, and they also provided "technicians a tremendous opportunity for . . . enormous improvement through practical perservering economic and social planning."[3]

One survey began in 1933 when a joint committee from the Department of the Interior and the Department of Agriculture went to Arizona to study conditions on the Navajo reservation. Under the leadership of Hugh Bennett, director of the Bureau of Chemistry and Soil in the Agriculture Department, it concluded that the Navajos had overgrazed, destroying several hundred thousand acres of range and causing rapid soil erosion.* Approximately 60 percent of the silt deposited in the Colorado River came from the Navajo reservation. This threatened the usefulness of Boulder Dam and the whole economy of southern California.[4]

During a July 1933 tribal council meeting at Fort Wingate, New Mexico, Collier told the Navajos about the crisis they faced. He explained to the delegates that they could save their range from further destruction only by sharply reducing the number of sheep and goats, altering range privileges, fencing off grazing areas for soil experimentation, and starting an intensive revival of subsistence irrigation farming. Collier warned the council that it could not veto these policies but that he wanted to act with their consent. Faced with little choice, the delegates adopted this first stock reduction program, which caused a tremendous amount of stress in a tribe that measured social status and gained daily subsistence from domestic stock. Conflict and turmoil became a way of life on the reservation for the next twelve years.[5]

Four months later, on October 30, 1933, at Tuba City, Arizona, Collier submitted a more detailed program to the tribal council. He told the Navajos that they must reduce 400,000 sheep and goats but pointed out that the Federal Surplus Relief Corporation had allotted money to purchase much of this livestock, and the government would compensate any income the Indians lost by relief work. He then pointed out the need for other changes such as replacing boarding schools with day schools, developing irrigation projects, and consolidating the six existing agencies into one headquarters. After much debate the council agreed to all of these proposals except stock reduction, which it promised to urge on the tribe.[6]

The Federal Surplus Relief Administration eventually purchased over 86,000 head of sheep, but it handled rather badly this first attempt at stock reduction.[7] By reducing the Navajo stock on a flat rather than graduated scale, the government ignored the minimum number of animals needed by a family for subsistence. While wealthy Navajos culled their herds and eliminated worthless stock, many small owners found their reduced herds completely inadequate. A similar reduction in the goat population deprived families of a source of milk.[8]

In March 1934, the bureau again brought the problem of sheep reduction before the tribal council. Collier and James Stewart, chief

---

*The Hoover administration had previously made a study which reached the same conclusion. It recommended that the Navajos reduce their stock, but took no action because of inadequate funds and insufficient general concern. Alden Stevens, "Once They Were Nomads," *Survey Graphic* 30 (February 1941): 64–67.

of the Indian Office Land Division, promised the councilmen that the speedy reduction of 150,000 goats and 50,000 sheep would insure passage of the Navajo boundary bill that called for the extension of reservation land in New Mexico. The council adopted this plan but insisted that the government omit families with less than 100 sheep or goats from this program. A short time later, Chee Dodge, a Navajo leader, wrote Secretary Ickes criticizing Collier for promising the passage of a bill which in fact depended on the action of Congress. Dodge warned that the failure to keep such promises would destroy the Indians' confidence in the government.[9]

This prediction became a reality when Congress failed to pass the bill, leaving 8,000 Navajos, who were living on the public domain in New Mexico, in "utter chaos." A series of unfortunate events caused these Indians to see their livestock reduced from 100,000 to 37,000. A blizzard in 1932 had decimated many sheep, and whites often provided the Indians with whiskey in return for valuable breeding stock. Furthermore, the Soil Conservation Service lacked the authority both to prevent Spanish-Americans and Anglos from trespassing on Indian property and to develop water sources until Congress settled the boundary dispute. Instead of using caution in this situation, zealous government agents by 1936 had eliminated approximately 12 percent of the Navajo herds in New Mexico, thus allowing whites to use Indian land.[10]

Navajo suspicion of the government increased when Collier created land management districts on the reservation with authority to set the maximum carrying capacity for livestock. The commissioner ended this order by warning the Indians that if after a reasonable time the tribe refused to reduce their herds sufficiently to end overgrazing, he would take the necessary steps to protect their well-being.[11] This contradicted his earlier pronouncement that he would not use compulsion to recast the Indians' economic life, and it resembled the arbitrary orders issued by the bureau during the twenties.

Collier's poor relationship with the Navajos worsened when he involved the Fruitland irrigation project (located on the San Juan River east of Shiprock, New Mexico) in the stock reduction dispute. In 1933, a representative from the bureau told the Navajos that each family at Fruitland would receive twenty acres of land if it agreed to donate one day of free labor each week until the completion of the project.[12] Three years later, after the Navajos finished most of the work, bureau officials suggested that the Indians select a committee to assign twenty-acre allotments. The committee began its work and, consequently, many Indians began to put up fences and plow their land.[13]

However, on April 15, 1936, Superintendent E. R. Fryer held a special meeting to tell the Navajos that new orders called for the assignment of only ten acres and anyone accepting this land must dispose of his sheep and goats. Collier had changed the bureau's position because he worried about providing subsistence living for some of the 4,000 Indian families who owned neither sheep or land. No matter what the justification, the individuals who worked on this project became incensed over the commissioner's failure to keep faith with them about the promised twenty acres. They refused to accept smaller allotments and influenced other Indians from moving into this area.[14]

The restructuring of Navajo administration added to this turmoil. At the beginning of the New Deal, Collier had used PWA funds to start the construction of a new tribal headquarters seven miles south of Ft. Defiance, Arizona, to replace inadequate facilities at Gallup, New Mexico. Collier planned to name this capital *Nee Alneeng* which meant "center of the Navajo world." This phrase, however, irritated many Indians because it was also one of several words for hell; so Collier changed the name to Window Rock. More importantly, the Navajos objected to the replacement of their six jurisdictions with twenty-five subdivisions under the control of one agency. This created confusion and made it difficult for them to consult with their superintendent.[15]

The leader of the Navajo resistance to Collier's policies was Jacob C. Morgan, a missionary and member of the tribal council, who had previously opposed the Wheeler-Howard bill. Morgan launched his campaign against stock reduction at hearings before the House Indian Affairs Committee during May 1936. He complained that Collier had cut stock across the board with little consideration for the small owners who were forced to reduce their herds by almost half. This violated the agreement made two years earlier, which exempted any family having less than 100 livestock, and many Indians who lived in remote areas of the reservation failed to secure relief work. Morgan indicated that the Soil Conservation Service had fenced off grazing areas for experimentation but reneged on its promise to pay the Indians five cents per head for sheep removed from this land. He attacked Collier for refusing to give the Navajos twenty acres of land on the Fruitland irrigation project and for firing Allen Neskahi from his job with the conservation corps after he criticized the commissioner's handling of this matter.[16]

Morgan's testimony had little impact on government policy, but he gained support on the reservation when Collier announced plans to reorganize the tribal council in order to make it more representative and to gain support for his stock reduction program. On November 24, 1936, the council acquiesced to Collier's proposal by abolishing itself and creat-

National Archives

Navajos waiting for an afternoon session of the Tribal
Council, Window Rock, 1939.

ing an executive committee to select local leaders to sit on a constitutional assembly. Led by Henry Taliman, a Navajo, and Father Berard
Haile, a local priest, this committee picked seventy individuals from a
list of 250 submitted by the Indians. At Haile's insistence most of these
delegates were headmen or traditional leaders who would supposedly
support Collier.[17]

The constitutional assembly met at Window Rock during April 1937.
Chee Dodge, an older patriarch of the tribe, praised the revision of the
old council, and he received support from Superintendent Fryer and Taliman, who introduced a resolution making the assembly a provisional
council with the authority to draft a constitution. But Morgan objected
to this procedure because he believed that the entire tribe should have
voted on whether or not to disband the old council. Superintendent Fryer

squelched this opposition by warning that the secretary of the interior had created the council in 1923 and thus he could abolish it and create a new assembly. Unimpressed with this explanation, Morgan questioned whether white election procedures were held in this manner, and he bolted the convention with several other delegates.[18]

Morgan received support from Matthew K. Sniffen, the secretary of the Indian Rights Association, who publicly castigated Collier in several editorials in *Indian Truth*. Sniffen accused the commissioner of using a "big stick" to force the Navajos to accept his conservation program. He claimed that when the council refused to act as a rubber stamp body by objecting to drastic stock reduction and day schools, Collier reorganized it and handpicked a slate of candidates who would support the bureau. Sniffen believed the Navajos were quite capable of choosing their own leaders through "bona fide" popular elections.[19]

Criticism of Collier's policies continued during June 1937, when Morgan took a delegation of thirteen Navajos to Washington, D.C., in order to testify before the Senate Indian Affairs Committee. They asked Congress to implement a five point program which would bring the Navajos real self-government.[20] Outlined by Paul Palmer, their attorney from New Mexico, it requested Collier's removal from office, the reestablishment of the old tribal council, giving the council authority to deal with all matters affecting the Navajos, the firing of Superintendent Fryer and other bureau officials on the reservation, and a return to the six jurisdictions rather than one central agency. Palmer criticized the bureau for wasting money on extravagant projects, while some Indians still ate prairie dogs; and he condemned the day schools where teachers taught Navajos how to dance but neglected reading.[21]

Obviously disturbed by this hostile testimony, Collier's face "showed emotion," and he interrupted Palmer to demonstrate that his statements were filled with numerous errors.[22] The commissioner pointed out that the Navajo council had supported his program of stock reduction, range control, and the consolidation of six jurisdictions into one agency. In order to help the Navajos implement stock reduction, the government had spent $1.8 million in wages on public works and soil conservation projects to supplement their incomes, built thirty-seven new day schools for their benefit, and the curriculum in these schools taught students how to read English as well as practical matters related to everyday life.[23]

This defense, however, failed to prevent continued conflict on the Navajo reservation. In August 1937, a crisis arose after Navajo policemen arrested and beat up Hosteen Tso, Morgan's brother-in-law, and two other Indians for refusing to dip their sheep to remove scabies.[24] One year later, tension again surfaced when the tribal council requested a reduction of the Navajo horse population from 70,000 to 30,000 in order to make room for more sheep. Collier added to this crisis by suggesting that the horse reduction would not "injure the economic royalists among the tribe but it would greatly benefit the Navajos as a whole."[25]

The commissioner, despite his previous inflexibility, implemented a policy of reconciliation during the summer of 1938 by calling for a popular election to create a third tribal council. The Navajos demonstrated their irritation over Collier's stock reduction program when they chose Morgan for the position of tribal chairman. In his inaugural address, Morgan warned that he refused to act as a puppet of the bureau but emphasized the need for compromise and reconciliation. Superintendent Fryer responded to this overture by admitting before the council that he had made mistakes and wanted to cooperate in the future.[26]

This tranquility ended in October 1940 when maverick Navajos under the leadership of Dashne Cheschillege formed the Navajo Indian Rights Association which eventually claimed to have 6,000 members. Cheschillege, an educated Navajo and one of Morgan's rivals, continued to oppose stock reduction although the tribal council had reached an agreement with the bureau in this matter. Frustrated over Morgan's refusal to cooperate with his association, Cheschillege wrote President Roosevelt a letter requesting Collier's resignation because his theories seemed communistic.[27] He sent similar protests to Mrs. Eleanor Roosevelt who discussed the Navajo situation in her column, "My Day," in the *Washington Daily News.**

Concerned over this continued agitation, Secretary Ickes asked President Roosevelt to intervene in the Navajo crisis. The chief executive responded by writing an open letter to the Navajos which warned that in order to prevent soil erosion they must make the necessary sacrifices by reducing their sheep, goats, and horses. He asked the Indians to cooperate with the government and abide by the laws and regulations passed by their tribal council.[28] Roosevelt's intervention calmed the unrest on the reservation, but Collier had minimal success with the Navajos because the struggle over stock reduction dwarfed all other issues.†

Besides his problems with the Navajos, Collier faced frustration among the Pueblos, who had shown only mild interest in the Indian Reorganization Act. The first manifestation of unrest occurred at Taos

---

*Collier doubted if Mrs. Eleanor Roosevelt was antagonistic to his program but she thought he might have been "over-enthusiastic, idealistic, or hopeful." The commissioner felt that the president believed his concepts were developed too exclusively from Southwestern data. John Collier to Raymond Armsby, June 15, 1937, Collier Papers.

† President Roosevelt was also probably responding to a critical letter he received from the Indian Rights Association asking for drastic action to stop the chaos and demoralization among the Navajos. *New York Times,* August 29, 1938, p. 21.

over the use of peyote by the Native American Church. As early as 1917 conservative officers at Taos had split the Pueblo into two factions by persecuting peyote users who threatened their ancient traditions. This hostility appeared again during the New Deal because conservative leaders insisted that self-government gave them unlimited authority to destroy the Native American Church. Consequently, on February 12, 1936, Antonio Mirabal, an Indian law enforcement officer, displayed his federal badge and gun in order to enter a house where a peyote ceremony was about to start. Mirabal placed his gun at the chest of John Reynal, the cult's leader, confiscated the supply of peyote, arrested three leaders of the Native American Church, and confined them in the filthy pueblo jail.*

The peyote church members immediately sought legal aid, but bureau officials persuaded them to settle the dispute within the Pueblo. A short time later, a trial was held at a council meeting and Mirabal acted as prosecutor and judge. He fined fifteen peyote men $100 each and Geronimo Gomez $225 after Gomez justified peyote worship and questioned the legality of the court's proceedings. Because they did not have any money, Mirabal confiscated approximately 300 acres of their irrigated land. In addition, he claimed that the peyote men had failed to "unwitch" a psychotic named Alvino Montoya and he used this charge to imprison some of the defendants.[29]

When the Indians continued to fight over the use of peyote, Collier traveled to New Mexico in order to meet with the governor and tribal council on June 16, 1936. He told the Indians that he wanted to preserve their ancient institutions but they must respect freedom of conscience. Before departing, Collier arranged a meeting at Albuquerque between Mirabal and Gomez. They agreed to implement voluntarily a plan which affirmed the principle of religious liberty while allowing the council to restrict the activities of the Native American Church. The peyote men gained the right to practice their religion in a remote part of the village; in return, they promised to observe kiva life, administer peyote only to healthy Indians, and to refrain from all proselytizing.[30]

Much to Collier's dismay, the peyote controversy made up only part of the growing Pueblo dissatisfaction. In 1935, Collier had reorganized their administration by consolidating the northern, southern, and Zuni jurisdictions into the United Pueblo Agency with headquarters at Albuquerque. In place of the three superintendents, Collier appointed as general superintendent, Sophie Aberle, a medical doctor who had

*Throughout this episode Mirabal received advice from Mabel Dodge Luhan and her husband, Antonio. John Collier, "Memorandum for Secretary Ickes, June 1, 1936," Collier Papers.

lived among the Pueblos for seven years to conduct health and anthropological studies. Furthermore, he announced that the bureau would seek
assistance from the Soil Conservation Service to help the Indians rehabili-
tate their eroded range lands.[31]

These changes proved especially unpopular at Zuni, where the governor of the Pueblo complained that the government had promised when
they voted for the IRA to consult with them. Instead, Collier had
appointed a woman superintendent without their consent, transferred a
trusted doctor to Santa Fe, and put them under the United Pueblo Agency
although they had little in common with the rest of the Pueblo Indians.[32]
The Zunis were also apprehensive about stock reduction — especially
Aberle's decision to allow Spanish-American stockmen to share grazing
rights on newly acquired submarginal land.[33]

Mabel Dodge Luhan, who had persuaded Collier to visit New Mexico in 1920, supported the Zunis by creating unrest among the Taos
Indians over the appointment of Aberle, a woman she considered old
fashioned and lacking the natural instincts of a good superintendent.[34]
Luhan broke with Collier because he had neglected to implement important programs such as preventive medicine and the suppression of peyote.*
She found it disturbing that they should have opposing loyalties, but suggested that Collier had become too remote from the Indians.†

Luhan's first major attack against the commissioner came on April
6, 1936, during an All Pueblo Council meeting held at Santo Domingo,
where she used her husband Antonio Luhan, to discredit Aberle. Collier
attended this gathering in order to discuss the IRA, livestock reduction
and the control of soil erosion, but two delegates from Taos requested
time to register complaints.[35] Antonio Luhan claimed that the new Taos
day school lacked furniture and teaching equipment, and that several
girls had returned home pregnant from the Santa Fe boarding facility.
He received support from Antonio Mirabal who indicated that the Indians
felt uneasy about bringing these grievances before Aberle because she
was a woman.[36]

---

*Mrs. Luhan had disliked peyote since 1914 when one of her friends in New
York City took this drug, became neurotic and incoherent. Mabel Dodge Luhan,
Movers and Shakers, Vol. 3 (New York: Harcourt and Brace, 1936), pp. 265–67.

†The commissioner believed that Luhan's desire to obtain land was another
motive behind her hostility. In 1934, some Indians at Taos had received land par-
celled out within the Tenorio Tract. Most of this property had passed under the
control of the Luhan family, so Collier issued an order stopping irrigation work on
the Tenorio Tract until Taos officers agreed to an equitable distribution of land
use rights. The confiscation of irrigated land in the peyote episode was, in part,
retaliation by the Luhans against Collier's order. John Collier, "MSS. on the Pueblos,
May 22, 1936," Collier Papers; and Mabel Dodge Luhan to John Collier, March 10,
1936, Collier Papers.

Collier defended Aberle at this All Pueblo Council meeting and several Indians sided with him, but he showed impatience because of the earlier peyote controversy. A few days later he wrote Mirabal a letter claiming that all the Pueblos except Taos and Zuni supported his policies. Collier pointed out that what Mirabal said as an individual was his own concern; on the other hand, if his stubborn opposition continued, he would have to terminate his employment with the bureau.[37] When the Indian refused to recant, the commissioner eliminated his salary from the government payroll.

The dismissal of Mirabal demonstrated Collier's intolerant side and provided Mrs. Luhan with another issue. On May 5, 1936, she sent a lengthy letter to the editor of the Santa Fe *New Mexican,* which implied that the Indians' request for the removal of Aberle was consistent with a clause found in the original Wheeler-Howard bill. They had called the All Pueblo Council meeting because of resentment over consolidating the pueblos and putting them under the direction of an inexperienced woman. Luhan suggested that the Indians who supported Collier at this gathering were government employees, and indicated that the commissioner had resorted to political blackmail by firing Mirabal.[38]

Collier replied to Luhan's statement in an interview with an Associated Press reporter. He called her statements "incredibly inaccurate" because the bureau paid salaries to only three of the seventeen representatives on the All Pueblo Council and these men were interpreters.[39] He suggested that her real motive for criticizing him stemmed from the false belief that she would "run the show and not from behind the curtains" once he became commissioner.[40] These countercharges, however, only aggravated a tense situation and caused Luhan to send a list of her grievances to Senator Elmer Thomas, chairman of the Senate Indian Affairs Committee.[41]

Thomas responded to Luhan's charges by holding a committee hearing at the Santa Fe Federal Court Building during August 1936. Antonio Mirabal spoke for the Taos Indians, and he explained that they resented Collier's appointment of a woman for superintendent as well as his attempts to prevent their suppression of peyote at the Pueblo. Mirabal claimed that dissatisfaction existed because the new Taos day school lacked equipment, several young girls had become pregnant at the unsupervised Santa Fe boarding school, and government officials permitted outside livestock and tourists to overrun their sacred Blue Lake area.[42]

Collier appeared before this hearing to refute Mirabal's charges. He explained that the bureau intervened in the peyote matter, not to coerce the Indians, but to help them settle their differences. As far as the pregnancies were concerned, seven of the eight Mirabal referred to originated during vacation when the girls stayed at home. The commissioner admitted that the Taos day school, built with PWA funds, lacked the necessary equipment and teachers, but appropriations had lagged behind construction. He defended Superintendent Aberle by pointing out that all the Pueblos except Taos and Zuni, which objected to his consolidation program, had supported her at various All Pueblo Council meetings.[43]

After these hearings ended, Collier decided to have a showdown with Mirabal and other conservatives at Taos over the peyote controversy. On September 18, 1936, Collier sent a letter to Secretary Ickes which recommended drastic action because the Taos officers had refused to abide by the earlier voluntary agreement to cease their opposition to the Native American Church. The commissioner suggested that Ickes inform the governor that if he refused to return the confiscated land, the government would invoke section 17 of the Pueblo Lands Act which prohibited alterations in land title without the secretary of the interior's approval.[44]

Ickes agreed with Collier's position and notified the Taos governor to end all religious persecution. The secretary told the Indians that he found it intolerable to imprison members of the Native American Church and take their property for a purely religious offense. Therefore, he would have to invoke section 17 of the Pueblo Lands Act, to invalidate all land transfers, and he directed the officers to make good any damages or losses caused by their seizure of this property. Santano Sandoval, the governor of Taos, replied that he could not subscribe to Collier's compromise formula without violating New Mexico state law which outlawed the use of peyote and he demanded a federal court hearing — but Ickes remained adamant.[45]

Although Collier had successfully protected the rights of the Native American Church, this episode proved unfortunate because it forced him to use the arbitrary methods he had deplored during the twenties.* Charles de Y. Elkus, a Defense Association lawyer, summed up the situation correctly when he warned that it threatened to ruin the commissioner's close relationship with the Pueblos. According to Elkus, Collier used political indiscretion by firing Mirabal, while the appointment of a woman superintendent created needless hurdles. He pointed out that the commissioner

---

*Matthew K. Sniffen, secretary of the Indian Rights Association, found Collier's position ironic. In 1925, Collier had defended the officers at Taos when they persecuted Christian progressives with little concern for that religious minority. Ten years later he followed the position of Commissioner Charles H. Burke who had tried to curtail the power of conservative tribal leaders. Matthew K. Sniffen, "Religious Liberty," *Indian Truth* 13 (December 1936): 2–3.

had implemented too many new programs with unrealistic ideas, instead he should have paid more attention to administrative details.[46]

Unhappily for the Indians, Collier failed to follow this advice and adopt a more modest posture. On March 1, 1937, in an editorial written for *Indians at Work,* he further deteriorated his position with Congress by defending President Roosevelt's unpopular court-packing proposal. Collier agreed with his chief executive that the deficiency of personnel had resulted in overcrowded dockets, and to prove his point he cited the inability of Defense Association lawyers to obtain a hearing in order to overturn the niggardly decisions of the Pueblo Lands Board. He doubted whether the present overburdened court could "meet its responsibility if every Justice among the nine were a Solomon of wisdom and a Napoleon of execution."[47] Unlike the president, Collier suggested that the fundamental reason for the court proposition was clearly an issue of social policy — "to insure a court possessed of a frame of mind receptive toward modern solutions for modern problems."[48]

This editorial brought a sharp reaction from Senator Bennett Champ Clark of Missouri, who helped form the conservative Democratic-Republican coalition which stymied New Deal reform. From the floor of the Senate, Clark accused Collier of using public funds "for propagandizing purposes." He pointed out that the commissioner's editorials in *Indians at Work* had supported court-packing, attempted to influence congressmen in favor of the IRA, and defended conservation programs. This was an "open and flagrant violation" of section 201 of the United States Criminal Code which meant that Collier had committed a misdemeanor and should be removed from office.[49]

Senator Burton K. Wheeler agreed with Clark but expressed little surprise that Collier wanted to line up the Indians "to pack the court with additional judges."[50] He explained that long before the president sent his message to Congress, Collier had formulated the Wheeler-Howard bill which tried to reorganize the lower courts by creating a federal court of Indian affairs. The senator admitted that he sponsored this legislation because he favored letting the Indians "carry on their own affairs." But he soon became disillusioned after Collier sent a "lot of uplifters" from Chicago and New York, who never saw an Indian except in a moving picture show, to impose their social theories on the Indians. When the tribes objected to these policies, Collier continued "the same old practice of controlling Indian councils that was in vogue under the Harding administration."[51]

Because he disliked the Indian New Deal, Wheeler had introduced a bill on February 24, 1937, which recommended that Congress repeal the IRA. He favored this legislation because many Indians resented "being herded like cattle" on to reservations where the bureau treated them like "some special kind of creature."[52] He pointed out that many Blackfeet disapproved of the act and over 500 Flatheads had sent a petition asking for exclusion from all of its provisions. Wheeler charged that the bureau had given tribal organizations powers beyond the scope authorized by the IRA and discriminated against Indians who failed to support this measure.[53]

There were other important factors, however, which caused Wheeler's hostility. A proud sensitive man, he found President Roosevelt's appointment of Homer Cummings for attorney general distasteful because Cummings had associated with Bruce Kremer, an individual close to the Anaconda interests, whom Wheeler had fought all his life. The senator became especially irritated when Cummings failed to promote public development of the Flathead power site, and he resented Collier's behind the scenes negotiations which thwarted his efforts to expose the attorney general's conservatism.[54] More importantly, Wheeler feared that the New Deal's recognition of particular social groups would divide rather than unite the country. He favored a moralistic approach to reform which stressed nineteenth century individualism pitted against the evils of centralized power.

Collier thought that Wheeler wanted to repeal the IRA because of his general irritation with the administration, and he refuted the senator's reasoning in a press release.[55] The commissioner questioned whether the IRA segregated the Indians any more than white people who made "themselves a class apart by forming municipal organizations or entering into business partnership." He indicated that chartered tribes received not only rights specified in the act, but all powers previously granted to them by earlier law. As far as discrimination was concerned, Collier claimed that an analysis of the bureau's allocation of funds since the passage of the IRA revealed that tribes who voted against it had been supplied with more money on a per capita basis.[56]

The commissioner stressed that certain of Wheeler's charges contained only partial truths. He agreed that the full-blood Blackfeet, a minority of the tribe, had expressed discontent with the IRA, but their complaint stressed that the mixed-bloods used this legislation in order to assimilate the tribe too rapidly. He discredited the senator's statement that 500 Flatheads had petitioned for the IRA's repeal; instead, they wanted per capita payments to help alleviate poverty. To further disprove Wheeler's allegations, Collier pointed out that this tribe had supported him on three separate occasions by voting for the IRA, by adopting a constitution, and by establishing a charter.[57]

Much to his surprise, Collier received support from the Indian Rights Association. Matthew K. Sniffen, its secretary, claimed that patient educational work would have achieved better results than Collier's "fanfare methods" that promised instant salvation, but he opposed complete repeal because it would leave the Indians in a state of uncertainty and add to existing confusion. Sniffen defended the IRA since it provided needed benefits such as extending restrictions on allotted lands, money for education and land purchases, and a revolving credit fund.[58]

Several other welfare groups joined the Indian Rights Association and they helped defeat Wheeler's bill. The National Association on Indian Affairs and the American Indian Defense Association issued a joint statement praising the IRA, the product of more than ten years of reform activities. These associations found Wheeler's action "incomprehensible" because of his earlier progressive record, but warned that as long as the Indians owned land, attacks by predatory whites would continue.[59] Mrs. Edith Murphy, state chairman of Indian welfare for the California Federation of Women's Clubs, added her voice of protest against the repeal of the IRA, and she was supported by Winifred Codman, the national vice-chairman on Americanism for the Daughters of the American Revolution, who claimed that Collier's policies had brought about a positive psychological change in the Indians' attitude toward life.[60]

Although pleased with the defeat of Wheeler's bill, Collier became increasingly concerned about the activities of the Oklahoma-based American Indian Federation. The mentality of the AIF became clear when thirty delegates met at Salt Lake City on July 23–25, 1936.[61] Led by Joseph Bruner, their president, and O. K. Chandler, a mixed-blood Indian who had been superintendent of the Quapaw Agency, they attacked Collier for supposedly opening the gates to communism with the IRA, encouraging the decline of Christianity, and appointing radicals to his staff.* Approximately 100 pamphlets were spread on two large tables and only a few of them mentioned Indians. The remainder dealt with the dangers of bolshevism inherent in the New Deal.†

At first a paper organization, the federation gained support by pro-

---

*Collier believed that O. K. Chandler's hostility came from his resentment over not receiving a position with the bureau. The commissioner refused his request because Chandler's civil service status had been revoked by the Hoover administration for illegally trading with the Indians while superintendent of the Quapaw Agency. John Collier to Senator Joseph O'Mahoney, May 23, 1936, NA, RG 75, File on the American Indian Federation.

†One pamphlet contained a speech by Paul Joseph Goebbels, the Nazi Party chieftain, called "Communism With the Mask Off." "List of Books, Pamphlets and Handouts on Display at the Annual Convention of the American Indian Federation, Chamber of Commerce Building, Salt Lake City, July 23–25, 1936," NA, RG 75, File on the American Indian Federation, 1933–1937.

moting a cash claims settlement. Leaders of the AIF solicited from Indians one dollar for themselves and the same amount for each ancestor; in return they promised to persuade Congress to pass legislation to pay the Indians $3,000 for each dollar spent. Upset that Collier had failed to secure passage of a bill introduced in 1935, which recommended the creation of an Indian Claims Commission, 4,664 Indians fell victims to the federation's scheme.[62]

Senator Elmer Thomas from Oklahoma and Representative Usher Burdick from North Dakota temporarily raised their hopes by introducing similar bills at the federation's request. This legislation provided for the final discharge of federal supervision over members of the AIF who owned land allotments, and it paid these Indians $3,000 cash as a final settlement for their claims against the United States. All other enrolled individuals could participate in this agreement one year after the bill passed, but federal guardianship would continue for other Indians who maintained their vested tribal property rights.[63]

Collier immediately attacked the AIF proposal as a cleverly designed racket to victimize unsuspecting Indians. Worried that it might succeed, however, he secured assistance from Secretary Ickes who asked Thomas and Burdick to withdraw their support for the bill because it financed right-wing activities and would cost the government over $900 million.[64] Senator Thomas, who was sensitive about the political power of the AIF in his state, refused to respond, but Representative Burdick dropped his sponsorship after further consideration. He agreed that the bill contradicted itself by attempting to liberate individual Indians while at the same time perpetuating tribal relations.[65]

This setback failed to deter leaders of the federation, who joined with Nazi groups to gain support for their crusade to abolish the Indian New Deal. The German government had decreed that Indians belonged to the Aryan race and it sent Colin Ross, a commentator for Nazi newspapers, on trips to Mexico and the United States where he issued press releases claiming that the Indians suffered as suppressed minorities. Ross predicted that the Indians in South America would soon overthrow their oppressors and establish an Indo-America affiliated with Germany.[66]

This propaganda appealed to leaders of the federation such as Elwood A. Towner, a mixed-blood Indian and attorney from Portland, Oregon, who used the German-American Bund to discredit Collier. Known as Chief Red Cloud, he dressed in full Indian costume, wearing a headdress of white, green, and lavender feathers with a thunderbird design or swastika in the center of his forehead. Towner told audiences attending his lecture tours on the West Coast, that Nathan Margold and other Jews in the Interior Department drew up the IRA.* He called Collier a "Jew-loving Pink Red" who associated with Roger Baldwin, the legal advisor of the "communist-inspired" American Civil Liberties Union. Towner labelled President Roosevelt a Jew whose real name was "Rosenfelt," and he advocated a dictatorship based on Hitler's form of government, so that the Indians could "eliminate" the Jews from the bureau.[67]

Besides the German-American Bund, the AIF cooperated with other fascist groups such as the James True Associates and Pelly's Silver Shirts. According to Collier, James True, one of the "most vicious Nazi pamphleteers in the United States," had circulated his members to raise money for Mrs. Alice Lee Jemison, a district president of the federation.[68] She received additional support from William Dudley Pelly, whose Silver Shirt organization centered in Asheville, North Carolina. He published a booklet entitled, "Indians Aren't Red; The Inside Story of Administration Attempts to Make Communists of the North Carolina Cherokees," which claimed that Collier had used the bureau as the vanguard for a new social order and he filed a lawsuit claiming that Collier illegally used government funds to publish *Indians at Work* for propaganda purposes.[69]

This affiliation with extremist groups brought unexpected dividends when isolationist members of the Senate Indian Affairs Committee such as Elmer Thomas, Lynn Frazier, and Burton K. Wheeler supported the AIF to embarrass the Roosevelt administration.† They allowed federation leaders to appear before their hearings and permitted A. A. Grorud, the committee's special attorney, to use his office as a center for the activities of Mrs. Jemison and Joseph Bruner.[70] This resulted in favorable committee action on a bill introduced by Lynn Frazier, in 1939, which exempted from the IRA the following Indian groups: the Pine Ridge,

---

*Elwood A. Towner's accusations were aimed at such other Jews in the bureau as Felix Cohen, Ward Shepard, Robert Marshall, and Walter Woehlke. Collier had appointed these individuals because their ethnic background caused them to sympathize with his effort to restore community life on the reservations. Hazel W. Hertzberg, *The Search For an American Indian Identity: Modern Pan-Indian Movements* (Syracuse: Syracuse University Press), p. 311.

†Senator Burton K. Wheeler openly associated with members of the federation at speeches before the America First Committee, while his son John Wheeler collaborated with F. G. Collett, the executive representative for Indians of California, an organization that affiliated with Pelly's Silver Shirts and the German-American Bund. The American Indian Federation also received support from Congressman Martin Dies of Texas, chairman of the House Committee on Un-American Activities. On November 24, 1938, Collier was summoned to appear before the Dies committee to refute charges by Alice Lee Jemison that the bureau had come under communist influence. *New York Times,* November 24, 1938, p. 1; "The Notarized Testimony of Stella Von Bulow, October 18, 1941," NA, RG 75, File on Michael Harrison; and Michael Harrison to Miss Winifred Pomeroy, October 13, 1941, NA, RG 75, File on Michael Harrison.

Elwood A. Towner places an Indian headdress on a leader of the German-American Bund.

Standing Rock, Cheyenne River, and Yankton Sioux tribes, all Indian
groups in Nevada and California, the Eastern Band of Cherokees in North
Carolina, the Indians on the Colorado River reservation in Arizona, and
the Navajos in New Mexico. In fact, however, some of these tribes had
already rejected this legislation.*

The committee report which accompanied the bill summarized
charges made by the federation against Collier. It warned that the IRA
had tried to force the Indians back into a primitive state by creating communal governments which discouraged private ownership of property
and inheritance rights. This report accused bureau officials of intimidating
Indians who opposed the act through arrests and imprisonment, while the
few tribes that adopted constitutions and charters became involved in
factional disputes. Finally, the report criticized Collier for trying to establish a "state or nation within a nation," an act contrary to the principles
of the American Republic. The committee believed that the Indians had
to stand alone as citizens because their greatest achievement would come
by adopting white civilization.[71]

When this repeal bill passed the Senate, Collier made a dramatic
appearance before the House Indian Affairs Committee, during June 1940,
to block its passage. He told the congressmen that the Senate report which
accompanied the bill contained "the style of language, and even in places
the favorite particular slogans and phrases" of the AIF and other "fifth
column" groups such as Pelly's Silver Shirts, the German-American
Bund, and the James True Associates. Collier implied that a careless
Senate Indian Affairs Committee had been "encircled and captured" by
these organizations.[72]

This testimony caused John Schafer of Wisconsin, a member of the
House Indian Affairs Committee, to draw up legislation which reflected
the position of the more moderate Indian Rights Association. It continued the IRA but permitted dissatisfied tribes which had adopted constitutions and charters to hold elections to annul all such obligations,
including corporate loans, trust agreements, and leases of their land.
After this bill reached the floor of the House, Francis Case from South
Dakota inserted a provision allowing tribes to accept particular sections
of the IRA, such as educational loans and the Sioux Benefits, while

---

*Lynn Frazier's omnibus legislation combined several individual bills introduced
by Senators Pat McCarran of Nevada, James Murray of Montana, Dennis Chavez
of New Mexico, and Representative John McGroarty of California, which would
have abolished the IRA in their states. John Collier, "Six Efforts in Congress to
Destroy the IRA." March 4, 1937, NA, RG 75, Records Concerning the Wheeler-
Howard Act, Part 8; and Congressional Record, 76th Cong., 3rd Sess., January 18,
1940, 86, Part 1: 469.

rejecting self-government.[73] This amended legislation passed the House and was sent to a conference committee but the conferees failed to agree on a compromise solution.

Collier had narrowly avoided a major defeat, but he found it difficult to prevent the negative impact of World War II on his reforms. The bureau experienced the greatest loss of personnel in its history when over 800 regular employees left for military service or transferred to agencies more directly connected with the war. The great exodus of approximately 50 percent of the able-bodied Indian men from the reservations to the armed forces or to war industries added to the demise of the New Deal's tribal self-government and cooperative economic programs.[74]

The war also destroyed most of Collier's efforts to improve Indian health conditions. Secretary Ickes warned the director of the budget that the bureau faced "an actual breakdown of its medical service" and requested authority to employ physicians and dentists who had not attained full citizenship for the duration of the war.[75] By 1944, there existed 100 vacancies for full and part-time doctors as well as 188 openings for nurses. Collier thought this situation alarming because "it was impossible to provide Indians even the most essential medical care," while restrictions in local transportation, due to the rubber shortage, further limited the effectiveness of remaining health personnel.[76]

Similarly, the bureau's conservation effort suffered because reduced appropriations brought a suspension of capital investment on the reservations. This ended the construction of roads and buildings, and irrigation work diminished in order to conserve materials vital to war projects. In 1942, Congress scuttled the Indian Division of the Civilian Conservation Corps and public relief projects such as the WPA which assisted Indians. Collier agreed that these activities were secondary to the successful conclusion of military campaigns, but he warned that accelerated erosion continued to destroy Indian and other lands throughout the nation.[77]

Interdepartmental cooperation between the Collier administration and other government agencies drastically declined after 1941 when the Bureau of the Budget compelled the removal of the Indian Service to the Merchandise Mart in Chicago to make room for war related activities. There Indian Service employees found it difficult to communicate with the Civil Service Commission, the United States Public Health Service, and the Soil Conservation Service.[78] The transfer to Chicago thus prevented the daily contacts needed with Congress to safeguard Indian interests.*

---

*Collier and a few bureau officials did manage to remain in Washington.

Embittered by the bureau's forced exile, Collier believed that the Bureau of the Budget wanted to usurp the power of the cabinet and control social policy. He feared this shift of power because its "anonymous young men" trained in administrative science knew little about "the dramatic flow of government at its terminal points into the life of the people."[79] In a lengthy letter sent to Secretary Ickes, the commissioner complained that his loyal and conscientious staff had become demoralized because they refused to believe the war justified so drastic a move as pulling up families "by the roots" and moving them half way across the continent. This removal impaired efficiency at a time when the government needed to scrutinize every penny, and he feared that "those who contrived this plan" wanted to make it permanent.[80]

Nevertheless, Collier continued his reform attempts by trying to revive Indian nationalism throughout the western hemisphere. In 1938 he drafted a resolution, presented before the Eighth International Conference of the American Nations at Lima, Peru, that recommended the establishment of an Inter-American Indian Institute.[81] This paved the way for the first Pan-American conference on Indian life, held at Patzcuaro, Mexico, for ten days during the spring of 1940. Fifty-six official delegates from nineteen American republics, seventy-one social scientists, and forty-seven Indians representing various tribes met to collaborate on the problems of the 30 million Indians in the western hemisphere.*

The conference met as a general assembly at the Caltzontizin Theatre but most work was done in smaller sessions in the Patzcuaro Public Library, where social scientists presented over one hundred papers on education, health, law, economics, and Indian culture. After listening to these papers, the delegates drafted seventy-two resolutions that furnished the basis for a hemisphere-wide policy. They included suggestions that each American republic create an agency to help its Indians build a viable economic life by providing them with needed land, water, credit, and cooperative farming techniques. The delegates recommended that their governments protect Indian culture, utilize native languages in community oriented educational programs, grant Indian women social equality, develop schools of rural medicine, and establish anthropology departments at state universities to train experts in native administration.[82]

The Patzcuaro Conference created by international agreement a permanent Inter-American Indian Institute to serve as a clearinghouse

---

*Only Paraguay and Canada failed to send official delegates. *The Final Act, The First Inter-American Conference on Indian Life,* Patzcuaro, Mexico, April 14–24, 1940, (Washington: Office of Indian Affairs, 1940), pp. 7–10, Elmer Thomas Papers.

for maintaining collaboration between the American nations on matters affecting Indians. Authorized to collect and distribute scientific investigations applicable to the solution of Indian problems, the institute published two bilingual journals, the quarterly *America Indigena* and the bi-monthly *Boletín Indigenista,* to foster the interchange of information on programs being developed throughout the hemisphere.[83]

The meeting at Patzcuaro provided for establishment of an affiliated National Indian Institute by each member nation. On November 1, 1943, President Roosevelt signed an executive order setting up a National Indian Institute in the United States. The tasks of this organization consisted of promoting the cooperation of learned societies in the fields of Indian administration, developing research projects, and publishing bibliographies on Indian matters. However, Jed Johnson, chairman of the House Subcommittee on Interior Appropriations, refused to allocate money for the institute because he was reluctant to increase the budget to assist Indians in other countries.[84] Consequently, President Roosevelt wrote a letter to Nelson Rockefeller, coordinator of Commercial and Cultural Relations between the American Republics, and secured $32,000 to privately finance the project.[85]

The National Indian Institute, under the direction of Collier, sponsored an Indian Personality Study by the Committee on Human Development at the University of Chicago. Supervised by Professor W. Lloyd Warner, this investigation used social scientists to discover the impact of the New Deal on selected tribes and to suggest proposals for increasing the effectiveness of Indian administration. In 1944, with only one monograph finished, the Committee on Human Development terminated its contract with the bureau for a variety of reasons, including the development of tension between Collier and Warner and the inability of the anthropologists to make administrative recommendations.*

But this problem failed to deter Collier, who made arrangements for the completion of the administrative phase of the study with the Society for Applied Anthropology. The final results, published in Laura

---

*Between 1941 and 1946, the Indian Bureau contributed $36,000 to cover the expense of this study. The completed monographs included Clyde Kluckhohn and Dorothea Leighton, *The Navajo* (Cambridge: Harvard University Press, 1947); Gordon MacGregor, *Warriors Without Weapons: A Study of the Society and Personality Development of the Pine Ridge Sioux* (Chicago: University of Chicago Press); Laura Thompson and Alice Joseph, *The Hopi Way* (Chicago: University of Chicago Press, 1944); Jane Chesky, Alice Joseph, and Rosamond Spicer, *The Desert People: A Study of the Papago Indians* (Chicago: University of Chicago Press, 1949); and Laura Thompson, *Personality and Government, Findings and Recommendations of the Indian Administration Research* (Mexico City: Ediciones Del Instituto Indigenista Inter-Americano, 1951).

Thompson's *Personality and Government,* recommended that the bureau should completely decentralize its services, making local Indian communities basic administrative units for medical and educational programs. It proposed that Indian Service personnel use existing tribal life patterns and personality structures to develop community organizations to solve economic and social problems.[86]

The minimal impact of Collier's attempt to internationalize the Indian New Deal became apparent in 1943 when Elmer Thomas submitted a report from the Senate Indian Investigating Subcommittee. It advocated the abolition of the bureau rather than continuing Collier's policies which supposedly promoted segregation, made the Indian a guinea pig for experimentation, tied the Indian to the land in perpetuity, and made him "satisfied with all the limitations of primitive life." In order to end such practices and liquidate the bureau within three years, the subcommittee recommended that Congress distribute tribal funds on a per capita basis, eliminate the trust status of allotted and inherited lands, transfer bureau divisions such as the Forestry and Medical Service to other federal agencies, close all boarding schools, and refuse to finance bureau activities.*

Being preoccupied with the war, Congress never seriously considered this report. But it assisted Jed Johnson, who wanted to slash funds for the bureau because he considered Collier a radical who should be tried under the Hatch Act.[87] Since 1935, Johnson had managed to eliminate almost all IRA monies authorized for tribal organization and land purchase, reduce funds for the Indians Arts and Crafts Board to a bare minimum, and cut expenditures for Indian timber and range conservation to less than one-fourth the figure required by the National Forest Service for identical work. This niggardly attitude was reflected in the 1945 appropriation bill which removed $2 million from the bureau's budget, making it $3.6 million smaller than the amount spent for fiscal year 1932.[88]

Collier believed that the "anti-intellectual tyranny" and "proto-fascist determination" embodied in Johnson's subcommittee had critically diminished the productiveness of the Indian Bureau, so he directed his zeal for preserving the culture of minority groups toward the Japanese-Americans who were placed in detention camps during World War II.[89] Vice-President Henry A. Wallace, at the commissioner's instigation, suggested at a cabinet meeting that the president give Collier the job of

---

*Burton K. Wheeler, Dennis Chavez, and Henrik Shipstead also signed this report. Senate Report 310, 78th Cong., 1st Sess., May 24, 1943, NA, RG 75, Fort Worth Federal Records Center.

handling the War Relocation Authority because of his expertise in community living. Secretary Ickes agreed with this proposal, but Roosevelt, whose attention was focused on military planning, never acted on this recommendation. Instead, he offered a compromise solution which allowed Collier to supervise 20,000 Japanese at the Poston relocation facility on the Colorado River reservation in western Arizona.[90]

Several reasons compelled Collier to involve the Indian Bureau in the activities of the Poston camp. He hoped to use the Japanese agricultural experience to put 25,000 acres of land under cultivation. This would help irrigate the Indian reservation, enable the Japanese to raise surplus foods to feed American troops, and allow them to build check dams and similar projects on open range lands.[91] Collier believed that the Poston experience might yield "scientific results" concerning American administration of former Japanese islands in the Pacific Ocean.[92]

In addition Collier wanted to create a community atmosphere at Poston in order to restore Japanese morale and faith in democracy. In June 1942, he told the Japanese evacuees that their camp would be a social experiment to demonstrate for the whole country "the efficiency and splendor of the cooperative way of living."[93] In order to implement this program he obtained the services of the Eastern Cooperative League and the Rochdale Institute of New York City. From August to September 1942, members of these two organizations helped the evacuees establish an adult educational program, municipal councils for self-government, recreation facilities, consumer cooperatives, and a community credit organization.[94]

The commissioner, however, failed to fulfill most of his objectives because they conflicted with the policy of Dillon S. Myer, the director of the War Relocation Authority. Under Myer's guidance, the WRA abandoned the utilization of 25,000 acres of Indian land for the production of surplus food and implemented a subsistence program which provided for the maximum development of 5,000 acres of land. Myer disliked the Poston experiment in cooperative living because he thought the relocation centers could never "be developed into normal communities."[95] He preferred the dispersal of the Japanese from the camps to all parts of the country in order to accelerate their assimilation into the normal life of the nation and prevent their return to "little Tokyos" after the war.[96]

The commissioner, on the other hand, stressed group activities and the Japanese-American's cultural heritage. He desired to keep the evacuees in the camps for the duration of the war and then send them back to the West Coast. These fundamental disagreements, plus an unfortunate riot in which Japanese militants played martial music and

waved flags, caused the bureau to withdraw from the Poston project.[97]
This pleased the Mohave and Chemehuevi Indians who lived on
the Colorado River reservation. They resented the Japanese-American
intruders and disliked Collier because he had turned their land into a
relocation site. The Colorado River Indians' hostility also stemmed from
the commissioner's previous plans to colonize large numbers of Hopis
and Navajos on their reservation to take advantage of a $12 million irri-
gation project. They claimed that their constitution adopted under the
IRA gave them the power to decide whether other Indians could settle
on the reservation. But Collier remained adamant because legislation
enacted after the Civil War authorized colonization.[98] The gap between
the promise of self-government and the reality of federal paternalism once
again became apparent.

As the war progressed, Collier's attention turned to the problem of
dependent peoples throughout the world. On January 15, 1943, he wrote
an unanswered memorandum to the president suggesting the creation
of a civilian training program responsible for "relief, rehabilitation, and
the administration of occupied and liberated areas."[99] Collier wanted to
create an institute of ethnic democracy in the Interior Department to
train colonial personnel in the art of democratic government. He believed
that it could serve "as a laboratory of ethnic relations," based on the
colonial record of the Indian Bureau during the last twelve years, to help
solve the problem of governing pre-literate and pre-industrial people.[100]
The commissioner's interest in the Far East started when he met
Dr. Laura Thompson, who worked with him on the Indian Personality
Study. Miss Thompson was a distinguished anthropologist who had
engaged in field research on Fiji and Guam. Their professional relationship soon developed into a love affair. After divorcing his first wife,
Collier married Laura during August 1943, in Reno, Nevada.* This
brought a cruel remark from Jed Johnson, who publicly claimed that
Collier should resign because he had used government funds to establish
legal residence in Nevada.[101]
Restless over his increasing ineffectiveness as commissioner and

---

*Dr. Laura Thompson had an impressive academic record. She received her
A.B. degree from Mills College, Oakland, and her Ph.D. from the University of
California. An assistant ethnologist for the Bishop Museum in Honolulu, she became
a research associate for the Institute of Pacific Relations in 1937 at the University
of Hawaii. Thompson also served as an anthropologist on the Community Survey
of Education for the territory of Hawaii. Her scholarly publications included
Archaeology of the Mariana Islands, Guam and Its People and *Fijian Frontier.*
"Laura Thompson Bride in Nevada," *Honolulu Star Bulletin,* August 28, 1943, NA,
RG 75, Suitland, Maryland.

concerned with the wider cause of ethnic democracy, Collier submitted his resignation to the president on January 10, 1945. He explained to Roosevelt that "working under your leadership and that of Secretary Ickes through these twelve years has been the most stimulating, developing, and fulfilling experience of my entire life." [102] Nevertheless, he wanted to do justice to the Pan-Indian movement and study the area of ethnic relations as it related to the creation of a stable post-war world. Collier indicated that existing conditions made it impossible for him to meet the legitimate demands of the Indian race. The removal of the bureau to Chicago had created "all but insurmountable difficulties and problems," while an excellent legislative program had "undergone progressive nullification through recent appropriation cuts." [103]

The president accepted this resignation with regret on January 22, 1945. Roosevelt told Collier that the one achievement of his administration in which he took great pride was the new orientation in Indian affairs. The president praised Collier for doing an outstanding job in one of the most difficult offices in the federal government. Far less criticism would have come if he merely accepted the status quo; instead Collier had added to the Indians' worth and dignity by protecting their cultural values, religious freedom, and property rights. Roosevelt suggested that if the Indians possessed greater self-respect and a stronger feeling of solidarity with the rest of the country, it was because Collier really believed in the Sermon on the Mount, the Declaration of Independence, and the Constitution.[104]

Collier deserved Roosevelt's praise, but in retrospect the Indian New Deal had serious shortcomings. Collier's attempt to implement John Marshall's legal doctrine that Indian tribes were sovereign entities capable of exercising all powers of self-government not relinquished by treaties or acts of Congress proved difficult to implement after fifty years of assimilation. Many Indians rejected the notion of being treated as a separate class and Collier failed to convince Congress that the preservation of native heritage, with its cooperative institutions, would enhance the Indian's ability to cope with modern life.

The commissioner had limited success as an administrator because he overestimated his capacity to reconstruct Indian affairs and introduced too many ideas which often created confusion. The abolition of the Board of Indian Commissioners, a move that accelerated reform in the short run, bitterly divided white philanthropists and deprived the Indians of possible assistance in the tumultuous post-war period. Collier demonstrated inflexibility by firing Indians from the bureau who opposed his policies, and he created unnecessary problems when he appointed a woman superintendent to head the Pueblos.

Several other mistakes hurt the commissioner as well. The consolidation of the Navajo and the New Mexico Pueblo jurisdictions into single administrative units resulted in division instead of unity. His use of other governmental agencies such as the Soil Conservation Service often added to this turmoil by starting interdepartmental conflict, especially on the Navajo reservation. Furthermore, the commissioner's tendency to impose his ideas on the Indians contradicted the principle of cultural diversity and caused some of them to join the destructive American Indian Federation.

On the other hand, if the mark of a good administrator were to consist of creativity instead of careful organization, Collier merited high praise for his resourcefulness. He attracted to government service social scientists who used the IRA to bring about deliberate changes in tribal life, who understood that the Indians must participate in American society in their own way, and who recognized the importance of group life in securing constructive acculturation to prevent personality disintegration. More importantly, Collier raised critical questions about whether the Indians would make progress by repudiating their own heritage: he provided them with a vision of collective action and showed them the possibility of hemisphere-wide Pan-Indianism to effectively insure the economic and spiritual survival of all Indians.

Nevertheless, Collier found it impossible to control the larger historical forces which stalemated the Indian New Deal. The inability of the Roosevelt administration to solve the poverty associated with the Great Depression made it difficult for the Indians to concentrate on self-government. The growth of a conservative coalition in Congress put Collier on the defensive when it slashed appropriations and introduced bills to repeal the IRA.

Particularly detrimental was the defection of congressmen such as Burton K. Wheeler and Lynn Frazier, who concerned themselves with preserving individualism and limiting the evils of centralized power. During the twenties they had joined Collier in order to fight an unresponsive Indian bureaucracy and big businessmen who threatened native oil and water power sites. Naturally, they became disillusioned with Collier's romanticism and brand of progressivism which tried to organize the Indians on a collective basis. This split among the progressive forces and the confusion that resulted from Collier's Indian policy helped end reform and paved the way for successful attempts to terminate the government's guardianship over certain Indian tribes after World War II.

In spite of these obstacles, Collier had attacked almost every Indian problem with vigor during his twelve years in office. He ended the allotment policy, restored several million acres of land at various reservations, and started long needed conservation programs. Aware that the government must build its Indian program around the dynamic potentials of group life, he secured passage of the IRA which allowed many tribes to assume some measure of political and economic control over their own affairs, as well as guaranteeing religious freedom and lifting the ban on native ceremonies. He reawakened in the souls of many natives, not only pride in being Indian, but hope for the future as Indians. Joseph W. Hayes, a Chickasaw, expressed this sentiment when he praised Collier because "every morning our children will be Indians."[105] Henry Roe Cloud, a Winnebago, expressed similar feelings by indicating that Collier had built up the pride of his people so they could feel they had "a great history, and great thoughts, and great ideas and inspirations in our hearts." Cloud believed that during the New Deal the Indians could walk with their heads up "instead of looking down all the time."[106]

10. The Quest Continues

Collier remained in Washington, D.C., after his resignation in order to take up the cause of dependent groups throughout the world. Influenced by his earlier experience with the Indians, he thought that social scientists could help pre-literate people use their communal institutions to promote progress. And because he was convinced that the government must develop an enlightened colonial administration that provided for self-government, Collier quickly opposed the cold war foreign policy of President Harry S Truman.*

In July 1945 Collier organized the Institute of Ethnic Affairs and became its president.[1] Incorporated under the laws of the District of Columbia as a non-profit organization, the institute had approximately 200 members, including several individuals associated with the Indian New Deal. Some of the more important members were Collier's wife, Laura Thompson; Felix Cohen, associate solicitor of the Interior Department; Rene d'Harnoncourt, chief curator at the Museum of Modern Art; Clyde Kluckhohn, a Harvard anthropologist; Dorothea Leighton, a psychiatrist; and D'Arcy McNickle, an employee at the Indian Bureau.†

The institute's charter, written by Collier, proposed to use social scientists in order to engage in "action-research" that would inform the average citizen about "ethnic tension, maladjustments, conflicts, or

---

*Historians have generally neglected Collier's role as an opponent of the cold war. See Thomas G. Paterson, ed., *Cold War Critics* (Chicago: Quadrangle Books, 1971).

†Several social scientists joined the institute's directorate. They were Louis Adamic, author of *My Native Land;* Evans Carlson, retired Brigadier General of the Marine Corps; Dr. John Cooper, chairman of the anthropology department at Catholic University of America; Allan Harper, an Indian Bureau employee; Dr. Harold Lasswell, law professor at Yale; Dr. Kurt Lewin, director of the Research Center for Group Dynamics at the Massachusetts Institute of Technology; Carey McWilliams, a liberal author; Dr. Philleo Nash, an anthropologist; Dr. Saul Padover, a historian and authority on Thomas Jefferson; and Dr. Paul Fejos, director of the Viking Fund. John Collier, "Memorandum on the Needs of the Institute of Ethnic Affairs, May 6, 1946," Collier Papers; and "The Directorate of the Institute of Ethnic Affairs," Collier Papers.

neglected group opportunities." Its main objective was to develop the art of administering human affairs by joining the "scientist's passion for discovering truth" with the people's dream of an energetic, democratic society. Since he was especially interested in the people who lived under American colonial rule, Collier intended to train administrators to work with these dependent minority groups.[2]

At a speech given before the Women's Alliance of the Unitarian Church at Wilmington, Delaware, on October 29, 1945, Collier elaborated on the goals of his institute. He claimed that social diversity was the creative force of history as seen by the genius of Christianity, which blended Hebraic morality, Greek philosophy, Oriental mysticism, and Roman law. But this cross-fertilization of cultures had come under attack with the advent of the machine age which predisposed mankind to concentrate on selfish material advantages and power struggles. Unfortunately, a spiritual bankruptcy ensued permitting the growth of Nazism and fascism — ideologies that reduced the human soul into a "monster idiot" and threatened to destroy the future of man on earth.[3]

Collier warned that this peril reemerged after the successful conclusion to World War II in the form of isolationism, anti-Semitism, hatred toward the Japanese, and intolerance of Indian culture. In order to cure this social sickness, he maintained, people had to find a way to implant in their children the passion that life was splendid, a house of many mansions, where different races needed one another. Collier suggested that his audience take a practical step in this direction by writing their congressmen. Their letters should insist that the United States take the lead in the colonial problem by allowing its dependencies self-government under United Nations trusteeship and ending the forty-five year "scandal of military rule" over Guam and Samoa.[4]

While he worked to implement the institute's program, Collier received assistance from Secretary Ickes, who appointed him as an alternate advisor to the United States delegation on trusteeship matters at the first session of the United Nations General Assembly which met at London. Collier departed for Great Britain on board the *Queen Elizabeth* during the first week of January 1946, and he helped Abe Fortas, an Interior Department undersecretary, formulate plans for American support of the pertinent chapters of the United Nations charter, setting forth the responsibilities of governments toward their colonies and territories.*

*Collier helped Abe Fortas compose a letter which asked Harold L. Ickes to persuade President Truman to make a statement about the importance of social welfare and self-government for dependent peoples, as well as an announcement that the United States would reexamine its colonial administration to determine whether or not it met the obligations of the United Nations Charter. The White House refused to answer this query. John Collier to Secretary Harold L. Ickes, January 4, 1946, Collier Papers.

Once they reached London, Collier and Fortas attended meetings of the General Assembly's Trusteeship Committee in the wartime chamber of the House of Lords. There they drafted a "Resolution on Non-Self-Governing Peoples" which reminded the delegates that they must accept "as a sacred trust" sections of the United Nations Charter that obligated them to establish an international trusteeship system and to promote "to the utmost the well-being of the inhabitants of these territories."[5] John Foster Dulles, who led the American delegation, endorsed this resolution because he understood the potential of rebellion from "backward" peoples. Nevertheless, Collier feared that his vision was limited by "a Wall Street investment lawyer's values."[6]

Unimpressed with other members of the American delegation (he found the Navy advisors "uninformed and lazy," while the Army's representatives were "dogmatic, myopic, and insolent"), Collier claimed that undesirable personality traits surfaced when military officials came in a crowd to the trusteeship conferences where they monopolized the conversation. Argument could not move their closed minds any more than "a dressed-up burro."[7]

Collier complained that Secretary of State James Byrnes wanted to prevent the United States "from initiating any policy or substantive matter."[8] This became apparent when fifty nations discussed the question of colonialism. Debate continued for a number of days and little progress took place because American delegates refused to reveal their intentions toward the newly acquired Marianas, Marshall, and Caroline islands. But one by one countries such as Great Britain, France, Belgium, Australia, New Zealand, and Holland decided to support a resolution that called for the creation of trusteeships.[9] Collier thought that the United States acquiesced on this issue because it "did not want Russia to reap all the propaganda benefits."[10]

Collier returned home upset with the equivocal position taken by the American government and appeared before the President's Committee on Civil Rights on May 14, 1946. He warned that on Guam, Samoa, and the Micronesian islands recently acquired from Japan, the Navy refused to grant the natives civil liberties. It subjected them to the arbitrary edicts of Navy governors, which resulted in a government of men not law. The situation was especially bad in Guam where the natives were paid substandard wages, denied their right to jury trial, and had their property taken for military use without compensation.[11]

Aware that his testimony would have little immediate impact, Collier helped organize groups such as the National Peace Conference, the Catholic War Veterans, and the United Nations Council of Philadelphia behind an effort to clarify American policy. On August 30, 1946, they sent a joint telegram to President Truman urging him to place the Japanese mandated islands under General Assembly trusteeship and govern them through a civilian agency. Collier thought this action necessary because military rule, except during national emergencies, contradicted democratic principles.[12]

The president, evidently under pressure from the military to act cautiously in this matter, failed to respond, so Collier criticized his foreign policy in the institute's *Newsletter*. Particularly harsh was his suggestion that the Navy had followed the Russian example in Eastern Europe by arbitrarily evacuating thousands of Japanese, generations of whom had lived in Micronesia, back to the main island.[13] In order to embarrass the administration he published a speech given by Harold L. Ickes, who had since resigned as secretary of the interior.* It claimed that the time had come for the State Department to restore civilian government in the Pacific and cease its infatuation with the "pleasant tinkle of brass and the luster of gold braid."[14]

Ickes continued to help Collier's cause by writing an article for *Collier's* magazine entitled "The Navy at Its Worst." Ickes indicated that since the Spanish-American War, the naval government in Guam had exiled Roman Catholic priests from the island, prohibited religious processions, established segregated schools that forbade the use of the Chamorro language, and subjected the natives to arrest and imprisonment "without jury trial in rump naval courts." He suggested that conditions were just as bad in Samoa because military officials had outlawed native religious feasts and imprisoned Samoan leaders who protested against this decision.[15]

Collier added fuel to this fire by sending a letter to the *New York Times* which challenged a naval report presented to the United Nations in July 1946 justifying military government on Guam. He warned that the Navy had misled the public because its "so-called experimental farm" provided food only for military personnel, while native owners who had their farms confiscated for this project never received compensation. He indicated that the Navy's concept of vocational education consisted of manual labor, and he pointed out that military officials had failed to return privately owned buses expropriated for military use during the war.[16]

Secretary of the Navy James Forrestal responded to this growing criticism in a rebuttal published by the *New York Times*. It stated that

---

*Disillusioned with the Truman administration, Harold L. Ickes resigned on February 12, 1946. He was especially upset with Truman for recommending the appointment of Edwin Pauley, a wealthy California oil producer, as undersecretary of the Navy. Walter Johnson, *1600 Pennsylvania Avenue: Presidents and People Since 1929* (Boston: Little, Brown and Company, 1960), p. 226.

Guam and Samoa were not subject to United Nations trusteeship because President William McKinley had placed them under naval control in 1898. More importantly, he defended continued military presence at these islands because they made up a mutually supporting base network that protected American national security. Forrestal rejected the notion that the Navy had neglected to protect native interests, and he cited a recent speech by former President Herbert Hoover who claimed the Navy had administered these Pacific possessions "completely without blemish."[17]

President Truman answered his critics on November 6, 1946, by announcing that he would place the Marianas, Marshall, and Caroline islands under a strategic trusteeship. This meant that the Security Council had responsibility for these dependencies, but in practice left the United States Navy as the sole administering authority. Angry over the president's announcement, Collier wrote an editorial in the institute's *Newsletter* calling Truman's decision "a miserable disappointment." He termed the concept of strategic trusteeship "virtual annexation" and rejected the "militarist" argument that the former mandated Japanese islands, located 6,000 miles from San Francisco and over 2,000 miles from the Soviet Union, provided security for the United States.[18]

Because the president still remained evasive about the status of Guam and Samoa, Collier increased his pressure on the administration by starting publication of a mimeographed newspaper entitled the *Guam Echo*. It provided information concerning American foreign policy for the 350 Guamanians who had joined the institute and ran feature articles that called for civilian control of the island. Encouraged by Collier's support, the Guam Congress, which had only advisory power, passed a resolution requesting federal legislation that would grant them full citizenship and self-government.[19]

Secretary Forrestal, concerned by this turmoil, appointed a special three-man civilian committee headed by Dr. Ernest Hopkins, president emeritus of Dartmouth College, to investigate conditions on Guam and Samoa.* The Hopkins committee visited these islands during March 1947 and discovered that many of Collier's allegations were valid. It found that on Guam the Navy had failed to dispose of war damage claims, dragged its heels on rehabilitation of the island, refused to compensate natives for confiscated land, raised bus fares too high, and engaged in racial discrimination. To correct these abuses, the committee recommended that Congress create a career group of colonial administrators,

---

*The other two committee members were Maurice Tobin, former governor of Massachusetts, and Dr. Knowles Ryerson, dean of the University of California's College of Agriculture. John Collier, "Analytical Summary of the Hopkins' Committee Report on Guam and American Samoa, May 11, 1947," Collier Papers.

give the Guamanians and Samoans full citizenship rights, and pass legislation creating self-government. It also proposed that the Navy, with its efficient administration and communications system, be given general control over the islands.[20]

Despite this last proposal, which seemed inconsistent with the rest of the report, Collier praised the Hopkins committee for taking "one of the longest strides toward democracy" in the history of American colonial rule.[21] His analysis proved correct because Congress used the Hopkins Report to draft the Guam Organic Act of 1950, which granted the natives citizenship rights and a civilian government under the jurisdiction of the Interior Department.[22]

Satisfied that his fight on behalf of the Pacific islanders had brought positive results, Collier discovered that it also "awakened embittered resistance in Naval top echelons" because Secretary Forrestal persuaded "former subordinates" in the Treasury Department to revoke the tax exempt status of his institute.[23] Collier received the bad news on November 20, 1946, from Fred Martin, acting deputy commissioner of the Internal Revenue Department, who claimed that the institute devoted too much time to propaganda in order to influence legislation, thus violating section 101 of the Internal Revenue Code.[24] Collier immediately appealed this decision but was rebuffed by Joseph Nunan, commissioner of Internal Revenue, who cited his telegram to Truman and the institute's program of action-research to prove that it was a political rather than scientific organization.[25] This ruling proved disastrous for Collier, preventing future solicitation from foundation funds.

Although beset with growing financial difficulties, Collier managed to secure a grant-in-aid from the Viking Fund in New York to investigate Spanish treatment of Indians in the New World, as part of a wider study of colonialism. He published this research during 1947 in a book entitled *Indians of the Americas,* which began with the Indians of prehistory, traced the Spanish conquest of the Incas and Aztecs, and discussed the Indians north of the Rio Grande. Throughout the text Collier indicated that the Indians possessed qualities needed by the Occident, which found itself spiritually impoverished by the "Cartesian Century" and the Industrial Revolution. These qualities included "a romantic view" of life where the gods "walked on every road of man," a passion for the earth, reverence for the human personality, psychological maturity, and "intensity" with tranquility.[26]

Collier's main thesis stressed that these traits, which stemmed from communal living experiences, had triumphed after centuries of oppression. Even the cruel Spanish conquest had failed to snuff out this collective spirit because the Indians of Paraguay, when given a chance by the Jesuits who followed the utopian vision of Friar Bartolomé de Las Casas, developed a cooperative commonwealth early in the seventeenth century. Similarly, the natives of Mexico during that country's revolution quickly adopted the *ejido* communal agricultural program, while the North American Indians used the Indian Reorganization Act to show that the "individual fares best" as a member of a group. Collier then described the activities of the Inter-American Indian Institute, predicting that Indian societies would join in an international federation and become the major embodiment of the worldwide "cooperative movement."[27]

Another by-product of Collier's research was the publication of a pamphlet called *America's Colonial Record*. It provided a historical survey of American imperialism starting with the conquest of the Indians, and including the acquisition of colonies during the Spanish-American War, as well as the acquisition of possessions such as Alaska, Hawaii, and the Pacific islands. Collier, who wanted to help dependent peoples, admitted that colonial rule brought certain rewards such as political sophistication, education, and public health. But he deplored the absence of a single federal agency to deal with these administrative matters. This had resulted in a laissez-faire economic policy that benefited business monopolies while it impoverished the local population.[28]

Collier cited American relations with the Philippines to prove his point. After the Spanish-American War, the United States worked to give its colony complete political freedom, which culminated in 1934 when President Franklin D. Roosevelt signed the Philippines Independence Act. This legislation provided for total self-government after a ten-year period. But the land monopoly by the cacique class imposed peonage on the masses, while American business interests were allowed to operate under a free trade system that caused economic dependency and encouraged the growth of "commercial feudalism" based on the sugar cane industry.[29]

According to Collier, this relationship continued under the guidance of General Douglas MacArthur after the United States reconquered the Philippines. He appointed to his staff a former collaborator with the Japanese, Manuel Roxas, because of his devotion to crushing the radical Hukbalahap peasants who favored agrarian reform. Later in 1946, the Army backed Roxas' candidacy for the presidency and soon after his successful election he laid "the foundation for a totalitarian regime," by disqualifying opponents in the Philippine Congress in order to ratify the American-sponsored Bell Act. This legislation allowed United States citizens and business enterprises to exploit mineral and natural resources on the islands. Collier believed that it demonstrated the bankruptcy of American colonial rule and tied the country's fate to "the feudal and monopolistic interests."[30]

Mrs. John Collier, Sr.

As professor of sociology and anthropology at CCNY, Collier
instilled humanistic values in his students.

Although Collier was perceptive in his analysis, his opinions brought
little financial support for the institute, so in 1947 he accepted the offer
to become visiting professor of sociology and anthropology at the City
College of New York, a position which became permanent during the following year.[31] Collier's teaching responsibilities included a course called
"Non-Literate and Non-Industrial Peoples in the Western World" covering the integrative value systems of ancient village communities in Asia,
Micronesia, India, Africa, and the American Southwest. He also talked
about humanistic social planning on behalf of peoples — such as the
Jesuit utopia in Paraguay, English indirect colonial rule, the Soviet treatment of nationalitites under Lenin, and the Indian New Deal.[32]

Collier also focused on the trends that threatened to destroy the
fabric of civilization. He told his students that post-war drift toward "free-
enterprise, cartelization and industrial statism" forced economic colonialism on non-industrialized peoples who could obtain capital only by
surrendering control over their own economies. Collier warned that
"exploitively planned industrialization" caused cultural and personality
disorientation which prevented world-wide social planning and intensified nation-state power struggles by building mass support through the

techniques of "hate, fear, and chauvinism." If these trends were not reversed, he feared, mankind would "destroy itself through a final world war."[33]

Along with his teaching duties, Collier simultaneously directed the Institute of Ethnic Affairs. In the summer of 1947 he secured funds from the Pacific Science Board and helped the Navy begin a Saipan Personality Study, using psychiatrists to conduct inkblot socio-psychological tests on 200 children. But Collier spent most of his time writing articles for the institute's *Newsletter* which attacked such evils of colonialism as South Africa's "pigmentocracy" where skin color determined a person's rights.[34]

Collier had almost given up hope for an enlightened American foreign policy toward the third world when President Truman announced in his inaugural address, on January 20, 1949, that the United States should embark on a Point Four program for "making scientific advances and industrial progress" available for the improvement and growth of underdeveloped areas. The chief executive indicated that he planned to create a special Committee on Economic Foreign Policy that would consult with private agencies such as overseas business firms and the Rockefeller Institute.[35]

In order to implement this directive, the State Department contacted several groups, including the Institute of Ethnic Affairs. Collier agreed to make studies of three northeastern African countries in preparation for Point Four assistance, but his ideal of using social scientists in dependent areas to create a viable community life had little in common with government objectives. According to Truman, Point Four would help poor nations raise their standard of living, create stable economies for American investment, and make them safe from Communism.[36]

Because he had little sympathy for the president's cold war policies, which forced the world "into hostile ideological camps," Collier sent a protest letter to the *New York Times*.[37] He attacked W. V. Tubman, the president of Liberia, for running a "one party regime" and excluding the opposition Reformation Party, led by Dihdwo Twe, from the May 1951 presidential race. Collier suggested that the State Department's refusal to act on Twe's request to send observers who would insure a free election meant that the United States had turned its back on the "Ghandi of Liberia" and stood as a "silent partner in the killing of democracy."[38] Angered by this exposure of an embarrassing situation, the State Department abruptly canceled the institute's Point Four project.[39]

Collier, being frustrated in his attempts to assist dependent peoples, increasingly turned his attention back toward the American Indian. In 1949, he wrote the text to *Patterns and Ceremonials of the Indians of the Southwest,* which contained over 100 beautiful sketches and lithographs of native life by Ira Moskowitz. The central theme of the book suggested that the southwestern Indian societies were "mountain peaks of a submerged social continent." According to Collier, these Indians possessed "a time sense different" from the clockwork pace found in the modern mechanized world. This allowed them to develop a group life marked by a passion for color, extreme hospitality, giving rather than receiving, and a "diffused spirituality which found God everywhere" — in short, they lived in a "dream of God."[40]

Explaining the particular institutional and spiritual genius of various tribes, Collier suggested that the Navajos affirmed the buoyant life through a multitude of highly structured rituals such as Blessing Way, while the Rio Grande Pueblos were conservationists who dealt with the land in a spirit of reciprocity instead of exploitation. The Pueblos also demonstrated the practicality of multilingual cultural pluralism and their sacred dramas like the Red Deer Dance provided group cohesion and a belief "in the power of ideals to move events." Finally, Collier praised the Apaches for their political and economic achievements under the Indian Reorganization Act, and he claimed that the Zunis possessed great organizational principles found in the concept of "the midmost," which forecast a future "democratic, pluralistic and holistic world-order."[41]

Although the publication of this book symbolized Collier's renewed interest in Indian affairs, he had never forgotten their cause. Previously he had written several articles for *America Indigena* such as "Indianismo vs Racism" where he warned that the post-war generation had to make a choice between a "monistic world" and one that searched for "contrasting and mutually enriching values." Collier believed that the Indianismo movement had strengthened the latter alternative by taking an "anti-racist and anti-authoritarian" posture at one of the most crucial periods in history.[42] He also remained on the governing board of the Inter-American Indian Institute, but was forced to resign from this position in May 1946 because of his teaching responsibilities and the hostility of the State Department which never supplied him with travel funds.[43]

This setback did not prevent Collier from carrying on the work of the National Indian Institute. Representative Jed Johnson continued to block its appropriations in the House, so Secretary Ickes transferred the National Indian Institute to the Institute of Ethnic Affairs in 1946. As director of the National Indian Institute, Collier cooperated with the Navy's Bureau of Medicine, which sent Dr. Michel Pijoan to Nicaragua in order to establish a health clinic for Indians. Another project, cosponsored with the State Department, was the beginning of a linguistic survey by Dr. Antonio Goubaud, director of Guatemala's Indian Institute, among the natives in that country. Little else was accomplished, however, due to the lack of financial support which forced Collier to return the responsi-bility for operating the National Indian Institute back to the Interior Department.[44]

Collier's career as a critic of the Indian Bureau resumed in 1949 after the Senate passed the Navajo-Hopi Rehabilitation bill. Based on long range proposals submitted by Interior Secretary Julius A. Krug for meeting the needs of two tribes who had made little progress during the New Deal, this measure was supported by the Indians and most welfare groups. It proposed to spend $88,570,000 over a ten-year period to pro-vide a coordinated program against poverty, illiteracy, inadequate roads, and poor health. This legislation was amended in the House at the insis-tence of Representative Antonio Fernandez from New Mexico, who inserted section nine, placing the Navajos and Hopis under the jurisdic-tion of state laws and courts. When these conflicting bills reached the joint conference committee, the Senate conferees accepted the House version and added a proviso that required the federal government to pay 80 percent of the social security subsidy for Indian applicants in Arizona and New Mexico.[45]

Worried that this bill would harm the Indians, Collier attacked its provisions in an article published in the *Nation*. He warned that sec-tion nine, "the malign heart" of the bill, placed the Indians under state laws, threatened their ceremonial life, and would destroy tribal cohesion.[46] In a similar action, he wrote a letter to the New York *Herald Tribune*, suggesting that the bill cleared "a royal road to Indian spoliation" because it violated the Navajo Treaty of 1868, a document that guaranteed fed-eral jurisdiction. Collier also objected to special federal social security benefits because they set a dangerous precedent where the government classified applicants according to race. He pointed out that previously both Arizona and New Mexico had refused to grant the Indians social security payments but a recent court decision refuted their position, so they added this obnoxious "Jim Crow amendment."[47]

More importantly, Collier and other white friends such as Mrs. Eleanor Roosevelt, Harold L. Ickes, and Oliver LaFarge notified the Navajos that they should raise objections about this legislation.[48] The tribal council reacted by holding a stormy two-day meeting during October 1949 where it renounced an earlier endorsement and requested that the president kill the bill. Truman responded with a veto, explaining that his decision was influenced by the attitude of the Indians who disliked section nine although they favored the rehabilitation program. Conse-quently, Congress passed this bill again on April 1, 1950, without this provision or the rider that called for special social security benefits for the states of Arizona and New Mexico, and the president signed it.[49]

Truman's firm handling of this dispute pleased Collier, but "initiatives frightening to the Indians came with a bursting speed," after Secretary of the Interior Oscar Chapman appointed Dillon S. Myer to the position of Indian commissioner in May, 1950.[50] Myer, who had been director of the War Relocation Authority during World War II, saw the reservations as prisons rather than self-governing communities which fit in with the government's plans to move in the direction of integrating all minority groups. He believed that the Citizenship Act of 1924 was one of the "most important milestones" in Indian affairs and hoped to promote assimilation by gradually withdrawing all "segregated" bureau services. Because America had become an urban nation, Myer felt it would be a mistake to "think of all Indians as an agricultural people." Instead, the government needed to initiate a large scale vocational program to relocate them into the more prosperous cities.[51]

Myer immediately dramatized his new policy by firing William Zimmerman, who had been assistant commissioner since 1933. This purge of former New Dealers accelerated when he secured the resignations of Theodore Haas, the bureau's chief counsel, who helped produce the *Handbook of Federal Indian Law,* Willard Beatty, head of Indian education, Joseph McCaskill, manager of the Indian Arts and Crafts Board, and Walter Woehlke, area director of the Phoenix office. In a parallel action, Myer refused to meet with the commissioner's Advisory Committee, which Collier had created in order to consult with citizens and social scientists interested in Indian matters.[52]

Myer again repudiated past reform by issuing thirty-six regulations for attorneys' contracts with Indian tribes. The commissioner announced that, except for the Indian Claims Commission established in 1946, he would decide what lawyers the Indians should hire and determine their fees.* In another move aimed at the Indian New Deal, Myer issued a memorandum to bureau officials urging them to implement programs that would abolish unnecessary services.[53] In other actions he supported a bill to terminate federal supervision over the California Indians, discouraged self-government at the Mescalero Apache Indian reservation in New Mexico, issued grazing permits on the Montana Blackfoot reservation without the required legal consent of the tribal council, and refused to secure the approval of the Indians at San Ildefonso Pueblo before selling a section of their property.[54]

---

*This action voided section 16 of the Indian Reorganization Act which allowed tribes authority in these matters. John Collier, "Indian Bureau Reverts to Obsolete Policy of Spoliation, November 28, 1950," Collier Papers.

Upset with these decisions, Collier stated they were similar to the "authoritarian, racist, and stereotyped administration" Myer had directed for the Japanese-Americans during the Second World War. He warned in an institute bulletin that the discredited "one formula solution" of liquidating the bureau and assimilating the Indians would only result in the alienation of their land, and he called for a return to the "bilateral trusteeship" policy followed by both Hoover and Roosevelt. They had successfully made the Indian Service experimental and pragmatic with regard to minority problems, involved other federal agencies to execute the government's guardianship obligation, and promoted tribal self-government.[55]

In order to arouse opposition against the bureau, Collier started publication of the *Southwest Indian News Letter* in February 1951. It carried articles by tribal leaders such as Clarence Wesley, chairman of the San Carlos Apache tribal council, who indicated that his people favored self-government and wanted the bureau to improve their educational facilities. Collier provided a column called "legislative roundup," which discussed bills related to the Indians, and he wrote editorials that criticized Myer for constant interference with the tribes' legal affairs, despite protests from many Indians, the American Association on Indian Affairs, the Civil Liberties Union, and a committee of the American Bar Association.[56]

This widespread criticism caused Secretary Chapman to conduct Department of the Interior hearings concerning the bureau's regulations that authorized the commissioner to control attorneys' contracts. Forty-four witnesses appeared at this proceeding, including twenty-five tribal delegates who represented over 200,000 Indians, and most of them testified against Myer's policy.[57] Collier, who was unable to attend, submitted a statement by the Institute of Ethnic Affairs, warning that these regulations frustrated "the entire principle of democratic self-government."[58] In response to this public outcry, Secretary Chapman withdrew Myer's directive, but he failed to formulate new guidelines which left the situation in chaos.

Pleased that he had helped discredit Myer, Collier found the "social reality" of the early fifties worse than the twenties. During that period reformers easily demonstrated to Congress the evils of men like Albert B. Fall, "the proud buccaneer" who belonged to the "rotten Harding cabinet." In addition, they received large donations from wealthy progressives, while Congress had men like James A. Frear who were "towers of strength." But after World War II, the public remained apathetic because of the cold war, high taxes, and the difficulty of making Myer "the chief villain and displaying his corpse."[59] Collier indicated that these trends became clear when he hired a public relations firm to solicit new members for the institute. After spending $1,000 and mailing appeals to 19,500 persons, he had secured only $280.[60]

Much to Collier's dismay, other problems plagued the institute. His program of research-action made it an "ugly duckling" unable to solicit money from foundations, while the members from Guam stopped their annual $5,000 contribution after Congress passed the Guam Organic Act.[61] Collier discovered that other welfare organizations such as the American Association on Indian Affairs and the Indian Rights Association preempted his fund-raising potential. Therefore, he had to cease publication of the institute's *Newsletter* and the *Southwest Indian News Letter,* which duplicated newspapers issued by tribal councils.*

Undeterred by these failures, Collier tried to secure the selection of a new Indian commissioner during the 1952 presidential campaign. He wrote letters to both Dwight D. Eisenhower and Adlai Stevenson, requesting that they refuse to reappoint Dillon S. Myer.[62] When Eisenhower won the election, Collier sent him another letter during the interregnum in an effort to influence Republican policy. Published in the *Nation,* it asked the new administration to stop the "social genocide" that Myer had spread through Indian group life with his withdrawal and relocation programs. Collier stressed that the reservations and "other homelands" consisted of genuine and permanent communities where the Indians were citizens rather than prisoners. He asked the president to study the reform heritage of the Hoover-Roosevelt years and repudiate those who considered ethnic differences "anti-American, un-Christian, outmoded, and perhaps disloyal or barbarous."[63]

This message had little influence on the president, who proceeded to establish a businessman's administration in Washington. For the important position of secretary of the interior, he chose Douglas McKay, a wealthy Chevrolet automobile dealer who had become governor of Oregon. McKay agreed that Myer should depart, and he appointed Glenn L. Emmons, a banker from Gallup, New Mexico, as commissioner. This change proved political rather than substantive because Emmons reaffirmed his predecessor's program by allowing H. Rex Lee, a Myer appointee, to remain as assistant commissioner. McKay also appointed Orme Lewis, who favored the assimilation objectives in vogue during the twenties, as associate secretary of the interior.[64]

---

*Collier still hoped that tribal newspapers such as the one issued by the San Carlos Apaches would continue to fight for Indian rights. He also realized the potential power of the National Congress of American Indians that he helped create during the twilight of the New Deal. John Collier, "Southwest Indian News Letter Discontinued," *Southwest Indian News Letter,* July 1953, Collier Papers.

Lewis explained Eisenhower's Indian program at a seminar held in conjunction with the intertribal ceremonies at Gallup, New Mexico. He pointed out that the department's basic objective, which McKay approved, was to rapidly terminate federal responsibility over Indian affairs. The government planned to accomplish this objective by transferring the bureau's services to the states and through a distribution of tribal assets to individual Indians. Lewis believed the latter necessary because it would relieve "the overburdened budgets of many state and local agencies." In his final remarks he criticized those who used the question of group identity as a pretext for keeping the Indians under a federal paternalism because it limited their freedom as citizens. Instead, the government should get "out of the business of administering Indian affairs."[65]

In order to implement these ideas, Lewis sent letters to Senator Arthur Watkins from Utah and Representative William Henry Harrison from Wyoming, requesting that they help the bureau carry out its termination policy. Harrison, a relative of the Indian-fighting former president of the same name, responded by introducing House Concurrent Resolution 108 which repudiated the Indian Reorganization Act.[66] It declared that Congress intended to free the Indians from federal control, end their wardship status, and subject them to the same laws and privileges other citizens enjoyed. This resolution, which the Senate adopted, declared it "the sense of Congress" that the Indian tribes in California, Florida, New York, and Texas should be released from federal supervision, including individual tribes such as the Montana Flatheads, the Oregon Klamaths, the Wisconsin Menominees, the Potawatomie of Kansas and Nebraska, and the Chippewas who resided on the Turtle Mountain reservation in North Dakota.[67]

A few days later, on August 15, 1953, Congress strengthened this resolution with legislation known as Public Law 280. It subjected all Indians living on reservations in California, Minnesota, Nebraska, Oregon and Wisconsin, except the Red Lake Band of Chippewas in Minnesota, the Warm Springs tribes of Oregon, and the Menominee tribe of Wisconsin, to the criminal and civil laws of their respective states. Public Law 280 authorized any state at its own discretion and without Indian consent to substitute state law codes for tribal custom.[68]

Collier heard about this legislation while vacationing at Block Island, Rhode Island. He immediately wrote a letter to Milton Eisenhower, an acquaintance during the New Deal, and asked him to persuade his brother to veto the bill. Collier warned that Congress had acted without prior committee hearings and provided the Indians with little chance to protest. He stressed that the bill "flagrantly flaunted the spirit of President Eisenhower's commitment to the Indians" by destroying federal trusteeship obligations. Collier claimed that it would create "a dragon nest of legal and administrative confusion," cause frustration and defeat among the Indians, and ruin the goodwill accumulated in Latin America with the founding of the Inter-American Indian Institute.[69]

Evidently this plea had some impact on Eisenhower, who publicly scolded Congress. He called the bill "a most un-Christian approach" that would destroy the Indians' "effective self-government." The president objected to sections six and seven which allowed the states to impose their criminal and civil jurisdiction without the Indians' consent, but his Whig conception of the presidency, which minimized executive leadership, prevented Eisenhower from vetoing this measure. And he showed political naiveté by asking Congress to amend it during the next legislative session in order to require tribal consultation before subjecting the Indians to state jurisdiction.[70]

Collier, who was seventy years old and near retirement, agreed with the president's qualms but found it incomprehensible that he refused to veto the bill. Shocked into action, he helped organize a symposium at the fifty-second annual meeting of the American Anthropological Association, on December 30, 1953, which defended the twenty-year record of the Indian Reorganization Act.[71] Collier also issued institute bulletins that attacked the policy of termination because it violated trusteeship commitments found in treaties, executive orders, Supreme Court decisions, and legislative statutes.[72]

In another effort to stir up public opinion, Collier wrote several magazine articles.[73] The most important one, published in the *Christian Century,* described the reform initiatives started by Hoover and Roosevelt which established tribal self-government and emphasized the importance of cultural diversity. Collier stated that since 1950 the government had renewed the "century of dishonor" with its relocation and withdrawal programs. Three years later, this trend became a "compulsive torrent" because Orme Lewis and other appointees in the Interior Department "stampeded through Congress" Public Law 280 and House Concurrent Resolution 108. Refusing to follow the president's advice to amend this law in order to obtain the Indians' consent, they drew up ten new termination bills that turned Indian treaties into "unhoused ghosts" and abolished several of the constitutions and charters formed under the Indian Reorganization Act.[74]

Being unimpressed with these arguments, members of the Eighty-Third Congress passed six termination laws which affected scattered bands of Indians in western Oregon, the Alabama-Coushattas in Texas, the Utes and Paiutes in Utah, the Wisconsin Menominees, and the Klamath of Oregon.[75] Collier again tried to secure a presidential veto by sending a letter to Eisenhower which never went beyond the White House staff.[76] After the president signed these bills into law, Maxwell Rabb, his administrative assistant on minority viewpoints, sent Collier a reply. It claimed that the termination bills had solid support from the Indians and indicated that the administration favored consultation with the tribes. Their consent, however, was not necessary in order to implement legislation that the government favored.[77]

This response irritated Collier, who became more despondent after learning that the Eisenhower administration had removed restrictions on 1.6 million acres of allotted land and had frozen $6 million in the IRA's revolving credit fund.[78] But his struggle against this "felonious nonsense" helped groups such as the American Association on Indian Affairs and the Indian Rights Association in their struggle to arouse public opinion against termination.[79] This forced Secretary of the Interior Fred A. Seaton, who replaced McKay at the start of Eisenhower's second term, to publicly reject the termination of any tribe without its consent.[80]

Collier planned to continue his fight to assist the Indians but academic turmoil at the City College of New York diverted his attention. The Department of Sociology and Anthropology had split into factions after its chairman, Professor Burt W. Aginsky, brought in new personnel who favored dynamic and experimental sociology. Near the end of spring semester 1954, this conflict increased when conservative members of the department, who were on the powerful college-wide appointments committee, filed charges against Collier in a confidential memorandum.[81]

They requested that the administration not rehire their colleague, who had reached the retirement age of seventy, because he involved students in research projects for the "radical" Institute of Ethnic Affairs, instigated "violent controversies" such as opposition to naval rule in the Pacific, and criticized current Indian policy. These charges forced Collier to resign, but he felt vindicated when the administration appointed his wife to fill the empty position.[82]

Before he left campus, Collier delivered a dramatic farewell address to his students. He talked about the present condition and future of American society, indicating that the rise of technology and the Industrial Revolution had brought consequences unforeseen by John Locke and the classical economists. The preoccupation of Occidental man with the acquisition of economic power had resulted in the First World War, which ended the liberal optimism of the nineteenth century, and World War II — a conflict that culminated in the "supremely irritational act" of deliberately dropping the atomic bomb on an "already practically conquered Japan." In the wake of this horror, America rushed forward into the cold war and fell victim to the "hate and fear" symbolized by McCarthyism, the witchhunt of Attorney General Herbert Brownell, and the "incompetent leadership" of President Eisenhower.[83]

Collier told his students that the overriding question for the twentieth century was whether they would surrender to technology and the creation of totalitarianism or make technology serve them "in the re-ordering of human life toward beauty and joy for everybody." He saw little immediate hope in either Russia or the United States for the revitalization of community life, but believed that if the two superpowers would give "the world time and elbow room" perhaps the human spirit would flourish, again in the third world. Especially hopeful was the art of living, the elan vital, found in the kibbutzim of Israel.[84]

Collier continued to pursue his teaching career after retiring from New York City College. First, he presented a series of talks during a summer seminar for foreign students at the Merrill-Palmer School for social workers in Detroit, Michigan. There he discussed the importance of preindustrial societies because they were creative, religious, poetic, and uninterested in the mere acquisition of wealth. Another theme dealt with his effort during the Indian New Deal to restore community life.[85] Finished with his classes in Detroit, Collier returned to New York in order to teach a semester at Columbia University where he reiterated many of the same ideas.[86]

There he found it difficult to concentrate on teaching because of a personal crisis. During the late spring of 1955, his wife, Laura, flew to Juarez, Mexico, and obtained a consent divorce based on mental incompatibility. Laura, twenty-four years younger than her husband, and devoted to an active professional career, wounded Collier deeply by this decision.[87] In a state of mental depression, he traveled to Block Island in order to recuperate at a small cottage on the beach. He found some solace by swimming in the ocean, but wrote Elizabeth S. Sergeant, a close friend, that he was "more unproductive than anytime in almost a lifetime."[88]

His spirits improved when the John Hay Whitney Foundation provided money making it possible for him to accept the position of visiting professor of anthropology at Knox College in Galesburg, Illinois, for the 1955–56 academic year. Always popular with the students, he became even more well-known for the large foxhound he walked around the campus after finding the animal near death in a ditch. Collier held his undergraduate classes at Old Main Hall where he tried to instill student participation through a passionate communication of ideas rather than a catalogue of facts. He conducted seminars at his home in the same atmosphere, often focusing the sessions on social research applied to community achievements at the local level.[89]

While at Knox College, Collier prepared a paper which he planned to deliver before the Institute on Minority Groups at the University of Rochester. Collier was unable to attend because of illness, but Theodore Haas, a colleague during the thirties, read this paper for him. It stressed the cooperative nonexploitative nature of Indian societies and traced the history of the Indian Reorganization Act which sought to establish a "living, evolving, and experimental" bilateral relationship between the government and the tribes.[90] Unfortunately, President Eisenhower had undercut this reform by signing Public Law 280 which pushed the Indians toward "a kind of social, cultural, and spiritual self-genocide." In this paper Collier admitted that many Indians had resisted such pressures, but expressed doubt about the survival "of any ever self-renewing democracy in our national life," because of prevailing "pressure group controls, public administration stereotypes, and the windherdedness of national electorates."[91]

His year at Knox College ended, Collier returned to Taos, New Mexico, in order to live close to the Pueblo Indians. On January 26, 1957, at Ranchos de Taos, he married Grace Volk, a woman he had met at the Institute of Ethnic Affairs.[92] They lived in a small adobe home at Talpa, three miles from the Indian Pueblo, on the most remote and exposed reach of the Taos plateau against the edge of the Sangre de Cristo mountain range. There Collier enjoyed the company of his son John, Jr., his daughter-in-law Mary, and their three sons. He found additional pleasure in the rugged landscape of northern New Mexico believing it equal "to any on the Planet." But he worried about a drought that had killed cottonwood trees around Santa Clara and pine trees up in the nearby mountains.[93]

Collier reminisced with old friends around Taos. He had heard that Mabel and Tony Luhan had become alcoholics and "entirely gone to pieces," but his impoverished Spanish neighbors remained very charming.[94] Collier talked a great deal with Antonio Mirabal, "the soul of the Pueblo," and was pleased when the Indians introduced themselves to him in the town plaza. He thought that the inner life of Taos Pueblo had intensified since his first visit thirty-seven years ago and he noticed little physical change at all.[95]

Although he suffered from several bouts with pneumonia, Collier maintained an active interest in the Indians. With the assistance of Grace, he wrote a manuscript analyzing the termination of federal guardianship over the Klamath and Menominee tribes. In it he deplored the "fanatical and arrogant" record of Eisenhower's Indian program which forcibly dismembered human groups, violated sacred treaties, and devastated two great forests.[96] He also evaluated several books concerning the Indians

Mrs. John Collier, Sr.

Professor Collier jokes with a newspaper reporter at Knox College.

of South America, the Sioux, and the betrayal of the Five Civilized Tribes for the *Saturday Review*.[97]

In August 1959, Collier began to write a brief column each week for *El Crepusculo,* a Taos newspaper. His topics ranged from the plight of the Negro in Southwest Africa to the threat of DDT on animal and human life, but most of his attention centered on the Indian. Repeating a theme he had focused on throughout his life, Collier claimed that the Southwestern tribes held social mysteries that would prove useful to the white world, which had failed to merge individual desires "into group fulfillments" that endured.[98] He pointed out that Pueblo culture permitted "intensity with tranquility" or a feeling within the self that the individual and group were "totally acceptable and of equal value," while the best in any person "must be used for the good not of one but all who were members of the community."[99]

According to Collier, these Indians had developed the "principle of unanimity" which entailed long discussion and brooding meditation rather than majority rule. Collier claimed that, if given a chance to operate, this principle would result in startling social achievements such as the successful effort of Acoma Pueblo during the New Deal to reduce its livestock from 33,000 to 8,500 in order to implement conservation techniques that preserved tribal existence.[100] Just as important, the Hopis had developed a "reverence for life," lost by technological man, because their society consisted of a web of relationships between man and nature which ideally functioned "harmoniously and positively for the good of all."[101]

Collier suggested that in recent years the Navajo tribal council had become an institution which every state, county, and township might study with profit. Through planned social action, the Navajos furnished dramatic disproof of the fixed notion that dark-skinned people were fundamentally incompetent and needed to have "their native ways stamped out and their souls saved by white men." Starting in 1933, the council had remained faithful to its task of reducing the tribe's livestock despite social stress and errors made by the Indian Bureau. Even more impressive, the Navajos used their oil income during the post-war period to work for the group's benefit by creating a scholarship trust fund, credit for needy individuals, a tribal forest products industry, and an irrigation program to train farmers.[102]

Although completing his series for *El Crepusculo* during the first part of 1960, Collier continued to exhibit intellectual vigor by preparing a memoir of his life. He published it three years later at the age of seventy-nine. Entitled *From Every Zenith,* it provided an impressionistic account of his social work at the People's Institute, the crusade to reform Indian affairs, the Indian New Deal, and his activities as president of the Institute for Ethnic Affairs. Collier claimed that the main purpose in writing this book was to record "the attempted devising of mental and social structures to enable the measureless potentials of community life to vibrate and flow into modern man."[103]

He recalled that his life had been spent in a quest to develop social organizations that would sustain public greatness by uniting "men, great and humble, with common purposes and endeavors."[104] He followed this course because Prince Peter Kropotkin's book, *Mutual Aid,* had demolished the tenets of social Darwinism and demonstrated that men worked best in groups. Collier explained that the communal instinct described by Kropotkin resided just below the threshold of man's social consciousness and when it was encouraged the human landscape changed "from a bleak winter to a flowering spring time."[105] To support this contention, he described the partial success in bringing the "common folk" of New York into a gemeinschaft mode of life, as well as his use of Indian groups to implement conservation techniques and revive "grass roots" democracy during the New Deal.[106]

Collier admitted that these attempts to create "a community of man

Mrs. John Collier, Sr.

John Collier reading his memoir, *From Every Zenith,* at his Taos, New Mexico, home, 1966.

with man, and man with earth" had fallen victim to the cold war community of conformism, self-serving mediocrity, and militarism. Nevertheless, he believed that future world survival depended upon an acceptance of the sociological concept held by the Pueblos and other preliterate societies; that adherence to the notion of shared social good was central to the creation of an adequate human personality which contained the enduring qualities of courage, joy, loyalty, and forbearance.[107]

During the last few years of his life, Collier wrote several articles about the American Indian, and he found immense satisfaction when the Department of the Interior presented him with its Distinguished Service Award on his eightieth birthday in 1964.* This citation described him

---

*Consult John Collier, "Indians' Heritage," *Americas* 14 (September 1962): 34–38; and David Brower, ed., *Wildlands in Our Civilization* (San Francisco: Sierra Club, 1964), pp. 115–27. Collier also revised *Patterns and Ceremonials of the Indians of the Southwest* and published it under the title *On the Gleaming Way* (Denver: Sage Books, 1962).

as a "humanitarian, conservationist, poet, and teacher." It stated that his twelve years as Indian commissioner had "brought the hope of a better day and a brighter future to a whole people."[108]

Because of poor physical health, Collier decided to make one last request from the officers of Taos Pueblo. He wrote them a letter which stated:

> I have done what I could for your people across forty years (and shall do what I may in any years ahead) although in a thousand years I could not repay my debt to you. I have never asked any return from your Pueblo, but I do ask one service of you, for myself, and for my wife, Grace Collier.
>
> It is, that when either of us dies, and then when the other dies, you shall remove our bodies at once to the Pueblo, and shall bury our bodies somewhere on the mesa to the North of the Pueblo, leaving no marker or monument.
>
> The funerary laws of New Mexico do not apply to your Pueblo land. Their requirements, which are designed to make undertakers prosperous, have no application to you or to your lands. In the same way, the mournful ceremonialism of funerals in the white world have no place in your Indian world or to my wife, Grace, and myself.
>
> If for whatever reason you might not be able to do what I am asking, then our request to our non-Indian friends is that our bodies shall be cremated immediately, and without ceremony or any lamenting. Our souls or selves may have become extinct or may have gone their ways to other tasks in the universe. Our bodies belong only to the good earth — and if feasible, to the Indian good earth.[109]

Collier died four days after his eighty-fourth birthday at 12:30 a.m. on May 8, 1968. His last experience before death was listening to songs by Indian friends who stood at his bedside. The Taos Indians, however, found it impossible to honor his last request but they did participate in a special memorial service where friends offered prayers and eulogies in Tewa, Spanish, and English. Collier's remains were buried in the cemetery of the Spanish-American Presbyterian Church in a spot overlooking the beautiful Ranchos de Taos Valley and the mountains beyond.[110]

11. The Collier Legacy

Collier's death ended a remarkable career — a career which demonstrated the strengths and weaknesses of twentieth century social reform in the United States. Characteristic of many American reformers, Collier believed that society would advance to higher levels of progress through creative planning and the revitalization of group living. This evolutionary, positivist world view was the dynamic behind Collier's successful efforts to promote social justice. But it also caused him to believe erroneously that he could create a cooperative commonwealth by combining the attributes of preindustrial ethnic cultures with the requirements of a capitalist civilization.

While in New York City during the Progressive era, Collier became part of a small elite of altruistic settlement workers who believed that the salvation of urban America depended on the benevolence and direction of the expert. They brought efficiency, rationality, and scientific planning to philanthropy in order to end poverty and class antagonism and to restore a sense of community lost in an industrial age.[1]

Collier contributed to this effort by using sociology and biology to solve social problems. Intrigued with Lester Frank Ward's imprecise concept of sociocracy, or the scientific control of social forces through the collective mind of society, Collier thought he could develop an art of governing human affairs which allowed the people to determine the goals of the group. He reasoned that once intellectuals found a way to release the unconscious democratic will of the people, Prince Peter Kropotkin's evolutionary law of mutual aid would take effect.

Being deeply influenced by advances in psychiatry, Collier saw the importance of subjective values and the role of the unconscious in human behavior. This enabled him to envision the possibility of using dance, pageantry, and theatre to unite men once again. And he applied this insight at the People's Forums and his Training School for Community Workers in order to understand and control the immigrant masses.

Collier's concern over the cultural atomization on Manhattan's lower east side led to his participation in the effort to transform the public school into a community center. He hoped that the socialized school, which offered a potential substitute for the small town church and meeting hall, would serve as a magnet where citizens could attend social events, engage in recreation, and discuss public issues. But the immigrant neighborhood was constantly flooded with newcomers, and it offered only a geographic setting for temporary group activities.[2]

Besides this dilemma, Collier had a romantic impulse, far removed from his effort to implement scientific philanthropy, that limited his success. He wanted to apply a system of primary group ties found in an older village-oriented America to an unstable industrial order. This impractical wish of returning to a simple arcadian life that probably never existed proved impossible in a city where ethnic tensions aggravated class divisions. Effective face to face relationships depended on a relative similarity of background and economic status.[3]

Other problems plagued Collier as well. Idealistic about the latent communal impulse inherent in human nature, he underestimated the resilience of the bourgeois values held by the individuals he tried to organize. Most immigrants came to the United States because they rejected the poverty associated with their rural homeland. They supported the People's Institute in order to improve their standard of living but showed little interest in the creation of lasting neighborhoods. Instead, they favored social mobility and merging into the mainstream of American society.

Just as important, Collier never worked out the inconsistencies inherent in the use of social scientists to restore a sense of community. Ideally, the people determined their own social objectives, but a tendency always existed toward elitism, manipulation, and repression. Collier did listen to the opinions expressed at the People's Forums, but there were no immigrant leaders on the institute's staff determining the agenda. Since he was better at directing than listening, he contradicted his own principles by trying to influence popular ideas through the National Board of Censorship, an agency that regulated the movie industry. When the immigrants lost interest in his reform initiatives, he toyed with the notion of having the federal government enforce social planning through the National Community Councils of Defense.

Collier's previous interest in establishing a gemeinschaft mode of life for the immigrants naturally attracted him to the American Indian. The romantic side of his personality led him to conclude that the Pueblos and other tribes in the Southwest held mystical properties of community that he had searched for in New York and California. Because he wanted to preserve this attribute for the benefit of all mankind he easily accepted the myth of the noble savage. He perceived the Pueblo Indians as living in a Golden Age, untainted by the corruptions of the modern world. Comparing their civilization to that of the ancient Greeks, he claimed that they had "achieved democracy, the rule of love, and a social ideal of beauty." Not interested in money or power, they lived close to nature and possessed superior social institutions that enabled them to build cooperative commonwealths.[4]

These romantic ideas, which paralleled those of Frederick Engels, the utopian socialist theoretician who praised the virtues of primitive communism, and Lewis Henry Morgan, a Rochester lawyer and ethnologist who wrote about the democratic aspects of the Iroquois Confederacy, had little basis in reality. It was true that the Pueblo Indians had developed egalitarian communal societies, but they resembled theocracies more than democracies. And Collier's perception of the peaceful Pueblo failed to take into account contradictory universal human traits such as suspicion, hostility, and constant bickering.[5]

Furthermore, he neglected to analyze the degree to which other tribes failed to fit his simplified generalizations about Indian life. The Chippewas, for example, lived in loosely connected villages; the Northwest Coast Indians had cultures that valued status and wealth; while the Navajos and Sioux were highly individualistic. Nor did Collier foresee the difficulty of reviving the community life of the Five Civilized Tribes, who had watched their governments disintegrate from the pressures of removal, internal dissension, and land allotment.

Nevertheless, once he became commissioner, Collier formulated the Wheeler-Howard bill, a measure that demonstrated his desire to implement scientific colonial administration and build societies where Indians lived in communal bliss. This legislation, consistent with Collier's earlier approach to minorities, contained contradictory trends of thought. It demonstrated that he looked to the future by insisting that the Indians adopt sophisticated technological skills in order to survive in the twentieth century; yet, at the same time, it revealed that Collier was essentially retrogressive in his attempts to resurrect a utopian Red Atlantis which, if it ever existed, could never be revived. Collier faced two directions at once by asking the Indians to accept the requirements of a complicated industrial order while concurrently asking them to restore their tribal heritage.[6]

Collier quickly discovered that his earlier perception of Indian life as a vibrant group endeavor was exaggerated. A few tribes understood his effort to strengthen their institutions, but many others favored the policy of assimilation. He learned at the Indian congresses that no widespread demand existed to relinquish land allotments. After the passage of the IRA, the reality of tribal life became clearer as the Indians struggled with the problems associated with self-government. It often consisted of extreme cultural conservatism that resisted any change, factionalism, discord between full and mixed bloods, and lack of community leadership.

Despite his harsh criticism of federal paternalism during the twenties, Collier often imposed his personal will and philosophy on the Indians. When several tribes showed a reluctance to accept the IRA, Collier counted in favor of the proposal those Indians who refused to vote. The use of social scientists to draw up constitutions and charters was another example of compelling the Indians to accept white ideas instead of listening to native viewpoints. Recognizing this error, Collier tried to correct it by initiating the Indian Personality Study.

In his zeal to create tribal solidarity, Collier often promoted conformity rather than community. He showed little concern for individual rights by drafting the original Wheeler-Howard bill, a bill that permitted the government arbitrarily to acquire restricted allotted land and abolish heirship. And he frequently denied the validity of minority viewpoints if they conflicted with his plans. This became apparent when he refused to provide constructive outlets for members of the American Indian Federation whose concept of community followed the voluntary associational relationships common to whites, rather than extended kinship patterns.

In addition, Collier imposed his ideas of scientific government and religious freedom on the Pueblo Indians. He fashioned the United Pueblo Agency, in part to promote efficiency, and appointed a woman social scientist as superintendent. But most of the Pueblos showed little interest in these reforms, preferring the older system which provided them with more autonomy. By insisting that the Taos Indians had a right to their traditional culture but not to their long standing religious intolerance concerning the Native American Church, Collier exposed yet another inconsistency in his notion of self-government.

His authoritarian tendencies were best revealed in his posture toward the Navajos. He demanded that they accept day schools when it was obvious they preferred boarding facilities. The Navajos were also compelled to adopt his conservation program which included rational planning and the careful use of their land. But they showed a violent revulsion at the grass roots level against his approach to resource management which started reservation-wide stock reduction and the fencing off of their grazing areas for soil experimentation. This resistance caused Collier to reorganize the tribal council in order to make it more complaisant, a response similar to the action of Albert B. Fall, the former secretary of the interior.

Collier's dream of creating energetic Indian communities depended upon the success or failure of the bureau's educational program. Under the leadership of W. Carson Ryan and Willard Beatty, the professional standards of the teachers improved and the children at day schools studied a curriculum that dealt with the difficulties of rural life. But tribes such as the Navajo and the Pine Ridge Sioux favored the continuation of their boarding schools, where instructors had taught patriotism, character development, and the work ethic.[7] More importantly, the bureau's progressive education policy often emphasized the restoration of traditional Indian values rather than preparing the tribes for the complexities of the contemporary world, while Congress refused to appropriate the large sums of money necessary for the training of adult Indians in the sophisticated administrative skills required to make the IRA function properly.[8]

The inability of Collier to secure passage of an Indian Claims Commission bill, due to opposition from the Bureau of the Budget, further harmed his drive to promote Indian self-government.[9] The Nez Percé, many California Indians, and the Sioux, all expressed a desire at the Indian congresses to have their claims against the government settled before accepting the IRA. When the Indian Claims Commission measure became stalled in Congress, the Sioux on the Pine Ridge reservation divided between those who wanted strict adherence to their treaty obligations and those who favored cooperation with the government. Other Indians succumbed to the proposal of the American Indian Federation which promised a $3,000 cash settlement for their claims against the United States. They believed that Collier was more inclined to dispensing bounty and platitudes than defending their legal rights.

Unfortunately, the commissioner's concern about promoting his conception of Indian welfare sometimes caused him to neglect the government's duty to honor its treaty obligations. In the original Wheeler-Howard bill he failed to define clearly the Indians' existing water, mineral, and hunting rights. By not insisting that the Navajos have one school for every thirty children, he violated their Treaty of 1868.[10] Even during his previous career as a critic of the Indian Bureau, Collier seemed more interested in the scientific management of the Indians' natural resources than in demanding that they had the prerogative of refusing white exploitation altogether. He also remained evasive about the Indians' right to vote and other benefits implicit in the Indian Citizenship Act of 1924.

Collier's difficulty in administering what he created further complicated matters. He had little control over the Indian Bureau agents at the
local level. Fearful of losing their jobs if the IRA succeeded, many of
them remained paternalistic and uncooperative. Self-government was all
but impossible on a number of reservations because of bad roads and the
long distances between population clusters. Other reservations, such as
Ft. Berthold in North Dakota, held the remnants of several tribes, thus
giving rise to internal dissension. Another problem stemmed from the
complicated procedure for adopting constitutions and charters, which
entailed several votes before the Indians secured money from the revolving
credit fund. By the time this process ended, many tribes had lost interest
in the IRA.[11]

In many ways, Collier's Indian policy was part of the reform vision
held by Secretary of Agriculture Henry A. Wallace and other New Deal
social liberals. The commissioner wanted to build a cooperative commonwealth through a managerial reorganization of society. He believed that
the Indians could assist other Americans in bringing about the good society
where personal relationships and ethical values found in an earlier America
merged with the benefits of an industrial state.[12] Yet his social engineering
only centralized the machinery of control in the Indian Bureau and often
led to coercion rather than promotion of social justice or spontaneous
community endeavors. The reconciliation of local democracy at the tribal
level with the bureaucratic expertise needed in Washington, D.C., to run
a complex colonial policy was a fundamental challenge that Collier failed
to meet.

Despite these shortcomings, Collier's career contained many impressive achievements. Throughout his life he took the middle ground between
the extremes of unregulated capitalism and totalitarian socialism.[13]
Whether working with immigrants, Indians, or natives from Micronesia,
Collier perceived the need for national planning to secure progress in a
society beset with constant change. Impatient when his plans were
thwarted, Collier sometimes became a domineering person, but he always
remained committed to his dream of devising methods where local groups
could participate in their fate, thus insuring the preservation of grass roots
democracy. And, in general, Collier insisted on retaining individual freedom by permitting people voluntarily to accept or reject the social discipline necessary for community living.

This administrative technique of combining social control with traditional ideas about local self-government often had remarkable success.
Thousands of immigrants participated in the neighborhood activities of
the People's Institute. They played an active role in the Progressive movement and helped chart the course of American liberalism. Similarly, the

natives on Guam and Samoa responded to Collier's Institute of Ethnic Affairs by demanding the end to naval rule and the creation of civilian self-government.

During the New Deal, Collier again demonstrated the potential of his approach to public administration. Many tribes used the IRA and other federal programs formulated by social scientists, to assume some control once again over their future. They benefited when Collier implemented special civil service regulations that allowed him to hire Indians for bureau jobs. He appointed individuals such as Robert Yellowtail, the superintendent of the Crow reservation in Montana, to high level positions, while the number of Native Americans employed by the bureau increased from approximately 3o percent to 65 percent.[14]

One of Collier's significant accomplishments took place in the area of conservation. He assisted in the formation of the Indian Emergency Work program which started the process of rebuilding the eroded land base on several reservations. He brought in advisors from the Soil Conservation Service to help draw up plans for tribal resource management, tried to implement sustained yield forestry, and persuaded the Navajos and other Indians of the dreaded but necessary task of reducing their livestock to prevent erosion. Because he remembered the "passion" with which Taos Pueblo guarded its sacred Blue Lake, and recalling his hikes in the Appalachian Mountains, Collier created several roadless and wilderness areas to provide a spiritual sanctuary for Indians.[15]

Collier understood that cultural diversity was a dynamic force in history. He hoped that the immigrants, Japanese-Americans, and the natives of Micronesia would enrich the potential alternatives for American society. This awareness that different races needed one another turned Collier's attention toward the Indian. Sensing the universal significance of tribal life, Collier questioned the wisdom of the government's assimilation policy which tried to turn the Indian into a white man. He raised the pregnant hypothesis that tribal institutions should be preserved and studied because they contain the lost attributes of communal experience, the beauties of art, a passion for the earth, reverence for the human personality, and the profound values of comparative religion.

This insight, together with a humanitarian concern for the downtrodden, started Collier on a crusade during the twenties to assist the Indian. An extremist over the issue of native rights, he helped the Pueblos defeat the Bursum bill and formed the American Indian Defense Association, an organization that promoted the preservation of Indian civilization. As executive secretary of the association, Collier defended Indian religious dances and tribal self-government, helped prevent the confiscation of oil and water power sites on the Navajo and Flathead reservations, pushed for a Senate investigation of the Indian Bureau, and formulated legislative programs that were enacted during the New Deal.

Collier will always be remembered as a mover and shaker of Indian history during his twelve years as commissioner. Because he had a poetic insight into the grandeur of Indian culture, Collier encouraged a sense of personal dignity and self-respect among many Indians. They understood his prediction that in the future their art forms would profoundly influence "the sense of the beautiful throughout the white race," while their "ancient, deep, universal love of the earth" would continue "to draw to them in fellow sharing, all who are young, all who have youth in their souls."[16]

Collier was one of those rare reformers who combined a moral passion for worthy causes with the scientist's respect for technical expertise.[17] He protected the Indians' religious freedom, brought them under President Roosevelt's public relief programs, set up an Arts and Crafts Board, ordered the codification of Indian law, used social scientists who respected traditional native culture, and demonstrated the potential of hemisphere-wide Pan-Indianism. The Indian Reorganization Act was a flawed product that failed to meet the needs of a diversified population, but it did stop land allotment and set up mechanisms for self-government, as well as providing needed credit facilities and allowing the Indians time to define their role in American society.

Vine Deloria, a noted Sioux author, indicated that the sons and daughters of parents who were influenced by Collier's Indian New Deal eventually supported the goal of cultural independence.[18] During the decades of the sixties and seventies they demanded that the Indian Bureau consult with them about its programs. This contemporary protest movement brought the growth of Indian nationalism, the stirrings of native religion, a reawakened sense of tribalism, and Pan-Indianism.[19] It would have pleased Collier, who devoted his long life to the Indians' cause, to know that some of the ideas he favored were still having an impact on history.

Bibliographical Essay

Manuscripts

The records that concern John Collier are voluminous and another author might discuss the same subject from a different perspective. The Papers of the People's Institute located in the Manuscript Division of the New York City Public Library provide the most important source for Collier's career as a social worker. This collection consists of several scrapbooks that have newspaper clippings relating to the institute's activities and a box of its publications. Correspondence folders describe Collier's involvement with the National Board of Review, the Training School for Community Workers, and the community center movement. The New York Public Library has a complete file of Collier's *People's Institute Bulletin* and the *Civic Journal*.

Most of this research was based on the John Collier Papers in the Western Americana Collection at Yale University Library. An enormous holding, it has over ninety boxes of manuscripts written by Collier, including an unpublished book entitled "Crowds, Groups and the Great Society," personal correspondence, minutes of the All Pueblo Councils, and newspaper clippings. Valuable sources pertaining to Indian reform during the twenties include American Indian Defense Association legislative bulletins and a complete set of its journal, *American Indian Life*. From the New Deal years there are the biweekly reports by Commissioner Collier to Secretary Harold L. Ickes and Department of the Interior press releases. Especially important for an understanding of the Institute of Ethnic Affairs is material reflecting Collier's attitude about United Nations' trusteeships, Guam, Samoa, Liberia, Point Four, and the government's termination policy toward the Indians. Finally, the John Gallup Collection of American Literature at Yale contains Collier's correspondence with Mable Dodge and Elizabeth S. Sergeant, which furnished insights into all aspects of his life.

The National Archives at Washington, D.C., provides another major source of Collier Papers centering around the Office File of Commissioner Collier and records concerning the Indian Reorganization Act. The office file includes Collier's public correspondence, manuscripts of his personal writing, reports by bureau personnel, newspaper clippings, and Interior Department memoranda. Particularly significant are the sections dealing with the alleged Nazi infiltration of the American Indian Federation, the reaction of missionaries to the Indian New Deal, stock reduction on the Navajo reservation, the Taos peyote warfare, the Indian Personality Study, and the internment of Japanese-Americans on Indian lands. There are a few pre-1933 documents, including Collier's poetry and embryonic but often vitriolic articles in rough manuscript such as "What the Armistice Means to Me." The boxes relating to the Indian Reorganization Act deal with the reaction of Indians and whites to this legislation. They contain minutes of tribal congresses and completed questionnaires detailing the effect of land allotment on tribal organization and economic life.

Other significant holdings in the National Archives are the Records of the Board of Indian Commissioners and the Private Papers of Herbert J. Hagerman. The former usually offer a critical assessment of Collier's activities and a defense of the bureau's policy of assimilation. Hagerman compiled the latter while he was special commissioner to the Navajos (1923–1932) and a representative of the secretary of the interior on the Pueblo Lands Board (1926–1932). The most important materials for this volume include Hagerman's collection of printed pamphlets and mimeographed releases of the American Indian Defense Association. His personal correspondence with Kenneth Roberts, a writer for the *Saturday Evening Post,* provides a colorful discussion of Coolidge politics, while the folder on the "Collier-Frazier Inquisition" contains Hagerman's defense in the successful effort to remove him from office.

The Franklin D. Roosevelt Library at Hyde Park has a small but significant collection on the Indian New Deal. The president's penciled notations and letters about the Wheeler-Howard bill are especially interesting. These papers demonstrate the close cooperation between Collier, Ickes, and Roosevelt in their successful effort to pass legislation repealing the Dawes General Allotment Act of 1887. They offer some information about the Pan-American Indian movement.

The following manuscript collections furnish additional data about Collier and the American Indian. The Louis C. Cramton Papers at the Michigan Historical Collection focus on the Flathead Indian water power site controversy, Hoover's attempt to increase the allotment for food and clothing at boarding schools, and the Middle Rio Grande Conservancy District. The Elmer Thomas Papers at the University of Oklahoma's

Western History Collection show the opposition of lawyers to the Wheeler-Howard bill and give information about the first Inter-American Conference on Indian Life held at Patzcuaro, Mexico, as well as providing minutes of the Indian congresses held in that state. The Hugh Scott Papers and the Bronson Cutting Papers at the Library of Congress relate to Indian matters during the twenties and thirties.

Public Documents

Among the numerous published government documents, the essential items on Indian reform are hearings of the House and Senate Indian Affairs Committees, as well as the Public Lands and Surveys Committee for the conflict over the Bursum bill. More important are the volumes of testimony compiled by the Senate Indian Investigating Committee between 1927 and 1945. They make for verbose and tedious reading but reach more deeply and diversely into the Indian problem than any other public documents. The *Congressional Record* provides a source of great value for Collier's activities during the twenties because such men as Representative James A. Frear and Senator Burton K. Wheeler inserted into it lengthy criticisms of the Indian Bureau by the American Indian Defense Association. It has the best concise account of the aims of the Indian Reorganization Act, Collier's support of President Roosevelt's court-packing plan, and Wheeler's eventual disillusionment with the Indian New Deal.

Another important source for Collier's narrative of Indian events is the annual reports of the secretary of the interior. A twelve volume series of pamphlets issued by the Indian Bureau between 1933 and 1945, entitled *Indians at Work,* describes the efforts to implement the Indian Reorganization Act, conservation programs, and public relief on the reservations. Anthropologists, conservationists, lawyers, and Indian Service personnel contributed feature articles, while Collier wrote editorials much broader in scope. They dealt with court-packing, social planning, and foreign policy, offering a neglected source of information about the goals and purposes of the New Deal. Indispensable for understanding Indian policy is Felix Cohen's *Handbook of Federal Indian Law* (Washington, D.C., 1942).

Books

The best surveys of recent Indian history are: Angie Debo, *A History of the Indians of the United States* (Norman, Oklahoma, 1970); Harold E. Fey and D'Arcy McNickle, *Indians and Other Americans* (New York, 1959); William T. Hagan, *American Indians* (Chicago, 1961); and Lyman Tyler, *Indian Affairs: A Study of the Changes in Policy of the United States Toward Indians* (Provo, Utah, 1964). Herbert O. Brayer sheds light on New Mexico's tangled land situation in *Pueblo Land Grants of the Rio Abajo* (Albuquerque, New Mexico, 1938). Hazel Hertzberg, *The Search for an American Indian Identity: Modern Pan-Indian Movements* (Syracuse, New York, 1971), gives an excellent analysis of Indian progressives who formed the Society of American Indians in the decade before the First World War. They identified with the goals of white society and were typical of those Indians who opposed Collier. Lawrence Kelly, *The Navajo Indians and Federal Indian Policy, 1900–1935* (Tucson, Arizona, 1968), is critical of Collier and his associates. This book amounts to a defense of the Republican-run Indian Bureau but is a well researched and a long needed contribution to the sparse historiography on the American Indian in the first part of the twentieth century. G. E. E. Lindquist's *The Red Man in the United States* (New York, 1923) contains information compiled by Protestant churches to assist their missionaries and is important for its investigation of conditions on the reservations in the early twenties. Lewis Meriam's *The Problem of Indian Administration* (Baltimore, Maryland, 1928), a private investigation launched by the bureau during the same period, offers a more critical approach and recommended reforms that were enacted by Herbert Hoover and Franklin D. Roosevelt.

John Collier's memoir, *From Every Zenith* (Denver, Colorado, 1963), contains an account of Indian reform from 1920 to 1945, but is too optimistic and lacks documentation. His other books, *Indians of the Americas* (New York, 1947) and *On the Gleaming Way* (Denver, Colorado, 1962), also explain events that culminated in the Indian New Deal. Robert Gessner's *Massacre: A Survey of Today's American Indian* (New York, 1931) offers an indictment of Indian policy during the twenties, while J. P. Kinney's *Facing Indian Facts* (Laurens, New York, 1973) provides a scathing criticism of Collier's reform efforts. Angie Debo, *And Still the Waters Run* (Princeton, New Jersey, 1940), discusses the shortcomings of the Oklahoma Welfare Act. D'Arcy McNickle's *Indian Man: A Life of Oliver La Farge* (Bloomington, Indiana, 1971) is a sensitive biography about one of Collier's close associates. Oliver La Farge supplies significant information on recent Indian history in *As Long as the Grass Shall Grow* (New York, 1940) and *The Changing Indian* (Norman, Oklahoma, 1942). George Boyce, *When Navajos Had Too Many Sheep* (San Francisco, 1974), shows the limitations of Collier's conservation and educational programs in the Southwest, while Margaret Szasz, *Education and the American Indian; The Road to Self-Determination, 1928–1973* (Albuquerque, 1974), and Evelyn Adams, *American Indian Education* (New York, 1946), provide further details on this important subject. J. B. Gittler (ed.) in *Understanding Minority Groups* (New York, 1956) describes a symposium on ethnic affairs with a contribution by Collier. Walter Daniels (ed.), *American Indians* (New York, 1957); William Brophy and Sophie Aberle, *The Indian: America's*

Unfinished Business (Norman, Oklahoma, 1966); Vine Deloria, *Custer Died for Your Sins: An Indian Manifesto* (New York, 1969); Wilcomb Washburn, *Red Man's Land — White Man's Law* (New York, 1971); and Theodore W. Taylor, *The States and Their Indian Citizens* (Washington, 1972), all discuss the government's policy of terminating the Indian reservation system.

Periodicals

The *New York Times* follows closely Collier's crusade to reconstruct Indian affairs. It criticizes the bureau's ban on native religious dances and carries his protests in the letters to the editor column. Favorable toward the New Deal, the *Times* publicizes the Indian Reorganization Act and federal relief programs on the reservations. But the hundreds of clippings from Yale University and the National Archives offer much more information about Collier, especially his activities in the Southwest.

Any serious student of recent Indian history must read with care the monthly journals of the two major Indian welfare groups. *Indian Truth,* published by the conservative missionary-oriented Indian Rights Association, praises the government's policy of assimilating the Indian and disapproves of Collier's tendency to treat the Native American as a separate social group. Nevertheless, it takes a stand against the policies of Albert B. Fall and the scandals that prevailed in the twenties. Collier's journal, *American Indian Life,* which openly attacks the bureau, provides an indispensable account of the American Indian Defense Association and the origin of the ideas that culminated in the Indian New Deal.

The best single article pertaining to this study is Randolph Downes, "A Crusade for Indian Reform 1922–1934," in the *Mississippi Valley Historical Review* (December 1945). It suggests that the Indian New Deal was the result of over a decade of struggle aimed at stopping the landlessness and pauperization stemming from land allotment. Downes proves perceptive, but he fails to focus on Collier's American Indian Defense Association as the main instigator of reform or to discuss the fundamental difference between Collier and the officials in the Hoover administration.

Contrary to Downes' thesis, Elizabeth Green in "Indian Minorities Under the American New Deal," *Pacific Affairs* (December 1935), claims that the New Deal with its emphasis upon ethnic diversity and the advent of anthropologists, represented a complete reorientation of Indian policy. Donald Young in "Minority Peoples in the Depression," *Social Science Research Council Bulletin,* no. 31, (1937), also stresses that the Indian Reorganization Act was an extreme departure in the American procedure of handling ethnic groups. John Collier offers a detailed account of these changes in "United States Indian Administration as a Laboratory of Ethnic Affairs," *Social Research* (September 1945). The new emphasis on cultural pluralism, the use of social sciences, and the revival of Indian nationalism are described in the bimonthly *Boletín Indigenista* and the quarterly *America Indigena,* journals that provided Collier and his associates with an outlet for their writings on the Indian.

In addition, the following scholarly articles offer insights concerning the themes of this book. They include: Calvin Gower, "The CCC Indian Division," *Minnesota History* (Spring 1972); Lawrence Kelly, "Choosing the New Deal Indian Commissioner: Ickes vs. Collier," *New Mexico Historical Review,* (January 1975); Lawrence Kelly, "The Navajo Indians Land and Oil," *New Mexico Historical Review* (January 1963); Donald Parman, "The Indian and the Civilian Conservation Corps," *Pacific Historical Review* (February 1971) and "J. C. Morgan: Navajo Apostle of Assimilation," *Prologue,* (Summer 1972); Michael T. Smith, "The Wheeler-Howard Act of 1934: The Indian New Deal," *Journal of the West,* (July 1971); Gary Stein, "The Indian Citizenship Act of 1924," *New Mexico Historical Review* (July 1972) and "Tribal Self-Government and the Indian Reorganization Act of 1934," *Michigan Law Review* (April 1972); Margaret Szasz, "Indian Reform in a Decade of Prosperity," *Montana: The Magazine of Western History* (Winter 1970); Eugene Trani, "Hubert Work and the Department of the Interior, 1923–1928," *Pacific Northwest Quarterly* (January 1970); B. T. Quinten, "Oklahoma Tribes, the Great Depression and the Indian Bureau," *Mid-America,* (January 1967), and Peter Wright, "John Collier and the Indian Welfare Act of 1936," *Chronicles of Oklahoma,* (Autumn 1972).

Several liberal periodicals consistently support Collier's reform initiatives. The *Survey* under the leadership of Paul Kellogg and Haven Emerson carries articles on the deplorable state of the Indian as early as 1922. The *Sunset Magazine* influenced by Walter Woehlke, a close friend of Collier, published few issues, from November 1922 until June 1924, without at least one article denouncing the Indian Bureau. The *Nation* is critical of the Republican Indian programs during the twenties, a defender of the Indian New Deal, and hostile toward the policy of termination followed by both Presidents Harry S Truman and Dwight D. Eisenhower. *Good Housekeeping* assists Collier by featuring emotional stories in the spring of 1929 and 1934 aimed at mobilizing the women of America to demand Indian reform. *Collier's* magazine offers favorable accounts of the Indian New Deal, and it sides with the dependent peoples in Micronesia, Guam, and Samoa in their struggle for self-government during the cold war.

Many conservative magazines support the Indian Bureau, especially the policies of President Herbert Hoover. The *Southern Workman* (complete file in the Yale Divinity School Library), published by the Hampton Normal and Agricultural Institute in Virginia, devotes its issues to the interests of underdeveloped races and provides a forum for a discussion of the Indian. J. Henry Scattergood, assistant commissioner under

Hoover and a member of the Indian Rights Association, was a Hampton Trustee. Under his guidance this periodical favors the assimilation of the Indian into white society. The *Saturday Evening Post* consistently sides with the Republicans by carrying feature articles by Hubert Work and Ray Lyman Wilbur. It violently attacks Collier and the Indian New Deal, on April 1, 1939, in Flora Warren Seymour's "Thunder Over the Southwest." Other publications that back the bureau are *Current History* and the *Missionary Review of the World*.

Some periodicals refuse to enter the political controversy but support both Hoover and Roosevelt in their effort to help the American Indian. In 1929 the *National Conference on Social Work* established a committee dealing with the Indian which resulted in articles by Charles J. Rhoads, Lewis Meriam, and John Collier. The *Progressive Education Magazine* devotes its February 1932, issue to a discussion of reform at Indian Bureau schools. Between 1929 and 1940, *School and Society* also describes the government's progressive educational programs.

Theses

The following theses were helpful: Arthur Bach, "Administration of Indian Resources in the United States," Ph.D. thesis, University of Iowa, 1942; Rudolph Xavier Foley, "Origins of the Indian Reorganization Act of 1934," Ph.D. thesis, Fordham University, 1937; John Leiper Freedman, "The New Deal for Indians: A Study in Bureau-Committee Relations in American Government," Ph.D. thesis, Princeton, 1952; Lawrence Kelly, "The Navajos and Federal Indian Policy, 1913–1934," Ph.D. thesis, University of New Mexico, 1961; Anton Long, "Senator Bursum and the Pueblo Lands Act of 1924," M.A. thesis, University of New Mexico, 1949; Donald Parman, "The Indian Civilian Conservation Corps," Ph.D. thesis, University of Oklahoma, 1967; F. A. Pollock, "Navajo-Federal Relations as a Social Cultural Problem," Ph.D. thesis, University of Southern California, 1942; M. C. Sykes, "A History of Attempts of the United States Government to Re-establish Self-Government Among the Indians," M.S. thesis, Bowling Green University, 1950; and Graham Taylor, "The New Deal and The Grass Roots," Ph.D. thesis, University of Pennsylvania, 1972.

Abbreviations

Collier Papers	The Private Papers of John Collier, Yale University Library, New Haven, Conn.
Cramton Papers	The Private Papers of Louis C. Cramton, University of Michigan, Ann Arbor
Elmer Thomas Papers	Elmer Thomas Papers, Western History Collection, University of Oklahoma, Norman
FDRL	Franklin D. Roosevelt Library, Hyde Park, New York
Hagerman Papers	The Private Papers of Herbert Hagerman, National Archives, Washington, D.C.
La Farge Papers	Oliver La Farge Papers, Humanities Research Center, University of Texas, Austin
NA	National Archives, Washington, D.C.
NYPL	New York Public Library
RG	Record Group

Notes

CHAPTER 1: DISCOVERING A RED ATLANTIS

1. John Collier, *From Every Zenith* (Denver: Sage Books, 1963), p. 115; and *El Crepusculo*, September 10, 1959, Taos, New Mexico, The Private Papers of John Collier, Yale University Library (hereafter referred to as Collier Papers).
2. *El Crepusculo*, September 10, 1959, Collier Papers.
3. Ibid.
4. Ibid. For an excellent portrayal of Mabel Dodge Luhan's (she married Antonio Luhan in 1923) bohemianism and rejection of Western society consult Christopher Lash, *The New Radicalism in America, 1889–1963* (New York: Vintage Books, 1965), pp. 104–40.
5. John Collier, "The Red Atlantis," *Survey* 49 (October 1, 1922): 16; Collier, "The Pueblos' Last Stand," *Sunset* 50 (February 1923): 19; and Collier, "Plundering the Pueblo Indians," *Sunset* 50 (January 1923): 21.
6. John Collier, "Our Indian Policy," *Sunset* 50 (March 1923): 13.
7. Consult Allen Davis, *Spearheads for Reform: The Social Settlements and the Progressive Movement, 1890–1914* (New York: Oxford University Press, 1967).
8. John Collier, *Indians of the Americas*, abridged ed. (New York: The New American Library, 1947), p. 7.
9. For a discussion of this idea see Mary Austin, "The Indivisible Utility," *Survey* 55 (December 1, 1925): 301–6.
10. Collier, *From Every Zenith*, pp. 15–23; and Laura Thompson, "John Collier, A Biographical Sketch," Collier Papers.
11. Interview with Mrs. John Collier, Sr., July 1971, Paterson, New Jersey.
12. Collier, *From Every Zenith*, pp. 23–24; and Thompson, "John Collier, A Biographical Sketch," Collier Papers.
13. John Collier, "Autobiographical Sketch, July 23, 1959, Ranchos de Taos, New Mexico," Collier Papers.
14. *Atlanta Journal*, January 21, 1901, Collier Papers.
15. Collier, *From Every Zenith*, pp. 34–35.
16. Ibid., pp. 27–30.
17. Ibid., pp. 29, 37.
18. John Collier, *The Indwelling Splendor* (Johnsville, Pennsylvania: Stone House Press, 1911), p. 11.

19. John Collier, *From Every Zenith,* pp. 37–38; and John Collier to Laura Thompson, March 2, 1942, Collier Papers.
20. Peter Kropotkin, *Mutual Aid, A Factor in Evolution* (London: William Heinemann, 1907), pp. 2–6, 90–97, 112, 121–22.
21. Collier, *From Every Zenith,* p. 239.
22. John Collier, *On the Gleaming Way* (Denver: Sage Books, 1962), p. 159.
23. Collier, *From Every Zenith,* p. 41.
24. James Hulse, *Revolutionists in London: A Study of Five Unorthodox Socialists* (Oxford: Clarendon Press, 1970), pp. 78–81, 93–94.
25. Collier, *From Every Zenith,* pp. 38–39.
26. John Collier, "The Mystery of Lester F. Ward, August-September, 1916," New York Public Library (hereafter referred to as NYPL), Training School for Community Workers Folder, Records of the People's Institute.
27. Collier, *From Every Zenith,* p. 40; and Sidney Fine, *Laissez Faire and the General Welfare State* (Ann Arbor: University of Michigan Press, 1965), p. 263.
28. John Collier, "The Mystery of Lester F. Ward," NYPL, Training School for Community Workers Folder, Records of the People's Institute.
29. Collier, *From Every Zenith,* pp. 45–48.
30. Ibid., pp. 50–52.
31. Ibid., pp. 59–63.
32. Ibid.
33. Ibid., p. 65.
34. Collier, *Indians of the Americas,* abridged ed., pp. 12–16.
35. John Collier, "Organized Laity and the Social Expert: The Meaning of Public Community Centers," *National Conference on Social Work* (1917), pp. 465–69.
36. Ibid.; and Collier, *Indians of the Americas,* abridged ed., p. 14.
37. John Collier, "People's Institute," *Independent* 72 (May 30, 1912): 1144–48.
38. Charles Sprague Smith, *Working With the People* (New York: A. Wessels Co., 1908), xiii–xiv.
39. Ibid., pp. 11–15.
40. Collier, "The People's Institute," *Independent* 72 (May 30, 1912): 1144–48.
41. Smith, *Working With the People,* pp. 50–58, 62; and John Collier, "People's Institute," *World Today* 41 (February 1909): 175.
42. Collier, "People's Institute," *World Today* 41 (February 1909): 175.
43. John Collier, "Leisure Time, The Last Problem of Conservation," *The Playground* 6 (June 1912): 93–98.
44. Ibid.; John Collier, "City Planning and the Problem of Recreation," *Annals of the American Academy of Political Science* 51 (January 1914): 208–15; and John Collier, "The Place of Recreation in a Religious Program," *Association Seminar* (May 1914), reprint, NYPL, Box of the Publications of the People's Institute, Records of the People's Institute.
45. John Collier, "New York's Problem of the Nickelodeon," *New York Press,* February 23, 1908, NYPL, Scrapbook 8, Records of the People's Institute.
46. Ibid.
47. Isaac Russell, "Two Million Dollars Worth of Films You Will Never See," *New York Mail,* October 2, 1915, NYPL, Scrapbook 11, Records of the People's Institute.
48. John Collier, "Should the Government Censor Motion Pictures," *Playground* 6 (July 1912): 129–32.
49. Collier, *From Every Zenith,* p. 72.
50. Edward J. Ward, ed., *The Social Center* (New York: D. Appleton and Co., 1913), pp. 241–51.
51. Collier, *From Every Zenith,* p. 72; and John Collier, "Moving Pictures, Their Function and Proper Regulation," *Playground* 4 (October 1910): 236–37.

52. The New York City Public Library has a complete file of *The People's Institute Bulletin.*

53. John Collier, editor, *Civic Journal,* October 9, 1909, p. 3.

54. Both the Library of Congress and the New York City Public Library have files of the *Civic Journal.*

55. John Collier, "Francisco Ferrer," *Civic Journal,* October 16, 1909, p. 3.

56. John Collier, "Announcement," *Civic Journal,* December 25, 1909, p. 4.

57. John Collier and Edward Barrows, *The City Where Crime Is Play* (New York: The People's Institute Press, 1914), pp. 11, 25–27.

58. *Seventeenth Annual Report of the People's Institute,* 1914, NYPL, Box of the Publications of the People's Institute, Records of the People's Institute.

59. John Collier and Clinton Childs, "Summary of the Results to Date of the Social Center Experiment at Public School 63," NYPL, Correspondence Folder, Community Center Schools, 64 A, Records of the People's Institute; and Collier, *The City Where Crime Is Play,* pp. 7–9.

60. "The Old Puppet Show is to be Restored to Flavor," *New York Times,* May 4, 1913, NYPL, Scrapbook 4, Records of the People's Institute.

61. John Collier, "Pageant to Bring Together All the Different Races of New York," *New York Press,* March 15, 1914, NYPL, Scrapbook 3, Records of the People's Institute.

62. Ibid.

63. Ibid.

64. "Plan Pageant for Immigrants," *New York Globe,* May 9, 1914; and "Pageant of Nations Reviewed by 15,000," *New York Times,* NYPL, Scrapbook 4, Records of the People's Institute.

65. Mabel Dodge Luhan, *Movers and Shakers* (New York: Harcourt and Brace, 1936), 3: 323.

66. Collier, *From Every Zenith,* pp. 105–6; and Henry F. May, *The End of American Innocence* (Chicago: Quadrangle Books, 1964), pp. 302–21.

67. John Collier to Mabel Dodge, April 26, 1914, John Gallup Collection of American Literature, Yale University Library.

68. Collier, *From Every Zenith,* pp. 82–83, and John Collier to Mabel Dodge, May 21, 1914, John Gallup Collection of American Literature, Yale University Library.

69. Collier, *From Every Zenith,* p. 83; and John Collier to Mabel Dodge, May 23, 1914, John Gallup Collection of American Literature, Yale University Library; and Hulse, *Revolutionists in London,* pp. 19, 96–97.

70. John Collier, *Shadows Which Haunt the Sun Rain* (Johnsville, Pennsylvania: Stone House Press, 1917), pp. 43–45.

71. John Collier to Mabel Dodge, April 26, 1914, John Gallup Collection of American Literature, Yale University Library.

72. Collier, *From Every Zenith,* p. 83; and Thompson, "John Collier, A Biographical Sketch," Collier Papers.

73. John Collier, "The Stage, A New World," *Survey* 36 (June 3, 1916): 259; and Collier, "For a New Drama," *Survey* 36 (May 6, 1916): 137–41.

74. Ibid.

75. Ibid.

76. Collier, *From Every Zenith,* pp. 66–67; and Mrs. John Collier, "The Cooperative Home School," Collier Papers.

77. Isadora Duncan, *Isadora* (New York: Award Books, 1968), pp. 22, 35, 39, 143.

78. Collier, *From Every Zenith,* pp. 106–9.

79. John Collier to Dr. Edward Sanderson, director of the People's Institute, August 8, 1916, NYPL, Training School for Community Workers Folder, 109 B, Records of the People's Institute.

80. Ibid.

81. "The New York Training School for Community Workers, General Announcements of the Opening Session, 1915–1916," NYPL, Box of the Publications of the People's Institute, Records of the People's Institute.

82. John Collier, "New Kind of Job Open to You, If You Have a Pioneer's Gift," *Evening Mail,* August 24, 1915, NYPL, Scrapbook 10, Records of the People's Institute.

83. John Collier, "Community Work as a Career," undated, NYPL, Correspondence Folder, The Community Center, Records of the People's Institute.

84. Collier, *From Every Zenith,* p. 84; and John Collier, "New Kind of Job Open to You," *Evening Mail,* August 24, 1915, NYPL, Scrapbook 10, Records of the People's Institute.

85. John Collier to Dr. Edward Sanderson, February 5, 1917, NYPL, Training School for Community Workers Folder, 109 B, Records of the People's Institute.

86. Ibid.; and "Manuscript on the Training School for Community Workers," NYPL, Training School for Community Workers Folder, 109 B, Records of the People's Institute.

87. Collier, *From Every Zenith,* p. 84; and John Collier to Dr. Edward Sanderson, February 5, 1917, NYPL, Training School for Community Workers Folder, 109 B, Records of the People's Institute.

88. *The Nineteenth Yearbook of the People's Institute,* 1917, NYPL, Box of the Publications of the People's Institute, Records of the People's Institute.

89. John Collier, "Criticisms of the Training School," undated, NYPL, Training School for Community Workers Folder, 109 A, Records of the People's Institute.

90. "Manuscript on the Financial Problems of the Training School," undated, NYPL, Training School for Community Workers Folder, 109 A, Records of the People's Institute.

91. *New York Times,* April 16, 1916, 6, p. 10; and Collier, *From Every Zenith,* p. 83.

92. *New York Times,* April 21, 1916, p. 4.

93. John Collier, *The Community Center,* February 3, 1917, NYPL, Correspondence Folder, Community Center Bulletin, Records of the People's Institute.

94. John Collier, "The Next Great Step in Social Legislation," *The Community Center,* February 24, 1917, NYPL, Correspondence Folder, Community Center Bulletin, Records of the People's Institute.

95. *Nineteenth Yearbook of the People's Institute,* 1917, NYPL, Box of the Publications of the People's Institute, Records of the People's Institute.

96. *New York Times,* September 27, 1917, p. 10, and December 3, 1917, p. 13.

97. "Special Defense Number, Organizing Community National Service in the Public School Buildings," *The Community Center,* June 1917, NYPL, Correspondence Folder, Community Center Bulletin, Records of the People's Institute.

98. John Collier, "School Buildings as Coordinating Places in the Civil Energies of the War," *American City* 16 (June 1917): 588–90.

99. John Collier, "The Crisis of Democracy," *The Community Center,* June 1917, NYPL, Correspondence Folder, Community Center Bulletin, Records of the People's Institute.

100. John Collier, "What Armistice Day Means to Me" (undated), National Archives, Record Group 75 (hereafter referred to as NA, RG), Office File of Commissioner Collier, Chronological File of Letters Sent, 1943–1944, Envelope 3.

101. Collier, *From Every Zenith,* p. 90.

102. Ibid., p. 115.

103. John Collier, "Crowds, Groups and the Great Society, With a Study of the American Community Movement," pp. 49–50, Collier Papers.

104. Collier, *From Every Zenith,* p. 117.

105. John Collier, "Crowds, Groups and the Great Society, With a Study of the American Community Movement," p. 371, Collier Papers; and John Collier, "The Crisis of Democracy," *The Community Center,* June 1917, NYPL, Correspondence Folder, Community Center Bulletin, Records of the People's Institute.

106. Collier, *From Every Zenith,* p. 118.

107. Ibid., p. 126.

108. Ibid., pp. 93–94.

109. John Collier, "The Red Atlantis," *Survey* 49 (October 1922): 15.

110. Edward Nehls, *D. H. Lawrence: A Composite Biography,* 3 vols. (Madison: University of Wisconsin Press, 1958), 2: 197–99, 487.

111. Mary Austin, "How I Found the Thing Worth Waiting For," *Survey* 61 (January 1, 1929): 434–38; and Collier, *From Every Zenith,* p. 155.

112. Diana Trilling, *The Selected Letters of D. H. Lawrence* (New York: Farrar, Strauss and Cudahy, 1958), p. 211.

113. For a discussion of the shortcomings of other settlement workers consult Roy Lubove, *The Professional Altruist: The Emergence of Social Work as a Career, 1880–1930* (New York: Atheneum, 1969); and Otis L. Graham, Jr., *The Great Campaigns: Reform and War in America, 1900–1928* (Englewood Cliffs, N.J.: Prentice-Hall, 1971).

114. Roy Lubove, *The Progressives and the Slums: Tenement House Reform in New York City, 1890–1917* (Pittsburgh: University of Pittsburgh Press, 1962), pp. 72–73.

CHAPTER 2: PROTEST FROM THE PUEBLOS

1. John Collier, *From Every Zenith,* (Denver: Sage Books, 1963), pp. 127–28.

2. U.S., Congress, House, Committee on Indian Affairs, *Hearings, on H.R. 13452 and H.R. 13674, Pueblo Land Titles,* 67th Cong., 4th Sess., 1923, p. 180.

3. Stella Atwood, "The Case for the Indians," *Survey* 49 (October 1, 1922): 7–11; and House, *Hearings, on H.R. 13452 and H.R. 13674,* 67th Cong., 4th Sess., 1923, pp. 74–75.

4. House, *Hearings, on H.R. 13452 and H.R. 13674,* 67th Cong., 4th Sess., 1923, pp. 180–83.

5. Ibid., pp. 184–85.

6. Collier, *From Every Zenith,* pp. 131–32.

7. U.S., Congress, Senate, Subcommittee on Public Lands and Surveys, *Hearings, on S. 3865 and S. 4223, Pueblo Indian Lands,* 67th Cong., 4th Sess., 1923, pp. 2–3, 219.

8. Ibid., pp. 53–58.

9. House, *Hearings, on H.R. 13452 and H.R. 13674,* 67th Cong., 4th Sess., 1923, pp. 17–18.

10. Felix Cohen, *Handbook of Federal Indian Law* (Washington: Government Printing Office, 1942), pp. 389–90; and Anton Long, "Senator Bursum and the Pueblo Lands Act of 1924," (M.A. thesis, University of New Mexico, 1949), p. 7. For a detailed picture of the non-Indian encroachment that threatened the Pueblos at Nambe, San Ildefonso, San Juan, Santa Clara, Tesuque, and Taos grants consult John Collier, "The American Congo," *Survey* 50 (August 1, 1923): 469; and Witter Bynner, "From Him That Hath Not," *Outlook* 133 (January 17, 1923): 126.

11. Senate, *Hearings, on S. 3865 and S. 4223,* 67th Cong., 4th Sess., 1923, pp. 49–50.

12. Indian Rights Association, *Thirty-Ninth Annual Report of the Board of Directors of the Indian Rights Association,* 36 (Philadelphia: Indian Rights Association, 1921), p. 44; and Robert Yard, "New Mexico Aflame Against Two Bills," *Outlook* 133 (January 17, 1923): 124.

13. Senate, *Hearings, on S. 3865 and S. 4223,* 67th Cong., 4th Sess., pp. 173–74.
14. Ibid., pp. 35–52.
15. Ibid., pp. 4–5; and *Congressional Record,* 67th Cong., 4th Sess., December 21, 1922, 64, part 1: 806–9.
16. Senate, *Hearings, on S. 3865 and S. 4223,* 67th Cong., 4th Sess., 1923, pp. 6–7.
17. Ibid., pp. 140–43; and *Congressional Record,* 67th Cong., 2nd Sess., September 11, 1922, 62, Part 12: 12324–25.
18. Ibid.
19. House, *Hearings, on H.R. 13452 and H.R. 13674,* 67th Cong., 4th Sess., 1923, pp. 136–37.
20. *New York Times,* January 7, 1923, 8, p. 6.
21. House, *Hearings, on H.R. 13452 and H.R. 13674,* 67th Cong., 4th Sess., 1923, p. 106; Atwood, "Case for the Indians," *Survey* 49: 15–20.
22. John Collier to Walter Woehlke, January 1, 1923, Collier Papers; Collier, "Plundering the Pueblo Indians," *Sunset* 50 (January 1923): 23; and House, *Hearings, on H.R. 13452 and H.R. 13674,* 67th Cong., 4th Sess., 1923, p. 209.
23. Erna Fergusson, "Crusade from Santa Fe," *North American Review* 242 (December 1936): 379; "Blue Book, Shall the Pueblo Indians of New Mexico be Destroyed," Collier Papers; House, *Hearings, on H.R. 13452 and H.R. 13674,* 67th Cong., 4th Sess., 1923, pp. 105–6; and *Congressional Record,* 67th Cong., 4th Sess., February 3, 1923, 64, Part 3: 2976.
24. Laura Thompson, "A Portrait of John Collier," Collier Papers.
25. For biographical sketches of these poets and writers, consult *Who's Who in America* (Chicago: A. N. Marquis Company, 1966, 1968); Edward Nehls, *D. H. Lawrence: A Composite Biography* 3 vols. (University of Wisconsin Press, 1957–1959), 2: 197–99, 487; and Fergusson, "Crusade from Santa Fe," *North American Review* 242 (December 1936): 377–78.
26. Witter Bynner, "From Him That Hath Not," *Outlook* 133 (January 17, 1923): 125–27; Alice C. Henderson, "Death of the Pueblos," *New Republic* 33 (November 29, 1922): 11–13; Elizabeth S. Sergeant, "Principales Speak," *New Republic* 33 (February 7, 1923): 273–75; "The Last First Americans," *Nation* 116 (November 29, 1922): 570; and House, *Hearings, on H.R. 13452 and H.R. 13674,* 67th Cong., 4th Sess., 1923, pp. 12–13.
27. Fergusson, "Crusade from Santa Fe," *North American Review* 242 (December 1936): 377–78; and "Justice for the Pueblo Indians," *Science* 56 (December 8, 1922): 665. For a summary of the nationwide newspaper protest against the Bursum bill, see "The Pueblo Indians to be Robbed of Their Heritage," *Current Opinion* 74 (February 1923): 213–14; and "Pueblos Plea for Justice," *Literary Digest* 76 (February 17, 1923): 17. *New York Times,* November 26, 1922, 4, p. 6, and December 24, 1922, 4, p. 3; and House, *Hearings, on H.R. 13452 and H.R. 13674,* 67th Cong., 4th Sess., 1923, pp. 241–43.
28. House, *Hearings on H.R. 13452 and H.R. 13674,* 67th Cong., 4th Sess., 1923, p. 234.
29. Senate, *Hearings, on S. 3865 and S. 4223,* 67th Cong., 4th Sess., 1923, pp. 109–10; and *New York Times,* November 19, 1922, 2, p. 6; and January 7, 1923, 8, p. 6.
30. *Congressional Record,* 67th Cong., 4th Sess., December 21, 1922, 64, Part 1: 809–10.
31. House, *Hearings, on H.R. 13452 and H.R. 13674,* 67th Cong., 4th Sess., 1923, p. 185; Collier, *Indians of the Americas,* abridged ed., p. 250; Senate, *Hearings, on S. 3865 and S. 4223,* 67th Cong., 4th Sess., 1923, pp. 120–21, and Collier, *From Every Zenith,* p. 132.
32. John Collier, "The Pueblos' Last Stand," *Sunset* 50 (February 1923): 65–66.
33. Ibid.
34. Senate, *Hearings, on S. 3865 and S. 4223,* 67th Cong., 4th Sess., 1923, pp. 77, 120–21.
35. Ibid.

36. Ibid., pp. 173–74, 254.

37. Ibid., pp. 123, 274–75.

38. *Congressional Record,* 67th Cong., 4th Sess., December 21, 1922, 64, Part 1: 806–9.

39. Senate, *Hearings, on S. 3865 and S. 4223,* 67th Cong., 4th Sess., 1923, p. 254.

40. Ibid., pp. 123, 275–76; *New York Times,* December 27, 1922, p. 29; and Burl Noggle, *Teapot Dome, Oil and Politics in the 1920's* (Baton Rouge: Louisiana State University Press, 1962), p. 51.

41. *New York Times,* January 3, 1923, p. 19.

42. John Collier to Irvine Lenroot, January 18, 1923, Collier Papers.

43. House, *Hearings, on H.R. 13452 and H.R. 13674,* 67th Cong., 4th Sess., 1923, pp. 238–39; and Collier, *From Every Zenith,* p. 132.

44. *New York Times,* January 15, 1923, p. 28; and "Proceedings of the Pueblo Indian Council Held at the Pueblo of Santo Domingo New Mexico, January 17, 1924," p. 20, Collier Papers.

45. House, *Hearings, on H.R. 13452 and H.R. 13674,* 67th Cong., 4th Sess., 1923, pp. 240–41.

46. Senate, *Hearings, on S. 3865 and S. 4223,* 67th Cong., 4th Sess., 1923, pp. 114–19.

47. Ibid., pp. 109–14.

48. Ibid., pp. 132–51.

49. Ibid.

50. Ibid.

51. Ibid., pp. 66, 82–107.

52. John Collier, "No Trespassing," *Sunset* 50 (May 1923): 15.

53. House, *Hearings, on H.R. 13452 and H.R. 13674,* 67th Cong., 4th Sess., 1923, pp. 189–93.

54. Ibid., pp. 183, 253–55, 278–79.

55. *New York Times,* January 25, 1923, p. 9; House, *Hearings, on H.R. 13452 and H.R. 13674,* 67th Cong., 4th Sess., 1923, pp. 407–13; and John Collier to the Economic Club of New York, February 16, 1923, Collier Papers.

56. *New York Times,* January 21, 1923, 7, p. 4; and March 4, 1923, 7, p. 14.

57. Collier, "The Pueblos' Last Stand," *Sunset* 50 (February 1923): 21.

58. *Nashville Tennessean,* January 16, 1923, Collier Papers; and New York *Journal of Commerce and Commercial Bulletin,* January 16, 1923, p. 6.

59. Collier, *From Every Zenith,* p. 133.

60. Herbert Corey, "He Carries the White Man's Burden," *Collier's* 71 (May 12, 1923): 13.

61. House, *Hearings, on H.R. 13452 and H.R. 13674,* 67th Cong., 4th Sess., 1923, pp. 1–2.

62. Ibid., pp. 10–29, 270–71.

63. Ibid., p. 160.

64. Ibid., pp. 87–88, 90–99.

65. Ibid., pp. 75–78.

66. Ibid., pp. 180–84.

67. Ibid., pp. 186–87, 204, 222–25.

68. Ibid.

69. Ibid., pp. 348–51.

70. Ibid., pp. 399–401.

71. Ibid., pp. 399, 407.

72. John Collier, "Pueblos' Land Problem," *Sunset* 51 (November 1923): 15, and *Congressional Record,* 67th Cong., 4th Sess., March 3, 1923, 64, part 6: 5544.

73. *Congressional Record,* 67th Cong., 4th Sess., February 28, 1923, 64, Part 5: 4876–77.
74. "Francis Wilson's Reply to Collier," Santa Fe *New Mexican,* September 1923, Collier Papers; and *Congressional Record,* 67th Cong., 4th Sess., February 28, 1923, 64, Part 5: 4878.
75. John Collier, "To the Senate Investigating Committee, 1932," Collier Papers.
76. Collier, *From Every Zenith,* pp. 135, 153.
77. "Minutes of the First Meeting of the Board of Directors of the American Indian Defense Association, May 18, 1923," Collier Papers; and Collier, *From Every Zenith,* p. 158.
78. "Announcement of the Purposes of the American Indian Defense Association," Collier Papers.
79. Ibid.
80. Ibid.
81. *Congressional Record,* 72d Cong., 1st Sess., March 10, 1932, 75, Part 5: 5677.
82. "Proceedings of the Pueblo Indian Council Held at the Pueblo of Santo Domingo, New Mexico, January 17, 1924," Collier Papers; and John Collier, "Pueblos' Land Problem," *Sunset* 51 (November 1923): 101.
83. Ibid.
84. Mrs. Stella Atwood to Miss E. S. Sergeant, July 21, 1923, Collier Papers; and John Collier, "The American Congo," *Survey* 50 (August 1923): 476.
85. John Collier to the Governors and Councils and Delegates to the All Pueblo Council, September 11, 1923, Collier Papers.
86. John Collier, "Lenroot Bill Sentence of Death for the Pueblos," Santa Fe *New Mexican,* September 22, 1923, Collier Papers.
87. John Collier to the Board of Directors of the American Indian Defense Association, September 19, 1923, Collier Papers.
88. John Collier to Elizabeth S. Sergeant, January 1, 1924, Collier Papers.
89. John Collier to the Board of the American Indian Defense Association, September 19, 1923, Collier Papers.
90. "Proceedings of the Pueblo Indian Council Held at the Pueblo of Santo Domingo, New Mexico, January 17, 1924," Collier Papers.
91. "Department of the Interior Press Release, May 11, 1923," Board of Indian Commissioners, General Correspondence, 1919–1933, NA, RG 75.
92. Indian Rights Association, *Forty-First Annual Report* (Philadelphia: Indian Rights Association, 1923), p. 40.
93. John Collier, "The Red Slaves of Oklahoma," *Sunset* 52 (March 1924): 95.
94. Ibid., 95; and Indian Rights Association, *Forty-First Annual Report,* (Philadelphia: Indian Rights Association, 1923), p. 40.
95. John Collier, "The Red Slaves of Oklahoma," *Sunset* 52 (March 1924): 99–100.
96. Indian Rights Association, *Forty-First Annual Report* (Philadelphia: Indian Rights Association, 1923), pp. 40–46.
97. John Collier, "The Red Slaves of Oklahoma," *Sunset* 52 (March 1924): 97–98.
98. "Board of Indian Commissioners, Minutes of the Annual Meeting, Washington, D.C., January 22–23, 1924," NA, RG 75.
99. Ibid.; and Collier, "The Red Slaves of Oklahoma," *Sunset* 52 (March 1924): 99–100.
100. Elizabeth S. Sergeant, "The Red Man's Burden," *New Republic* 37 (January 16, 1924): 201.
101. Collier, "The Red Slaves of Oklahoma," *Sunset* 52 (March 1924): 100.
102. G. E. E. Lindquist, *The Red Man in the United States, An Intimate Study of the Social, Economic and Religious Life of the American Indian* (New York: George H. Doran Company, 1923), p. xi.
103. Ibid., pp. 125, 156–57, 192, 205, 261, 288, 292, 300–301.

104. Ibid., pp. 392–93.

105. Ibid., p. 36.

106. Ibid., pp. 62, 73.

107. Ibid., p. 68.

108. Elizabeth S. Sergeant, "The Red Man's Burden," *New Republic* 37 (January 16, 1924): 201.

109. "Proceedings of the Pueblo Indian Council Held at the Pueblo of Santo Domingo, New Mexico, January 17, 1924," Collier Papers.

110. *New York Times,* January 31, 1924, p. 13.

111. *New York Times,* February 3, 1924, 2, p. 7; and February 9, 1924, p. 14.

112. "Proceedings of the Pueblo Indian Council Held at the Pueblo of Santo Domingo, New Mexico, January 17, 1924," Collier Papers.

113. John Collier, "The Accursed System," *Sunset* 52 (June 1924): 82–83; and John Collier, "Statement Regarding Misrepresentations, March 8, 1924," Collier Papers.

114. U.S., *Statutes at Large,* Vol. 43, Part 1: 639–42.

115. Ibid.

116. Ibid.

117. Ibid.

118. John Collier, "Statement Regarding Misrepresentations, March 8, 1924," Collier Papers.

119. John Collier to the Board of Directors of the American Indian Defense Association, September 19, 1923, Collier Papers.

CHAPTER 3: INDIAN DANCES DEFENDED

1. Indian Rights Association, *Forty-First Annual Report* (Philadelphia: Indian Rights Association, 1923), pp. 20, 27.

2. Ibid., *Thirty-Ninth Annual Report,* 1921, pp. 8–9.

3. Ibid., pp. 10–11.

4. M. K. Sniffen, ed., *Indian Truth* 1 (April 1924): 3–4.

5. U.S., Congress, House, Committee on Indian Affairs, *Hearings, on H.R. 7826, Reservation Courts of Indian Offenses,* 69th Cong., 1st Sess., 1926, pp. 86–88.

6. "Board of Indian Commissioners, Minutes of the Fall Meeting, Mohonk, New York, October 20–21, 1920," NA, RG 75, Records of the Board of Indian Commissioners.

7. Charles H. Burke to Senator James Wadsworth, Jr., March 15, 1924, Collier Papers.

8. Charles H. Burke, "Indians Making Progress Learning the White Man's Way," *School Life* 9 (June 1924): 241–42.

9. Collier, "Persecuting the Pueblos," *Sunset* 52 (July 1924): 50; and J. P. Kinney, *Facing Indian Facts* (Laurens, New York: The Village Printer, 1973), pp. 32–34.

10. Indian Rights Association, *Forty-First Annual Report* (Philadelphia: Indian Rights Association, 1923), p. 26.

11. Collier, "Persecuting the Pueblos," *Sunset* 52 (July 1924): 50; and Kinney, *Facing Indian Facts,* pp. 35–40.

12. Collier, "Persecuting the Pueblos," *Sunset* 52 (July 1924): 92.

13. Indian Rights Association, *Forty-First Annual Report* (Philadelphia: Indian Rights Association, 1923), pp. 42–43.

14. Hubert Work, "Our American Indians," *Saturday Evening Post* 196 (May 31, 1924): 92.

15. John Collier, "Our Indian Policy," *Sunset* 50 (March 1923): 93.

16. John Collier and Ira Moskowitz, *American Indian Ceremonial Dances* (New York: Bounty Books, 1972), pp. 173–81.

17. U.S., Congress, House, Committee on Indian Affairs, *Hearings, on H.R. 13452 and H.R. 13674, Pueblo Land Titles,* 67th Cong., 4th Sess., 1923, p. 212.

18. Ibid., p. 235.

19. *New York Times,* December 2, 1923, 9, p. 8.

20. *New York Times,* December 16, 1923, 8, p. 6.

21. *Indian Truth* 1 (April 1924): 3; and *New York Times,* November 16, 1924, 9, p. 12.

22. John Collier to Mrs. John D. Sherman, September 16, 1924, Collier Papers.

23. William E. Johnson (pamphlet), 1923, Collier Papers.

24. William E. Johnson, "Those Sacred Indian Ceremonials," *The Native American* 24 (September 20, 1924): 173–77.

25. William E. Johnson (pamphlet), 1923, Collier Papers.

26. *New York Times,* December 20, 1923, p. 6; and October 26, 1924, 8, p. 12.

27. John Collier, *The Indian and His Religious Freedom* (pamphlet), July 2, 1924, Collier Papers.

28. Collier, "Persecuting the Pueblos," *Sunset* 52 (July 1924): 92–93.

29. The Governor and His Council of the Pueblo and the Tribe of Taos to Commissioner Charles H. Burke, May 7, 1924, Collier Papers.

30. *Indian Truth* 1 (May 1924): 1.

31. Ibid. (June 1924): 2.

32. Ibid. (May 1924): 1.

33. Ibid. (October 1924): 3.

34. John Collier to the Members of the Board of Directors, May 22, 1924, Collier Papers.

35. *Indian Truth* 1 (June 1924): 6.

36. John Collier, *From Every Zenith* (Denver: Sage Books, 1963), p. 141.

37. Collier, *The Indian and Religious Freedom* (pamphlet), July 2, 1924, Collier Papers.

38. Ibid.

39. Collier, *From Every Zenith,* p. 141.

40. John Collier to Mrs. John D. Sherman, September 16, 1924, Collier Papers.

41. Collier, *The Indian and Religious Freedom* (pamphlet), July 2, 1924, Collier Papers.

42. Ibid.

43. *New York Times,* November 16, 1924, 9, p. 12.

44. *Indian Truth* 1 (November 1924): 3.

45. John Collier to Bishop (?) Cantwell, November 18, 1924, Collier Papers.

46. Ibid.

47. John Collier, "Do Indians Have Rights of Conscience," *Christian Century* 42 (March 13, 1925): 346–49.

48. "From the Pueblo Indians of New Mexico to the President of the United States, the Congress, and Our Friends the American People, August 31, 1925," Collier Papers.

49. John Collier to the Pueblo Tribal Officials, November 22, 1925, Collier Papers.

50. "From the Pueblo Indians of New Mexico to the President of the United States, the Congress, and Our Friends the American People, August 31, 1925," Collier Papers.

51. John Collier, ed., *American Indian Life,* September-December 1925, pp. 1–4.

52. U.S., Congress, Senate, Committee on Indian Affairs, *Hearings, on S. Res. 341,* 69th Cong., 2nd Sess., 1927, p. 69.

53. House, *Hearings, on H.R. 7826, Reservation Courts of Indian Offenses,* 69th Cong., 1st Sess., 1926, pp. 1–2.

54. Ibid., pp. 18–27.
55. Ibid.
56. Ibid., p. 39.
57. Ibid., pp. 72–77.
58. Ibid., pp. 111–12.
59. Ibid., p. 91.
60. Ibid., pp. 91–93.
61. Ibid., pp. 86–88.
62. Ibid., pp. 94, 96, 100.
63. Ibid., pp. 14, 76.
64. Ibid., pp. 6, 170–71.
65. John Collier to Scott Leavitt and John Harreld, chairmen of the Committees on Indian Affairs, March 11, 1926, Collier Papers.
66. Ibid.
67. *The Great Falls Tribune*, October 9, 1926, Collier Papers.
68. New Mexico *Tribune*, December 11, 1926, Collier Papers.
69. Santa Fe *New Mexican*, November 15, 1926, Collier Papers.
70. John Collier to the All Pueblo Council, 1926, Collier Papers.
71. New Mexico *Tribune*, December 11, 1926, Collier Papers.
72. For an excellent discussion of conservation objectives during the Progressive period consult Samuel P. Hays, *Conservation and the Gospel of Efficiency: The Progressive Conservation Movement, 1890–1920* (Cambridge: Harvard University Press, 1959).

CHAPTER 4: A PROVISIONAL REVOLUTION

1. *Congressional Record,* 69th Cong., 1st Sess., January 11, 1927, 68, Part 2: 1435.
2. Indian Rights Association, *Fortieth Annual Report* (Philadelphia: Indian Rights Association, 1922), pp. 28–29.
3. M. K. Sniffen, ed., *Indian Truth* 1 (February 1924): 2.
4. U.S., Congress, Senate, Subcommittee of the Committee on Indian Affairs, *Hearings, on S. 3159, Development of Oil and Gas Mining Leases on Indian Reservations,* 69th Cong., 1st Sess., 1926, pp. 52–54.
5. *Indian Truth* 1 (February 1924): 2.
6. Indian Rights Association, *Fortieth Annual Report,* (Philadelphia: Indian Rights Association, 1922), pp. 28–32; and *Indian Truth* 1 (June 1924): 4.
7. Senate, *Hearings, on S. 3159,* 69th Cong., 1st Sess., 1926, pp. 52–54; and *Congressional Record,* 69th Cong., 2nd Sess., January 11, 1927, 68, Part 2: 1435.
8. Indian Rights Association, *Forty-First Annual Report,* (Philadelphia: Indian Rights Association, 1923), pp. 22–23.
9. Lawrence C. Kelly, *The Navajo Indians and Federal Indian Policy, 1900–1935* (Tucson: University of Arizona Press, 1968), p. 77.
10. Indian Rights Association, *Forty-Second Annual Report,* (Philadelphia: Indian Rights Association, 1924), pp. 27–28.
11. Ibid.
12. U.S., Congress, Senate Document 53, *Indian Affairs Laws and Treaties,* vol. 4 (Washington: Government Printing Office, 1929), pp. 1056–61.
13. Ibid.
14. *Congressional Record,* 68th Cong., 2nd Sess., December 30, 1924, 66, Part 1: 998–99.
15. Ibid., March 3, 1925, Part 5: 5433.
16. *Congressional Record,* 69th Cong., 2nd Sess., January 11, 1927, 68, Part 2: 1435.

17. Kelly, *The Navajo Indians and Federal Indian Policy*, pp. 78–80.
18. Indian Rights Association, *Forty-Fourth Annual Report*, (Philadelphia: Indian Rights Association, 1926), pp. 16–17.
19. U.S., Congress, House Committee on Indian Affairs, *Hearings, on H.R. 9133, Leasing of Executive Order Reservations*, 69th Cong., 1st Sess., 1926, pp. 23–24.
20. Kelly, *The Navajo Indians and Federal Indian Policy*, p. 80.
21. *New York World*, March 22, 1927, Collier Papers.
22. Ibid.
23. Consult the following American Indian Defense Association bulletins written by Collier: "The Albert B. Fall Title Cancellation Scheme Revived, March 1, 1926"; "The Pima Tragedy and the Oil Leasing Scandal, April 16, 1926"; and "The Renewed Attack Against Indian Ownership of Executive Order Reservations, February 2, 1928," Collier Papers.
24. John Collier, "The Albert B. Fall Indian Title Cancellation Scheme Revived, March 1, 1926," Collier Papers.
25. John Collier to the editor of the *New York World*, March 31, 1926, Collier Papers, and John Collier to the *New York Herald Tribune*, April 17, 1926, Collier Papers. Several other newspapers carried adverse columns concerning the Indian Oil bill. Consult David Lawrence, "Congress Astir Over Indian Rights," *Evening Sun*, April 2, 1926; Jay B. Nash, "Indian Defense Association Denounces Proposed Exploration of Reservations," *Fresno California Republican*, April 9, 1926; and "Indian Oil Land Grab Charged," *Los Angeles Times*, April 11, 1926.
26. Senate, *Hearings, on S. 3159*, 69th Cong., 1st Sess., 1926, pp. 67–76.
27. *Congressional Record*, 68th Cong., 2nd Sess., January 29, 1925, 66, Part 3: 2642–46; and Kelly, *The Navajo Indians and Federal Indian Policy*, p. 77.
28. *Congressional Record*, 69th Cong., 1st Sess., March 23, 1926, 67, Part 6: 6108–18.
29. Ibid., May 26, 1926, 67, Part 9: 10092–96, and Ibid., 2nd Sess., February 2, 1927, 68, Part 3: 2793–94.
30. Stella Atwood to Calvin Coolidge, March 27, 1926, Collier Papers.
31. *New York World*, June 3, 1926, Collier Papers.
32. John Collier, "American Indian Defense Association Legislative Bulletin, June 9, 1926," Collier Papers.
33. *Washington Star*, February 27, 1926, Collier Papers.
34. Judson King, "Scheme Before Congress to Loot Rich Indian Lands" (undated), *Labor*, Collier Papers.
35. *Congressional Record*, 69th Cong., 1st Sess., June 8, 1926, 67, Part 10: 10911–13.
36. *Indian Truth*, 3 (July 1926): 1.
37. Ibid., 4 (March 1927): 1.
38. John Collier, ed., *American Indian Life*, April-June 1926, pp. 1–2.
39. Felix Cohen, *Handbook of Federal Indian Law*, (Washington: Government Printing Office, 1942), pp. 248–49.
40. Collier, *American Indian Life*, October-November 1927, pp. 1–2.
41. *Congressional Record*, 69th Cong., 1st Sess., February 24, 1926, 67, Part 4: 4469–470.
42. Ibid., February 17, 1926, 67, Part 4, 4152.
43. Ibid., February 4, 1926, 67, Part 3: 3326–31.
44. Ibid.
45. Ibid., February 17, 1926, 67, Part 4: 4152.
46. Ibid., February 24, 1926, 67, Part 4, 4469.
47. *Indian Truth*, 3 (October 1926): 3.
48. *Congressional Record*, 69th Cong., 2nd Sess., January 11, 1927, 68, Part 2: 1434.

49. Ibid., 1st Sess., February 26, 1926, 67, Part 5: 4597–98.

50. John Collier, "American Indian Defense Association Legislative Bulletin, June 9, 1926," Collier Papers.

51. *Congressional Record,* 69th Cong., 1st Sess., March 4, 1926, 67, Part 5: 5034–35.

52. Ibid., 5035–50.

53. Ibid., 2nd Sess., January 4, 1927, 68, Part 1: 1067–68.

54. "Indian Affairs Given Hearing" (undated), Collier Papers.

55. *Congressional Record,* 69th Cong., 2nd Sess., January 10, 1927, 68, Part 2: 1401–03.

56. Ibid., January 11, 1927, 68, Part 2: 1437.

57. U.S., Department of the Interior, *Annual Report of the Secretary of the Interior,* (Washington: Government Printing Office, 1927), pp. 12–20.

58. Ibid., 1926, pp. 1–4; and U.S., Department of the Interior, *Annual Report of the Commissioner of Indian Affairs,* (Washington: Government Printing Office, 1924), pp. 2, 20.

59. *Annual Report of the Secretary of the Interior,* 1927, p. 12.

60. *Annual Report of the Secretary of the Interior,* 1927, pp. 13–20.

61. U.S., Congress, Senate Subcommittee on Indian Affairs, *Hearings, on S. Res. 431, A General Survey of the Condition of the Indians in the United States,* 69th Cong., 2nd Sess., 1927, pp. 1–2.

62. Ibid., pp. 6–8.

63. Ibid., p. 43.

64. Ibid., pp. 37–47.

65. Ibid.

66. Ibid., pp. 91–94.

67. Kelly, *The Navajo Indians and Federal Indian Policy,* p. 145.

68. Cato Sells, "Personal Communication from a Private Investigator, April, 1920," NA, RG 75, Fort Worth Federal Records Center, Box 355158; and Angie Debo, *And Still the Waters Run* (Princeton: Princeton University Press, 1940), pp. 338–40.

69. Debo, *And Still the Waters Run,* p. 341.

70. Ibid., p. 346; and *New York Times,* August 10, 1927, p. 25.

71. U.S., Congress, Senate, *Hearings, on S. Res. 79, Condition of the Indians in the United States,* 70th Cong., 1st Sess., 1928, pp. 6–7, 17–19.

72. Ibid., pp. 49–56.

73. *New York Times,* January 8, 1929, p. 28.

74. Kelly, *The Navajo Indians and Federal Indian Policy,* pp. 147–48.

75. *Congressional Record,* 70th Cong., 1st Sess., February 4, 1928, 69, Part 3: 2477–79; and "Power Plant on Flathead Is Opposed" (undated), Louis C. Cramton Papers, University of Michigan, Michigan Historical Collection (hereafter referred to as Cramton Papers).

76. *Congressional Record,* 70th Cong., 1st Sess., February 4, 1928, 69, Part 3: 2480.

77. Collier, *American Indian Life,* August 26, 1927, p. 1; and John Collier, "Manuscript on the Flathead Power Site, 1928," Collier Papers.

78. *Congressional Record,* 71st Cong., 2nd Sess., February 18, 1930, 72, Part 4: 3896.

79. John Collier, "Manuscript on the Flathead Indians, 1927," Collier Papers.

80. John Collier to Lewis Gannett, February 10, 1928, Collier Papers.

81. John Collier, "The Pending Flathead Indian Outrage, February 28, 1927," Cramton Papers.

82. Ibid.; John Collier, "To Members of the Senate and House, December 20, 1927," Cramton Papers; and Collier, *American Indian Life,* August 27, 1927, pp. 1–4.

83. John Collier, "Manuscript on the Flathead Indians, 1927," Collier Papers.

84. John Collier to Calvin Coolidge, February 14, 1927, Collier Papers.

85. John Collier to Calvin Coolidge, July 25, 1927, Collier Papers.

86. Consult the following issues of the *New York Times;* June 22, 1927, p. 1; June 28, 1927, p. 2; and August 18, 1927, p. 1.

87. *New York Times,* August 18, 1927, p. 1. For a discussion of the Indian Citizenship Act see Gary Stein, "The Indian Citizenship Act of 1924," *New Mexico Historical Review,* 67, (July 1972): 257–74.

88. *Congressional Record,* 70th Cong., 1st Sess., February 21, 1928, 69, Part 3: 3329–40; and John Collier, "Manuscript on the Flathead Power Site, 1928," Collier Papers.

89. U.S., Congress, Senate, Committee on Indian Affairs, *Hearings, on S. 700, The Middle Rio Grande Conservancy District,* 70th Cong., 1st Sess., 1928, pp. 4–6.

90. John Collier to Several Newspaper Associations, February 22, 1928, Cramton Papers.

91. *Hearings, on S. 700,* 70th Cong., 1st Sess., 1928, pp. 2–4.

92. Ibid.

93. Ibid., pp. 30–36.

94. Ibid., p. 22.

95. *Congressional Record,* 70th Cong., 1st Sess., February 6, 1928, 69, Part 3: 2571.

96. Ibid., February 15, 1928, 69, Part 3, 3056–58.

97. John Collier, "Recall This Bill and Protect the Pueblo Indians, February 8, 1928," Cramton Papers.

98. Consult the following Defense Association legislative bulletins written by John Collier: "The Acknowledged Facts Which Condemn the Pending Rio Grande Pueblo Conservancy Bill, February 19, 1928," Cramton Papers; "To the Several Newspaper Associations, February 22, 1928," Cramton Papers; and "The Indian Bureau's Conservancy Scheme Is Finally Exposed, December 21, 1928," Collier Papers.

99. *Congressional Record,* 70th Cong., 1st Sess., January 12, 1928, 69, Part 2: 1393.

100. Ibid., March 1, 1928, 69, Part 4: 3836–54.

101. John Collier, "The President's Veto Has Been Asked for the Pueblo Conservancy Bill, March 6, 1928," Collier Papers.

102. Ibid.; and *Albuquerque Journal,* March 23, 1928, and March 25, 1928, Collier Papers.

103. Institute for Government Research, *The Problem of Indian Administration* (Baltimore: The Johns Hopkins Press, 1928).

104. Ibid., pp. 3, 11–13, 25, 29–34.

105. Ibid., p. 41.

106. Ibid., p. 39.

107. Ibid., pp. 41–42.

108. Collier "Now It Can be Told," *American Indian Life* 44 (June 1928): 1–17.

109. James Frear to John Collier, May 6, 1929, Collier Papers.

110. John Collier, "The Proof That the Indian Effort Succeeds, January 4, 1928," Collier Papers.

CHAPTER 5: HERBERT HOOVER'S NEW ERA

1. Haven Emerson, "Our Indian Citizens, Their Crisis, A Letter Addressed to the Presidential Candidates and a Supporting Statement, October 6, 1928," NA, RG 75, Office File of Commissioner Collier, 1933–1945, Envelope 4.

2. Herbert Hoover to the Gentlemen of the American Indian Defense Association, October 20, 1928, Collier Papers.

3. American Indian Defense Association, "For President, Vote for Governor Alfred E. Smith," Collier Papers.

4. M. K. Sniffen, ed., *Indian Truth* 6 (May 1929): 1–3.

5. *New York Times,* March 14, 1929, p. 17; and "Board of Indian Commissioners Bulletin 333, Mr. E. B. Meritt, April 9, 1929," Hugh Scott Papers, File on Indian Affairs, January–May 1929, Box 51, Library of Congress.

6. "Memorandum: The Reorganization of Indian Administration and the Indian Commissionership, January 5, 1929," Hugh Scott Papers, File on Indian Affairs, January–May 1929, Box 51, Library of Congress.

7. *Indian Truth* 6 (May 1929): 1–3.

8. John Collier, ed., *American Indian Life,* May 1929, p. 1.

9. Vera Connolly to John Collier, January 23, 1929, Collier Papers.

10. Vera Connolly's articles included "Cry of a Broken People," *Good Housekeeping* 88 (February 1929): 30–31; "We Still Get Robbed" (March 1929): 34–35; and "End of the Road" (May 1929): 44–45.

11. Institute for Government Research, *The Problem of Indian Administration* (Baltimore, Md.: The Johns Hopkins Press, 1928), pp. 52–55.

12. John Collier, "The Immediate Tasks of the American Indian Defense Association, December 10, 1929," Collier Papers.

13. Collier, *American Indian Life,* July 1930, p. 7.

14. *Congressional Record,* 72nd Cong., 1st Sess., March 10, 1932, 75, Part 5: 5677–78.

15. *Indian Truth* 8 (March 10, 1931): 1.

16. B. T. Quinten, "Oklahoma Tribes, The Great Depression and the Indian Bureau," *Mid America* 49 (January 1967): 29–43.

17. *New York Times,* March 30, 1931, p. 3.

18. The most extensive and perceptive analysis of the new spirit in Indian education is W. Carson Ryan and Rose Brant, "Indian Education Today," *Progressive Education Magazine* 9 (February 1932): 82–182. Lewis Meriam, "Indian Education Moves Ahead," *Survey* 66 (June 1, 1931): 253–57, describes favorably the educational progress made during the Hoover administration. Other valuable accounts of Indian education are located in the issues of *School and Society* from January 19, 1929, to December 17, 1932.

19. *Congressional Record,* 71st Cong., 3rd Sess., March 2, 1931, 74, Part 7: 6801–802.

20. *Indian Truth* 8 (March 10, 1931): 2–3.

21. Edgar Eugene Robinson and Paul Carroll Edwards, eds., *The Memoirs of Ray Lyman Wilbur, 1875–1949* (Stanford, Calif.: Stanford University Press, 1960), pp. 479–80.

22. "New Indian Office Policy Announced," *Washington Star,* March 28, 1929, Hugh Scott Papers, File on Indian Affairs, January–May 1929, Box 51, Library of Congress.

23. Ray Lyman Wilbur, "Uncle Sam Has a New Indian Policy," *Saturday Evening Post* 222 (May–June 1929): 5.

24. John Collier, "Our Indians We Should Know," *California Southland,* October 1927, NA, RG 75, Envelope 4.

25. John Collier to the Guggenheim Foundation, December 1, 1932, Collier Papers.

26. Collier, *From Every Zenith,* pp. 354–55; and John Collier, "Mexico's Indian Service, Methods and Results, 1931," Collier Papers.

27. John Collier, "Mexico: A Challenge," *Progressive Education Magazine* 9 (February 1932): 95–98; and Collier, *American Indian Life,* July 1931, pp. 32–34.

28. John Collier, "A.I.D.A. Legislative Bulletin, Cramton Defies the President and Indian Children are Doomed to Disease and Death from Undernourishment and Privation unless the Senate Saves Them," Collier Papers.

29. For a portrayal of Cramton consult Ruby A. Black, "New Deal for the Red Man," *Nation* 130 (April 2, 1930): 388–90.

30. John Collier, "A.I.D.A. Legislative Bulletin, Cramton Defies the President and Indian Children are Doomed to Disease and Death from Undernourishment and Privation unless the Senate Saves Them," Collier Papers.
31. John Collier to Charles de Y. Elkus, May 1, 1930, Collier Papers.
32. John Collier to Charles de Y. Elkus, May 2, 1930, Collier Papers.
33. John Collier, "A.I.D.A. Legislative Bulletin, Cramton Defies the President and Indian Children are Doomed to Disease and Death from Undernourishment and Privation unless the Senate Saves Them," Collier Papers.
34. Ibid.
35. Ruby A. Black, "New Deal for the Red Man," *Nation* 130 (April 2, 1930): 388–90; Louis C. Cramton to Mrs. Joseph L. Smith, March 19, 1930, Cramton Papers; and *Indian Truth* 8 (March 1931): 1–2.
36. John Collier, "A.I.D.A. Legislative Bulletin, Authority to Flog Indian Boarding School Children is Re-established by Commissioner Rhoads, April 21, 1931." Collier Papers.
37. John Collier, "Senators and Indians," *Survey Graphic* 61 (January 1, 1929): 425–26.
38. Ibid.
39. John Collier, "A.I.D.A. Legislative Bulletin, Authority to Flog Indian Boarding School Children is Re-established by Commissioner Rhoads, April 21, 1931." Collier Papers.
40. Ibid.
41. Ibid.
42. *New York Times,* May 23, 1930, p. 16, and May 24, 1930, p. 19.
43. Ray Lyman Wilbur to Haven Emerson, May 7, 1930, Hugh Scott Papers, File on Indian Affairs, January–June 1930, Box 51, Library of Congress.
44. *New York Times,* May 23, 1930, p. 16.
45. John Collier, "Monopoly in Montana," *The New Freeman,* May 3, 1930, Collier Papers.
46. Ibid.
47. John Collier, "A.I.D.A. Legislative Bulletin, The Flathead Power Site Decision at the Verge of Irreparable Injury to the Public and the Indians, April 4, 1930," Collier Papers; and John Collier, "The Flathead Water Power Lease," *New Republic* 64 (August 20, 1930): 20–21.
48. "Department of the Interior Press Release, May 19, 1930," Cramton Papers.
49. *Congressional Record,* 72nd Cong., 1st Sess., March 10, 1932, 75, Part 5: 5679.
50. John Collier to Haven Emerson, February 4, 1930, Collier Papers.
51. John Collier to Secretary Wilbur, May 27, 1930, Collier Papers.
52. Mary Austin to the editor of the *Saturday Review,* August 15, 1931, Collier Papers.
53. Mary Austin to John Collier, April 27, 1930, and April 18, 1930, Collier Papers.
54. John Collier to Mary Austin, April 18, 1930, Collier Papers.
55. Mary Austin to John Collier, April 27, 1930, Collier Papers.
56. *New York Times,* December 15, 1929, p. 5.
57. *Washington Post,* December 8, 1929, Collier Papers.
58. John Collier to Charles de Y. Elkus, January 9, 1931, Collier Papers.
59. Lawrence Kelly, *The Navajo Indian and Federal Indian Policy, 1900–1935* (Tucson: University of Arizona Press, 1968), p. 62.
60. Erna Fergusson, "Senators Investigate Indians," *American Mercury* 23 (August 1931): 464–68.
61. John Collier to Charles Fahy, February 6, 1931, Collier Papers.
62. Letter to Fremont Older, San Francisco *Call-Bulletin,* February 6, 1932, Collier Papers; and "Improper Guardianship," *Nation* 134 (February 3, 1932): 132.

63. John Collier, "Manuscript on Hagerman," Collier Papers.

64. John Collier, "A.I.D.A. Legislative Bulletin, The New Course of Action by the Pueblos With Respect to Their Lands Adversely Held by White Settlers," Collier Papers.

65. Ibid.; and "Minutes of the All Pueblo Council Meeting Held at Santo Domingo Pueblo, May 5, 1931," Collier Papers.

66. John Collier to John Haynes, December 18, 1930, Collier Papers.

67. U.S., Congress, Senate, Subcommittee of the Committee on Indian Affairs, *Hearings, on S. Res. 79, Survey of Conditions of The Indians In the U.S.*, 71st Cong., 3rd Sess., 1931, pp. 4371–73.

68. John Collier, "Manuscript on Hagerman," Collier Papers.

69. John Collier, "A.I.D.A. Legislative Bulletin, January 30, 1932," Collier Papers.

70. *Albuquerque Journal,* December 12, 1931, and January 30, 1932, Collier Papers.

71. "Meeting of the Council of All the New Mexico Pueblos at Santo Domingo, August 20, 1932," Collier Papers.

72. *New Mexico Tribune,* January 26, 1932, Collier Papers.

73. *Congressional Record,* 72nd Cong., 1st Sess., March 10, 1932, 75, Part 5: 5670.

74. Kelly, *The Navajo Indians and Federal Indian Policy,* pp. 16–36, 115–28.

75. Ibid.

76. Ibid.

77. John Collier, "The Case Behind Herbert Hagerman, as Established to Date, February 5, 1931," Collier Papers.

78. John Collier, "The Indian Bureau Charged with Deception or with Being the Victim of Deception in the Matter of Navajo Land Adjustments, February 6, 1931," Collier Papers.

79. Albert B. Fall to Governor Herbert Hagerman, January 2, 1923, Western Union Telegram, NA, RG 316, Private Papers of Herbert Hagerman (hereafter referred to as Hagerman Papers), File on the Correspondence with Albert Fall, 1923.

80. Herbert Hagerman to the Gentlemen of the Indian Rights Association, March 28, 1934, NA, RG 316, Hagerman Papers, File on the Wheeler-Howard bill, Series I, Item 49.

81. John Collier, "Highlights of the Case for Removing Hagerman from the Government Payroll, February 29, 1932," Collier Papers.

82. F. S. Donnell to the editor of *Collier's,* February 28, 1934, NA, RG 316, Hagerman Papers, File on the Wheeler-Howard bill, Series I, Item 49.

83. Ibid.; and Kelly, *The Navajo Indians and Federal Indian Policy,* p. 69.

84. John Collier, "The Case Against Herbert Hagerman, as Established to Date, February 5, 1931," Collier Papers; and Albuquerque *New Mexico Herald,* October 15, 1923, Collier Papers.

85. John Collier, "Highlights of the Case for Removing Hagerman from the Government Payroll, February 29, 1932," Collier Papers; and *Congressional Record,* 72nd Cong., 1st Sess., March 9, 1932, 75, Part 5: 5547–49.

86. John Collier, "The Fate of the Navajos," *Sunset Magazine* 52 (January 1924): 62.

87. Ibid.

88. John Collier to Charles Fahy, February 6, 1931, Collier Papers.

89. John Collier to Lewis Meriam, January 23, 1931, Collier Papers; and Senate, *Hearings, on S. Res. 79,* 71st Cong., 3rd Sess., 1931, p. 4366.

90. John Collier, "Rebuttal Testimony on the Navajo Oil Leasing Record of Herbert Hagerman," Collier Papers.

91. Ibid.; and John Collier to Lynn Frazier, September 9, 1931, Collier Papers.

92. Kenneth B. Nowells to H. H. Hill, U.S. Bureau of Mines, September 28, 1923, NA, RG 316, Hagerman Papers, Miscellaneous Correspondence of Hagerman's Removal, Series I, Item 10.

93. Kenneth B. Nowells, "Report on Development Accomplished in the Hogback Field by the Midwest Refining Company with Miscellaneous Notes on Structures to be Leased by the Navajos, October 13, 1923," NA, RG 316, Hagerman Papers, Miscellaneous Correspondence of Hagerman's Removal, Series I, Item 10.

94. John Collier, "Rebuttal Testimony on the Navajo Oil Leasing Record of Herbert Hagerman," Collier Papers.

95. Herbert Hagerman to W. F. Cantelou, March 11, 1931, NA, RG 316, Hagerman Papers, File on the Collier-Frazier Inquisition, Part 1, 1931.

96. Herbert Hagerman to Evan W. Estep, March 12, 1931, Hagerman Papers, File on the Collier-Frazier Inquisition, Part 1, 1931.

97. Kenneth B. Nowells, "To Whom It May Concern," Hagerman Papers, File on the Collier-Frazier Inquisition, Part 1, 1931.

98. Oliver La Farge, "A Gross Injustice," *New York Times,* January 28, 1931, p. 20.

99. Ibid.

100. *New York Times,* February 15, 1931, p. 20; and *Congressional Record,* 72nd Cong., 1st Sess., March 16, 1932, 75, Part 6: 6224.

101. Erna Fergusson, "Crusade From Santa Fe," *North American Review* 242 (December 1936): 385–86.

102. Ibid.

103. Witter Bynner to the editor of the *Nation,* February 24, 1931, NA, RG 316, Hagerman Papers, File on the Collier-Frazier Inquisition, Part I, 1931.

104. Joe Sena, "Collier and the Indians," *La Revista de Taos,* NA, RG 316, Hagerman Papers, File on the Collier-Frazier Inquisition, Part 1, 1931.

105. "Elimination of Hagerman a Blunder by Congress," Santa Fe *New Mexican,* July 7, 1932, Collier Papers.

106. John Collier to Haven Emerson, February 4, 1931, Collier Papers.

107. *Congressional Record,* 72nd Cong., 1st Sess., March 19, 1932, 75, Part 5: 5547–49. For a detailed account of Collier's dissatisfaction with the Hoover administration consult John Collier, "The Indian Bureau's Record," *Nation* 135 (October 5, 1932): 303–305.

108. *Congressional Record,* 72nd Cong., 1st Sess., March 10, 1932, 75, Part 5: 5677.

109. John Collier, *From Every Zenith* (Denver: Sage Books, 1963), p. 148.

CHAPTER 6: THE INDIAN NEW DEAL BEGINS

1. John Collier, ed., *American Indian Life,* January 1933, pp. 1–5.

2. Ibid.

3. John Collier to Judge Richard Hanna, December 26, 1932, Collier Papers; John Collier to the Governor and the Pueblos of Santo Domingo, December 31, 1932, Collier Papers; and *New York Times,* April 15, 1933, p. 3.

4. "Minutes of the Annual Meeting of the Board of Indian Commissioners, January 11–12, 1933, Washington, D.C.," NA, RG 75, Records of the Board of Indian Commissioners.

5. John Collier to Charles de Y. Elkus, January 4, 1933, Collier Papers.

6. John Collier, "An Open Letter Sent to a Number of Limited Friends, January 1, 1933," Collier Papers.

7. John Collier to the Governor and the Pueblos of Santo Domingo, December 31, 1932, Collier Papers.

8. Ibid.

9. Collier, *American Indian Life,* January 1933, pp. 1–5.

10. U.S., Congress, Senate, Committee on Indian Affairs, *Hearings, Condition of the Indians in the United States,* 72nd Cong., 2nd Sess., 1933, p. 25.

11. Haven Emerson, "A Statement in Support of the Resolution of the Board of Directors of the American Indian Defense Association Endorsing John Collier for Appointment as Commissioner of Indian Affairs, February 24, 1933," NA, RG 75, Office File of Commissioner John Collier, Chronological File of Letters Sent, Envelope 3.

12. John Collier to Dr. John Haynes, January 30, 1933, Collier Papers.

13. John Collier to Charles de Y. Elkus, January 31, 1933, Collier Papers.

14. Berton Staples to Henry A. Wallace, June 15, 1934, NA, RG 16, Records of the Office of the Secretary of Agriculture.

15. Harold L. Ickes, "The Federal Senate and Indian Affairs," *Illinois Law Review* 24 (January 1930), 577.

16. Ibid.

17. *Washington Post,* September 1, 1935, Collier Papers.

18. *Congressional Record,* 73rd Cong., 1st Sess., April 21, 1933, 77, Part 2: 2102–3.

19. Ibid.

20. Harold L. Ickes, *The Secret Diary of Harold Ickes: The First Hundred Days, 1933–1936* (New York: Simon and Schuster, 1953), p. 19; and John Collier, *From Every Zenith* (Denver: Sage Books, 1963), p. 171.

21. *New York Times,* April 16, 1933, p. 10; and *Indian Truth* 10 (June 1933): 1.

22. John Collier to Dr. John Haynes, April 10, 1933, Collier Papers.

23. "People in the Limelight," *New Republic* 112 (March 5, 1945): 319.

24. *Congressional Record,* 73rd Cong., 1st Sess., April 21, 1933, 77, Part 2: 2103.

25. M. Corey, "Lo, the Poor Indian Bureau," *Nation's Business* 33 (February 1945): 31; and "People in the Limelight," *New Republic* 112 (March 5, 1945): 319.

26. "People in the Limelight," *New Republic* 112 (March 5, 1945): 319.

27. M. K. Sniffen, ed., *Indian Truth* 10 (May 1933): 2–3.

28. Ibid.

29. John Collier, "Talk to the Returned Students of the Navajos at Fort Wingate, New Mexico, July 7, 1933," NA, RG 316, Hagerman Papers, File on the Wheeler-Howard bill, Series 1, Item 49.

30. U.S., Department of the Interior, *Annual Report of the Secretary of the Interior: Report of the Commissioner of Indian Affairs* (Washington: Government Printing Office, 1933), p. 101; and U.S., *Statutes at Large,* Vol. 68, Part 1: 108–11.

31. *New York Times,* May 26, 1933, p. 2; and "Executive Order, Abolition of the Board of Indian Commissioners, May 25, 1933," NA, RG 75, Records of the Board of Indian Commissioners.

32. Warren K. Moorhead to Samuel A. Eliot, June 2, 1933, NA, RG 75, Records of the Board of Indian Commissioners, General Correspondence, 1919–1933.

33. Harold L. Ickes, "Memorandum for Commissioner Collier, July 29, 1933," Collier Papers.

34. Felix Cohen, *Handbook of Federal Indian Law* (1942; reprint ed., Albuquerque: University of New Mexico Press, 1972), pp. vii–xxix.

35. Donald Lee Parman, "The Indian Civilian Conservation Corps," (Ph.D. diss., University of Oklahoma, 1967), pp. 28–29.

36. Calvin Gower, "The CCC Indian Division," *Minnesota History* 43 (Spring 1972): 4–6.

37. J. P. Kinney, "I.E.C.W. on Indian Reservations," *Journal of Forestry* 31 (December 1933): 911–13; "CCC Activities for Indians," *Monthly Labor Review* 49 (July 1939): 94–95; and "Indians in CCC Camps," *Missionary Review of the World* 56 (December 1933): 61. For an average day at camp consult L. C. Schroeder, "Indian Conservation Camps," *Recreation* 28 (August 1934): 249–52.

38. *Congressional Record,* 75th Cong., 1st Sess., June 28, 1937, 81, Part 6: 6381–83.

39. John Collier to Henry A. Wallace, January 6, 1934, NA, RG 16, Records of the Office of the Secretary of Agriculture; and Henry Wallace to John Collier, September 26, 1933, NA, RG 16, Records of the Secretary of Agriculture.

40. John Collier to C. E. Faris, May 14, 1934, Collier Papers.

41. Rexford Tugwell to John Collier, September 29, 1933, NA, RG 16, Records of the Secretary of Agriculture.

42. *New York Times,* November 11, 1934, 4, p. 6; and December 15, 1936, p. 27.

43. Harold L. Ickes to Rexford Tugwell, June 22, 1934, Collier Papers; and *Indians at Work,* October 15, 1935, pp. 1–6.

44. *Indians at Work,* November 15, 1934, p. 35.

45. *New York Times,* November 28, 1933, p. 2; and U.S. Treasury Department, *Combined Statement of Receipts and Expenditures,* 1934, p. 110.

46. U.S., Department of the Interior, *Annual Report of the Secretary of the Interior* (Washington: Government Printing Office, 1935), pp. 124–25.

47. *Indians at Work,* December 15, 1933, pp. 3–4; and February 15, 1934, pp. 1–6.

48. *New York Times,* January 21, 1934, 4, p. 6.

49. Ibid., September 23, 1934, 12, p. 9; and *Indians at Work,* June 15, 1935, p. 8.

50. *New York Times,* August 17, 1941, 10, p. 8.

51. *Indians at Work,* February 15, 1934, pp. 31–32; and Alden Stevens, "Whither the American Indian," *Survey Graphic* 29 (March 1940): 170–71.

52. "Department of the Interior Press Release, August 22, 1933," Collier Papers; and "Window Rock Site for the Navajo Capitol," NA, RG 316, Series 1, Item 49, File on the Wheeler-Howard bill.

53. *Indians at Work,* November 15, 1934, pp. 37–38; and December 15, 1933, pp. 7–8.

54. *New York Times,* July 15, 1934, 4, p. 2.

55. William E. Leuchtenburg, *Franklin Roosevelt and the New Deal* (New York: Harper and Row, 1963), pp. 125, 130.

56. John Collier to Henry A. Wallace, September 18, 1935, NA, RG 16, Office File of the Secretary of Agriculture.

57. Aubrey Williams to President Franklin D. Roosevelt, November 4, 1936, NA, RG 51, Box I-7, Bureau of the Budget Records.

58. *New York Times,* April 24, 1938, 2, p. 4; and *Annual Report of the Secretary of the Interior,* 1939, pp. 62–64.

59. *Indians at Work,* August 15, 1936, p. 5; and *New York Times,* July 18, 1936, p. 1; and August 5, 1936, p. 1.

60. *New York Times,* February 27, 1936, p. 1; and *Annual Report of the Secretary of the Interior,* 1937, p. 205.

61. *New York Times,* September 25, 1935, p. 5; and Aubrey Williams to Franklin D. Roosevelt, November 4, 1936, Franklin D. Roosevelt Library (hereafter referred to as FDRL), File No. 6–C.

62. *Annual Report of the Secretary of the Interior,* 1936, pp. 184–85; Ibid., 1937, pp. 220–21; Ibid., 1938, p. 20; and Ibid., 1939, p. 33.

63. *Indians at Work* June 15, 1935, p. 2; and Harold L. Ickes to Franklin D. Roosevelt, December 19, 1935, FDRL, File No. 6–C.

64. Harold L. Ickes to Franklin D. Roosevelt, December 19, 1935, FDRL, File No. 6–C.

65. U.S., Congress, House, Committee on Indian Affairs, *Hearings, on H.R. 6234, General Welfare of the Indians of Oklahoma,* 74th Cong., 1st Sess., 1935, p. 21.

66. U.S., Congress, House, Committee on Indian Affairs, *Hearings, on H.R. 7781, Indian Conditions and Affairs,* 74th Cong., 1st Sess., 1935, pp. 142–43.

67. John Collier to Thomas Dodge, February 4, 1935, NA, RG 75, File on J. C. Morgan; and "Indians Get Small Part of Conservation Cash in the Southwest," NA, RG 316, Series 1, Item 49, File on the Wheeler-Howard bill.

68. William Endersbee, "Soil Conservation on Indian Lands," *Indians at Work,* September-October 1944, p. 13.
69. Ibid., May-June 1945, pp. 18–20.
70. *Annual Report of the Secretary of the Interior,* 1933, pp. 108–9.
71. Ibid., pp. 99–100
72. Ibid., pp. 108–9.
73. Ibid., p. 103.
74. John Collier to Chester Hanson, October 14, 1936, Collier Papers.
75. *Annual Report of the Secretary of the Interior,* 1933, pp. 72–79.
76. Collier, *American Indian Life,* April 1934, p. 14; and Willard Beatty, "Uncle Sam Develops a New Kind of Rural School," *Elementary School Journal* 41 (November 1940): 185–94.
77. *Annual Report of the Secretary of the Interior,* 1935, p. 129.
78. Ibid., 1934, p. 87; and Vera Connolly, "End of a Long, Long Trail," *Good Housekeeping* 98 (April 1934): 256.
79. Flora Warren Seymour, "Thunder over the Southwest," *Saturday Evening Post* 211 (April 1, 1939): 71.
80. Collier, *From Every Zenith,* p. 195; "Indianizing the Red Man; Tribal Ways of Life Stressed in Reservation Schools," *Newsweek* 17 (April 14, 1941): 77; and John Collier to Senator William King, August 18, 1937, NA, RG 75, Suitland, Maryland.
81. Willard Beatty, "Uncle Sam Develops a New Kind of Rural School," *Elementary School Journal* 41 (November 1940): 185–94.
82. The best accounts of Indian education during the New Deal are Evelyn Adams, *American Indian Education* (Morningside Heights, New York: King Crown Press, 1946); Willard Beatty, *Selected Articles from Indian Education, 1936–43* (Oklahoma: Chilocco Agricultural School Printing Press, 1944); and Margaret Szasz, *Education and the American Indian, The Road to Self-Determination, 1928–1933* (Albuquerque: University of New Mexico Press, 1974).
83. Adams, *American Indian Education,* pp. 91–92.
84. Willard Beatty, "Uncle Sam Develops a New Kind of Rural School," *Elementary School Journal* 41 (November 1940): 192–93; and Collier, *From Every Zenith,* p. 196.
85. Collier, *From Every Zenith,* p. 196.
86. Alden Stevens, "Whither the American Indian?" *Survey Graphic* 29 (March 1940): 171–73; and George Boyce, *When Navajos Had Too Many Sheep: The 1940's* (San Francisco: Indian Historian Press, 1974), pp. 110–11.
87. Boyce, *When The Navajos Had Too Many Sheep,* pp. 94–97, 117.
88. Joseph Cash and Herbert T. Hoover, *To be an Indian: An Oral History* (New York: Holt, Rinehart and Winston, 1971), p. 126.
89. Collier, *American Indian Life,* April 1934, p. 15; and *Annual Report of the Secretary of the Interior,* 1934, pp. 93–94.
90. *Annual Report of the Secretary of the Interior,* 1936, p. 174.
91. Ibid., p. 94; and Adams, *American Indian Education,* pp. 85–88.
92. *New York Times,* October 15, 1933, 2, p. 2; and John Collier to Harold L. Ickes, August 4, 1933, NA, RG 48, Office File of Harold L. Ickes, Part 1, 1933–1935, Miscellaneous Correspondence Relating to the Indian Office.
93. "Minutes of the Annual Meeting of the Board of Indian Commissioners, January 11–12, 1933, Washington, D.C.," NA, RG 75, Records of the Board of Indian Commissioners.
94. Flora Warren Seymour to Dr. Samuel Eliot, July 4, 1933, NA, RG 75, Records of the Board of Indian Commissioners.
95. John Collier to Harold L. Ickes, August 4, 1933, NA, RG 48, Office File of Harold L. Ickes, Part 1, 1933–1935, Miscellaneous Correspondence Relating to the Indian Office.

96. *New York Times,* October 15, 1933, 2, p. 2.

97. John Collier to Harold L. Ickes, August 4, 1933, NA, RG 48, Office File of Harold L. Ickes, Part 1, 1933–1935, Miscellaneous Correspondence Relating to the Indian Office.

98. *New York Times,* October 17, 1933, p. 24.

99. John Collier to Dr. Harry Hummer, October 5, 1933, Collier Papers.

100. *New York Times,* November 12, 1933, 4, p. 7.

101. Ibid.; and Collier, *American Indian Life* April 1934, p. 15.

102. John Collier, "Regulations for Religious Worship and Instruction, January 30, 1934," NA, RG 75, File on Religious Freedom.

103. Ibid.

104. "Parents of Pine Ridge Indian Children Protest Collier Plan to Discontinue Mission Schools," *Rapid City Daily Journal,* April 23, 1934, NA, RG 75, Part 9, Records Concerning the Wheeler-Howard Act.

105. E. C. Routh to John Collier, November 21, 1934, NA, RG 75, File on Religious Freedom.

106. John Collier, "Interview Given to the Associated Press Representative, November 2, 1934," NA, RG 75, File on Adverse Propaganda.

107. John Collier to Ben Dwight, February 19, 1936, NA, RG 75, File on Religious Freedom.

108. John Collier, "Talk to the Students of Bacone College, March 22, 1934," NA, RG 16, Records of the Office of the Secretary of Agriculture.

109. John Collier to Burton K. Wheeler, January 31, 1934, Collier Papers.

110. John Collier to Hiram Johnson, January 31, 1934, Collier Papers.

111. *Congressional Record,* 73rd Cong., 2nd Sess., April 5, 1933, 78, Part 6: 6148.

112. Szasz, *Education and the American Indian: The Road to Self-Determination,* pp. 89–105.

113. Lawrence Kelly, *The Navajo Indians and Federal Indian Policy, 1900–1935* (Tucson: University of Arizona Press, 1968), pp. 128–29.

114. *American Indian Life,* April 1934, pp. 14–15.

115. Connolly, "End of a Long, Long Trail," *Good Housekeeping* 98 (April 1934): 249.

CHAPTER 7: THE FAILURE TO CREATE A RED ATLANTIS

1. Vera Connolly, "End of a Long, Long Trail," *Good Housekeeping* 98 (April 1934): 249–50.

2. M. K. Sniffen, ed., "Washington Conference," *Indian Truth* 11 (February 1934): 3–4.

3. John Collier to Professor Forrest Clements, November 20, 1933, NA, RG 75, Part 10–A, Records Concerning the Wheeler-Howard Act.

4. Ralph Linton to John Collier (undated), NA, RG 75, Part 10–A, Records Concerning the Wheeler-Howard Act.

5. Oliver La Farge to John Collier, December 5, 1933, NA, RG 75, Part 10–A, Records Concerning the Wheeler-Howard Act.

6. Ibid.

7. John Collier to Superintendents, Tribal Councils and Individual Indians, "Indian Self-Government," January 20, 1934, NA, RG 75, Kiowa Indian Agency, Box 361697, Federal Records Center, Fort Worth, Texas.

8. Ibid.

9. Ibid.

10. W. O. Roberts to John Collier, January 31, 1934, NA, RG 75, Records Concerning the Wheeler-Howard Act.

11. O. H. Lipps to John Collier, January 25, 1934, NA, RG 75, Records Concerning the Wheeler-Howard Act.

12. P. W. Danielson to John Collier, February 15, 1934, NA, RG 75, Records Concerning the Wheeler-Howard Act.

13. Carpio Martinez to John Collier, February 10, 1934, NA, RG 75, Records Concerning the Wheeler-Howard Act.

14. "Resolution of the Eastern Band of Cherokees in North Carolina to John Collier, February 14, 1934," NA, RG 75, Records Concerning the Wheeler-Howard Act.

15. Ibid.

16. Henry Lee Tyler to the Honorable Commissioner of Indian Affairs, February 20, 1934, NA, RG 75, Records Concerning the Wheeler-Howard Act.

17. Ray Clamore, chairman of the Cheyenne-Arapaho Tribal Council, to John Collier, February 15, 1934, NA, RG 75, Records Concerning the Wheeler-Howard Act.

18. John Buckman, president of the Ft. Belknap Tribal Council, to John Collier, February 7, 1934, NA, RG 75, Records Concerning the Wheeler-Howard Act.

19. See the following letters: Forrest Stone, superintendent of the Blackfeet Agency, to John Collier, February 8, 1934; John Snake and other Shawnees to John Collier, February 10, 1934; Edwin Cloud, Ute chief, to John Collier, February 12, 1934; and Barney Rickard, secretary of the Colville Indian Association, to John Collier, February 27, 1934, NA, RG 75, Records Concerning the Wheeler-Howard Act.

20. John Collier, *Indians at Work,* September 15, 1933, pp. 1–5.

21. John Collier, "The Purposes and Operations of the Wheeler-Howard Indian Rights Bill, February 19, 1934," Library of Congress, Bronson Cutting Papers, Box 30.

22. John Collier, *American Indian Life,* July 1931, pp. 32–38.

23. Bartolomé de Las Casas, *History of the Indies,* ed. Andree M. Collard, (New York: Harper and Row, 1971), pp. ix–xiv.

24. John Collier, *Indians of the Americas,* abridged ed., (New York: New American Library, 1947), pp. 67–78.

25. "H.R. 7902, A Bill to grant Indians living under Federal tutelage, the freedom to organize for purposes of local self-government and economic enterprise, to provide for the necessary training of Indians in administrative and economic affairs; to conserve and develop Indian lands; and to promote more effective justice in matters affecting Indian tribes and communities by establishing a Federal Court of Indian Affairs, February 12, 1934," NA, RG 75, Records Concerning the Wheeler-Howard Act.

26. John Collier, "The Purposes and Operation of the Wheeler-Howard Indian Rights bill, February 19, 1934," Library of Congress, Bronson Cutting Papers, Box 30.

27. H.R. 7902, February 12, 1934, NA, RG 75, Records Concerning the Wheeler-Howard Act.

28. Collier, *Indians of the Americas,* abridged ed., pp. 89–98; and Connolly, "End of a Long, Long Trail," *Good Housekeeping* 98 (April 1934): 251–52.

29. H.R. 7902, February 12, 1934, NA, RG 75, Records Concerning the Wheeler-Howard Act.

30. Ibid.

31. Ibid.

32. Ibid.

33. U.S., Congress, House, Committee on Indian Affairs, *Hearings, on H.R. 7902, Readjustment of Indian Affairs,* 73rd Cong., 2nd Sess., 1934, pp. 315–17.

34. John Collier, "The Purpose and Operation of the Wheeler-Howard Indian Rights Bill, February 19, 1934," Library of Congress, Bronson Cutting Papers, Box 30.

35. House, *Hearings, on H.R. 7902,* 73rd Cong., 2nd Sess., 1934, pp. 33–36, 64.

36. Ibid., pp. 64–65.

37. U.S., Congress, Senate, Committee on Indian Affairs, *Hearings, on S. 2755, To Grant Indians the Freedom to Organize,* 73rd Cong., 2nd Sess., 1934, pp. 33–49.

38. Ibid.

39. Ibid.

40. Ibid., p. 35.

41. Ibid.

42. John Collier, "For The Press, Meeting at the Secretary's Office, February 16, 1934," NA, RG 75, Records Concerning the Wheeler-Howard Act, Envelope 3.

43. Ibid.

44. "Collier Goes Slowly on His Indian Plan, March 3, 1934," NA, RG 75, Records Concerning the Wheeler-Howard Act, Part 9; "200 Indians Gather for Big Parley," NA, RG 75, Records Concerning the Wheeler-Howard Act; and "Minutes of the Indian Congress, Rapid City, South Dakota, March 2, 1934," p. 3, NA, RG 75, Records Concerning the Wheeler-Howard Act.

45. "Minutes of the Indian Congress, Rapid City, South Dakota, March 2, 1934," p. 4, NA, RG 75, Records Concerning the Wheeler-Howard Act.

46. Ibid., pp. 5–14, 23.

47. Ibid., pp. 15–18.

48. Ibid., pp. 47–54, and March 3, 1934, pp. 22–25, 40–41.

49. Ibid., March 3, 1934, pp. 29–30.

50. John Collier, "Memorandum for Secretary Ickes, April 18, 1934," NA, RG 75. Records Concerning the Wheeler-Howard Act.

51. John Collier to the editor of the *Catholic Daily Tribune,* April 18, 1934, NA, RG 75, Records Concerning the Wheeler-Howard Act, Part 6–BB; and John Collier, "Memorandum for Secretary Ickes, April 18, 1934," Collier Papers.

52. "Minutes of the Indian Congress, Rapid City, South Dakota, Special Evening Session, March 3, 1934," pp. 1–7, NA, RG 75, Records Concerning the Wheeler-Howard Act.

53. Ibid., pp. 20–23.

54. Ibid., March 4, 1934, pp. 12–13, 18–19, 27–28.

55. Ibid., pp. 4–7, 29, 31; and "Afternoon Session," March 5, 1934, pp. 1–2.

56. "Proceedings of the Conference at Chemawa, Oregon, March 8, 1934," pp. 10–14, 28–29, NA, RG 75, Records Concerning the Wheeler-Howard Act.

57. "Proceedings of the Conference at Chemawa, Oregon, March 9, 1934," pp. 54, 56–57, NA, RG 75, Records Concerning the Wheeler-Howard Act.

58. Ibid., pp. 43, 62, 65, 70.

59. "Minutes of the Special Session of the Navajo Tribal Council, Fort Defiance, Arizona, March 12–13, 1934," NA, RG 75, Records Concerning the Wheeler-Howard Act, Part 2–A.

60. John Collier, "Indians at Work," *Survey Graphic* 23 (June 1934): 260–65; and Alden Stevens, "Once They Were Nomads," *Survey Graphic* 30 (February 1941): 64–67.

61. "The Missionaries View on the Wheeler-Howard bill, Resolutions Adopted by a Group of Missionaries at Ft. Defiance, Arizona, March 13, 1934," NA, RG 75, Records Concerning the Wheeler-Howard Act, Part 6-BB.

62. Berton Staples, president, United Traders Association, to John Collier, April 3, 1934, NA, RG 75, Records Concerning the Wheeler-Howard Act.

63. House, *Hearings, on H.R. 7902,* 73rd Cong., 2nd Sess., 1934, p. 384.

64. Ibid., pp. 380–82.

65. "Minutes of the Indian Congress, Phoenix, Arizona, March 16, 1934," pp. 1–23, 32, NA, RG 75, Records Concerning the Wheeler-Howard Act.

66. Ibid., pp. 25, 37, 35, 45–46, 66, 70–75.

67. "Proceedings of the Conference for the Indians of Southern California, March 17-18, 1934, Riverside, California," pp. 13, 34-37, 40, 47-48, 54, 65-66, NA, RG 75, Records Concerning the Wheeler-Howard Act.

68. "Minutes of the Meeting at Anadarko, Oklahoma, March 20, 1934," NA, RG 75, Kiowa Agency, Box 361697, Federal Records Center, Fort Worth, Texas.

69. Ibid.

70. "Minutes of the Meeting Held at Miami, Oklahoma, March 24, 1934," NA, RG 75, Records Concerning the Wheeler-Howard Act, Part 2-A.

71. "Proceedings of the Conference for the Indians of the Five Civilized Tribes of Oklahoma, March 22, 1934, Muskogee, Oklahoma," pp. 1-4, NA, RG 75, Records Concerning the Wheeler-Howard Act.

72. "Collier Attack Made by Bruner," Tulsa *Daily World*, May 3, 1934, NA, RG 75, Records Concerning the Wheeler-Howard Act, Part 5-B; and Joseph Bruner to John Collier, May 28, 1934, NA, RG 75, Records Concerning the Wheeler-Howard Act.

73. "Proceedings of the Conference for the Indians of the Five Civilized Tribes of Oklahoma, March 22, 1934, Muskogee, Oklahoma," p. 67, NA, RG 75, Records Concerning the Wheeler-Howard Act.

74. Ibid., pp. 7-8, 13-18, 22.

75. "Collier Would Revise Bill for Five Civilized Tribes," *Morning Examiner* (Bartlesville, Oklahoma), NA, RG 75, Records Concerning the Wheeler-Howard Act, Part 5-A.

76. "Proceedings of the Conference for the Indians of the Five Civilized Tribes of Oklahoma, March 22, 1934, Muskogee, Oklahoma," pp. 42-43, 60-61, 67-68, NA, RG 75, Records Concerning the Wheeler-Howard Act, and John Collier to Jenkin Lloyd Jones, associate editor, *Tulsa Tribune*, May 7, 1934, Collier Papers.

77. M. K. Sniffen, ed., "Stop, Look and Consider," *Indian Truth* 11 (March 1934): 1-3.

78. John Collier to Jonathan Steere, March 30, 1934, NA, RG 75, Records Concerning the Wheeler-Howard Act, Part 6-BB.

79. Sniffen, "The Future of the Indians," *Indian Truth* 11 (May 1934): 1-7.

80. G. E. E. Lindquist, "The Government's New Indian Policy, Proposed Revival of Tribalism Seen from the Missionary Angle," *Missionary Review of the World* 57 (April 1934): 182-83.

81. Flora Warren Seymour, "Trying It on the Indian," *New Outlook* 163 (May 1934): 22-25.

82. "Department of the Interior, Memorandum for the Press, April 15, 1934," Collier Papers.

83. Senate, *Hearings, on S. 2755*, 73rd Cong., 2nd Sess., 1934, pp. 66-69, 96, 101, 146, 151, 177.

84. Ibid., pp. 97-98, 52, 156, 239.

85. Ibid., p. 310-11.

86. "Indian Group Attacks Werner's Activities," NA, RG 75, Records Concerning the Wheeler-Howard Act; and Harold L. Ickes," Memo for Colonel McIntyre, May 4, 1934," FDRL, File No. 6-C.

87. "Selfish Groups Block Indian Aid, Collier Claims," Washington *Daily News*, April 20, 1934, NA, RG 75, Records Concerning the Wheeler-Howard Act, Part 6-B.

88. Harold L. Ickes, "To All Employees of the Indian Service, April 30, 1934," NA, RG 75, Records Concerning the Wheeler-Howard Act, Part 7.

89. John Collier, "Memorandum for Secretary Ickes, February 21, 1934," FDRL, File No. 6-C.

90. Henry A. Wallace to John Collier, April 20, 1934, NA, RG 16, Records of the Office of the Secretary of Agriculture.

91. Franklin D. Roosevelt to Edgar Howard and Burton K. Wheeler, April 28, 1934, FDRL, File No. 6-C.

92. *Congressional Record,* 73rd Cong., 2nd Sess., May 22, 1934, 78, Part 9: 9268.
93. *Congressional Record,* 73rd Cong., 2nd Sess., June 12, 1934, 78, Part 10: 11122–37.
94. U.S., *Statutes at Large,* Vol. 68, June 18, 1934, pp. 984–88.
95. For an excellent discussion of Indian progressives, who formed the Society of American Indians and identified with the goals of white society consult Hazel Hertzberg, *The Search for an American Indian Identity: Modern Pan-Indian Movements* (Syracuse, N.Y.: Syracuse University Press, 1971).
96. Ibid., pp. 315–16.

CHAPTER 8: A PARTIAL RESTORATION OF TRIBAL SOVEREIGNTY

1. John Collier, *Indians of the Americas,* abridged ed. (New York: New American Library, 1947), p. 155; and John Collier, *Indians at Work,* October 15, 1934, pp. 2–3.
2. "Address Given by Commissioner Collier on Indian Day of the Four Nations Celebration at Niagara Falls, New York, September 4, 1934," *Indians at Work,* September 15, 1934, pp. 19–21, and June 1, 1934, p. 9.
3. John Collier, "Address Given at the 50th Anniversary Ceremonies of the Haskell Institute, November 11–12, 1934," *Indians at Work,* December 1, 1934, pp. 36–45.
4. *Indians at Work,* July 1, 1934, p. 12.
5. Collier, "A. E. at Washington," *Indians at Work,* January 15, 1935, pp. 1–7; and John Collier, *From Every Zenith* (Denver: Sage Books, 1963), p. 199.
6. U.S., Congress, House, Subcommittee of the Committee on Indian Affairs, *Hearings, on H.R. 7781, Indian Conditions and Affairs,* 74th Cong., 1st Sess., 1935, pp. 43–47, 108–9.
7. Ibid., p. 59.
8. Theodore Haas, *Ten Years of Tribal Government Under IRA* (Washington: U.S. Indian Service, 1947), p. 41.
9. Ibid., p. 3.
10. Roman Hubbell to John Collier, June 16, 1935, Collier Papers.
11. John Collier, "A Message to the Navajo People, June 21, 1935," NA, RG 75, Navajo Documents from Commissioner Collier's File.
12. Haas, *Ten Years of Tribal Government Under IRA,* pp. 21–30. For a list of tribes who adopted constitutions under authority other than the IRA consult Theodore Taylor, *The American Indians And Their States* (Washington: Government Printing Office, 1972), pp. 233–45.
13. Skudder Mekeel, "An Appraisal of the IRA," *American Anthropologist* 46 (April 1944): 207–9.
14. "U.S., Department of the Interior, Office of Indian Affairs, Constitution and By-Laws for the Blackfeet Tribe of the Blackfeet Indian Reservation, Montana, December 13, 1935"; and "Constitution and By-Laws of the Oglala Sioux Tribe of the Pine Ridge Reservation, South Dakota, January 15, 1936," NA, RG 75, Records of the Bureau of Indian Affairs.
15. "Corporate Charter of the Rosebud Sioux Tribe, South Dakota, March 16, 1937," NA, RG 75, Records of the Bureau of Indian Affairs.
16. U.S., Congress, House, Subcommittee on Indian Affairs, *Hearings, on H.R. 5753, Conditions on Sioux Reservations,* 75th Cong., 1st Sess., 1937, p. 7.
17. "Constitution and By-Laws of the Oglala Sioux Tribe of the Pine Ridge Reservation, South Dakota, January 15, 1936," NA, RG 75, Records of the Bureau of Indian Affairs.
18. U.S., Congress, House, Committee on Indian Affairs, *Hearings, on H.R. 8360, Condition of Indians in the United States,* 74th Cong., 2nd Sess., 1936, p. 35; and House, *Hearings, on H.R. 5753,* 75th Cong., 1st Sess., 1937, pp. 1–5.

19. House, *Hearings, on H.R. 8360,* 74th Cong., 2nd Sess., 1936, pp. 12-14, 22-23.

20. Ibid., pp. 5-8, 36.

21. House, *Hearings, on H.R. 5753,* 75th Cong., 1st Sess., 1937, pp. 8-11.

22. Jay B. Nash, ed., *The New Day for the Indians: A Survey of the IRA of 1934* (New York: Academy Press, 1938), pp. 22, 43-44.

23. D'Arcy McNickle, *Indian Man: A Life Of Oliver La Farge* (Bloomington: Indiana University Press, 1971), p. 107; and Haas, *Ten Years of Tribal Government Under IRA,* p. 14.

24. Collier, *From Every Zenith,* p. 218.

25. Oliver La Farge, "Notes for Hopi Administrators, February, 1937," pp. 1-8, Oliver La Farge Papers, Humanities Research Center, University of Texas, Austin, Texas (hereafter referred to as Oliver La Farge Papers); and McNickle, *Indian Man,* p. 112.

26. "Constitution and By-Laws of the Hopi Tribe, Arizona, December 19, 1936," NA, RG 75, Records of the Bureau of Indian Affairs.

27. Ibid.

28. La Farge, "Notes For Hopi Administrators," pp. 3-4, 8-9, 13, Oliver La Farge Papers.

29. Frank Waters, *Book of the Hopi* (New York: Ballantine Books, 1963), pp. 384-87.

30. La Farge, "Notes for Hopi Administrators," p. 10, Oliver La Farge Papers.

31. La Farge, "Notes for Hopi Administrators," pp. 10, 22, Oliver La Farge Papers.

32. John Collier to Mr. (?) McCray, June 28, 1938, Collier Papers.

33. Collier, *From Every Zenith,* p. 218.

34. Nash, *The New Day for the Indians,* pp. 19-20.

35. "Washington Notes: Senator Wheeler Turns Conservative," *New Republic* 90 (April 7, 1937): 261-62.

36. Nash, *The New Day for the Indians,* pp. 19-20; and "Corporate Charter of the Confederated Salish and Kootenai Tribes of the Flathead Reservation, Montana, April 25, 1936," NA, RG 75, Records of the Bureau of Indian Affairs.

37. Collier, *From Every Zenith,* p. 182.

38. "Constitution and By-Laws of the Jicarilla Apache Tribe of the Jicarilla Apache Indian Reservation, New Mexico, August 4, 1937," NA, RG 75, Records of the Bureau of Indian Affairs.

39. Collier, "Indians Come Alive," *Atlantic Monthly* 170 (September 1942): 79; and Nash, *The New Day for the Indians,* pp. 20-21.

40. M. K. Sniffen, ed., "Loans," *Indian Truth* 16 (November-December 1939): 2-3.

41. Haas, *Ten Years of Tribal Government,* pp. 18, 27; and U.S., Department of Commerce, *Federal and State Indian Reservations* (Washington: Government Printing Office, 1971), p. 273.

42. "Constitution and By-Laws of the Pueblo of Santa Clara, December 20, 1935," NA, RG 75, Classified Correspondence Files, United Pueblos, Records of the Bureau of Indian Affairs.

43. *Indians At Work,* March 15, 1937, pp. 1-6.

44. House, *Hearings, on H.R. 7781,* 74th Cong., 1st Sess., 1935, pp. 14-21.

45. Ibid., pp. 863-66.

46. Ibid., pp. 867-71, 881.

47. Ibid., pp. 19-21.

48. Ibid., pp. 881-97.

49. Ibid., pp. 32-37, 502-7.

50. Donald Parman, "J. C. Morgan: Navajo Apostle of Assimilation," *Prologue* 4 (Summer 1972): 83-86.

51. House, *Hearings, on H.R. 7781,* 74th Cong., 1st Sess., 1935, pp. 217-323.

52. Ibid., pp. 357, 774-77.

53. Ibid., pp. 767–68.
54. "To the American Citizenship of the United States," NA, RG 75, File on the American Indian Federation, 1933–1937.
55. House, *Hearings, on H.R. 7781,* 74th Cong., 1st Sess., 1935, p. 540.
56. Ibid., pp. 56–57.
57. Ibid., pp. 52, 763.
58. Ibid., p. 682.
59. Ibid., p. 669.
60. Ibid., pp. 659–62, 690–94.
61. Ibid., p. 718.
62. Ibid., pp. 742–56.
63. Ibid., pp. 746–47; 756–57.
64. Ibid., pp. 751–54, 757–58.
65. Ibid., pp. 648–49.
66. Ibid., pp. 730–33.
67. John Collier to Senator William King, August 18, 1937, NA, RG 75, Suitland, Maryland.
68. John Collier, "Memorandum for Secretary Ickes, March 6, 1935," Collier Papers.
69. Angie Debo, *A History of the Indians of the United States* (Norman: University of Oklahoma Press, 1970), p. 294.
70. "Meeting Held at Muskogee, Oklahoma, October 15, 1934," Elmer Thomas Papers, Western History Collection, University of Oklahoma (hereafter referred to as Elmer Thomas Papers).
71. Felix Cohen, *Handbook of Federal Indian Law* (Washington: Government Printing Office, 1942), p. 455.
72. "Meeting Held at Miami, Oklahoma, October 16, 1934," Elmer Thomas Papers.
73. "Meeting Held at Muskogee, Oklahoma, October 15, 1934," Elmer Thomas Papers.
74. Ibid.
75. Ibid.
76. "Meeting Called by Senator Elmer Thomas with Commissioner John Collier and the Indians, Pawnee, Oklahoma, October 18, 1934," Elmer Thomas Papers.
77. "Meeting Held at Shawnee, Oklahoma, October 19, 1934," Elmer Thomas Papers.
78. "Meeting Held at Anadarko, Oklahoma, October 23, 1934," Elmer Thomas Papers.
79. U.S., Congress, House, Committee on Indian Affairs, *Hearings, on H.R. 6234, General Welfare of the Indians of Oklahoma,* 74th Cong., 1st Sess., 1935, pp. 1–4.
80. Ibid., pp. 75, 197.
81. Ibid., pp. 75, 90–93, 197.
82. Ibid., pp. 70–71.
83. Ibid., pp. 151, 172.
84. Ibid., p. 191.
85. Ibid., pp. 64, 181, 186.
86. Ibid., pp. 65–66, 154–55, 163, 192–93.
87. Haas, *Ten Years of Tribal Government,* pp. 43–45.
88. Ibid.
89. Cohen, *Handbook of Federal Indian Law,* p. 455.
90. Angie Debo, *And Still the Waters Run* (Princeton, N.J.: Princeton University Press, 1940), pp. 377, 387.

91. Ibid., p. 373; and Sniffen, "Indian Loans," *Indian Truth* 16 (November-December 1939): 2–3. For an analysis of the impact of the Oklahoma Welfare Act consult Angie Debo, *The Five Civilized Tribes of Oklahoma: Report on Social and Economic Conditions* (Philadelphia: Indian Rights Association, 1951), pp. 1–35.

92. Cohen, *Handbook of Federal Indian Law*, pp. 413–14.

93. Haas, *Ten Years of Tribal Government*, p. 42.

94. Ibid., pp. 29–30.

95. Debo, *A History of the Indians of the United States*, p. 322.

96. Cohen, *Handbook of Federal Indian Law*, pp. 414–15.

97. Debo, *A History of the Indians of the United States*, pp. 323, 331.

98. *New York Times,* May 26, 1935, 7, p. 10.

99. *New York Times,* August 12, 1934, 4, p. 6.

100. House, *Hearings, on H.R. 7781,* 74th Cong., 1st Sess., 1935, pp. 1029–35.

101. Collier, *From Every Zenith,* p. 194.

102. "The Development of Indian Arts and Crafts," *Monthly Labor Review* 46 (March 1938): 655–58; and Frederick H. Douglas and Rene D'Harnoncourt, *Indian Art of the United States* (New York: The Museum of Modern Art, 1941).

103. Collier, *From Every Zenith,* p. 194; and *New York Times,* August 17, 1941, p. 8.

104. U.S., Department of the Interior, *Forest Conservation on Lands Administered by the Interior Department, Part 2: Forestry on Indian Lands* (Washington: Government Printing Office, 1940), pp. 84–85.

105. *New York Times,* December 17, 1937, p. 24.

106. John Collier, *On the Gleaming Way* (Denver: Sage Books, 1962), p. 116.

107. *Indians at Work,* January 1941, pp. 1–3.

CHAPTER 9: THUNDER OVER THE SOUTHWEST

1. Samuel P. Hays, *Conservation and the Gospel of Efficiency, 1890–1920* (Cambridge, Mass.: Harvard University Press, 1959), pp. 2–3; and *Indians at Work,* September 15, 1933, pp. 1–5.

2. Consult Richard Hofstadter, *The Age of Reform* (New York: Random House, 1955), pp. 302–8.

3. U.S., Department of the Interior, *Annual Report of the Secretary of the Interior: Report of the Commissioner of Indian Affairs* (Washington: Government Printing Office, 1935), pp. 141–44.

4. John Collier, "Memorandum for Secretary Ickes, May 7, 1936," NA, RG 75, Records of the Bureau of Indian Affairs.

5. John Collier, "Indians at Work," *Survey Graphic* 23 (June 1934): 260–65.

6. Lawrence Kelly, *The Navajo Indians and Federal Indian Policy, 1900–1935* (Tucson: University of Arizona Press, 1968), pp. 158–59.

7. Ibid., p. 160.

8. Alden Stevens, "Once They Were Nomads," *Survey Graphic* 30 (February 1941): 64–67.

9. Chee Dodge to Harold L. Ickes, April 26, 1935, NA, RG 75, Records Concerning the Wheeler-Howard Act.

10. U.S., Congress, House, Committee on Indian Affairs, *Hearings, on H.R. 8360, Condition of Indians in the United States,* 74th Cong., 2nd Sess., 1936, pp. 98–100.

11. John Collier, "Regulations Affecting the Carrying Capacity and Management of the Navajo Range, November 5, 1935," NA, RG 75, Navajo Documents from Commissioner Collier's file.

12. J. C. Morgan to Harold L. Ickes, May 15, 1936, NA, RG 75, File on J. C. Morgan.

13. House, *Hearings on H.R. 8360,* 74th Cong., 2nd Sess., 1936, pp. 79–80.

14. Ibid., pp. 89–96; and Harold L. Ickes to J. C. Morgan, June 1, 1936, NA, RG 75, File on J. C. Morgan.

15. Flora Warren Seymour, "Thunder Over the Southwest," *Saturday Evening Post* 211 (April 1, 1939): 23, 74.

16. House, *Hearings, on H.R. 8360,* 74th Cong., 2nd Sess., 1936, pp. 77–88.

17. Donald Parman, "J. C. Morgan: Navajo Apostle of Assimilation," *Prologue* 4 (Summer 1972): 92.

18. Ibid., 92–93.

19. M. K. Sniffen, "Navajo Tribal Council," *Indian Truth* 15 (January 1938): 1–3; and "False Reporting," *Indian Truth* 14 (March 1937): 2–3.

20. *Albuquerque Journal,* June 4, 1937, NA, RG 75, File on J. C. Morgan — Stock Reduction.

21. "Navajos Charge Southwest Turned Into Zoo," *Washington Post,* June 18, 1937, NA, RG 75, File on J. C. Morgan — Stock Reduction.

22. "Collier Denies Indians Forced to Pawn Beads," *Washington Post,* June 19, 1937, NA, RG 75, File on J. C. Morgan — Stock Reduction.

23. Collier, "Press Release, June 19, 1937," NA, RG 75, File on Morgan and Palmer.

24. Parman, "J. C. Morgan: Navajo Apostle of Assimilation," *Prologue* 4 (Summer 1972): 94; and E. R. Fryer to the Commissioner, August 8, 1937, NA, RG 75, File on Morgan and Palmer.

25. Santa Fe *New Mexican,* February 19, 1938, NA, RG 75, File on Morgan and Palmer.

26. Parman, "J. C. Morgan: Navajo Apostle of Assimilation," *Prologue* 4 (Summer 1972): 92–93.

27. Dashne Cheschillege to President Franklin D. Roosevelt, May 31, 1941, NA, RG 75, File on Navajo Stock Reduction; Eleanor Roosevelt, "Navajos Plead for Their People," *Washington Daily News,* June 12, 1941, NA, RG 75, File on Navajo Stock Reduction; and Ibid., "Irrigation Project Could Save Navajos," June 18, 1941, NA, RG 75, File on Navajo Stock Reduction.

28. Franklin D. Roosevelt to the Navajo People, June 19, 1941, FDRL, File No. 296.

29. John Collier, "Memorandum for Secretary Ickes, June 1, 1936," Collier Papers.

30. John Collier, "Memorandum for Secretary Ickes, June 24, 1936," NA, RG 75, File on Taos-Peyote Warfare.

31. "Department of the Interior Press Release, May, 1935," Collier Papers.

32. Sniffen, "Field Notes," *Indian Truth* 12 (November 1935): 1.

33. John Collier, "Pueblo MSS., May 22, 1936," Collier Papers.

34. Mabel Dodge Luhan to John Collier, March 10, 1936, Collier Papers.

35. Santa Fe *New Mexican,* May 11, 1936, Collier Papers.

36. Mabel Dodge Luhan to the editor of the Santa Fe *New Mexican,* April 30, 1936, Collier Papers.

37. John Collier to Antonio Mirabal, April 21, 1936, Collier Papers.

38. Mabel Dodge Luhan to the editor of the Santa Fe *New Mexican,* May 5, 1936, Collier Papers.

39. "Statement by Commissioner Collier to the Associated Press, May 12, 1936," Collier Papers.

40. John Collier to Joe (?), May 15, 1936, Collier Papers.

41. Mabel Dodge Luhan to Senator Elmer Thomas, May 22, 1936, Collier Papers.

42. Santa Fe *New Mexican,* August 21, 1936, Collier Papers.

43. "Statement by Commissioner Collier, August 24, 1936," NA, RG 75, File on Taos-Peyote Warfare.

44. John Collier, "Memorandum of Action on the Native American Church Matter at Taos Pueblo, September 18, 1936," NA, RG 75, File on the Navajo-Pueblo Boundary Hearings.

45. "Department of the Interior Memorandum for the Press, October 25, 1936," NA, RG 75, File on the Navajo-Pueblo Boundary Hearings; and Santano Sandoval to Harold L. Ickes, October 21, 1936, NA, RG 75, File on the Navajo-Pueblo Boundary Hearings.

46. Charles de Y. Elkus to John Collier, May 23, 1936, Collier Papers.

47. *Indians at Work,* March 1, 1937: 1–7.

48. Ibid.

49. *Congressional Record,* 75th Cong., 1st Sess., June 28, 1937, 81, Part 6: 6380–84.

50. Ibid., 6379–80.

51. Ibid.

52. *New York Times,* March 14, 1937, p. 16.

53. Ibid.

54. "Washington Notes: Senator Wheeler Turns Conservative," *New Republic* 90 (April 7, 1937): 261–62; and Gerald Johnson, "Wheeler Rides the Storm," *Collier's* 114 (July 8, 1944): 11.

55. John Collier to Oliva Cutting, March 25, 1937, Collier Papers.

56. John Collier, "Senator Wheeler and the Indian Reorganization Act, March 18, 1937," NA, RG 75, Records Concerning the Wheeler-Howard Act, Part 8.

57. Ibid.

58. Sniffen, "Proposed Repeal," *Indian Truth* 14 (April 1937): 1–4.

59. Dr. Haven Emerson and Oliver La Farge, "Joint Statement by the American Indian Defense Association and the National Association on Indian Affairs, March 12, 1937," Elmer Thomas Papers.

60. Mrs. Edith Murphy, "Resolution Against the Repeal of the IRA, March 30, 1937," Elmer Thomas Papers; and Winifred Codman to B. K. Wheeler and Lynn Frazier (undated), Elmer Thomas Papers.

61. "The 1936 Convention of the American Indian Federation," NA, RG 75, File on the American Indian Federation, 1933–1937.

62. Harold L. Ickes to Usher Burdick, April 26, 1936, NA, RG 75, File on Bruner and the Oklahoma Racket.

63. H.R. 5921, 76th Cong., 1st Sess., April 20, 1939, NA, RG 75, File on Bruner and the Oklahoma Racket.

64. John Collier, "Memorandum on S. 2206, April 21, 1939," NA, RG 75, File on Bruner and the Oklahoma Racket; and Harold L. Ickes to Usher Burdick, April 26, 1939, NA, RG 75, File on Bruner and the Oklahoma Racket.

65. Usher Burdick to Harold L. Ickes, May 1, 1939, NA, RG 75, File on the Oklahoma Racket.

66. *New York Times,* March 16, 1939, p. 20.

67. Elwood A. Towner, "Wake Up America," NA, RG 75, File on Alice Lee Jemison.

68. John Collier, "The American Indian Federation and the German-American Bund" (undated), NA, RG 75, File on the German-American Bund.

69. William Dudley Pelly, "Indians Are Not Red: The Inside Story of Administration Attempts to Make Communists of the North Carolina Cherokees," NA, RG 75, File on the Silver Shirts of America; and John Collier to Oliver La Farge, May 10, 1939, NA, RG 75, File on the German-American Bund.

70. John Collier to Senator Samuel Jackson, March 24, 1944, Collier Papers.

71. U.S., Congress, House, Committee on Indian Affairs, *Hearings, on S. 2103, Wheeler-Howard Act — Exempt Certain Indians,* 76th Cong., 3rd Sess., 1940, pp. 5–9.

72. Ibid., pp. 60–61, 86–92.
73. *Congressional Record,* 76th Cong., 3rd Sess., September 30, 1940, 86, Part 11: 12848–49.
74. *Annual Report of the Secretary of the Interior,* 1944, p. 237.
75. Harold L. Ickes to Harold Smith, September 21, 1942, Collier Papers.
76. *Annual Report of the Secretary of the Interior,* 1942, p. 256; Ibid., 1944, p. 237.
77. Ibid., 1944, p. 240.
78. John Collier, "Memorandum for the Secretary, December 30, 1941," Collier Papers.
79. John Collier, "The Permanent Establishments Are Being Forced Out of Washington by the Budget Bureau: Not to Meet War Requirements but for Different Reasons" (undated), Collier Papers.
80. John Collier, "Memorandum for the Secretary, December 30, 1941," Collier Papers.
81. John Collier to Elmer Thomas, February 28, 1940, Collier Papers.
82. *The Final Act, The First Inter-American Conference on Indian Life,* Patzcuaro, Mexico, April 14–24, 1940 (Washington: Office of Indian Affairs, 1940), pp. 7–10.
83. John Collier, "Radio Broadcast on the Future of the American Indian, October 27, 1941," Collier Papers.
84. "National Indian Institute," *Hispanic American Historical Review* 22 (May 1942): 427; and John Collier, "Memorandum for Secretary Ickes, January 24, 1945," Collier Papers.
85. Franklin D. Roosevelt to Nelson Rockefeller, January 30, 1941, FDRL, File No. 4205; and Nelson Rockefeller to Franklin D. Roosevelt, February 25, 1941, FDRL, File No. 4205.
86. Laura Thompson, *Personality and Government, Findings and Recommendations of the Indian Administration Research* (Mexico City: Ediciones Del Instituto Indigenista Inter-Americano, 1951), pp. 1–177. For other publications of the personality study see *Boletín Indigenista* 8 (March 1948): 19–35.
87. Jed Johnson to William Zimmerman, July 14, 1944, Collier Papers.
88. John Collier, "Memorandum for Secretary Ickes, January 24, 1945," Collier Papers; and *Indians at Work,* May-June 1944, pp. 1–5.
89. John Collier, "Memorandum for Secretary Ickes, December 5, 1944," Collier Papers.
90. John Collier, "Memorandum for the Secretary, March 4, 1942," NA, RG 48, Records of the Secretary of the Interior, Central Classified Files (1–188), File on Internment, Part 1; and Harold L. Ickes to Franklin D. Roosevelt, June 15, 1942, NA, RG 48, File on Internment, Part 2.
91. John Collier, "The Unrealized Food Production Capabilities at Japanese Relocation Centers, January 7, 1943," NA, RG 48, File on Internment, Part 2; and John Collier to Secretary Ickes, March 4, 1942, NA, RG 75, File on the Internment of Japanese on Indian Lands, 1942, Part 2.
92. John Collier to Milton Eisenhower, April 15, 1942, NA, RG 75, File on the Internment of Japanese on Indian Lands, 1942, Part 2.
93. John Collier, "Speech to Fellow Citizens and Fellow Americans, June 27, 1942," NA, RG 75, File on the Internment of Japanese on Indian Lands, Part 1.
94. Mary Ellicott Arnold and Lionel Perkins, "Report of the Rochdale Institute," NA, RG 75, File on the Internment of Japanese on Indian Lands, Part 2.
95. John Collier, "The Unrealized Food Production Capabilities at Japanese Relocation Centers, January 7, 1943," NA, RG 48, File on Internment, Part 2; and Dillon S. Myer, "Talk Before a Luncheon Meeting of the Commonwealth Club in San Francisco, California, August 6, 1943," NA, RG 75, File on the War Relocation Authority — Correspondence Concerning Evacuees.

96. Dillon S. Myer, "To All Project Directors, March 15, 1943"; and Dillon S. Myer to A. H. Leighton, September 21, 1943, NA, RG 75, File on the War Relocation Authority — Correspondence Concerning Evacuees.
97. John Collier, "Memorandum for the Secretary, March 4, 1942," NA, RG 48, File on Internment, Part 1.
98. J. P. Kinney, *Facing Indian Facts* (Laurens, New York: The Village Printer, 1973), p. 88.
99. John Collier, "Memorandum for the President, January 15, 1943," Collier Papers.
100. John Collier and Saul K. Padover, "Institute of Ethnic Democracy," *Common Ground* 4 (Autumn 1943): 3–7; and John Collier, "United States Indian Administration as a Laboratory of Ethnic Relations," *Social Research* 12 (September 1945): 265–68.
101. "Charges Collier Obtained Divorce at United States Expense," *Albuquerque Journal,* May 19, 1944, Collier Papers.
102. John Collier to Franklin D. Roosevelt, January 19, 1945, FDRL, File No. 6–C.
103. Ibid.
104. Franklin D. Roosevelt to Commissioner John Collier, January 22, 1945, FDRL, File No. 6–C.
105. "Proceedings of the Conference for the Indians of the Five Civilized Tribes of Oklahoma, March 22, 1934, Muskogee, Oklahoma," NA, RG 75, Records Concerning the Wheeler-Howard Act.
106. Collier, *American Indian Life,* April 1934, p. 13.

CHAPTER 10: THE QUEST CONTINUES

1. "Institute for Racial Democracy," Collier Papers.
2. *The Institute of Ethnic Affairs* (Washington, D.C., 1945), pp. 2–3, Collier Papers.
3. John Collier, "The Positive, Affirmative Meaning of Racial Differences: And What the Fascist Disease Is," October 29, 1945, Collier Papers.
4. Ibid.
5. John Collier, *Newsletter of the Institute of Ethnic Affairs,* April 6, 1946, Collier Papers (hereafter referred to as *Newsletter*); and Draft Resolution, "Non-Self-Governing Peoples," February 2, 1946, Collier Papers.
6. John Collier, "Confidential Memo, January 9, 1946," Collier Papers.
7. Ibid.
8. John Collier, "Confidential Memo, January 14, 1946," Collier Papers.
9. John Collier, "The First Stage Results," Collier Papers.
10. John Collier, "Memorandum for Mr. (?) Arnold, February 23, 1946," Collier Papers.
11. John Collier, "Statement on the Denials of Civil Rights on Guam and American Samoa, President's Committee on Civil Rights, May 14, 1946," Collier Papers.
12. Collier, *Newsletter,* September 1946, Collier Papers.
13. Ibid.
14. Harold L. Ickes, "Our Pacific Dependencies and the Peace Crisis — Naval Rule," *Newsletter,* June 1946, Collier Papers.
15. Harold L. Ickes, "The Navy at Its Worst," *Collier's* 118 (August 31, 1946): 22–23, 67.
16. John Collier to the editor of the *New York Times,* September 8, 1946, Collier Papers.
17. James Forrestal to the editor of the *New York Times,* September 24, 1946, Collier Papers.

18. Collier, "United States Trusteeship Draft: Analysis and Recommendation," *Newsletter,* December 1946, Collier Papers.
19. Collier, "Resolutions from Guam and Samoa," *Newsletter,* February 1947, Collier Papers.
20. Ibid.
21. Collier, "Hopkins' Committee Report," *Newsletter,* May 1947, Collier Papers.
22. Martha Jay to Herbert Rothschild, May 31, 1954, Collier Papers.
23. John Collier to the Members of the Board of Directors (undated), Collier Papers; and "Mr. Collier's Proposed Letter to the Directors and Members of the Institute" (undated), Collier Papers.
24. Fred Martin to the Institute of Ethnic Affairs, November 20, 1946, Collier Papers.
25. Joseph Nunan to the Institute of Ethnic Affairs, June 12, 1947, Collier Papers.
26. John Collier, *Indians of the Americas,* abridged ed. (New York: The New American Library, 1947), pp. 11, 22, 99.
27. Ibid., pp. 73-76, 93, 170, 186.
28. John Collier, *America's Colonial Record* (London: Fabian Publications, Ltd., 1947), 5-6, 33.
29. Ibid., 6-14.
30. Ibid.; and John Collier, "Has Roxas Betrayed America," *Saturday Review of Literature* 30 (January 11, 1947): 15.
31. John Collier, *From Every Zenith* (Denver: Sage Books, 1963), p. 408.
32. "Tentative Program of a Course on Non-Literate and Non-Industrial Peoples in the Modern World," Collier Papers.
33. Ibid.
34. Collier, "Institute to Conduct Research on Saipan," *Newsletter,* June-July 1947, Collier Papers; and "Trusteeship Confronting the United Nations General Assembly," *Newsletter,* November 1946, Collier Papers.
35. Harry Truman, *Years of Trial and Hope,* Vol. 2, (New York: Signet Books, 1965), pp. 267-69.
36. Ibid.; Collier, *From Every Zenith,* p. 335; and Collier, "Knowing the Native Community," *Newsletter,* March-April 1949, Collier Papers.
37. Collier, "The Scientist's Responsibility in the World Crisis," *Newsletter,* July-August 1948, Collier Papers.
38. John Collier, "Governing Liberia," *New York Times,* June 10, 1951, Collier Papers.
39. Collier, *From Every Zenith,* pp. 335-36.
40. Consult the revised edition: John Collier, *American Indian Ceremonial Dances* (New York: Bounty Books, 1972), pp. 20, 31, 35, 147.
41. Ibid., pp. 43, 11, 119, 129, 169-70, 175.
42. John Collier, "Indianismo vs Racism," *America Indigena* 5 (July 1945): 241-46; and Collier, "Indian Day," *America Indigena* 6 (June 1946): 99-109.
43. John Collier, "Autobiographical Sketch, July 23, 1959," Collier Papers.
44. Collier, *From Every Zenith,* pp. 362-65; Oscar Chapman to John Collier, January 20, 1950, Collier Papers; and "Functions of the National Indian Institute Transferred," *Boletín Indigena* 6 (March 1946): 35-36.
45. D'Arcy McNickle, *Indian Man* (Bloomington: Indiana University Press, 1971), pp. 148-49; and George A. Boyce, *When Navajos Had Too Many Sheep* (San Francisco: Indian Historian Press, 1974), pp. 239-40.
46. John Collier, "Beleaguered Indian," *Nation* 169 (September 17, 1949): 276-77.
47. "Hour of Crisis for American Indians," *New York Herald Tribune,* October 4, 1949, Collier Papers.
48. John Collier, "Press Release, October 9, 1949," Collier Papers; and Collier, *From Every Zenith,* p. 370.

49. McNickle, *Indian Man*, pp. 150–51.

50. Collier, *From Every Zenith*, p. 371.

51. "Address by Commissioner of Indian Affairs Dillon S. Myer, Before the Western Governors' Conference, Phoenix, Arizona, December 9, 1952," Collier Papers; and Donald McCoy and Richard Reutten, *Quest and Response: Minority Rights and the Truman Administration* (Lawrence: University of Kansas Press, 1974) pp. 302–6.

52. John Collier, "Memorandum for Governor Stevenson, October 18, 1952," Collier Papers.

53. Dillon S. Myer to All Tribal Council Members, October 10, 1952, Collier Papers.

54. John Collier, "Indian Bureau Reverts to Obsolete Policy of Spoliation, November 28, 1950," Collier Papers; and John Collier, "Memorandum for Governor Stevenson, October 18, 1952," Collier Papers; and Angie Debo, *A History of the Indians of the United States* (Norman: University of Oklahoma Press, 1970), p. 303.

55. John Collier, "Memorandum for Governor Stevenson, October 18, 1952," Collier Papers.

56. Clarence Wesley, "San Carlos Tribe Seeks Equal Rights," and John Collier, "Indian Rights Depend on Indian Leadership," *Southwest Indian News Letter*, February 1951, Collier Papers.

57. McNickle, *Indian Man*, pp. 159–60.

58. John Collier, "Statement of the Institute of Ethnic Affairs," *Southwest Indian News Letter*, January-February 1952, Collier Papers.

59. John Collier to Betty Cooper and Martha Jay, July 12, 1950, Collier Papers.

60. "Mr. Collier's Proposed Letter to the Directors and Members of the Institute" (undated), Collier Papers.

61. Ibid.; and John Collier, "To the Members of the Board of Directors" (undated), Collier Papers.

62. John Collier, "Memorandum for Governor Stevenson, October 18, 1952," Collier Papers; and John Collier to Milton Eisenhower (undated), Collier Papers.

63. John Collier, "Letter to General Eisenhower," *Nation* 176 (January 10, 1953): 29–30.

64. Merlo J. Pusey, *Eisenhower the President* (New York: Macmillan, 1956), pp. 64–65; and Debo, *A History of the Indians of the United States,* p. 304.

65. "Address by Orme Lewis, Associate Secretary of the Department of Interior, at a Seminar in Connection with the Intertribal Ceremonial, Gallup, New Mexico, August 13, 1953," Collier Papers.

66. Vine Deloria, *Custer Died for Your Sins: An Indian Manifesto* (New York: The Macmillan Company, 1969), pp. 62–63.

67. Theodore W. Taylor, *The States and Their Indian Citizens* (Washington: Government Printing Office, 1972), pp. 60–61.

68. William Brophy and Sophie D. Aberle, *The Indian: America's Unfinished Business* (Norman: University of Oklahoma Press, 1966), pp. 184–85.

69. John Collier to Milton Eisenhower, August 6, 1953, Collier Papers.

70. John Collier, "Statement of the Institute of Ethnic Affairs," July 8, 1954, Collier Papers.

71. William H. Kelly, *Indian Affairs and the Indian Reorganization Act: The Twenty Year Record* (Tucson: University of Arizona, 1954), pp. 1–39.

72. John Collier, "Terminating the American Indian, Institute of Ethnic Affairs Bulletin, February 13, 1954," Collier Papers.

73. Reprint, John Collier, "Return to Dishonor," *Frontier Magazine,* (June 1954), Collier Papers; John Collier, "Indian Takeaway," *Nation* 179 (October 2, 1954): 290–91; and reprint, John Collier, "Against Indians and Our Honor," *The Churchman* (1954), Collier Papers.

74. John Collier, "Back to Dishonor," *Christian Century* 71 (May 12, 1954): 578–80.

75. Debo, *A History of the Indians of the United States,* pp. 307–8.

76. John Collier to the Honorable Dwight D. Eisenhower, August 24, 1954, Collier Papers.

77. Maxwell Rabb to John Collier, September 2, 1954, Collier Papers.

78. Walter Daniels, ed., *American Indians* (New York: H. W. Wilson Company, 1957), pp. 115–16; and Debo, *A History of the Indians of the United States,* p. 312.

79. Debo, *A History of the Indians of the United States,* p. 311; and Collier, *From Every Zenith,* p. 377.

80. Debo, *A History of the Indians of the United States,* pp. 307, 315.

81. John Collier to Professor Burt W. Aginsky, May 1, 1952, Collier Papers; and John Collier to Harry Wright, president of the City College of New York (undated), Collier Papers.

82. "Professor Still Whoops It Up for Redmen," Collier Papers.

83. John Collier, "The Present and Future Citizen," May 27, 1954, Collier Papers.

84. Ibid.

85. John Collier, "The Nature of Man," *Merrill-Palmer Quarterly* 1 (Spring 1955): 111–17; and Ibid., "Values and the Introductions of Change" 2 (Fall 1955): 13–22.

86. "John Collier Memorial Is Established Here," Collier Papers.

87. John Collier to Elizabeth S. Sergeant, April 6, 1955, and July 10, 1955, Collier Papers.

88. John Collier to Elizabeth S. Sergeant, August 2, 1955, Collier Papers.

89. Collier, *From Every Zenith,* pp. 410–11.

90. Joseph Gittler, ed., *Understanding Minority Groups* (New York: John Wiley and Sons, 1956), pp. vii, 33–57.

91. Ibid.

92. "Wedding Announcement," January 26, 1957, Collier Papers.

93. John Collier to Elizabeth S. Sergeant, March 25, 19??, Collier Papers.

94. Ibid.; and John Collier to Elizabeth S. Sergeant, March 15, 1962, Collier Papers.

95. Ibid.

96. John Collier, "The Menominee of Wisconsin and the Klamath of Oregon Cases, April, 1957," Collier Papers.

97. Consult John Collier, "Richness to Dust in Two Decades," *Saturday Review* 40 (November 8, 1958): 33–34; John Collier, "Massacre of a Wondrous Culture," *Saturday Review* 42 (June 20, 1959): 16–17; John Collier, "Slow Recovery Since Wounded Knee," *Saturday Review* 46 (June 15, 1963): 31–32; and John Collier, "Fate of the Five Tribes," *Saturday Review* 49 (April 2, 1966): 39.

98. John Collier, "Our Mingling Worlds," *El Crepusculo,* January 7, 1960, Collier Papers.

99. Ibid., September 24, 1959.

100. Ibid., October 1, 1959.

101. Ibid. (undated).

102. Ibid., October 8, 1959 and October 15, 1959.

103. Collier, *From Every Zenith,* p. 10.

104. Ibid., p. 94.

105. Ibid., pp. 233, 239.

106. Ibid., pp. 93, 308–12.

107. Ibid., pp. 10, 466.

108. "John Collier, United States Official," *Washington Post,* May 9, 1968, D, p. 14.

109. John Collier to the Officers of Taos Pueblo (undated), Collier Papers.

110. *New York Times,* May 9, 1968, p. 47; and Mrs. John Collier, Sr., to Kenneth Philp, September 12, 1971.

CHAPTER 11: THE COLLIER LEGACY

1. Consult Roy Lubove, *The Professional Altruist: The Emergence of Social Work as a Career, 1880–1930* (New York: Atheneum, 1969).

2. Ibid., p. 175.

3. Roy Lubove, *The Progressives and the Slums: Tenement House Reform in New York City, 1890–1917* (Pittsburgh, Pa.: University of Pittsburgh Press, 1962), pp. 72–73.

4. John Collier, "The Pueblos' Last Stand," *Sunset* 50 (February 1923): 19–22; and John Collier, "The Red Atlantis," *Survey* 49 (October 1922): 16–17.

5. Peter Farb, *Man's Rise to Civilization as Shown by the Indians of North America from Primeval Times to the Coming of the Industrial State* (New York: Dutton and Co., 1968), pp. 83–89, 100.

6. Samuel P. Hays, *Conservation and the Gospel of Efficiency, 1890–1920* (Cambridge: Harvard University Press, 1959), p. 269.

7. D. S. Otis, *The Dawes Act and the Allotment of Indian Lands,* ed. Francis Paul Prucha (Norman: University of Oklahoma Press, 1973), pp. 66–72.

8. Alden Stevens, "Whither The American Indian?" *Survey Graphic* 29 (March 1940): 171–73.

9. John Blandford, Jr., "Bureau of the Budget, Memorandum for the President, June 2, 1941," File 2865, FDRL; and John Collier, *From Every Zenith* (Denver: Sage Books, 1963), pp. 296–97.

10. George Boyce, *When Navajos Had Too Many Sheep; The 1940's* (San Francisco: Indian Historian Press, 1974), p. 156.

11. Graham D. Taylor, "The New Deal and the Grass Roots" (Ph.D. diss., University of Pennsylvania, 1972), pp. 163–70.

12. Norman D. Markowitz, *The Rise and Fall of the People's Century: Henry A. Wallace and American Liberalism, 1941–1948* (New York: The Free Press, 1973), p. 1.

13. Ibid., p. 19.

14. John Collier, *From Every Zenith* (Denver: Sage Books, 1963), p. 227.

15. David Brower, ed., *Wilderness in Our Civilization* (San Francisco: Sierra Club, 1964), pp. 115–26.

16. John Collier, "Radio Broadcast on the Future of the American Indian, October 27, 1941," Collier Papers.

17. Otis L. Graham, Jr., *The Great Campaigns: Reform and War in America, 1900–1928* (Englewood Cliffs, N.J.: Prentice Hall, 1971), p. 129.

18. *New York Times,* March 8, 1970, 6, p. 54.

19. Stan Steiner, *The New Indians* (New York: Dell Publishing Co., 1968).

Index

Aberle, Sophie, 194–97
Abeyta, Pablo, 40
Acoma Pueblo, 27, 234
Adams, Olva, 52
African View (Huxley), 140
Aginsky, Burt W., 230
Agricultural Adjustment Administration (AAA), 122–23
Alabama-Coushatta Indians, 229
Alaska Native Industries Cooperative Association, 183
Alaska Reorganization Act (1936), 183–84
Albuquerque State Tribune, 65
Alfred, Thomas, 181
All Pueblo Council: and Albert Fall, 107; and Bursum bills, 36, 52; and Collier, 114, 195–97; defends religious freedom, 60; endorses Bratton-Cutting bill, 105; and Lenroot bill, 48; and peyote warfare, 64–65; repudiates Leavitt bill, 68–69; and Wheeler-Howard bill, 151–52
America Indigena, 207, 223
America's Colonial Record (Collier), 220
American Anthropological Association, 229
American Association for the Advancement of Science, 47
American Association on Indian Affairs, 226–27, 230
American Bar Association, 72, 226
American Civil Liberties Union, 135n, 173–74, 202, 226

American Horse, Ben, 165
American Indian Defense Association: against repeal of IRA, 200; attacks Lee's Ferry bridge, 78–79; attends Cosmos Club conference, 135, 154n; cooperates with Hoover appointees, 92–94; criticism of, 111, 173; criticizes Hoover administration, 100–101, 111; defends religious freedom, 61–62, 65, 68; dispute with Indian Bureau, 96–97; evaluates Collier, 114, 134; and Flathead Indians, 86, 100–101; and food and clothing allowance, 98–99; formation of, 46–47, 243; opposes Indian Oil bill, 75–77; and peyote warfare, 197; promotes arts and crafts, 184–85; and Pueblo Indians, 52; and Pueblo Lands Board, 198; and Pueblo Relief bill, 105, 118; purge of, 48–49; and reform, 91; rejects Leavitt bill, 65–66; rejects Lenroot bill, 47–49; and Rio Grande Conservancy, 88–89; supports Alfred E. Smith, 92; and Swing-Johnson bill, 102
American Indian Federation, 170–73, 200–202, 240, 241
American Indian Life (Collier), 46, 113
American Indian Survey, 51
American Power and Light Holding Company, 100
Anaconda Copper Company, 100
Anadarko Indian Congress, 153
Annette Islands, 184

Anthropologists, and IRA, 161–62, 164
Apache Indians, 179, 223
Arapaho Indians, 139, 153, 157n, 182n
Armstrong, Thomas, 178
Ashurst, Henry F., 144
Assiniboine Indians, 139, 184
Atlanta Charities, 8
Atlanta High School, 5
Atlanta Journal, 5
Atsina Indians, 139
Atwood, Stella: attends All Pueblo Council, 68; as chairwoman of Indian Welfare Committee, 26; and Collier, 26–27; and General Federation of Women's Clubs, 2, 39, 44, 48; joins American Indian Defense Association, 47; meets Albert B. Fall, 32; opposes Bursum bill, 32–33, 37, 39; opposes Indian Oil bill, 76; opposes Lenroot bill, 48; removed from Indian Welfare Committee, 62; testifies before Congress, 39, 43–44
Austin, Mary, 24, 34, 102, 102n
Ayres, Roy, 170n, 174

Bacone College, 84, 133
Bad Wound, Chief, 165
Bailey, Elmer, 84
Baldwin, Roger, 174, 202
Baptist General Convention, 132
Baptist Home Mission Society, 84
Barnett, Jackson, 84–85, 171
Barrows, Edward, 15
Baruch, Bernard, 50
Bates, Mattie, 19
Beard, Charles, 21
Beatty, Willard, 128, 225, 241
Bell Act, 220
Bennett, Hugh, 187
Bergson, Henri, 18
Better America Federation of California, 24
Bigman, Max, 149
Billingsley, M. W., 167, 167n
Birth of a Nation, 13
Blackfeet Indians, 140, 149, 165–66, 184, 199, 225
Blessing Way, 223
Blue Lake (New Mexico), 196
Blue Ridge Mountain (North Carolina), 18
Board of Indian Commissioners, 37, 56, 67, 113, 118–20, 128, 130, 154–55, 211, passim
Boletín Indigenista, 207

Bonneville Dam, 168
Borah, William, 35, 37
Boulder Dam, 188
Bratton, Sam G., 79, 105, 113
Bratton-Cutting bill, 105, 112
Brill, A. A., 21
Bronson, O. H., 47
Brosius, S. M., 32, 66
Brownell, Herbert, 231
Brumm, George, 68
Bruner, Joseph, 153, 171–72, 200, 202
Bryan, William Jennings, 50
Buck, Joe, 150
Bull, George White, 148
Bureau of Animal Husbandry, 123
Bureau of Catholic Education, 63
Bureau of Catholic Missions, 56, 60
Bureau of Chemistry and Soil, 187
Bureau of Ethnology, 162
Bureau of Indian Affairs: and Alaska Indians, 183–84; and American Indian Federation, 170–74, 200–204; appropriations for, 45, 82, 82n, 129, 130n, 156, 175–76, 208, 211; bans Indian dances, 56–60, 64–65; and Bursum bill, 45; and circular on Indian Self-Government, 136–40; and circular on Student Control, 99–100; consults with anthropologists, 161–62; convenes Indian congresses, 145–54; criticism of, 43, 45, 47, 60–63, 79–81, 83, 90, 97–102, 111, 132–33, 143–45, 154–57, 172–75, 181–82, 190–99, 224–25; defends religious freedom, 131–32; defense of, 51–52, 67–68, 81–84, 111–12; drafts Leavitt bill, 65–67; drafts Wheeler-Howard bill, 141–45; favors Rio Grande Conservancy bill, 88; educational policy of, 56, 96, 128–29, 241; establishes Pueblo Indian Council, 68–69; and Flathead Indians, 85–87, 100–101, 168–69; implements stock reduction, 187–93; and IRA, 162–68; investigation of, 81–85, 99–100, 103–110, 175, 208; and Japanese-American removal, 208–10; and Lee's Ferry bridge, 79–80; and Meriam Report, 90, 98, 129, 135; and Navajo Tribal Council, 108–9, 190–93; and Oklahoma Welfare Act, 176–83; and peyote warfare, 194, 197; and Pueblo Lands Act, 53; reforms of, 93–96, 118–34; repudiates New Deal reform, 225–230; sponsors personality study, 207–8; supports Indian Oil bill, 74–75

Bureau of the Budget, 45, 82n, 95, 104–5, 141, 156, 175, 176n, 205–6, 241, passim

Burdick, Usher, 107n, 174, 181, 201

Burke, Charles H.: assists missionaries, 56–57; attacks James A. Frear, 81; and Bursum bill, 28, 31, 39, 45; biographical sketch of, 28n; Circular 1665, 56; criticism of, 39, 60–61, 64–65, 115; criticizes John Collier, 83; curtails Indian dances, 56–57, 59–60; defends Indian Oil bill, 74–75; description of, 42–43; forbids corporal punishment, 99; and Indian dances, 58n; and Institute for Government Research, 83–84; and Jackson Barnett, 84–85, 171; meets with Montana Power Company, 85; Message to All Indians, 57; and Rattlesnake Dome, 108; rejects Jones-Leatherwood bill, 45; repudiates Albert B. Fall, 72; resignation from office, 90n, 92; supports Leavitt bill, 65; and Taos Pueblo, 60–61, 64, 197n; testifies before House Indian Affairs Committee, 45; visits Santa Clara Pueblo, 31

Bursum, Holm O., 30, 52

Bursum bill: 35, 43, 45, 54, 62, 77, 110, 166, 243; and Albert Fall, 28–34, 36–42; and Indian Affairs Committee, 42–45; introduced, 30; and Joy Survey, 31–32; and R. E. Twitchel, 28–32, 36, 40; and Committee on Public Lands and Surveys, 35, 38–41; opposition to, 32–36, 38–39, 40; provisions of, 32; second Bursum bill, 52

Bynner, Witter, 34, 47–48, 110–11

Byrnes, James, 216

Caddo Indians, 182n, 183

California Indian Plan, 93

California Indians, 139, 225, 241

Cameron, Ralph H., 77, 79

Cameron bill, 77

Canard, Roley, 183

Caroline Islands, 216, 218

Case, Francis, 164, 204

Catholic Daily Tribune, 148

Catholic War Veterans, 216

Century of Dishonor, A (Jackson), 90

Chandler, O. K., 200, 200n

Chapman, Oscar, 225–26

Chemawa Indian Congress, 149–50

Chemehuevi Indians, 210

Cherokee Indians, 139, 154, 178, 202

Cheschillege, Dashne, 193

Cheyenne Agency, 139

Cheyenne Indians, 153, 182n

Chicago Indian Rights Association, 38

Chickasaw Indians, 154, 178, 183, 213

Childs, Clinton S., 16

Chippewa-Cree Indians, 169

Chippewa Indians, 156n, 169, 228–29, 239

Choctaw Indians, 177–78, 183

Christian, George, Jr., 37

Christian Century, 63–64, 229

Christian Reformed Church, 151n, 173

Christian Science Monitor, 34

Circular 1665, 56–57

Circular on Indian Self-Government, 137–38

Circular on Student Control, 99–101

City College of New York (CCNY), 221–22, 230–31

City Where Crime Is Play, The (Barrows and Collier), 15

Civic Journal, 14–15

Civilian Conservation Corps (CCC), 120

Civil Service Commission, 205

Civil Works Administration (CWA), 123–24, 127, 165

Clark, Bennett Champ, 198

"Cliff Dwellers," 38

Cloud, Henry Roe, 147n, 213

Cochiti Pueblo, 3, 87

Codman, Winifred, 200

Coffey, Robert, 179

Cohen, Felix, 117, 120, 140n, 202n, 214

College de France, 9

Collier, Charles (brother), 5

Collier, Charles A. (father), 4

Collier, Mrs. Charles (daughter-in-law), 184

Collier, Grace (neé Volk), 232, 236

Collier, John: as adult educator, 23–24; *American Indian Life,* 46, 113; *America's Colonial Record,* 220; Appalachian camping trips of, 5–7, 18–19, 243; career as journalist, 9, 14–15, 22; childhood experiences of, 4–7; *The City Where Crime Is Play,* 15; criticism of, 45, 89, 110–12, 132–33, 154–55, 171–75, 189, 192, 193n, 195–200, 204, 208, 210, 237–42; death of, 236; description of, 16–17, 117; as director of National Board of Censorship, 12–14, 238; divorces of, 210, 231; education of, 5–7; evaluation of, 24–25, 112, 159–60, 185–86, 211–13, 237–44; as executive secretary of American Indian Defense

Collier, John *(cont.)*
Association, 46–47; *From Every Zenith,* 234; *Guam Echo,* 218; *Indians of the Americas,* 219–20; as lecturer at San Francisco State College, 26–27; marriages of, 9, 210, 232; *Newsletter,* 217–18, 222, 227; nomination for Indian commissioner, 113–17; *Patterns and Ceremonials of the Southwest,* 222–23; and People's Institute, 10, 12–17, 19-22, 25, 39, 237–38, 242; as president of Institute of Ethnic Affairs, 214; as professor at City College of New York, 221–22, 230–31; as research agent for Women's Federation, 27; resignation as Indian commissioner, 211; retirement of, 232–36; *Ruined Land,* 18; as social worker, 9–10, 23–24; *Southwest Indian News Letter,* 226–27; teaches at Knox College, 231–32; teaches at Merrill-Palmer School, 231; travels abroad, 9, 97, 206; writes for *El Crepusculo,* 233–34
Collier, Laura. *See* Thompson, Laura
Collier, Lucy (neé Wood), 9, 18–19, 210
Collier, Susie Rawson (mother), 4
Collier's, 217
Collins, William T., 52
Colorado River, 188
Colorado River reservation, 186n, 209–10
Columbia University, 20, 231
Colville reservation, 140, 157n
Commanche Indians, 153, 179
Committee of One Hundred, 49–52, 54, 57, 82
Committee on Economic Foreign Policy, 222
Committee on Human Development, 207
Committee on Public Lands and Surveys (Senate), 35–37, 39–41, 45–46, 52
Committee on the Judiciary (House), 95
Commonwealth Club, 65
Community Center, 22
Community Clearing House, 22
Congressional Record, 76, 111
Connolly, Vera, 93
Consumer movement, English, 169
Continental Oil Company, 108
Coolidge, Calvin: 52, 73, 80, 89; addresses Sioux Indians, 86–87; and Committee of 100, 51–52; and Indian dances, 54, 62; and Indian Oil bill, 76–78
Cooperative League, 162
Cooperative movement, European, 9, 10, 21
Cooper Union, 10, 12

Cosmos Club, 122, 135, 140, 154
Costo, Rupert, 153
Cotton States and International Exposition (1895), 4
Cramton, Louis C.: 82, 86, 110; amends Rio Grande Conservancy bill, 88–89; attacks Collier, 89; criticism of, 99, 101; criticizes Swing-Johnson bill, 102; fiscal conservatism of, 82n, 96, 99, 101; and food and clothing allowance, 98–99; and Meriam Report, 98; opposes Republican reform, 96–97
Crandall, C. J., 60, 64, 68
Creek Indians, 84, 153, 171, 173, 182n, 182–83
Crow Agency, 149
Crow Indians, 157n, 184
Crow reservation, 243
Crozier, Lucy Graham, 7–8
Crumbo, Woodrow, 124–25
Cummings, Homer, 168, 199
Curtis, Charles, 48, 52, 73, 89, 177
Cushing, Frank Hamilton, 58
Custer Park, 23
Cutting, Bronson, 105, 115, 163n

Dabb, Edith, 51–52, 58–59
Dallinger, Frederick, 74
Danielson, P. W., 139
Dartmouth College, 218
Daseney, Lucien, 178
Daugherty, Harry, 28, 30, 36–37, 42, 104
Daughters of the American Revolution, 200
Dawes General Allotment Act (1887), 47, 51, 56, 83, 87, 94, 97, 106, 114, 119, 127, 134–35, 141–42, 145–47, 155, 159, passim
Deloria, Vine, 244
Dennison, Adell, 178
Dewey, John, 19–20, 129
Disney, Wesley, 181–82
Dissette, Mary E., 59
Distinguished Service Award, 235
Dodge, Chee, 189, 191
Dodge, Mabel: and Collier, 1–2, 16–17, 18; and D. H. Lawrence, 24, 33–34; and Fifth Avenue salon, 17–19; and Isadora Duncan, 19–20; and writers, 24. *See also* Luhan, Mabel Dodge
Dodge, Thomas H., 173
Douglas, Lewis, 148
Dulles, John Foster, 216
Duncan, Isadora, 17, 19–20, 172
Durant, W. A., 177, 183

Eastern Association on Indian Affairs: defends Herbert Hagerman, 109; and Herbert Hoover, 93; opposes Leavitt bill, 66; opposes suppression of dances, 59; repudiates Bursum bill, 33, 35, 37–39; supports Lenroot bill, 46
Eastern Band of Cherokees, 139
Eastern Cooperative League, 209
Eastern Emigrant Cherokees, 154
Eastman, Max, 17
Eighth International Conference of American Nations, 206
Eisenhower, Dwight D., 227–32
Eisenhower, Milton, 228
Ejido agrarian reform, 97, 142, 220
El Crepusculo, 233–34
Elkus, Charles de Y., 47, 105n, 197–98
Emergency Relief Appropriations Act, 125
Emergency Relief Council, 125
Emerson, Haven, 22, 33, 77, 92, 100–101, 134
Emmons, Glenn L., 227
Enabling Act (1910), 28
Engels, Frederick, 239
Esherf, Shevky, 44
Eskimos, 7
Explorers Club, 38

Fahy, Charles, 117, 140n
Fall, Albert B.: appointment as secretary of interior, 28; appoints Herbert Hagerman, 103; appoints R. E. Twitchell, 28; and Collier, 116, 241; criticism of, 33–35, 37–40, 63, 76–77, 86; favors Indian omnibus bill, 72n; and Harry Daugherty, 37; and Jackson Barnett, 84; leases executive-order reservations, 69, 71–72; legacy of, 91, 104, 226; letter to New York Economic Club, 41; and Navajo Tribal Council, 107–9; and Rattlesnake Dome, 91, 107; resignation of, 42; retirement of, 38, 41–42, 54; sponsors Bursum bill, 28–32; testifies before Senate Public Lands and Surveys Committee, 40–41; threatens to evict settlers, 36–37; use of Joy Survey, 31–32; writes to William Borah, 37
Fechner, Robert, 120
Federal Emergency Relief Administration (FERA), 123, 165
Federal Power Commission, 85, 87, 100, 168

Federal Surplus Relief Administration, 188
Federal Surplus Relief Corporation (FSRC), 123, 188
Federal Water Power Act (1920), 86
Fejos, Paul, 214
Ferguson, Erna, 110
Ferrer, Francisco, 14–15, 172
Field, Neil B., 108
Fiji, 210
Fire Thunder, 148–49
Five Civilized Tribes: attend Muskogee Indian Congress, 153–54; condition of, 239; and Cosmos Club conference, 136; form National Indian Confederacy, 172; loss of land, 150–51; and Oklahoma Welfare Act, 182–83; and Thomas-Rogers bill, 177–78, 180; and Wheeler-Howard bill, 141n
Flathead Indians: 184, 186n, 199; and Montana Power Company, 85–87, 91, 100–101, 167–69, 243; and Wheeler-Howard bill, 150
Flathead Irrigation District, 85
Ford, James, 9, 21
Forrestal, James, 217–19
Fortas, Abe, 215n, 215–16
Fort Belknap reservation, 139, 149
Fort Berthold reservation, 242
Fort Yuma reservation, 153
Frankfurter, Felix, 115
Frazier, Lynn: 77, 86, 89, 109, 202; favors repeal of IRA, 204n, 212; and Senate Indian Investigating Subcommittee, 84, 94, 101, 103, 105, 111
Frear, James A.: 66; attacks Lee's Ferry bridge, 78–79; biographical sketch of, 76n; and Collier, 226; criticism of, 81; denounces Indian Bureau, 77, 80–81, 82–83; and Jackson Barnett, 84; and Leavitt bill, 66; opposes Indian Oil bill, 76–77; supports Progressive ticket, 76; testifies before Congress, 83
Frear bill, 66, 69
Free Folk Theatre of Berlin, 19
From Every Zenith (Collier), 234
Fruitland irrigation project, 189–90
Fryer, E. R., 190–93

Gadsden Purchase Treaty, 144
Gaelic Renaissance, 9
Gaynor, William Jay, 13–14
General Council of Progressive Christian Indians, 61, 63

General Federation News, 44
General Federation of Women's Clubs:
and Lenroot bill, 45–46, 48; attends
Cosmos Club conference, 135n;
biennial conference, 44; campaign
against Bursum bill, 32–33, 36–37,
39–40, 54; criticism of, 43–44; forma-
tion of Indian Welfare Committee,
26–27; and Indian dances, 61–62;
and Indian reform, 47, 91, 93; investi-
gation of Indian affairs, 27; Los
Angeles convention, 61–62; opposes
Indian Oil bill, 76; resignation of
Stella Atwood, 62; supports IRA, 200
General Land Office, 71, 74
General Leasing Act (1920), 71–75
General Reclamation Service, 95–96
German-American Bund, 201–2, 202n,
204
Gibson, Mrs. Frank, 26
Gila River Indians, 96
Gilbert, W. W., 179
Glavis, Louis, 108, 117
Goldman, Emma, 17
Gomez, Geronimo, 194
Good Eagle, 179
Goubaud, Antonio, 123
Grand Canyon, 79
Grand Coulee Dam, 168
Greenwich Village, 154
Grorud, A. A., 202
Gros Ventres Indians, 184
Grounds, Charles, 178
Guam, 210, 215–19, 227, 243
Guam Congress, 218
Guam Echo, 218
Guam Organic Act (1950), 219, 227
Gulick, Luther, 21

Haas, Theodore H., 120, 225, 232
Hagerman, Herbert: attacked by Senate
Indian Investigating Subcommittee,
103–10; biographical sketch of, 103;
criticized by Collier, 105–6, 108–9;
defended by Wilbur, 111–12; opposes
Wheeler-Howard bill, 155n; and
Pueblo Lands Board, 104; praised by
Oliver La Farge, 109–10; and Rattlesnake Dome, 107–10; removed from
government payroll, 111; reorganizes
Navajo Tribal Council, 107–8, 110;
self-defense of, 109; Santa Fe recep-
tion, 110–11; special commissioner
to Navajos, 103, 105–10; and United
States Pueblo Indian Council, 69

Hagerman, James, 103
Haida Indians, 184
Haile, Berard, 162n, 191
Handbook of Federal Indian Law
(Cohen), 120, 225
Hapgood, Hutchins, 17
Harding, Warren G., 32, 36–38, 42,
115n, 226
Harnoncourt, René d', 185
Harper, Allan, 154, 214n
Harreld, J. W., 68, 73–74
Harrison, E. M., 71, 73–74, 76
Harrison, William Henry, 228
Haskill Institute, 128, 147n, 161
Hastings, William, 158
Hatch Act, 208
Hauptmann, Gerhart, 19
Hayden, Carl, 74, 106
Hayden bill, 106
Hayes, Joseph W., 154, 178, 213
Haynes, John R., 47
Hayward Indian Congress, 155, 156n
Haywood, Bill, 17, 22
Henderson, Alice Corbin, 34
Hiawatha Insane Asylum, 130–31
Hill Indians, 125
History of the Indies (Las Casas), 140
Hitler, Adolph, 202
Hodge, F. W., 60
Hoffman, Frederick, 44
Hogback Dome, 109
Holy Rosary Mission, 148
Home School, 19
Hoover, Herbert: criticized by Collier,
101; defends American colonialism,
218; evaluation of, 112; and food and
clothing allowance, 99; and Johnson-
O'Malley bill, 133; legacy of, 226–27,
229; and Navajo Indians, 134, 188n;
and O. K. Chandler, 200n; and Rattle-
snake Dome, 91, 107; selects Indian
commissioner, 92–93; threatens to
veto Bratton-Cutting bill, 105
Hopi Indians, 55, 137, 166–67, 186, 210,
224, 234
Hopkins, Ernest, 218
Hopkins, Harry, 123
Hopkins committee, 218–19
Hopkins Report, 219
Hotevilla, 167
House Appropriations Committee, 96,
98, 148, 175–76
House Concurrent Resolution 108, 228–29
Howard, Edgar, 140, 157–58, 162
Hubbell, Roman, 163
Hughs, Monsignor William, 63

Hummer, Harry, 131
Hunter, Robert F., 144
Hunter-Martin claims, 144–45
Huxley, Julian, 140

Ickes, Anna W., 115, 135
Ickes, Harold L.: abolishes Board of
    Indian Commissioners, 118–20; and
    Alaska Indians, 184; appointed secre-
    tary of interior, 115; biographical
    sketch of, 115n; cancels reimbursable
    debts, 127; criticizes American
    colonialism, 215n, 217; directs Public
    Works Administration, 124–25; and
    Hiawatha Insane Asylum, 131; joins
    American Indian Defense Association,
    38; and Navajo Indians, 189; nomi-
    nation of Collier for commissioner,
    115–16; and peyote warfare, 197;
    resignation from office, 217n; selects
    Collier as United Nations advisor,
    215; stifles criticism of Indian Bureau,
    157–58; and Subsistence Homestead
    Division, 125; supports Wheeler-
    Howard bill, 158; transfers National
    Indian Institute, 223; and War Reloca-
    tion Authority, 209
Indian Affairs Committee (House):
    considers Leavitt bill, 65–68; criticizes
    Collier, 170–75, 186; hearings on
    Indian Oil bill, 74–76; hearings on
    Snyder bill, 42–45; and Indian dances,
    58; and IRA, 204–5; and Lee's Ferry
    bridge, 78; and Navajos, 190; opposes
    Wheeler-Howard bill, 143–44, 157–59;
    and Sioux, 165; and Thomas Rodgers
    bill, 181–82
Indian Affairs Committee (Senate),
    82–83, 88, 143–45, 156–57, 186, 192,
    202–4
Indian Art Fund, 102
Indian Art of the United States
    (Harnoncourt), 185
Indian Arts and Crafts bill, 94, 101–2,
    112
Indian Arts and Crafts Board, 185, 208,
    225, 244
Indian Claims Commission, 201, 225, 241
Indian Citizenship Act (1924), 87, 225,
    241
Indian Congresses, 145–154, 177–79,
    239
Indian Conservation Corps, 165, 175, 205
Indian court of claims, 95
Indian Emergency Conservation Work
    (IECW), 120–22, 122n, 126, 243

Indian Forestry Service, 174–75, 208
Indian Law Survey, 120
Indian Medical Service, 81–83, 130n,
    174, 208
Indian Office Land Division, 189
Indian Oil bill, 74–77, 80
Indian Oil Leasing Act (1924), 74–75,
    77–78
Indian Personality Study, 207, 210, 240
Indian Reorganization Act (IRA): and
    Apache Indians, 223; and anthropolo-
    gists, 161–62; attempted repeal of,
    198–200, 202–4, 204n, 225n, 229;
    and Blackfeet Indians, 165–66; con-
    gressional hostility to, 170, 173–76,
    204, 208; constitutions and charters,
    163–65; and cooperative economic
    enterprise, 169–70; criticism of,
    162–63, 170–73, 195; evaluation of,
    185–86, 211–13, 239–44; and Flat-
    head Indians, 167–69; and Hopi
    Indians, 166–67; Navajo rejection of,
    163; and Pine Ridge Sioux Indians,
    165; provisions of, 159; and Santa
    Clara Pueblo, 170
Indian Rights Association: 60, 91, 193n,
    197n; against repeal of IRA, 199–200,
    204; assists Herbert Hoover, 92–93;
    attends Cosmos Club conference, 135;
    contacts Calvin Coolidge, 73; criticizes
    Hubert Work, 61; and Dawes Act,
    94; disapproves of Indian dances,
    55–56, 60–63; distributes Sweet
    Report, 59; objects to Leavitt bill, 66;
    opposes leasing of executive-order
    reservations, 72–74; and Progressive
    Christian Indians, 61; rejects Bursum
    bill, 30, 32, 35, 35n, 54; rejects
    Wheeler-Howard bill, 154–55, 160;
    and reorganization of Navajo Tribal
    Council, 192; repudiates Lee's Ferry
    bridge, 79; and selection of Indian
    commissioner, 92–93, 113; supports
    Rhoads and Scattergood, 113; and
    termination, 230
Indians at Work, 122, 198, 202
Indians of the Americas (Collier), 219
Indian tribes. See specific Indian tribes
Indian Truth, 56, 155, 192
Indian Welfare Committee, 26–27, 43–44
Institute for Government Research,
    81–83, 90, 96, 114, 135. See also
    Meriam Report
Institute of Ethnic Affairs, 214, 222–23,
    226, 230, 232, 234, 243
Institute on Minority Groups, 232

Inter-American Indian Institute, 206–7, 220, 223, 229
Internal Revenue Department, 219
International Workers of the World (IWW), 17, 22
Iowa Indians, 179, 182n
Irish folk-revival, 162
Iroquois Confederacy, 239
Irving, Joe, 149
Ishadore, Chief, 150
Isleta Pueblo, 40, 62n, 88, 170

Jackson, Helen Hunt, 90
James, Frank, 179
James, William, 18
James True Associates, 202, 204
Janet, Pierre, 9
Japanese-Americans, 208–10, 243
Jemison, Alice Lee, 172–73, 202, 202n
Jesuits, 141, 148, 219, 221
Jicarilla Apaches, 169, 186
John Hay Whitney Foundation, 231
Johnson, Allen, 178
Johnson, Dana, 35
Johnson, Jed, 176, 207–8, 210, 223
Johnson, William E., 59, 62
Johnson-O'Malley bill, 133–34, 175
Jones, Andrius, 46
Jones, George, 183
Jones-Leatherwood bill, 38, 41–43, 45–46
Joy Survey (1913), 31–32, 37, 40, 45
Justice Department, 167

Kanine, Jim, 150
Karluck River (Alaska), 184
Kaw Indians, 153, 177–78
Ketcham, W. H., 56, 67
Kibbutzim, 231
King, Judson, 39, 43, 46, 77
King, William, 82, 111
Kiowa Indians, 153, 179, 186n
Kivahema, Joab, 167
Klamath Indians, 157n, 159n, 228–29, 232
Klamath reservation, 126
Kluckhohn, Clyde, 207n, 214
Knox, John C., 84
Knox College, 231–32
Kodiak Island, 184
Kootenai Indians, 150
Koshare Dance, 56
Kremer, Bruce, 199
Kropotkin, Prince Peter, 7, 10, 234, 237
Krug, Julius A., 224

Labor, 77
Lac du Flambeau reservation, 156n, 169
La Farge, Oliver, 109–10, 137, 154n, 166–67, 167n, 224
La Follette, Robert, 72n, 76
La Follette, Robert, Jr., 84, 86
Laguna Pueblo, 34, 170
La Pointe, Sam, 149
Las Casas, Bartolomé de, 140–41, 219
Lawrence, D. H., 24, 34
League of Women Voters, 48
Leavitt, Scott, 67–68
Leavitt bill, 65–69
Lee, H. Rex, 227
Lee, Robert E., 5
Lee's Ferry bridge, 78–80, 91, 127, 172
Leighton, Dorothea, 207n, 214
Lenroot, Irving, 40
Lenroot bill, 45–49, 54
Lewis, Orme, 227–29
Liberia, one-party government of, 222
Lincoln, Abraham, 38–39
Lindquist, G. E. E., 51, 120n, 132n, 153, 155
Linton, Ralph, 120n, 136–37, 162n
Lippmann, Walter, 17, 34
Lipps, O. H., 139
Little Bronzed Angel, 148
Locke, John, 230
Loco, John, 179
Lodge, Henry Cabot, 73
Lonewolf, Delos, 179
Lowe, Anna Laura, 84–85
Lowndes, Charles, 130
Luhan, Antonio, 2, 35, 195, 232
Luhan, Mabel Dodge, 194n, 195n, 195–96, 232. See also Dodge, Mabel
Lummis, Charles Fletcher, 62, 62n, 68

MacArthur, Douglas, 220
McCarthyism, 230–31
McCaskill, Joseph, 225
MacDougall, D. T., 47
McDougall, William, 20
McGroarty, John, 170n, 174, 181, 204n
McKay, Douglas, 227–28, 230
MacKenzie, F. A., 50
McKinley, William, 218
McKittrick, Margaret, 36, 47–50
McNaughton, Ray, 153
McNickle, D'Arcy, 214

Macon Telegraph, 9
Manchester Band of Pomo Indians, 169
Margold, Nathan, 105n, 114–15, 117, 140n, 201

Marianas Islands, 216, 218
Marshall, John, 211
Marshall, Louis, 89, 105n
Marshall, Robert, 120n, 185, 202n
Marshall Islands, 216, 218
Martin, Fred, 219
Martinez, Carpio, 139
Marx, Karl, 154
Masses, The, 17
Matthews, Brander, 7
Maytubby, Floyd, 183
Mekeel, Scudder, 164
Mellon, Andrew, 75
Menominee Indians, 156n, 228, 232
Merchandise Mart, 205
Meriam, Lewis, 90, 94, 114–15, 135
Meriam Report, 90–91, 93, 96, 98–99, 112, 129, 134. *See also* Institute For Government Research
Meritt, Edgar B.: attacks John Collier, 67; candidate for Indian commissioner, 113–15, 117; criticism of, 80–81, 115; defends Indian Bureau, 81–82; defends Lee's Ferry bridge, 79–80; favors private investigation of Indian affairs, 81; and Pueblo Indians, 45; and Rio Grande Conservancy bill, 88; supports Leavitt bill, 67; testifies before House Indian Affairs Committee, 45; transferred to budget department, 92
Merrill-Palmer School, 231
Mesa Land (Ickes), 115
Mescalero Apache Indians, 169, 169n, 186, 225
Metlakahtla Indians, 184
Metropolitan Oil Company, 108
Miami Indian Congress, 153
Miami Indians, 178
Micronesia, 216–17, 242–43
Middle Rio Grande Conservancy bill, 87–88
Midwest Oil Company, 108
Mirabal, Antonio, 194n, 194–97, 232
Missionaries: attack Wheeler-Howard bill, 151, 154, 163, 173; attend Committee of 100, 50; and Board of Indian Commissioners, 119; and circular on Indian Self-Government, 138; favor ban on Indian dances, 55–59, 63–64; and Jackson Barnett, 84; oppose John Collier, 131–33
Mission Indians, 153, 162, 173
Mitchell, Harry, 114
Mitchell, John Purroy, 19, 22
Mohave Indians, 152, 210
Moley, Raymond, 115

Monohan, A. C., 152
Montana Power Company, 85–87, 100–101, 167, 169
Montezuma, Carlos, 172
Montoya, Alcario, 35, 194
Moore, Paul, 80–81
Morgan, Jacob C., 126, 163, 173, 190–93
Morgan, Lewis Henry, 239
Mormons, cooperative living of, 143
Morris, William, 8, 18
Moskowitz, Ira, 223
Mowry, George, 27
Muntz, S. C., 108
Murdock, Abe, 170
Murphy, Blue, 178
Murphy, Edith, 200
Museum of Modern Art, 214
Museum of the American Indian, 60
Muskogee Indian Congress, 153–54
Muskrat, Ruth, 51–52
Mutual Aid (Kropotkin), 7, 10, 234
Myer, Dillon S., 209, 225–27

Nacoochee Valley (Georgia), 5
Nambe Pueblo, 104
Nantahala River (North Carolina), 18
Nash, Willard, 110
Nashville Tennessean, 42
Nation, 34, 224, 227
National Association on Indian Affairs, 135, 135n, 154n, 166, 200
National Board of Censorship, 238
National Community Center Conference, 3, 21–23
National Community Councils of Defense, 3, 22–23, 238
National Council of American Indians, 135n, 137
National Forest Service, 208
National Indian Confederacy, 153, 172
National Indian Institute, 207, 223–24
National Industrial Recovery Act (NIRA), 124–25
National Park Service, 79
National Peace Conference, 216
National Popular Government League, 39, 46, 77, 91
National Resources Board, 176, 178n, 187
National Youth Administration (NYA), 125, 127
Native American Church, 51, 64, 132, 194–97, 240. *See also* Peyote warfare
Navajo Arts and Crafts Guild, 185
Navajo boundary bill, 134, 163, 163n
Navajo-Hopi Rehabilitation bill, 224
Navajo Indian Rights Association, 193

Navajo Indians: and agency consolidation, 188, 192, 212; and Anna W. Ickes, 115; and Arts and Crafts Guild, 185; attend Indian Congress, 150–51; and Colorado River reservation, 210; dislike day schools, 128–29, 173; engage in conservation work, 121, 126, 240; and expansion of reservation, 134; and Herbert Hagerman, 103, 105–10; and Indian Bureau questionnaire, 137; and Indian Oil bill, 75, 243; land consolidation of, 122; and Leavitt bill, 66; and Navajo-Hopi Rehabilitation bill, 224–25; and Navajo Indian Rights Association, 193; and public relief, 123, 125–26, 128; question Lee's Ferry bridge, 78–80; and Rattlesnake Dome, 107–10; reorganization of tribal council, 107–9, 190–92, 234; roadless and wilderness areas of, 185; stock reduction of, 123, 187–93, 240–41; vote against IRA, 163, 204

Navajo Treaty of 1868, 224, 241
Navajo Tribal Council, 106–8, 137, 150–51, 173, 188–93, 224, 234
Nazi Party, 200
Neblett, Colin, 30, 64
Neskahi, Allen, 190
Newell Tunnel, 85–86, 101
New Mexico Association on Indian Affairs, 33, 35, 46–48, 93, 111, 155n
New Mexico Cattle Growers Association, 106
New Mexico District Court, 32
New Mexico Taxpayers Association, 103, 107
New Republic, 34
Newsletter, 217–18, 222, 227
New York Board of Education, 15, 22
New York City, 2, 3, 15, 18–19, 22, 24, 41, 46, 209, 237, passim
New York Economic Club, 41–42
New York Herald Tribune, 75, 224
New York *Journal of Commerce and Commercial Bulletin,* 42
New York Museum of Modern Art, 185
New York Press, 16
New York Sun, 116
New York Times, 34, 41, 58–60, 131, 185, 217, 222
New York World, 34, 75
Nez Percé Indians, 150, 241
Nichols, Jack, 181
Nietzsche, Friedrich Wilhelm, 8
Night Hawk Keetoowah Society, 154, 178, 182n, 182–83

Noggle, Burl, 42
Northern Cheyenne Indians, 169
Northwest Coast Indians, 239
Northwest Indian Congress, 149–50
Nowells, Kenneth B., 108–9
Nunan, Joseph, 219

Oakland Forum, 65, 81
Oklahoma Indian Credit Corporation, 180
Oklahoma Indians: and American Indian Federation, 171–72, 200n, 200–203, 240–41; and circular on Indian Self-Government, 139; criticize Collier, 132, 139, 158, 172; criticize Wheeler-Howard bill, 153–54; and Elmer Thomas, 156–57, 176–79; and Indian Bureau questionnaire, 136–37; and Indian Congresses, 153–54, 177–79; Jackson Barnett scandal, 84; languages of, 129; and Meriam Report, 135; and Oklahoma Welfare Act, 176, 182–83; and public relief, 121, 124–26; revival of arts and crafts, 185; support of missionaries, 132n, 132–33; and Thomas-Rogers bill, 179–82
Oklahoma *Tushkahomman,* 133
Oklahoma Welfare Act (1936), 176, 182, 184
Old Oraibi, 167
O'Malley, Thomas, 157, 181
Onondaga Indians, 125
Osage Indians, 141n, 153, 180
Otippoby, James, 153
Ottawa Indians, 153, 178, 178n
Outlines of Zuni Creation Myths (Cushing), 58
Outlook, 34

Pacific Science Board, 222
Pageant and Festival of Nations, 16–17
Paiute Indians, 229
Palmer, Moody, 178
Palmer, Paul, 192
Pan-American Conference on Indian Life, 206
Pan-Indianism, 206–7, 212, 223–24, 244
Papago Indians, 144, 152, 158, 158n
Papago reservation, 144, 158
Paraguay, cooperative living in, 141, 219, 221
Parker, Arthur C., 50
Parton, Lemuel, 115–16
Patterns and Ceremonials of the Indians of the Southwest (Collier and Moskowitz), 222
Patzcuaro Conference (Mexico), 206
Pawnees, 179, 182n

Pelly, William Dudley, 202
Pelly's Silver Shirts, 202, 202n, 204
Penitente cult, 58
People's Institute: activity at Cooper Union, 10, 12; *Civic Journal,* 14; Community Clearing House, 22; evaluation of, 24–25, 234, 238, 242; founded, 10; National Board of Censorship, 13; Pageant and Festival of Nations, 16–17; people's church, 11; people's forum, 10–12, 238; and Pueblo Indians, 38–39; school community centers, 15–16; Social Clinic for Unadjusted Children, 22; Training School for Community Workers, 20–21; Wingate Community Center, 21
People's Institute Bulletin, 14
Peoria Indians, 153, 182n
Perry, Reuben, 114
Personality and Government (Thompson), 208
Peyote warfare, 132, 193–97, 195n
Philippine Islands, self-government of, 11, 220
Phoenix Boarding School, 100
Phoenix Indian Congress, 152
Picuris Pueblo, 58, 104
Pijoan, Michel, 223
Pima Indians, 152
Pine, W. B., 84–85
Pine Ridge reservation, 132, 165, 186n, 241
Plains Indian Congress, 146–49
Poincaré, Henri, 18
Point Four program, 222
Pojoaque Pueblo, 170
Ponca Indians, 178, 153, 182n
Porter Springs (Georgia), 5
Poston relocation camp, 209
Potawatomie Indians, 125, 156n, 179, 182n, 228
Poyntz, Juliette, 19
President's Committee on Civil Rights, 216
Problem of Indian Administration (Meriam), 90, 135
Public Law 280, 228–29, 232
Public Works Administration (PWA), 124–25, 128–31, 165, 175, 184, 190, 197
Pueblo Defense Fund, 43
Pueblo Indians: 56, 58, 122, 184; acquire land, 126; and All Pueblo Council, 35–36, 47–48, 52, 60, 64, 68, 105, 107, 114, 151–52, 196; attend Indian Congress, 151–52; and Bursum bill, 28–46; and Bratton-Cutting bill, 105; and circular on Indian Self-Government, 139; and Collier's death, 236; and Committee of 100, 50–51; and

IRA, 170, 186, 194; and Indian Rights Association, 55–56; oppose Lenroot bill, 45–52; peyote warfare of, 64, 194, 196–97, 240; and Pueblo Lands Act, 53, 104–5, 111, 118; and Pueblo Relief bill, 105, 118; repudiate Leavitt bill, 68–69; revival of arts and crafts, 185; and Rio Grande Conservancy bill, 87–90; and Scott Report, 55, 59; social significance of, 2–3, 24, 159–60, 223, 233–35, 239; Spanish land grants threatened, 27–30; suppression of dances, 56–65; testify before Congress, 40; travel to East Coast, 38–39; and United States Pueblo Council, 69; and Wheeler-Howard bill, 151–52. *See also names of specific Pueblos*
Pueblo Lands Act (1924), 53, 104, 111, 197
Pueblo Lands Board, 65, 69, 105, 111, 118, 198
Pueblo Relief bill, 114, 118
Pyramid Lake reservation, 153

Quapaw Agency, 200, 200n
Quapaw Indians, 153, 178
Quinaielt reservation, 150

Rabb, Maxwell, 230
Rainbow Bridge (Arizona), 185
Rapid City Indian Congress, 146–49
Rattlesnake Dome, 91, 107–10
"Red Atlantis," 2, 160, 182, 239
Red Cloud, Chief, 201
Red Deer Dance, 223
Red Man in the United States (Lindquist), 51
Red Scare, 23, 54
Reed, John, 17
Reifel, Ben, 129
Renehan, A. B., 29, 31, 63
Resettlement Administration, 125–27, 176n
Reynal, John, 194
Rhoads, Charles J.: 93, 94, 98, 102, 120; and circular on Student Control, 99–100; criticism of, 98–100; evaluation of, 112; and reform effort, 94–95, 117
Rice Boarding School, 99
Rio Grande Conservancy District, 87–90
Riverside Indian Congress, 153
Roberts, W. O., 138
Robertson, Alice, 43–44
Robinson, Joseph T., 113, 116–17
Rochdale Institute, 209
Rockefeller, Nelson, 207
Rockefeller Institute, 222
Rogers, Will, 157
Romaro, Antonio, 39

Roosevelt, Eleanor, 114, 132, 193, 193n, 224
Roosevelt, Franklin D.: 4, 38, 140, 147, 172, 177, 210, 220, 226–27, 229, 244; abolishes Board of Indian Commissioners, 118–19; and Collier, 4, 112–13, 211; and court-packing proposal, 198; creates National Indian Institute, 207; criticism of, 202; endorses Wheeler-Howard bill, 158; and Indian conservation work, 120–21; and Navajo stock reduction, 193; and public relief, 123–26; selects Indian commissioner, 114–17; signs Indian Reorganization Act, 159; and War Relocation Authority, 208–9
Roosevelt, Theodore, 103
Rosebud Indian Agency, 138
Ross, Colin, 201
Roxas, Manuel, 220
Ruined Land (Collier), 18
Russell, George (A. E.), 162
Russian Revolution, 12, 23
Ryan, W. Carson, 96, 128, 241

Sac and Fox Indians, 179, 182n
Sacco and Vanzetti Horror (Collier), 89
Sacramento Agency, 125, 139
Saenz, Moises, 135, 172
Saint Elizabeth's Hospital, 130–31
Saipan Personality Study, 222
Sam, Thomas, 150
Samoa, 215–19, 243
San Carlos Apache Indians, 99, 152, 226, 227n
Sandia Pueblo, 88, 104
Sandoval, Santano, 197
Sandoval Case (1912), 29–30
San Felipe Pueblo, 88
San Francisco State College, 26–27
Sangre de Cristo Mountains (New Mexico), 232
San Ildefonso Pueblo, 35, 44, 152, 225
San Juan Pueblo, 29–30, 107, 108n, 139
San Juan River, 189
Santa Ana Pueblo, 61, 88
Santa Clara Pueblo, 29, 31, 130, 137, 152, 170, 232
Santa Fe Laboratory Museum, 102
Santa Fe New Mexican, 34, 48, 196
Santa Fe Railroad, 1, 105, 134
Santa Rosa reservation, 144, 153
Santa Ysabel reservation, 162
Santo Domingo Pueblo, 36, 45, 47, 56, 60, 64, 68–69, 88, 105, 114, 152, 195, passim

Saturday Review, 233
Saunkeah, Jasper, 153
Sawyer, Charles, 36–37, 42
Scattergood, J. Henry, 93, 98–101, 109, 112–13, 117, 135
Schafer, John, 204
Schuster, Fridolin, 35–37, 63
Scott, Hugh, 37, 50
Seaton, Fred A., 230
Second Urgency Deficiency bill, 85–86
Selby, Charles B., 85
Sells, Cato, 84, 181
Seminole Indians, 178, 183
Senate Committee on Public Lands and Surveys, 35–36, 38–41, 43, 45–46, 52
Senate Indian Investigating Subcommittee, 82–85, 99–100, 103–10, 112, 175, 208
Seneca Indians, 172–73, 178, 182n
Sergeant, Elizabeth S., 34, 36, 231
Seymour, Flora Warren, 120n, 128, 130, 155
Seymour, Ralph Fletcher, 47
Shale, Harry, 150
Shawnee Agency, 179
Shawnee Indians, 140, 178n, 181, 182n
Shepard, Ward, 120n, 202n
Sherman, Mrs. John D., 62
Shevky, Esherf, 44, 172
Shongopovi, 167
Sigurd the Volsung (Morris), 8
Silk, Samuel, 130–31
Sioux Benefits, 149, 156, 204
Sioux Indians: and public relief, 126; attend Indian Congress, 146–49; and ban on dancing, 56; and circular on Indian Self-Government, 138–39; education of, 129, 132, 241; and Indian claims, 241; individualism of, 239; and IRA, 164–65, 186; listen to Calvin Coolidge, 87; obtain buffalo, 184
Sisters of the Sacred Heart, 5
Sloan, Thomas, 179
Small, Robert, 179
Smith, Alfred E., 92
Smith, Charles Sprague, 10, 13
Smith, John, 178
Smithsonian Institution, 8
Smoot, Reed, 46
Sniffen, Matthew K.: 61, 79, 99, 192, 197n; as editor of Indian Truth, 56, 155; opposes repeal of Indian Reorganization Act, 199–200; rejects Wheeler-Howard bill, 154–55
Snyder, Homer, 42–43, 78
Snyder bill, 43

Social Clinic for Unadjusted Children, 22
Social Conservation Service, 187,
    189–90, 195, 205, 212, 243
Social Democratic Party, 19
Socialist League, 8
Social Psychology (McDougall), 20
Social telesis, 8, 12
Society for Applied Anthropology,
    207–8
Soil Erosion Service, 123
South Africa, racial policies of, 222, 233
Southern Ute Indians, 140
Southwestern Land and Cattle
    Company, 103
Southwest Indian News Letter (Collier),
    226–27
Spaulding vs *Chandler* (1896), 72
Spencer, Herbert, 9
Spinden, Herbert, 35, 162n
State Department, 217, 222–23
Steere, Jonathan, 155
Stevenson, Adlai, 227
Stewart, James, 188
Stone, Harlan, 73, 77
Storey, Moorfield, 72
Stowe, Harriet Beecher, 83
Strong, Duncan, 162
Subsistence Homestead Division, 125
Sun Dance, 56, 184
Sunset Magazine, 33, 33n, 43, 108
Survey, 32
Survey Associates, 33
Survey Graphic, 18
Swarthmore College, 96
Sweet, E. M., 55
Sweet report, 55, 59
Swing-Johnson bill, 93, 102–3, 112
Swinomish reservation, 125, 169

Taliman, Henry, 191
Talpa, New Mexico, 232
Tallulah Falls (Georgia), 5
Tammany Hall, 10, 14, 21, 22
Taos Pueblo, 58, 60–62, 64–65, 68–69,
    104, 118, 194–97, 232, 236, 240, 243,
    passim
Teapot Dome, 38, 70, 72, 77, 107, 110
Tesuque Pueblo, 28, 30, 35, 44, 185
Thomas, Elmer, 103, 116, 156, 158,
    176–79, 196, 201–2, 208
Thomas-Rogers bill, 179–182
Thompson, Laura, 207n, 207–8, 210,
    210n, 231
Thompson, Vern, 178
Tlingit Indians, 184
Tonkawa Indians, 153

Towner, Elwood A., 149n, 201–3, 202n
Town Hall, 41, 52, 76
Training School for Community
    Workers, 20–21, 238
Treaty of Versailles, 23
True, Clara D., 61–62
True, James, 202
Truman, Harry S, 214, 215n, 222,
    224–25
Tso, Hosteen, 192
Tubman, W. V., 222
Tugwell, Rexford, 122, 125–26
Twe, Dihdwo, 222
Twitchell, R. E., 28, 30–32, 36, 40

Umatilla Indians, 150
Umatilla reservation, 145
Uncle Tom's Cabin (Stowe), 83
Union League, 38
Unitarian Church, 215
United Traders Association, 151, 184
United Nations, 215–18
United Nations Charter, 215n, 215–16
United Nations Council of Philadelphia,
    216
United Pueblo Agency, 194–95, 240
United States Bureau of Education, 21
United States Criminal Code, 198
United States Public Health Service, 47,
    51, 174–75, 205
United States Pueblo Indian Council, 69
United States Reclamation Service, 97,
    175
University of Oklahoma, 129
University of Rochester, 232
Ute Indians, 229

Vance, Carolyn, 42
Viking Fund, 214n, 219
Villard, Oswald, 50
Vorse, Mary Heaton, 122
Vosburg, Kate, 27

Wald, Lillian, 16
Walker, Robert, 39
Wallace, Henry A., 122, 158, 208, 242
Walpi, 167
Warbasse, James P., 162, 162n
Ward, Edward J., 21–22
Ward, Lester Frank, 8, 12, 20, 140, 236
Warm Springs Indians, 228
Warner, W. Lloyd, 207
War Relocation Authority (WRA),
    209, 225
Warren, Nina Otero, 61, 63

Washington Daily News, 157, 193
Watkins, Arthur, 228
Weavers, The (Hauptmann), 19
Welsh, Herbert, 35, 55–56, 63, 72
Werner, Theodore, 143–44, 170n, 174
Wesley, Clarence, 226
Western Cherokee Indians, 154
Wheeler, Burton K.: 86, 103, 158n;
    affiliation with American Indian
    Federation, 202, 202n; attacks
    Charles H. Burke, 85; and court-
    packing, 198; favors repeal of IRA,
    198–99, 208n, 212; introduces
    Wheeler-Howard bill, 140; opposes
    Indian Oil bill, 76–77; repudiates
    Wheeler-Howard bill, 156, 198; and
    selection of Indian commissioner,
    113–14; and Senate Indian Investi-
    gating Subcommittee, 84, 103, 208n;
    supports American Indian Defense
    Association, 76
Wheeler, Walter, 100
Wheeler-Howard Act (1934), 95. *See
    also* Indian Reorganization Act
Wheeler-Howard bill: amendments to,
    155–56; congressional hostility
    toward, 143–45, 156–57; criticism
    of, 157–58, 198; debated at Indian
    Congresses, 145–54; endorsed by
    Franklin D. Roosevelt, 158; evalua-
    tion of, 159–60, 239–41; opposed by
    Indian Rights Association, 154–55;
    provisions of, 140–43; and revisions
    of, 158–59
White, Amelia E., 37, 47, 49, 66–67
White Cow Killer, Jacob, 149
Wilbur, Ray Lyman: advocates assimi-
    lation, 97; and Collier, 101, 111–12;
    defends Herbert Hagerman, 111–12;
    evaluation of, 112; and Flathead
    Indians, 100–101; and Indian educa-
    tion, 96; nomination of, 92; and
    Papago Indians, 144–45, 158; reform
    program, 95–96; rejects Bratton-
    Cutting bill, 105
Williams, James, 178
Williamson, William, 68

Wilson, Francis: 36; abandons Jones-
    Leatherwood bill, 43; and Albert B.
    Fall, 41; as attorney for Women's
    Federation, 33; break with Collier,
    46; and Sandoval case, 29; supports
    Lenroot bill, 45–46; testifies before
    Congress, 39–40
Wilson, John, 150
Wilson, Margaret, 16
Wilson, Woodrow, 16, 144
Window Rock, as Navajo capital, 190
Wind River reservation, 139
Wingate Community Center, 21
Winnebago Indians, 156n, 213
Winter, Mrs. Thomas, 48
Wirt, Emmit, 169
Woehlke, Walter, 33, 152, 202n, 225
Women's Alliance, 215
Woods Hole Marine Laboratory, 7
Wool Growers Association, 106
Work, Hubert: appointed secretary of
    interior, 49; creates Committee of 100,
    49–50; criticizes Congress, 82; disap-
    proves of Indian dances, 57; and
    executive-order reservations, 72–74;
    favors Lee's Ferry bridge, 78; and
    Flathead Indians, 85; and Institute
    for Government Research, 81–82;
    visits Taos Pueblo, 60–61
Works Progress Administration (WPA),
    125, 127, 205
World League of Alcoholism, 59
World War I, 54, 230
World War II, 205–6, 208, 212, 215,
    225–26, 230
Wyandotte Indians, 178, 178n, 182n

Yakima Indians, 150
Yellow, George, 149
Yellowstone National Park, 184
Yellowtail, Robert, 243
Young, Charles, 126
Young, James, 94
Young, S. A., 68

Zimmerman, William, 117, 150, 225
Zuni Indians, 58–60, 170, 194–97, 223